The Modes of Modern Writing

Metaphor, Metonymy, and the
Typology of
Modern Literature

David Lodge

A member of the Hodder Headline Group
LONDON

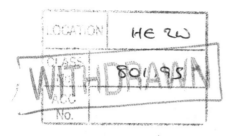

What does literature do and how does it do it. And what does English Literature do and how does it do it. And what ways does it use to do what it does.

Gertrude Stein

First published in Great Britain in 1977
First published in paperback 1979
Eleventh impression 2002 by Arnold,
a member of the Hodder Headline Group
338 Euston Road, London NW1 3BH
175 Fifth Avenue, New York, NY 10010

Co-published in the United States of America by
Oxford University Press, Inc.,
198 Madison Avenue, New York NY 10016

© 1977 David Lodge

British Library Cataloguing in Publication Data
A catalogue record for this book is available from the British Library

Library of Congress Cataloging-in-Publication Data
A catalog record for this book is available from the Library of Congress

ISBN 0 7131 6258 9

Printed and bound in India by
Replika Press Pvt. Ltd., 100% EOU, Delhi 110 040

Contents

Preface

The first part of this book considers some fundamental questions of literary theory and critical practice, illustrated by reference to a wide range of modern texts; questions such as, what is literature, what is realism, what is the relationship between form and content in literature, and what principles underlie the variety of literary forms, and the changes in literary fashion, in the modern era? To answer such questions, it is argued, we need a comprehensive typology of literary discourse—that is, one capable of describing and discriminating between all types of text without prejudging them. The second part of the book describes and explores a theory of language upon which such a typology may be based—Roman Jakobson's distinction between metaphor and metonymy—and applies it to the analysis of a number of short texts, including those examined in Part One. In Part Three, the theory is applied to a more discursive and historical study of the work of particular writers, or schools and generations of writers, in the modern period.

As is usually the case, the actual genesis of this book was not quite as straightforward as the above summary may suggest. Some years ago I accepted an invitation to contribute to a symposium entitled *Modernism*, edited for Penguin Books by Malcolm Bradbury and James McFarlane. My subject was to be 'The Language of Modern Fiction' and my starting point, in endeavouring to establish some common denominator in the language of novelists who seemed to be such varied and idiosyncratic stylists, was something I had often noticed in casual reading of the 'antimodernist' writers of the 1930s, such as Isherwood, Orwell and Greene, namely their marked preference for simile over metaphor in expressing figures of comparison. In the major modernist novelists such as Joyce, Lawrence and Virginia Woolf, it seemed to me that there was not the same bias, but on the contrary an abundance of metaphor. Some traces of this distinction will be found in what follows, but as my research progressed it was fairly quickly absorbed into what seemed a much more powerful theory.

Like, I suppose, most Anglo-American critics of my generation, I had for some years been making occasional, baffled forays into the foreign territory loosely known as 'structuralism', a word which began to be fashionable in the second half of the 1960s. Here, evidently, was an intellectual movement of rapidly growing influence and prestige, with much to say on the subject of literature and literary criticism. Clearly it could not be ignored. On the other hand, its major texts were difficult to obtain, often available only in a foreign language, and seldom seemed more intelligible when translated into English. Though predisposed to be sympathetic to a formalist and linguistic approach to literary criticism, I found a book like Roland Barthes's *Writing Degree Zero*—one of the first productions of the *nouvelle critique* to be translated—deeply and disturbingly alien in its cryptic, dogmatic style of discussion, unsupported by the kind of close reading which is so characteristic of Anglo-American formalist criticism. The same author's *Elements of Semiology* I found almost incomprehensible (and I wonder how many other readers were misled by that title, invitingly suggestive of a beginner's guide, and put off structuralism for life in consequence?). But I did salvage from that discouraging experience the memory of some allusion to Roman Jakobson's distinction between metaphor and metonymy. In working on my article for the Modernism book, I looked up the source, Jakobson's essay, 'Two Aspects of Language and Two Types of Aphasic Disturbances'. Lightning—and enlightenment—struck. The distinction between metaphoric and metonymic types of discourse not only seemed a much more effective way of distinguishing between the language of modernist and antimodernist fiction than metaphor/simile; it suggested the possibility of an all-embracing typology of literary modes. Jakobson's brief comment on the metonymic character of realistic fiction particularly excited me by its obvious explanatory power. Furthermore, Jakobson's article proved to be the key that unlocked for me some of the sealed doors of structuralism. Pondering it, I began to grasp the principles of, and see the usefulness of, the binary model of language and communication that underlies the whole structuralist enterprise from de Saussure onwards; Roland Barthes's criticism began to make more sense; and I was led back to investigate the origins of the *nouvelle critique* in the work of the Russian Formalists and the Czech Linguistic Circle, discovering the highly suggestive concepts of 'defamiliarization' and 'foregrounding' in the process.

All these ideas, and the whole tradition of thought about language and literature to which they belong, seemed to throw a good deal of light on the problems that had preoccupied me in my previous critical books, *Language of Fiction* (1966) and *The Novelist at the Crossroads* (1971), especially the problem of how to account aesthetically for the realistic novel—how to analyse its formal devices in terms proper to itself and not drawn from drama and poetry. These ideas, and even some of the primary texts in which they first appeared, had of course been available when I was working on those earlier books. René Wellek and Austin Warren refer briefly to the metaphor/metonymy distinction in their *Theory of Literature* (1949), and Roman Jakobson alluded to it in his paper 'Linguistics and Poetics' in the symposium *Language and Style* edited by Thomas A. Sebeok (1960), both of which books I used and referred to in *Language of Fiction*. The ideas were there, under my nose, and yet I did not see them because I was not looking for them. It needed the provocation of the *nouvelle critique* to make them visible to me some years later—and I think my experience has been shared by other English and American critics in the last decade. Although this book is in no sense a systematic introduction to or critique of structuralist criticism (for which the reader is directed to such books as Jonathan Culler's *Structuralist Poetics* (1975), Robert Scholes's *Structuralism in Literature* (1974), Frederick Jameson's *The Prison House of Language* (1972) and Stephen Heath's *The Nouveau Roman* (1972)) it does consciously attempt a synthesis of the two traditions of modern formalist criticism, the European and the Anglo-American. I hope that at least it will serve the function of making some of the concepts of the former tradition better known to exponents of the latter. In particular it seems to me that the importance and possibilities of the metaphor/metonymy distinction have not been adequately recognized even by those English and American critics (such as those named above) who have been most active in studying and disseminating structuralist criticism.*

I have always been a formalist critic, interested in the kind of questions posed by Gertrude Stein in the epigraph to this book, and drawn to the study of the novel partly because of the challenging resistance it seems to offer to formalist criticism. In *Language of Fiction* I took my stand on the axiom that novels are made of words, and argued that since language is self-authenticating in literary discourse in a way that does not apply to nonliterary discourse, all critical questions about novels must be ultimately reducible to questions about language. Though I think it is irrefutable in theory, this argument entailed certain methodological difficulties and

---

*The only book in English known to me which makes extensive use of Jakobson's theory is *The Story-Shaped World: Fiction and Metaphysics: Some Variations on a Theme* (1975) by my colleague at Birmingham, Brian Wicker, whose application of it is rather different from mine, his book being theological as well as literary in its orientation. I have come across a few articles which use or explore the distinction: Fred G. See, 'The Demystification of Style: Metaphoric and Metonymic Language in *A Modern Instance*' [on W. D. Howells] *Nineteenth Century Fiction* XXVIII (1974) pp. 379–403; Frederick Jameson, 'Wyndham Lewis as a Futurist', *Hudson Review* XXVI (1973) pp. 295–329; and (the most interesting from a theoretical point of view) Roger M. Browne, 'The Typology of Literary Signs', *College English* XXXIII (1971) pp. 1–17. No doubt there are others, but on the whole one is struck by how long it has taken for this idea to work its way into Anglo-American critical discourse. Its application to anthropology is better known, through the work of Edmund Leach, especially *Lévi-Strauss* (Fontana, 1970) and *Culture and Communication* (Cambridge, 1976).

disadvantages. In particular it seemed to entail abstaining from discussing a lot of interesting aspects of novels because they had been pre-empted by content-oriented criticism—or discussing them at the risk of seeming inconsistent. In the working out of the argument, language or style became opposed to such categories as plot and character. The great attraction of the structuralist variety of formalism, it seems to me, is that within its terms of reference this kind of antithesis is dissolved in a more comprehensive theory of literary forms. *Everything* is form, from the individual phrase or sentence, up to the structure of a plot or plot-type; and there is a homology between the smallest structural unit and the largest, because all involve the same basic processes of selection and combination, substitution and deletion. Wherever we cut into the literary text, and in whatever direction, we expose, not 'content', but a systematic structure of signs in which content is made apprehensible.

The *dis*advantage of *this* position, in turn, is that it applies through the whole of culture (i.e. everything that is not nature) and governs nonliterary and indeed nonverbal systems of signs as well as literature. A good deal of the most effective structuralist analysis has been employed upon such areas as fashion, food, advertising, and in the field of literary criticism upon work that would be considered beneath the notice of traditional literary studies, such as thrillers and detective stories. It thus leaves open the question of why we should be interested in literature at all. Structuralist critics, especially the French, have taken a somewhat dismissive stance towards the question of value in literature,* either because they deem it irrelevant to the methodology of formal analysis, or because they are ideologically motivated to undermine the traditional cultural prestige of literature as an institution. Thus, by a curious irony, extreme semiotic formalists and their natural opponents, the content-oriented critics, agree in denying that there is any significant discontinuity between life and art—the former on the ground that life is really no different from art, and the latter on the ground that art is really no different from life.

I suppose I am sufficiently conditioned by the Arnoldian tradition in English studies to feel that any critical method should be able to explain why literature is valued (in other words, what is special about it) as well as how it works. I begin therefore, by addressing myself directly to the question, 'What is Literature?' I fear this chapter may be found dry by some readers, especially if they are unfamiliar with the jargon of modern linguistics and impatient with literary theorizing; but I cannot encourage them to skip, since some basic terms used later are defined here. As soon as possible the theoretical issues are examined in relation to specific texts. It seemed desirable that these

---

*One must make an exception of Roland Barthes's more recent work, *S/Z* (Paris, 1970) and *Le Plaisir du Texte* (Paris, 1973) in which value is defined hedonistically and derived from plurality of signification.

texts should have, for purposes of comparison, a common theme. The choice of capital punishment as that theme was more or less accidental (it began with my noticing first the striking similarities, and then the significant differences, between Michael Lake's account of a hanging in the *Guardian* and Orwell's famous essay); but by the time I had finished the book I had become convinced that the 'condemned prisoner story', as Leonard Michaels calls it (see below, p. 232), has a special fascination for the modern literary imagination. Be that as it may, there is something to be said for testing a formalist critical approach on texts that would appear, more than most, to affect us primarily by virtue of their sombre and highly emotive 'content'.

Part Two is not so much a summary of Jakobson's theory, as a speculative expansion of it, a personal exploration of the hints, possibilities and gaps in that fascinating, cryptic, endlessly suggestive paper referred to above, especially the few densely packed pages headed 'The Metaphoric and Metonymic Poles'. The authors and groups of authors discussed in Part Three were selected with a view to illustrating the relevance of the metaphor/metonymy distinction to as many different types of modern writing as possible. I have not discussed contemporary British fiction at any length, because I have written fairly extensively about it before, but a short chapter on Philip Larkin partly covers the relevant phase of literary history. With the exception of that chapter, the focus of the book is upon prose fiction, because that is the form that interests me most and because to have attempted to do equal justice to poetry and drama would have resulted in an impossibly long book. I hope that the occasional asides and digressions about poetry and drama indicate the relevance of the general approach to these kinds of writing also.

Obviously my chief intellectual debt in the writing of this book has been to the work of Roman Jakobson, albeit to a very small part of it. References to other printed sources from which I have profited will be found in the text and notes. While the book was in preparation I addressed several audiences in England and abroad on aspects of its subject, and benefited from the discussions, formal and informal, that followed. I am especially grateful to colleagues, postgraduate students and undergraduates at the University of Birmingham with whom I have explored many of the ideas and texts discussed below, in seminars and in casual conversation. My research into the background of D. H. Lawrence's story, 'England, My England', was significantly assisted by Gabriel Bergonzi and James Boulton. Mas'ud Zavarzadeh generously kept me supplied with postmodernist texts from America. Finally, I owe a special debt of gratitude to those who read the complete text of this book, at one stage or another of its progress to publication, with eyes alert to errors and obscurities, and who gave me the benefit of their opinions and advice: Park Honan, Deirdre Burton, Helen Tuschling and my wife, Mary.

Parts of the essay in *Modernism*, edited by Malcolm Bradbury and James McFarlane, referred to above, and printed in a slightly different form in the *Critical Quarterly*, are embedded in this book; as are parts of a review-article on Gabriel Josipovici, 'Onions and Apricots; or, Was the Rise of the Novel a Fall from Grace?', also printed in the *Critical Quarterly*. The first chapter of Part One is a condensed version of an essay entitled 'What is Literature? A Despatch From The Front', originally published in *The New Review*.

Prefatory Note to the Second Impression

This Note will probably mean little to readers who are beginning the book for the first time, and they are recommended to turn back to it when they have reached the end of Part Two.

In section 5 of Part Two, entitled 'Poetry, Prose and the Poetic', I suggested that there was a certain discrepancy between two important papers by Roman Jakobson, 'Two Aspects of Language and Two Types of Linguistic Disturbances' (1956) and 'Linguistics and Poetics' (1960), namely, that the later paper defines literariness, or the poetic function of language, in terms ('the poetic function projects the principle of equivalence from the axis of selection into the axis of combination') that correspond to the account of metaphor, but not of metonymy, in the earlier paper.

On further reflection, prompted by Terence Hawkes's discussion of Jakobson in *Structuralism and Semiotics* (1977), and confirmed in conversation with Professor Jakobson himself, I wish to withdraw this criticism. Jakobson sees both metaphor and metonymy as figures of 'equivalence', though generated according to different principles. Thus, to use my own example (in section 1 of Part Two), in the sentence 'Keels ploughed the deep', *ploughed* is a metaphorical equivalent for the movement of the ships, derived from similarity, while *keels* and *deep* are synecdochic and metonymic equivalents for 'ships' and 'sea' respectively, derived from contiguity. The discrepancy of which I accused Jakobson was therefore of my own making, since I treated 'equivalence' and 'similarity' as homologous terms.

I am still of the opinion, however, that Jakobson's discussion of 'literariness' in the influential 'Linguistics and Poetics' is, in effect, biassed towards verse rather than prose, towards dominantly metaphorical writing rather than dominantly metonymic writing; and the celebrated definition itself contains a buried metaphor ('projects') which is more obviously applicable to the formation of metaphor than of metonymy. In my model sentence, *ploughed* violently and illogically forces one context (the earth, agriculture) into another (the sea, navigation); *keels* and *deep* do not have the same effect of transgression and rupture. Therefore, while I was wrong to attribute to Jakobson a theoretical inconsistency, this admission does not, I think, affect the main drift and purpose of this book, which was to redress the balance in literary criticism between analysis of metaphoric and metonymic techniques (something Jakobson himself has called for more than once); nor does it invalidate my own theoretical argument, for this was always closer to Jakobson's than I realised.

Although I did not use Jakobson's term, the underlying argument of the theoretical sections of Part One is that 'equivalence' in the most inclusive sense—repetition, parallelism, symmetry of every kind and on every linguistic level—is what makes a text 'literary', or, alternatively, what a literary reading of a text focusses on. As I try to show in the course of Parts Two and Three, the metonymic mode of writing, typically in the realistic novel, allows a pattern of equivalences to be developed in a text without radically disturbing the illusion of a pseudo-historical reality which is constructed on the axis of combination. There would appear to be two principal ways in which this is done. First, the metonymic signifier foregrounds the signified and thus makes its recurrence and interrelation with other signifieds in the text aesthetically functional: what the Prague School theorists call 'systematic internal foregrounding.' This need not involve actually using the rhetorical figures of metonymy or synecdoche, because a narrative text is always in a metonymic or synecdochic relation to the action it purports to imitate, selecting some details and suppressing (or deleting) many others. We notice and respond to the superintendent's manipulation of his stick in Orwell's 'A Hanging' because, out of all the manifold items of his dress and equipment that might have been described, 'stick' is the only one mentioned in the text. Second, the particular property or attribute of a given signified that is highlighted by a metonymic signifier connotes, by association or similarity, another signified not actually mentioned in the text, thus creating a quasi-metaphorical effect without the use of the rhetorical figure of metaphor. The sexual symbolism of the 'red columns' of the guillotine in Bennett's *The Old Wives' Tale* (III, iii, 4) would be an example. Both kinds of metonymically-generated equivalence are in fact extensively illustrated and discussed in the course of this book, though without being related to Jakobson's theory of literariness as explicitly as I would now wish. The argument advanced in section 8 of Part Two, 'The Metonymic Text as Metaphor', though still, I believe, valid, is not the only way of assimilating the metonymic to the poetic in Jakobson's scheme.

April 1979

Acknowledgements

Grateful acknowledgement is made for permission to quote from the following copyright sources: from *Collected Poems* by W. H. Auden, by permission of Faber & Faber Ltd and Random House Inc.; from *Lost in the Funhouse* by John Barth, by permission of Lurton Blassingame and Secker & Warburg Ltd; from *S/Z* by Roland Barthes, translated by Richard Miller, by permission of Jonathan Cape Ltd and Farrar, Straus, Giroux, Inc. (Translation © 1974 by Farrar, Straus, Giroux Inc. Originally published in France as *S/Z* © 1970 Editions Du Seuil, Paris); from 'Style and Its Image' by Roland Barthes, translated by Seymour Chatman, in *Literary Style* ed. Seymour Chatman, by permission of the translator and Oxford University Press, New York: from *Come Back, Dr Caligari*, by Donald Barthelme, by permission of Little, Brown & Co and A. D. Peters & Co Ltd, and from 'A Film' in *Sadness* by the same author, by permission of Jonathan Cape Ltd and Farrar, Straus, Giroux, copyright © by Donald Barthelme 1970, 1971, 1972 (this story originally appeared in the *New Yorker*); from *More Pricks Than Kicks* (All Rights Reserved. First published by Chatto & Windus, London, 1934), *Murphy*, *Watt* (All Rights Reserved) and *The Unnamable* (from *Three Novels* copyright © 1955, 1956, 1958 by Grove Press, Inc.) by permission of Calder & Boyars Ltd and Grove Press Inc.; from *The Old Wives' Tale* by Arnold Bennett, by permission of Mrs Dorothy Chesterton, Hodder & Stoughton Ltd and Doubleday & Co; from *Trout Fishing in America* by Richard Brautigan, copyright © 1967 by Richard Brautigan by permission of Jonathan Cape Ltd and Delacorte Press/Seymour Lawrence; from *The Naked Lunch*, copyright © 1959 by William Burroughs, by permission of Calder & Boyars Ltd and Grove Press Inc.; from *The Film Sense* by Sergei Eisenstin, by permission of Faber & Faber Ltd and Harcourt Brace Jovanovich, Inc.; from *Collected Poems 1909–1962* by T. S. Eliot, by permission of Faber & Faber Ltd and Harcourt Brace Jovanovich, Inc.; from *Collected Essays* and *The Confidential Agent* by Graham Greene, by permission of the author; from 'The Non-Intervenors' in *Several Observations* by Geoffrey Grigson, by permission of the author; from *Death in the Afternoon* and *Men Without Women* by Ernest Hemingway, by permission of the Executors of the Ernest Hemingway Estate, Jonathan Cape Ltd and Charles Scribner's Sons; from *Goodbye*

to Berlin and *Lions and Shadows* by Christopher Isherwood, by
permission of the Hogarth Press and New Directions Inc. and from *A
Single Man* by the same author, by permission of Methuen & Co and
Simon & Schuster Inc.; from 'Two Aspects of Language and Two
Types of Aphasic Disturbances' and 'Linguistics and Poetics' in
Selected Writings by Roman Jakobson, by permission of the author;
from *The World and the Book* by Gabriel Josipovici, by permission of
the author; from *Dubliners*, *A Portrait of the Artist as a Young Man*,
Ulysses and *Finnegans Wake* by James Joyce, by permission of the
Society of Authors, literary representative of the Estate of James
Joyce, Jonathan Cape Ltd, The Bodley Head, Viking Press, Inc. and
Random House, Inc.; from *The Less Deceived* by Philip Larkin by
permission of The Marvell Press, from *The Whitsun Weddings* by the
same author, by permission of Faber & Faber Ltd and from *High
Windows* by the same author, by permission of Faber & Faber Ltd and
Farrar, Straus, Giroux, Inc.; from 'England, My England' in *Collected
Short Stories* by D. H. Lawrence and *The Complete Short Stories of D.
H. Lawrence* Vol II, copyright 1922 by Thomas B. Selzer, Inc., 1950
by Frieda Lawrence, and from the first version of this story in *The
English Review*, October 1915, and from *Women in Love* by the same
author, and from a letter from D. H. Lawrence to Catherine Carswell,
by permission of Lawrence Pollinger Ltd, Viking Press Inc. and the
estate of the late Mrs Frieda Lawrence; the entire text of 'Michael
Lake Describes What The Executioner Actually Faces' in *The
Guardian* 9 April 1973, by permission of the author; from *Autumn
Journal* by Louis MacNeice, by permission of Faber & Faber Ltd and
Oxford University Press, New York; from 'In The Fifties' in *I Would
Have Saved Them If I Could* by Leonard Michaels, copyright © 1973,
1975 by Leonard Michaels, by permission of the author and Farrar,
Straus, Giroux, Inc. (This story first appeared in *Partisan Review*); the
entire text of 'A Hanging' in *Shooting an Elephant and Other Essays* by
George Orwell, copyright 1945, 1946, 1949, 1950, 1973, 1974, by
Sonia Brownell Orwell, also from *Coming Up For Air*, *Keep The
Aspidistra Flying* and *Inside The Whale* by the same author, by
permission of Mrs Sonia Brownell Orwell, Secker & Warburg Ltd,
Brandt & Brandt and Harcourt Brace Jovanovich, Inc.; from *A
Hundred Years of Philosophy* by John Passmore, by permission of
Duckworth & Co Ltd; from *Le Voyeur* by Alain Robbe-Grillet by
permission of Les Editions de Minuit, Paris, and from *The Voyeur*
translated by Richard Howard, by permission of Grove Press and
Calder and Boyars Ltd; from *The Making of Americans* by Gertrude
Stein, by permission of Harcourt Brace Jovanovich, Inc. and from
Look At Me Now And Here I Am by the same author, by permission of
Peter Owen Ltd; from *The Railway Accident and Other Stories* by
Edward Upward, by permission of William Heinemann Ltd; from *The
Waves, To the Lighthouse, Jacob's Room* and *Mrs Dalloway*, by Virginia
Woolf, by permission of the Hogarth Press and Harcourt Brace
Jovanovich, Inc.

Part One

Problems and Executions

1 What is Literature?

We all 'know' what literature is, but it is remarkably difficult to define. When the scholarly journal *New Literary History* recently devoted one of its issues (Autumn, 1973) to the question posed above, the majority of contributors agreed that no abstract, formal definition could be arrived at. Philosophers tell us that such 'essentialist' enquiries are fruitless,[1] that literature, like Wittgenstein's 'games' is a 'family-resemblance concept', the members of the family being linked by a network of overlapping similarities none of which is common to all of them.[2] This latter argument is difficult to refute, and has the attraction, for some, of giving a seal of philosophical approval to theoretical inertia. All games, however, have in common the capacity to be played; and though we lack an equivalent verb in poetics, it seems worthwhile (for reasons suggested in the Preface) enquiring whether there is anything *in* literature that causes or allows us to experience it *as* literature.

Most definitions of literature have, as Tzvetan Todorov observes,[3] been of two kinds: one stating that it is language used for purposes of imitation, that is to say, for the making of fictions, and the other stating that it is language used in a way that is aesthetically pleasing, that calls attention to itself as medium. Todorov attacks modern theorists, such as René Wellek and Northrop Frye, for sliding covertly between these two positions, because, he says, there is no necessary link between them and neither can be a satisfactory criterion for literature alone. I shall argue that there *is* a necessary connection, but it is certainly true that neither definition can stand alone. For, to take the first one, there is literature which is not fiction (e.g. biography) and fiction which is not literature (e.g. advertising in narrative form). Another difficulty with this definition of literature is that the concept of 'fiction' has to be stretched somewhat to cover propositions as well as descriptions, since a good deal of literature (e.g. lyrical and didactic poetry) consists of the former rather than the latter. Recent efforts to apply the speech-act philosophy of J. L. Austin to the theory of literature have enhanced our understanding of what is involved in fictional or mimetic utterance, but have not been able to explain how writing that is factual by intention can acquire the status of literature.[4] It would seem that we can identify literature with fiction only in the weak, negative sense that in the literary text, descriptions and propositions *need* not be put forward or accepted as 'true'.

The other type of definition, literature as language used in a way that is aesthetically pleasing, language that calls attention to itself as medium, has its roots in classical rhetoric, but persists into modern formalist criticism. At its most simple, this theory associates literature with a mere abundance of tropes and figures, and as such is easily refuted. Ruqaiya Hasan, another recent investigator of the problem, observes: 'it is highly doubtful if the frequency of such recognized devices in longer prose works is significantly different from that in, say, a feature article in a quality newspaper.'[5] Nor have the attempts of English and American 'New Critics' to identify literariness with one particular rhetorical device—metaphor, irony, paradox, ambiguity—been conspicuously successful. A more promising approach is the argument of the Czech school of structuralists that literary discourse is characterized by consistent and systematic foregrounding.

'Foregrounding' is the accepted English translation of the Czech word *aktualisace*, which was the central concept of the school of linguistics and poetics that flourished in Prague in the 1930s (to which Roman Jakobson belonged after he left Russia and before he moved to America). In this school of thought, the aesthetic is opposed to the utilitarian. Any item in discourse that attracts attention to itself for what it *is*, rather than acting merely as a vehicle for information, is foregrounded. Foregrounding depends upon a 'background' of 'automatized' components—that is, language used in customary and predictable ways so that it does *not* attract attention. Foregrounding was defined by Jan Mukařovský, the most distinguished of the Czech theorists, as 'the aesthetically intentional distortion of linguistic components'.[6] It is not peculiar to literature—the use of puns in casual conversation is an example of foregrounding; nor does it imply a single linguistic norm, for what is automatized in one kind of discourse will become foregrounded when transferred to another (for example, the use of a technical term in casual conversation). It is not the statistical frequency of foregrounded components that distinguishes literary discourse from nonliterary discourse, but the consistency and systematic character of the foregrounding and the fact that the background as well as the foreground, and the relationships between them, are aesthetically relevant, whereas in nonliterary discourse only the foregrounded components are aesthetically relevant. Furthermore the 'background' of literary discourse is dual: ordinary language ('the norm of the standard language') and the relevant literary tradition.[7]

To this may be added a third type of background: the linguistic norms established by the work itself. Thus, for example, T. S. Eliot's 'Sweeney Among the Nightingales' is foregrounded, first, as poetry against the background of the norms of the standard language, by the presence of metre and rhyme and certain archaic and literary lexical items such as 'the hornèd gate', 'Gloomy Orion', etc. Secondly it is foregrounded as a 'modern' poem against the background of the norms of nineteenth-century English lyric poetry by the inclusion of low subject matter and low diction:

> Gloomy Orion and the Dog
> Are veiled; and hushed the shrunken seas;
> The person in the Spanish cape
> Tries to sit on Sweeney's knees

and by the absence of explanatory links between the various events reported in the poem. And thirdly, the last stanza,

> And sang within the bloody wood
> When Agamemnon cried aloud,
> And let their liquid siftings fall
> To stain the stiff dishonoured shroud

is foregrounded against the background of the rest of the poem by the *absence* of poetic indecorum and by the switch of tense from present to past. At first we are struck by the contrast between the sordid present and the dignified, harmoniously beautiful mythical past to which we are swept by the emphatic 'sang'; then perhaps we recognize that 'liquid siftings' is not after all a metaphor for birdsong but a euphemism for bird-droppings, that the nightingales (representing the natural and aesthetic orders) are as indifferent to Agamemnon as to Sweeney, and that there is not all that much to choose between the two in terms of making a good death. It will be noted that what is foregrounded at one level becomes background at the next.

In the poetics of the Prague school, foregrounding defined in this way is a sufficient criterion of literariness, but Hasan thinks literary foregrounding requires some 'motivation' to explain it. This she finds in the 'unity' of literary texts, a unity of topic or theme that regulates the development of the discourse without being literally present in it:

In literature there are two levels of symbolization: the categories of the code of the language are used to symbolize a set of situations, events, processes, entities, etc. (as they are in the use of language in general); these situations, events, entities, etc., in their turn, are used to symbolize a theme or a theme constellation. I would suggest that we have here an essential characteristic of literary verbal structures. . . . So far as its own nature is concerned, the theme (or regulative principle) of a literary work may be seen as a generalization or an abstraction, as such being closely related to all forms of hypothesis-building. A certain set of situations, a configuration of events, etc. is seen not only as itself (i.e. a particular happening) but also as a manifestation of some deep underlying principle.[8]

This, as Hasan acknowledges, has much in common with Aristotle's definition of the poetic as expressing the universal in the particular. Aristotle, however, equates literature with fiction, to the exclusion of history and philosophy, and so, by implication, does Hasan's theory. It is not immediately obvious how it would, for instance, explain why Boswell's *Life of Johnson* and Pope's *Essay on Man* can be, and are, read as literature, since in these texts there seems to be no second level of symbolization, no second-order theme: Boswell is concerned only with the particular, Pope directly with the universal, and the language of the texts refers us immediately to these regulating themes or topics—Johnson in one case, man's place in the universe in the other. One could get round this difficulty only by saying that Boswell's *Life* is *really* about the nature of genius, or about the problems of writing biography; that the *Essay on Man* is *really* about the terror of the Augustan mind in the face of scepticism or about the problems of fitting philosophical statements into rhyming couplets—finding the regulative principle of the discourse in this kind of motivation. Certainly it is one of the characteristics of a 'literary' reading that we ask what a text is 'about' with the implication that the answer will not be self-evident. We do not merely decode the literary message—we interpret it, and may get out of it more information than the sender was conscious of putting into it. Unfortunately (for the purpose of defining literature) all discourse is open to the same kind of interpretation, as a lot of recent work in linguistics and cultural studies has shown. Roland Barthes's *Mythologies* (Paris, 1957) is a good example of how a second level of symbolization in Hasan's sense can be discovered in journalism, advertising and indeed non-verbal spectacles such as striptease and wrestling.

All one can say to reinforce Hasan's theory is that the literary text *invites* this kind of interpretation, and indeed requires it for its completion, whereas the nonliterary text does not invite it, and is in effect destroyed by it. When Barthes, for example, analyses the contrasting rhetorical strategies used in advertisements for cleaning fluids and detergents ('The implicit legend of [chlorinated fluid] rests on the idea of a violent, abrasive modification of matter; the connotations are of a chemical or mutilating type: the product "kills" the dirt. Powders, on the contrary, are separating agents: their ideal role is to liberate the object from its circumstantial imperfection: dirt is "forced out" and no longer killed . . .'[9]) he renders them impotent: what has been offered as reality is exposed as (in the derogatory sense) a myth. To interpret *Robinson Crusoe* as a myth of bourgeois individualism, however, (as Ian Watt has plausibly done)[10] in no way destroys the power of that story to excite and engage us on the realistic level but explains and enhances it; myth here is used in the honorific sense of a useful fiction, the narrative equivalent of a non-verifiable, non-falsifiable yet valid hypothesis.

We come back to the problem of showing that there is a necessary connection between the fictional and rhetorical definitions of literature. Mukařovský was very insistent that 'the question of truthfulness does not apply in regard to the subject matter of a work of poetry, nor does it even make sense . . . the question has no bearing on the aesthetic value of the work; it can only serve to determine the extent to which the work has documentary value'.[11] The referential dimension of works of literature is regarded by the Prague school as merely a 'semantic component' to be considered by the critic strictly in terms of its structural relationships with other components. The regularizing principle which Hasan looked for in theme or topic is, in their theory, the *dominant*—the component 'which sets in motion, and gives direction to, the relationship of all the other components'.[12] And since literature is not about the real world it must be about itself:

> In poetic language foregrounding achieves maximum intensity to the extent of pushing communication into the background as the objective of expression and of being used for its own sake; it is not used in the services of communication, but in order to place in the foreground the act of expression, the act of speech itself.[13]

A more celebrated and concise formulation of this principle is Roman Jakobson's assertion that the poetic (i.e., literary) function of language is 'the set towards the message for its own sake'. 'Message', here, stands for any act of verbal communication, which Jakobson has analysed in the following terms:

> The ADDRESSER sends a MESSAGE to the ADDRESSEE. To be operative the message requires a CONTEXT referred to . . . a CODE fully, or at least partially common to the addresser and addressee . . . and finally a CONTACT, a physical channel and psychological connection between the addresser and addressee. . . .

Jakobson proposes a typology of utterances according to which of these factors is dominant. Thus, the REFERENTIAL message (e.g. statements of fact) is characterized by the set (*Einstellung*) towards CONTEXT; the EMOTIVE message by the set towards the ADDRESSER (e.g. ejaculations) the CONATIVE message by the set towards the ADDRESSEE (e.g. orders); the PHATIC message by the set towards the CONTACT (e.g. conventional opening exchanges in telephonic communication); and the METALINGUAL message by the set towards the CODE (e.g. definitions of words). The POETIC message is characterized by the set towards the MESSAGE as such, 'for its own sake'.[14]

The usual objections to Jakobson's (and Mukařovský's) definition of the literary are that it is biased towards self-conscious and highly deviant kinds of literature (e.g. the modernist lyric), that it cannot account for kinds of literature in which the referential and communicative element appears to be central (e.g. realistic fiction or autobiography) and that it leads logically to the assertion that the subject matter of a work of literature is merely the pretext for bringing certain verbal devices into play.[15] It is on precisely such grounds that Stanley Fish rejects what he describes as Jakobson's 'message-minus' definition of literature. But he is equally scornful of 'message-plus' definitions that present literature as 'a more effective conveyor of the messages ordinary language transmits', for proponents of this view are 'committed to downgrading works in which the elements of style do not either reflect or support a propositional core'[16]—precisely the kind that are upgraded by the message-minus definition. For Fish and for Todorov, then, available definitions of literature fail because they exclude or downgrade texts pragmatically definable as literature. For Todorov the mistake is to make a dichotomy between literature and non-literature. He argues:

> from a structural point of view, each type of discourse usually referred to as literary has nonliterary relatives which resemble it more than do other types of discourse. For example, a certain type of lyric poetry has more rules in common with prayer than with a historical novel of the *War and Peace* variety. Thus the opposition between literature and nonliterature is replaced by a typology of the various types of discourse.[17]

He does not explain how, lacking a definition of literariness, we may distinguish between literary and nonliterary examples of the same type of discourse—between, say, a prayer that is not literature and a poem by Herbert that is; but he would probably say that this is a 'functional' (as distinct from a structural) distinction that depends upon the cultural values of readers at a particular time. Fish puts it more starkly: 'Literature . . . is an open category . . . definable . . . simply by what we decide to put into it.'[18] For him the mistake is to make a dichotomy between literary language and nonliterary or 'ordinary' language. '*There is no such thing as ordinary language,* at least in the naive sense often intended by that term . . . [T]he alternative view would be one in which the purposes and needs of human communication inform language and are constitutive of its structure.'[19] To deny that there is any difference between literary and nonliterary uses of language has, of course, serious consequences for criticism, for it is then difficult to insist upon the inseparability of form and content in literature.[20] There is, however, a confusion here between the linguistic form of a literary work and the function of its language in the communication of meaning. H. G. Widdowson usefully distinguishes between the two as 'text' and 'discourse', and observes that 'although literature need not be deviant as text it must of its nature be deviant as discourse'.[21] The best term we have for this deviance is, I believe, fictionality, in its most elastic sense. I suggest that literary discourse is either self-evidently fictional or may be read as such, and that what compels or permits such reading is the structural organization of its component parts, its systematic foregrounding. As Widdowson puts it:

> what distinguishes our understanding of literary discourse is that it depends upon our recognizing patterns of linguistic organization which are superimposed as it were on those which the code requires, and our inferring the special values that linguistic items contract as elements in these created patterns.[22]

We must, however, beware of equating literature with 'good literature', as Todorov and Fish do by implication. Another contributor to the *New Literary History* symposium, Dell Hymes, observes:

> there seems to be no special difficulty in categorizing as sculpture works which are great, routine, or amateurishly bad. It is not customary to say that something is not an opera on the ground that it is not great or good. Indeed, of what else except an opera could it be a bad instance? There is no evident reason to be different with regard to literature.[23]

In fact there *is* an evident reason, precisely in that some works of literature can be instances of something else; but Dell Hymes's hint will carry us a long way towards the solution of our difficulties. It is obviously true that 'literature' is a flexible category in that the sum of works included in it will vary from age to age and from person to person. But it is flexible only at its circumference. There are a great many texts which are and always have been literary because there is nothing else for them to be, that is, no other recognized category of discourse of which they could be instances. We may call them *axiomatically literary. The Faerie Queen, Tom Jones* and 'Among School Children' are examples of such texts; but so are countless bad, meretricious, ill-written and ephemeral poems and stories. These too must be classed as literature because there is nothing else for them to be: the question of their value is secondary. When, however, a text that belongs to another identifiable category of discourse is shifted by cultural consensus into the category of literature, value is the primary criterion. As Todorov says, any text can be given a 'literary reading' (which can only mean the kind of reading appropriate to the texts that are axiomatically literary)—but not all texts will emerge with credit from such a reading. This, however, does not affect the status of texts that are axiomatically literary. *Love Story* is literature whether you like it or not, and would be literature even if nobody liked it. But works of history or theology or science only 'become' literature if enough readers like them for 'literary' reasons—and they can retain this status as literature after losing their original status as history, theology or science. Thus it would be meaningful to say, for example, that a text by Freud is a work of literature as well as a work of science, or to say that even if it isn't acceptable as science it is nevertheless a work of literature; but it would be pointless to criticize it for *not* being a work of literature, because it was intended to be science, and only readers could make it into literature. (It would of course be quite legitimate to criticize *them* for doing so.) The main difference between the two kinds of text is that recognition of 'the set towards the message' is essential to interpretation in the first instance, optional in the second.

Although descriptions and propositions in literature may have the appearance of nonliterary descriptions and propositions, by virtue of sharing a common code, nevertheless the adequacy of what is said in literary discourse 'is not, in any straightforward sense, governed by any state of affairs prior to and independent of what is said'.[24] The systematic foregrounding of axiomatically literary texts often acts in the first place as a sign that this is the case—that the ordinary rules for determining truthfulness do not apply—by foregrounding the text as literature against the background of nonliterature. If such texts are successful, it is because the systematic foregrounding also supplies the place of the absent context of facts and logical entailments which validates nonliterary discourse; one might say that it folds the context back into the message, limits and orders the context in a system of dynamic interrelationships between the text's component parts—and thus contrives to state the universal in the particular, to speak personally to each reader and yet publicly to all, and to do all the other things for which literature has traditionally been valued. If a text which is *not* foregrounded as literature can nevertheless become literature by responding to a literary reading, it can only be because it has the kind of systematic internal foregrounding which makes all its components aesthetically relevant, 'patterns of linguistic organization which are superimposed as it were on those which the code requires'. (We find an intuitive recognition of this by the reading public in the fact noted by Northrop Frye that 'style . . . is the chief literary term applied to works of prose generally classified as non-literary'.[25]) It is this which allows us to read the text 'as if' the criteria of truthfulness did not apply. Boswell's Johnson then becomes something like a fictional character, and his *Life* is read as if it were a kind of novel—though without ceasing to be a biography: we read it on two levels at once, as literature and as history, whereas most other biographies of Johnson are merely history, and conceivably superior as such to Boswell's. Jonathan Culler suggests, in his thoughtful *Structuralist Poetics*, that 'Rather than say . . . that literary texts are fictional, we might cite this as a convention of literary interpretation and say that to read a text as literature is to read it as fiction.'[26]

I would accept this formulation as long as it is recognized that the convention of fictionality derives from texts that *insist* on being read as fiction. The qualification is important because Culler, like Todorov and Fish (though on different grounds), implies that 'literature' is wholly accountable in terms of the reading process—that it is indeed a category of reading procedures, not of the properties of texts. But to stress the dependence of literature upon particular modes of reading is only a half-truth, the other half of which is the dependence of those modes of reading on the existence of literature. The process is dialectical, as Sartre explained in *What is Literature?*

> The operation of writing implies that of reading as its dialectical correlative and these two connected acts necessitate two distinct agents. It is the conjoint effort of author and reader which brings upon the scene that concrete and imaginary object which is the work of the mind.[27]

To accept this version of the literary process does not entail accepting Sartre's prescription of literary *engagement*, because the contractual link between writer and reader which he defines as an appeal to 'freedom' could quite as well be defined as an appeal to something else—to intelligibility, for instance, to use a word Culler himself favours. The important point is that literature is not a body of texts which came into being accidentally, and which we have spontaneously decided to read in a certain way. Most of the discourse we read as literature is on one level the expression of an intentionality to write literature, and it is from such discourse that we derive the conventions of interpretation that Culler calls 'literary competence', which we can then turn experimentally upon discourse that does *not* express such intentionality. Writing requires reading for its completion, but also teaches the kind of reading it requires.

I am therefore accepting that literature is an open category in the sense that you can, in theory, put any kind of discourse into it—but only on condition that such discourse has something in common with the discourse you cannot take out of it: the something being a structure which either indicates the fictionality of a text or enables a text to be read as if it were fictional. I now propose to test this theory on a text chosen deliberately for the resistance it seems to offer to the theory.

2   George Orwell's 'A Hanging', and 'Michael Lake Describes . . .'

George Orwell's 'A Hanging'* is undoubtedly part of 'English Literature', but surely (it may be objected in the light of the preceding discussion) it is a factual document, and to say that it is literature because we can read it as if it were fiction can only deprive it of its main claim to be valued, namely that it is telling the truth, making us 'face the facts' of capital punishment.

*See Appendix A. Figures in square brackets refer to the numbered paragraphs of this text.

When I first read 'A Hanging' I certainly assumed that it was a true story, an eye-witness account. The more I studied it, the more I suspected that Orwell had added or altered some details for literary effect, but I did not doubt that the piece was essentially factual and historical. I think this is probably the response of most readers of 'A Hanging'—certainly nearly all the published commentary on it assumes that it is, like its companion piece 'Shooting an Elephant', a true story based on Orwell's own experience. The exception is the interesting biography of Orwell's early years, *The Unknown Orwell* (1972) by Peter Stansky and William Abrahams. They have interviewed Orwell's friend Mabel Fierz, who was largely responsible for getting *Down and Out in London and Paris* (1933) published and whom he met in 1930. They report:

> he appears to have told her things he told no-one else—from a literary point of view, the most sensational confidence was that his essay 'A Hanging' which came out in the *Adelphi* the next winter* was not, as it purported to be, an eye-witness account but a work of the imagination, for (she remembers him telling her) he had never been present at a hanging.[1]

Stansky and Abrahams have also talked to Orwell's colleagues in the Burmese police force, who agreed that

> It would have been most unusual, though not impossible . . . for him to have been present at a hanging. As Headquarters ASP [Assistant Superintendent of Police] at Insein his duties would not normally require his presence there.[2]

Writing in *The Road to Wigan Pier* (1937) about his experience of administering the British Empire, Orwell says, 'I watched a man hanged once. It seemed to me worse than a thousand murders'[3]— which appears to be a fairly clear reference to, and authentication of, 'A Hanging'. But Stansky and Abrahams show that Orwell, like most of us, did not always tell the strict truth, either in conversation or in print. So there is at least an element of doubt about the eye-witness authenticity of 'A Hanging', a possibility that it is a fiction.

To entertain this possibility may be a shock at first, involving a sense of having been deceived. But on reflection we can see, I think, that the factors which made us read the text as an eye-witness account are mainly *external* to the text. First, most of us read it, no doubt, in a volume of Orwell's essays, a context which implies that is a factual, rather than a fictional account. The volumes of essays in which it appeared, *Shooting an Elephant* (1950) and *Collected Essays* (1961) were, however, posthumous publications: Orwell himself was not responsible for placing 'A Hanging' in this non-fiction context. In his lifetime the piece was published only twice—in the *Adelphi* for August 1931 and in the *New Savoy* in 1946. Secondly, we read 'A Hanging' knowing that George Orwell was a police officer in Burma, a job which

*Actually August 1931.

he grew to detest and repudiate, but one that would plausibly enough involve him in witnessing an execution. We may, indeed, read 'A Hanging' with that reference in *The Road to Wigan Pier* at the back of our minds.

The original readers of 'A Hanging' in the *Adelphi* had no such knowledge of its author. 'Eric A. Blair', as the piece was signed (he did not adopt the name George Orwell until 1933) was known to them only as the author of a few book reviews in the same periodical and of a first-person sketch of a weekend spent in an English workhouse—'The Spike'—published in April 1931, and later incorporated into *Down and Out in Paris and London*. The text of 'A Hanging' itself gives no information about the 'I' figure who narrates: no explanation of why he is present at the hanging, or what his function is supposed to be. This absence would have been more striking to the original readers than it is to us, who read back into the text all the biographical information we have acquired about George Orwell/Eric Blair, much of which he himself supplied in his books from 1936 onwards. Stansky and Abrahams observe the same ambiguity about the 'I' figure in 'The Spike' and in *Down and Out*, which Orwell was writing at about the same time. They argue that the invention of this narrator, originally in 'The Spike', was the crucial technical breakthrough in Eric Blair's early struggles to find a style for himself that was not hopelessly derivative and conventionally 'literary'.

> The material he had accumulated until now had to be reinvented if he was to use it truthfully—which meant not a surface honesty but to get under the surface (any honest reporter could take care of the surface) and get down to the essence of it. He began to write in the first person without intervention: simply, I was there.[4]

But since the focus was to be on '*there*', the personal history of '*I*' had to be rigorously curtailed. (Stansky and Abrahams plausibly suggest that Blair adopted the pseudonym 'George Orwell' when *Down and Out* was published not, as he claimed, because he feared the book would be a failure, but to reinforce the anonymity of the narrator. They also show how he rather clumsily attempted to conceal the fact that he had collected much of the material by deliberately posing as a down-and-out).

It is very unlikely, at this date, that we shall ever be able to establish definitely whether Orwell attended a hanging or not, and more or less impossible that we should ever be able to check the particular circumstances of 'A Hanging' against historical fact. It may be completely factual, it may be partly based on experience, or partly on the reported experience of others, or partly fictional, or wholly fictional—though the last possibility seems to me the least likely. The point I wish to make is that it doesn't really matter. As a text, 'A Hanging' is self-sufficient, self-authenticating—autotelic, to use the jargon word. The internal relationships of its component parts are far more significant than their external references. In fact, when we examine the text carefully we see that these external references—to time, place, history—have been kept down to a minimum. There are no proper names except 'Burma' and the Christian name of the head warder. There are no dates. There is no explanation of the prisoner's crime. And it is because the external references of the text are reduced in this way that the internal relationships of its component parts— what has been referred to earlier as systematic foregrounding or patterns of linguistic organization—are correspondingly important, as I shall show.

'A Hanging' is literature, therefore, not because it is self-evidently fictional, but because it does not need to be historically verifiable to 'work'. Although it is possible, and perhaps natural in some circumstances, to read 'A Hanging' as history, the text will, I believe, survive the undermining of that assumption. It is equally satisfying, equally successful read as a true story or as a fiction or as something in between, and nothing we might discover about its relationship to history will affect its status as literature.

It may seem that I am making too simple a distinction here between fiction and history, and taking a naively positivistic view of the latter. But while it is true that historians construct fictions in the sense that they inevitably select and interpret 'the facts' according to conscious or unconscious ideological predilections, no neutral or total reconstruction of the past being possible, nevertheless history is based on the assumption that there is a body of facts to be selected from and interpreted, and that our understanding of an event can be improved or revised or altered by the discovery of new facts or the invalidation of old ones.[5] There is no way in which our understanding of 'A Hanging' could be improved or revised or altered by the discovery of new facts. In this respect it contrasts instructively with an account of a hanging by Michael Lake that appeared in the *Guardian* for 9 April, 1973 under the title 'Michael Lake Describes What the Executioner Actually Faces'.* This text has many features in common with 'A Hanging', and superficially the same narrative design: the procession to the scaffold, the numbed state of the condemned man, the abrupt operation of the gallows, the whisky and the macabre joking of the officials afterwards, the narrator's residual sense of guilt. 'Michael Lake Describes . . .' seems to me a good piece of journalism, and as a polemic against capital punishment perhaps more effective than Orwell's piece. But it *is* journalism, and remains this side of literature. Its effectiveness depends on our trust that it is historically verifiable. If we discovered that there was no such person as Walter James Bolton, or that Michael Lake had never attended a hanging, the text would collapse, because it would be impossible to read it, as one can read 'A

*See Appendix B.

Hanging', as an effective piece of fiction. Once its external references were cut, the comparative weakness of its internal structure would become all too evident. We should become aware of clichés, opportunities missed, a lack of variety in tempo and in intensity of feeling. Details like 'Mr Alf Addison, an old friend of mine' would no longer have any function and would become irritating irrelevancies. And perhaps we should feel we were being bullied into the desired response by crudely sensationalist means.

Correspondingly, 'A Hanging' has certain qualities which 'Michael Lake Describes . . .' hasn't got: a narrative structure, for instance, that is more than a mere sequence. The structure of Michael Lake's report is a chain of items linked in chronological order and suspended between an opening statement of polemical intent and a closing statement of personal feeling. The structure of 'A Hanging' is also chronological, but it is more complex: the inevitable movement towards the death of the condemned man is deliberately but unexpectedly retarded at two points: first by the interruption of the dog and secondly by the prisoner's invocation of his god. These delays heighten the tension, and they allow the moral protest against capital punishment to emerge out of the narrative instead of being merely signalled at the beginning and end. Another structural difference is that Orwell's piece goes on proportionately longer after the actual execution, enforcing the double concern of the writer: not only with what the execution does to the executed but also what it does to the executioners. In a sense, this extended ending is another form of retardation, since it retards the expected termination of the text.

'Retardation' is one of the basic devices that, according to the Russian Formalist Victor Shklovsky, enable narrative art to achieve the effect of 'defamiliarization' which he held to be the end and justification of all art:

> Habitualization devours objects, clothes, furniture, one's wife and the fear of war. 'If all the complex lives of many people go on unconsciously, then such lives are as if they had never been.' Art exists to help us recover the sensation of life; it exists to make us feel things, to make the stone *stony*. The end of art is to give a sensation of the object as seen, not as recognized. The technique of art is to make things 'unfamiliar', to make forms obscure, so as to increase the difficulty and the duration of perception. The act of perception in art is an end in itself and must be prolonged. *In art, it is our experience of the process of construction that counts, not the finished product.*[6]

Although the last statement leads logically to Shklovsky's celebration of *Tristram Shandy* as the supreme example of narrative art,[7] the quotation in the second sentence is from the diary of Tolstoy, from whom Shklovsky draws several of his illustrations. In other words, there is no incompatibility between the theory of 'defamiliarization' and realistic writing of the kind Orwell practiced—indeed 'A Hanging' illustrates the theory very well, for what Orwell is doing is defamiliarizing the idea of capital punishment—the idea, not the experience of it, since only the first is 'familiar'.

Michael Lake is trying to do the same thing, but by the comparatively crude method of filling out the familiar idea with unfamiliar details. He selects and describes aspects of the event he witnessed which will make us recoil from it: the possibility of Bolton's head being torn off by his own weight, the hypocrisy and/or irrelevance of the chaplain's prayers, the macabre fancy-dress of the executioner's get-up, Bolton's inarticulateness, and so on. But these details belong to quite disparate emotive categories—some are nauseating, some ironic, some pathetic—and Lake makes no attempt to relate them to each other. He fires the details at us on the principle of the shotgun: if a few miss the target, enough will hit it to make the desired effect. It would be difficult to say, on the evidence of the text, exactly what aspect of the proceedings was to him the most significant or indeed what it is, precisely, that makes capital punishment inhuman in his view.

There is no such difficulty in the Orwell text. The central paragraph [10] makes clear what the narrator feels to be wrong about capital punishment (though it is an 'unspeakable wrongness' he in fact proceeds to speak it). Interestingly, it is not the most gruesome or solemn part of the proceedings that provokes this realization, but a gesture so small and ordinary that most people, perhaps including Mr Lake, would never have noticed it (always supposing, of course, that it actually happened): the prisoner side-stepping the puddle. Why is this gesture so pregnant with meaning for the narrator? Because in the context of imminent death, it makes him understand what it is to be alive. Orwell has thus defamiliarized the idea of capital punishment by defamiliarizing something in fact much more familiar, much more veiled by habit: simply being alive. Implicitly the incident reveals that there is all the difference in the world between knowing *that* we shall die and knowing *when* we shall die. Human life exists in an open-ended continuum. We know that we shall die, but if we are healthy our minds and bodies function on the assumption that we shall go on living, and indeed they cannot function in any other way. The man instinctively avoids the trivial discomfort of stepping in the puddle on his way to the scaffold. His nails continue growing even as he falls through the air with a tenth of a second to live. So he is in the intolerable position of having to behave as if he is going to go on living, but knowing that he isn't going to. And the spectator is correspondingly impressed by the grim irony that all present are inhabiting the same continuum of experience, but that for one person it is not open-ended: 'he and we were a party of men walking together, seeing, hearing, feeling, understanding the same world'—the present participles emphasize the notions of continuity and community—'and in two minutes, with a sudden snap, one of us would be gone—one mind less, one world less.'

There is then, in this central paragraph, an emphasis on the idea of time in relation to life and death. 'Time is life, and life is time,' runs the lyric of a modern song.[8] 'Death,' said Wittgenstein, 'is not an event *in* life. We do not live to experience death.'[9] At the level of maximum abstraction that is what 'A Hanging' is about: the paradoxical relationships between the concepts death, life and time, in the context of capital punishment. For capital punishment in a sense seeks to subvert the logic of Wittgenstein's assertion, to force the experience of death into life. That is why it is, or may be held to be, inhuman and obscene. Michael Lake is dimly aware of these paradoxes—at least I think that is why he is shocked and incredulous that the chaplain is reading aloud the Burial Service over the living man. But he hasn't quite worked out what is shocking about it, and without Orwell's piece for comparison we might not have worked it out either.

Throughout 'A Hanging' there are repeated references to the theme of life/death/time which prepare for and sustain the explicit statement of it by the narrator in paragraph 10. In the first paragraph there is the reference to the other 'condemned men due to be hanged in the next week or two'. In paragraph 3, eight o'clock strikes, and the superintendent urges the warders to hurry up: 'The man ought to have been dead by this time. . . .' In paragraph 5 there is the remark that the prisoners can't get their breakfast until the execution is completed—a reference to the continuum of life/time that will go on without the condemned man.

Then comes the intervention of the dog. This of course is the vehicle for several kinds of ironic commentary on the action, but let us just note for the moment that it is a delay, an interruption of the proceedings and duly recorded as such by the narrator: 'It was several minutes before someone managed to catch the dog. Then we put my handkerchief through its collar and moved off once more . . .'[8]. The association of the narrator with the dog through 'my' handkerchief is interesting, perhaps a way of preparing for the narrator's moral recoil from the execution in the next paragraph, in which the personal pronoun 'I' is used for the first time, 'I' becoming distinguished from 'we'. This paragraph ends with the side-stepping of the puddle, which leads to the explicit reflection upon life/death/time in paragraph 10.

In paragraph 12 begins the second interruption or delay: the prisoner's prayer to his god. We are now in a position to appreciate the underlying function of these two delaying or 'retarding' incidents, which as we noted above constitute the main structural feature of the narrative. If the genre were romance, or at least a narrative more overtly fictional and 'literary', these delays might be welcomed by the narrator, and vicariously by the reader, as affording some time in which a reprieve might arrive, or some rescue be effected (one thinks of *The Heart of Midlothian* or *Adam Bede*). But of course no such possibility is hinted at in 'A Hanging'. Although the narrator, in paragraph 10, recognizes the 'unspeakable wrongness' of the execution, he has no intention of trying to stop it, and neither have any of the other people present. Therefore, although for the prisoner every cry is 'another second of life', this only draws out the agony. Since he must die, the quicker the better for everyone's comfort: 'the same thought was in all our minds: oh, kill him quickly, get it over, stop that abominable noise.' [13] To the narrator, the repetition of the god's name is not 'like a prayer or cry for help'—not, that is, like human speech—but 'steady, rhythmical, almost like the tolling of a bell'—in other words, a regular notation of passing time. 'Minutes seemed to pass.' The narrator wonders if the superintendent is allowing the man a fixed number of cries, 'fifty, or perhaps a hundred'. [13]

After the execution is carried out and the body of the man has been inspected, the Superintendent glances at his watch: 'Eight minutes past eight.' [16] In paragraph 17 the procession reverses itself, minus one. There is a reference to the other condemned men waiting to die, a reference to the other prisoners receiving their breakfast—recapitulations of details in the opening paragraphs. Now the unbearable contradictions of life/death/time have been temporarily resolved and an almost hysterical wave of relief and callous good-humour flows over the witnesses, temporarily melting away conventional barriers of caste, status and race. Dialogue—direct speech—suddenly begins to dominate narrative. 'I' is absorbed back into 'we', and the ironies of time are replaced by ironies of space: 'We all had a drink together, native and European alike, quite amicably. The dead man was a hundred yards away.' [24]

One might say that Orwell has achieved the 'defamiliarization' of capital punishment by 'foregrounding' the semantic component of time in his text. There is indeed a close connection between these two concepts—defamiliarization being opposed to habitualization in Russian Formalism as foregrounding is opposed to automatization in the poetics of the Prague school. It is to be noted, however, that the language in which the time motif is reiterated is not itself foregrounded in any obvious way either against the 'norm of the standard' or against the internal norms of the text itself (the nearest equivalent in 'A Hanging' to the foregrounded shift of tense in the last stanza of 'Sweeney Among The Nightingales' is the shift from 'we' to 'I' in paragraph 9).

To sum up the argument so far: 'Michael Lake Describes . . .' is not axiomatically a literary text and could only become one by responding satisfactorily to a 'literary' reading. This, I suggest, it could not do. Whether or not Orwell's 'A Hanging' is axiomatically a literary text is much more problematical and the answer probably depends upon the context in which it is read, and the expectations of the individual reader. It is not foregrounded as literature in any obvious way—indeed it could be said to disguise itself as nonliterature, to merge like a chameleon into the background of writing like 'Michael Lake Describes . . .', though there are certain significant absences in the text which perhaps operate as signs of literariness at an almost subliminal level, and covertly invite a 'literary' reading. That it responds satisfactorily to a literary reading there is no doubt, and I have tried to connect this with certain features of its internal structure. There is a lot more to be said about this text, and we shall return to it in due course. Meanwhile I wish to introduce another text into our discussion which will enable us to test Todorov's hypothesis that 'each type of discourse usually referred to as literary has nonliterary relatives which resemble it more than do other types of literary discourse'.

3 Oscar Wilde: 'The Ballad of Reading Gaol'

Oscar Wilde's poem has a good deal in common with the two prose texts discussed above in respect of subject matter and attitudes. Like them it is about the execution of a certain individual—in this case a trooper of the Royal Horse Guards convicted of murdering his wife or mistress and hanged at Reading Gaol, where Wilde himself was a prisoner at the time. The execution (which takes place at 8 a.m.) is the occasion of mounting horror and intolerable suspense, and there are many references to time:

> So we—the fool, the fraud, the knave—
>   That endless vigil kept,
> And through each brain on hands of pain
>   Another's terror crept.
>
> . . . .
>
> The moaning wind went wandering round
>   The weeping prison-wall
> Till like a wheel of turning steel
>   We felt the minutes crawl . . .
>
> . . . .
>
> We waited for the stroke of eight:
>   Each tongue was thick with thirst:
> For the stroke of eight is the stroke of Fate
>   That makes a man accursed.[1]

The attendant doctor has a watch

> whose little ticks
> Are like horrible hammer-blows.

There is comment on the paradoxical solicitude of the condemned man's warders:

> Who watch him lest himself should rob
> The prison of its prey

and on the reading of the Burial Service over the living man.

Like 'A Hanging' and 'Michael Lake Describes . . .', 'The Ballad of Reading Gaol' is both didactic and confessional: it seeks to condemn the institution of capital punishment, in which the narrator has no active role, and at the same time confesses his sense of guilt and complicity in the act. Unlike 'Michael Lake Describes . . .', however, and in a much more obvious and unproblematical way than 'A Hanging', 'The Ballad of Reading Gaol' is literature, and would be unhesitatingly identified as such by any reader. It is axiomatically a literary text because there is nothing else for it to be. This is not simply because it is a ballad (the ballad form, though usually a sign of literature, may be applied to nonliterary purposes, e.g. advertising); and certainly not because it is obviously fictional, for it is dedicated to 'C.T.W. Sometime Trooper of the Royal Horse Guards obit. H.M. Prison, Reading, Berkshire, July 7, 1896' and it was public knowledge at the time of publication that Oscar Wilde had been a convicted prisoner in the same gaol. To that extent the poem is more 'historical' than 'A Hanging'. We should be on firmer ground in tracing the poem's literariness to the way it states propositions which do not require our intellectual assent to be effective, for instance:

> For he who sins a second time
> Wakes a dead soul to pain,
> And draws it from its spotted shroud
> And makes it bleed again,
> And makes it bleed great gouts of blood,
> And makes it bleed in vain!

There is indeed in 'The Ballad of Reading Gaol' a heavy loading of religious sentiment, an appeal to transcendental and specifically Christian values (entirely absent from the Orwell and Lake texts) which, though no doubt more immediately accessible and appealing to a Christian reader, are not dependent on the reader's prior belief in or conversion to Christianity for their effectiveness. The poem is, to use I. A. Richards's logico-positivist term, a tissue of 'pseudo-statements'. The sterile and sordid operation of human justice is contrasted with the mysterious mercy and transforming grace of God, and the redemption of the condemned man is affirmed by associating him closely with the passion of Christ: not only by explicit assertion—

> How else but through a broken heart
> May Lord Christ enter in?

—but through an elaborate pattern of symbolism and allusion. The ministry of the prison chaplain is called 'the kiss of Caiaphas'; the last night before the execution is a kind of Gethsemane for the condemned man and for those who watch with him in spirit. There are metaphoric allusions to the Passion like 'And bitter wine upon a sponge/Was the savour of Remorse'; references to cocks crowing, to 'bloody sweats', the 'wounds of Christ' and the Good Thief. The gallows, like the Cross in typological and devotional tradition, is compared to a tree—

> And, green or dry, a man must die
> Before it bears its fruit!

The warders 'strip' and 'mock' the prisoner's corpse. And so on.

Perhaps the most interesting motif is the play on the colour red, and its 'opposite' white.* Northrop Frye, in a brief, brilliant comment on *The Faerie Queen*, has drawn attention to the archetypal and specifically Christian symbolism of these colours:

> St George's emblem is a red cross on a white ground, which is the flag borne by Christ in traditional iconography when he returns in triumph from the prostrate dragon of hell. The red and white symbolize the two aspects of the risen body, flesh and blood, bread and wine, and in Spenser they have a historical connection with the union of red and white roses in the reigning head of the Church. The link between the sacramental and the sexual aspects of the red and white symbolism is indicated in alchemy, with which Spenser was clearly acquainted, in which a crucial phase of the production of the elixir of immortality is known as the union of the red king and the white queen.'[2]

Wilde draws on a surprising number of these associations and combines them skilfully with the given facts of the action he is dealing with—for instance the red uniform of the guardsman:

> He did not wear his scarlet coat,
>   For blood and wine are red,
> And blood and wine were on his hands
>   When they found him with the dead,
> The poor dead woman whom he loved,
>   And murdered in her bed.

Here, in the very first stanza, Wilde introduces one of the keynotes of his poem. Literally the stanza seems to say that the soldier did not wear his scarlet uniform in prison because it would have reminded him of the blood and wine that covered his hands when he committed murder. But this is a slightly fanciful speculation rather than a statement of fact

*Archetypally, the opposite of white is black; but red can be opposed to white or black. It has been argued that these are universally the three most common colour terms: i.e. languages with only two basic colour terms have words for black and white, and languages with only three basic colour terms have words for black, white and red. See B. Berlin and P. Kay, *Basic Colour Terms* (Berkeley, 1969); cited by John Lyons, 'Structuralism and Linguistics', *Structuralism: An Introduction* ed. David Robey (Oxford, 1973), p. 16.

(presumably he would not have been allowed to wear his dress uniform in prison anyway). The logical force of 'for' is by no means immediately apparent to the reader, whose attention is more likely to be engaged by the emotive reverberations of the phrase 'blood and wine', which the ballad form permits Wilde to use twice in successive lines. Though the blood and wine are literal facts of the case, the idea of sacramental transubstantiation of one into the other, of the Eucharistic wine into Christ's redemptive Blood, can scarcely be kept out of the reader's mind, and thus the idea of religious transcendence is immanent in the poem from the very beginning. Though there is no mention of whiteness in the stanza it is implicit in the reference to the man's hands and to the woman murdered in her bed (connotations of sheets, nightclothes, naked flesh, death pallor, etc.). Whiteness is *kept* implicit in this way because Wilde wants to use it explicitly later on as an image of grace, redemption, transcendence. For instance, after the fine stanzas describing the burial of the man in quick-lime ('He lies, with fetters on each foot/Wrapt in a sheet of flame') the poet asserts that no seed will be sown on the grave for three years.

> They think a murderer's heart would taint
>   Each simple seed they sow.
> It is not true! God's kindly earth
>   Is kindlier than men know.
> And the red rose would blow more red,
>   The white rose whiter blow.
>
> Out of his mouth a red, red rose!
>   Out of his heart a white!
> For who can say by what strange way,
>   Christ brings His will to light. . . .

A few lines later, to recall the original symbolism of red = wine = blood, the rose is referred to as 'wine-red'. Towards the end of the poem we return to the image of its opening stanza:

> And with tears of blood he cleansed the hand
>   The hand that held the steel:
> For only blood can wipe out blood,
>   And only tears can heal:
> And the crimson stain that was of Cain
>   Became Christ's snow-white seal.

One does not have to be a stylistician to see that in linguistic form 'A Hanging' is much more like 'Michael Lake Describes . . .' than either is like 'The Ballad of Reading Gaol'. The latter displays a degree of systematization quite absent from the other two texts. In the first place there is the regularity of rhythm and repetition of sounds in rhyme which usually distinguishes verse from prose. And there are other kinds of linguistic schematization which though not peculiar to verse are present here in greater density than one finds in prose: tropes and figures of repetition, equation, symmetry, analogy and contrast. Just looking again at the first stanza, we find repetition of the same sounds in the rhymes *red—dead—bed*, repetition of *blood and wine*, repetition of *dead*, application of two semantically contrasting verbs to the same noun (a kind of zeugma) in the '*woman* whom he *loved*,/And *murdered*', an explicit equation of blood and wine in respect of colour, and an implicit equation of them by allusion to the Eucharist, and an emphatic parallelism of syntactical structure, each line constituting a clause in subject-predicate order and each line being in effect an expansion or explanation of an item in the preceding line. Thus *red* in line 2 explains the significance of *scarlet* in line 1, *on his hands* in line 3 explains the significance of *blood and wine* in line 2, *dead* in line 4 explains *blood* in line 3, *woman* in line 5 explains *the dead* in line 4, and *murdered* in line 6 explains *dead woman* (though not *loved*) in line 5. In these respects, the first stanza (which is also the first sentence) of the poem is a microcosm or model for the whole poem, which is built up in much the same way: the stanzas/sentences (there is always one sentence per stanza) are linked formally by the repetition of verbal formulae and semantically by the expansion of or variation upon the same set of themes.

It would be much more difficult to offer an equivalent account of 'A Hanging' and 'Michael Lake Describes . . .' because there seems to be much less linguistic systematization to get hold of. Indeed one of the first things a critic would probably say about the language of these texts is that on the whole their authors have deliberately *avoided* the various rhetorical devices of which Wilde makes such abundant use, in order to achieve accuracy and authenticity (or the illusion of these qualities). The structure of the discourse, such a critic might suggest, is derived not from rhetoric, not, that is, from the possibilities of linguistic form (e.g. the ballad in Wilde's case) but from reality, the structure of events described. Orwell himself seems to have believed this was indeed how such writing got written:

> What is above all needed is to let the meaning choose the word, and not the other way about. In prose, the worst thing one can do with words is to surrender to them. When you think of a common object, you think wordlessly, and then, if you want to describe the thing you have been visualizing, you probably hunt about until you find the exact words that seem to fit it.[3]

Though revealing about Orwell's literary aims, this description of the compositional process is wholly unsatisfactory. It is based on the fallacy that we can think without using verbal concepts and it therefore ignores the creative function of language in making 'reality' humanly intelligible.

Hangings are highly formalized social rituals and therefore have a more definite structure than most events involving human interaction; and it is certainly the case that both Orwell and Lake have modelled their texts on this structure more closely than Wilde. We have already observed, for instance, that Orwell and Lake follow the chronological order of events, whereas Wilde shifts his narrative about in time a good deal, so that we experience the actual execution not once but many times in the course of the poem. 'A Hanging' and 'Michael Lake Describes . . .' are, however, in no sense totally objective or comprehensive accounts of the events they purport to describe, simply because no such account is possible. There is more order in these texts than in the events they describe because, unlike the events, they are wholly constituted of language, and language is more systematic than nonlanguage. Orwell and Lake have produced their texts by making some selection and organization of the theoretically inexhaustible 'facts' of the events they describe, and it should be possible to analyse how this is done in language more positively than by saying that they have avoided the obtrusive patterning of Wilde's poem. In short, what we need is a definition of the type of discourse to which these texts belong—but a definition that will enable us to explain why one is literature and the other is not. For while Todorov's hypothesis holds good in that 'A Hanging' resembles 'Michael Lake Describes . . .' much more closely than it resembles 'The Ballad of Reading Gaol', the kind of reading which establishes 'A Hanging' as literature, and which (I have suggested) 'Michael Lake Describes . . .' cannot sustain, is essentially the same kind of reading as that which the 'Ballad' naturally invites. A 'literary' reading of the Orwell and Wilde texts alike is essentially a process of identifying and interrelating recurrent features which are thematically significant, the difference being that whereas these features are foregrounded by Wilde's poetic language, they are much less visible in the language of Orwell's text, either because the foreground-background perspective is much shallower or because the thematic motifs are deliberately buried in the background. In this respect, 'A Hanging' is like much realistic fiction. But what is realism?

4 What is Realism?

'Realism' (or 'realistic') is as problematical a term as literature/literary, and for much the same reasons. It is used sometimes in a neutrally descriptive sense and sometimes as an evaluative term; the particular instances to which it is applied will vary from one period to another and from one person to another;[1] and it is not exclusively aesthetic in application. Quite apart from the technical meaning of realism in philosophy, there is an ordinary use of 'realism/realistic' to denote a recognition of facts, usually unwelcome facts, which, though sometimes applied to art, is by no means exclusive to it (e.g. 'The Government had made a realistic assessment of the country's economic situation'). This use of realism usually implies approval and its negative is the disapproving 'unrealistic'. The specifically aesthetic use of 'realism', however, which has the meaning, roughly, of 'truth to life/experience/observation in representation', may be used either evaluatively or descriptively, and has two corresponding negatives, unrealistic and nonrealistic. If we say that a certain text is 'unrealistic' we normally mean that it has tried to be realistic and failed, and if we say that a text is nonrealistic we usually mean that the writer has deliberately chosen to write in the mode of, say, fantasy rather than realism.* But there are many literary texts where the question of realism as an aesthetic category does not seem to arise at all: lyric poetry of a thematic kind, for instance, and even much narrative poetry. It wouldn't make much sense to ask whether 'The Ballad of Reading Gaol' was realistic or not. It has its realistic passages:

> We tore the tarry rope to shreds
> 	With blunt and bleeding nails
> We rubbed the doors and scrubbed the floors
> 	And cleaned the shining rails:
> And, rank by rank, we soaped the plank,
> 	And clattered with the pails

and it has its nonrealistic passages—for example when the 'forms of Fear' and 'Shapes of Terror' are described as dancing and singing through the cells on the eve of the execution:

> With the pirouettes of marionettes,
> 	They tripped on pointed tread:
> But with flutes of Fear they filled the ear,
> 	As their grisly masque they led,
> And loud they sang, and long they sang,
> 	For they sang to wake the dead.

Yet there is no aesthetic conflict between these two very different narrative passages, no problem about accommodating them within the same work, because the 'Ballad' does not demand the kind of assent in which such a conflict could arise. It does not ask (despite the obvious influence of *The Ancient Mariner*) for a willing suspension of our disbelief—the central subject is, after all, a matter of historical fact, and there is no difficulty about accepting it as such. But neither does

---

*An alternative term, coined by Borges, is 'irrealism'. See, for instance, Tom Samet, 'Contemporary Irrealism', *Novel*, IX (1975) pp. 66–73.

the 'Ballad' ask us to agree, 'Yes, this is how it must have been'—it does not confine itself to historical fact, or make all its details consistent with historical fact, or seek to recreate the experience of historical fact. If Wilde had wanted to do these things he would have written in prose, the natural medium of history. He is not concerned to reconstruct or explain a given event, but to apprehend the event through the attributes and associations which it generates, and for this purpose the highly systematic nature of the ballad form is appropriate.

When applied in the aesthetic sense to nonfictional texts, 'realism' is nearly always an evaluative term which assigns a 'literary' status to the text. To say that 'Michael Lake Describes . . .' is 'realistic' in a neutrally descriptive sense would be a kind of tautology. This kind of writing is either true—true in the sense that the facts given are verifiable—or it is not, in which case it is worthless: nonrealism is not an option for the journalist. Of course, this 'truth' is mainly a matter of conventional trust between reader and writer (or reader and newspaper) but such trust is in part dependent upon the character of the discourse. It is necessary that there should be an absence of logical contradiction because this would throw doubt on the veracity of the report; and some hostages to verifiability must be given in the form of dates, names, etc. Beyond this, we might praise a journalistic report for being 'vivid' or 'sensitive' or 'evocative' or 'revealing', and these would be essentially literary judgments since we are normally in no position to compare a journalistic report with the events it describes (though we can sometimes compare it with other reports) and it is precisely through such judgments that historical or journalistic reports are accorded the status of literature. 'Realistic' is another such word. Consider, for example, Leonard Schapiro's comment on Alexander Solzhenitsyn's *The Gulag Archipelago* (1974):

> The book is shattering in its realism. The horrors, the degradation, the sufferings are described with an actuality which makes one feel that one is oneself present at what is happening. The realism recalls Tolstoy more than any other writer . . .[2]

It is clear from the context, if not from the quotation itself, that this is a literary judgment. In his review Schapiro deals with *The Gulag Archipelago* first as political history, and then as 'a literary work of genius' and it is under the latter heading that he makes the remark about realism. *The Gulag Archipelago*, Schapiro is saying, is history, but it transcends the limitations of historical method by recreating experience in the manner of a novelist (Tolstoy). This does not apparently undermine its status as history (though some historians might think it did).

There is always a suggestion of imagination, of illusion, of the fictive, in the word 'realistic' used as a term of praise, as can be seen by the way Schapiro pays his tribute to the effect: Solzhenitsyn 'makes one feel one is actually present at what is happening'. The writer, by projecting himself into where he is not (and often into where he has never been, because Solzhenitsyn is writing largely about other people's experiences) transports the reader to where *he* is not. This is perhaps the fundamental appeal of all realistic art—and it depends of course on the consumer knowing where he *really* is: reading a book or looking at a picture or watching a film or play. Although in a simple sense realism is the art of creating an illusion of reality, one hundred per cent success in this enterprise equals failure. *Trompe l'oeil* art only becomes art at the moment we recognize how we have been deceived, and it is considered a low form of art precisely because we cannot simultaneously enjoy the illusion and the knowledge that it is an illusion.

For obvious reasons, a verbal text can never be mistaken for the reality it refers to, as an object of visual or plastic art may be mistaken. Writing cannot imitate reality directly (as a film, for instance, can); it can only imitate ways of thinking and speaking about reality, and other ways of writing about it. A working definition of realism in literature might be: *the representation of experience in a manner which approximates closely to descriptions of similar experience in nonliterary texts of the same culture.* Realistic fiction, being concerned with the action of individuals in time, approximates to history: 'history is a novel which happened; the novel is history as it might have happened' as the Goncourt brothers put it.[3] Thus the realistic novel, from its beginnings in the eighteenth century, modelled its language on historical writing of various kinds, formal and informal: biography, autobiography, travelogue, letters, diaries, journalism and historiography.

With respect to fictional texts, then, the term 'realistic' may be used in the neutral, descriptive sense to mean that the discourse is broadly consistent with historical fact as known and mediated by the contemporary historical consciousness. In this sense both Tolstoy and, say, Anthony Powell, are realistic novelists, whereas Lewis Carroll and Thomas Pynchon are not. This realism is a convention which makes possible in the novel the qualitative realism attributed by Schapiro to Solzhenitsyn and Tolstoy, the power of making events, whether invented or factually based, convincingly 'present' to the reader. Paradoxically, whereas realism in the neutral sense indicates a fictional text's approximation to history, realism in the qualitative sense may indicate a historical text's approximation to fiction.

I am conscious here of Hayden White's objection to using an oversimplified concept of history as a route to a definition of realism:

> In my view the whole discussion of the nature of 'realism' in literature flounders in the failure to assess critically what a genuinely 'historical' conception of reality consists of. The usual tactic is to set the 'historical' over against the 'mythical' as if the former were genuinely *empirical* and the latter

were nothing but *conceptual*, and then to locate the realm of the 'fictive' between the two poles. Literature is then viewed as being more or less *realistic*, depending upon the ratio of empirical to conceptual elements contained within it.[4]

I admit to employing this tactic, but I do not see that White offers, in the end, a better one at this level of generality. He does indeed show that 'different historians stress different aspects of the same historical field'[5] because of their different ideological, argumentative, narrative and rhetorical predispositions, and that it is possible to develop a typology of historiography as richly varied as any typology of narrative literature. Nevertheless he concedes that all the varieties of nineteenth-century historiography can be seen as shades within the spectrum of a general professional orthodoxy about the aims and limits of history-writing, an orthodoxy to which only the philosophers of history, Marx and Nietzsche, offered a truly radical challenge. According to this orthodoxy,

> a 'historical account' would be any account of the past in which the events that occupied the historical field were properly named, grouped into species and classes of a distinctively 'historical' sort, and further related by general conceptions of causation by which changes in their relationships could be accounted for.[6]

Such a concept of history will serve as a point of reference for measuring realism in fiction. The radical alternatives proposed by Marx and Nietzsche perhaps correspond, respectively, to the radically nonrealistic fictional modes of metafiction (which destroys illusion by exposing its own structural principles) and mythopoeia (which sacrifices illusion to imagination).

If we hesitate to apply the word 'realistic' to 'A Hanging' it is because the word implicitly raises questions about where the text stands in relation to history and to fiction which, as we have seen, the text seems designed to elude. 'A Hanging' certainly has the effect of making us feel 'one is present at what is happening'. But we cannot be certain whether Orwell is recreating someone else's experience, or creating a fictional experience, or reporting an experience of his own. It purports to be the last of these, and probably most people read it as such: but in that case it would be either redundant or inappropriate to describe it as 'realistic'. What would a truthful account of what the writer actually saw and felt be, but realistic in the neutral sense? And if we say it is realistic in the qualitative sense, doesn't that imply that he has created the *illusion* of his being present at the hanging? I think myself that 'A Hanging' is best classified as an early example of a kind of writing that has been called recently 'the non-fiction novel' or the New Journalism,[7] a kind of writing in which the techniques of realistic fiction, which evolved out of the application of historical narrative methods to fictitious events, are in turn applied to historical events.

This would explain why it so closely resembles realistic fiction in form without being comfortably classifiable as such. To continue the discussion we need a more orthodox example of realistic fiction.

5 Arnold Bennett: 'The Old Wives' Tale'

Pursuing our somewhat morbid theme, let us take as a classic instance of an execution described in a realistic novel, Chapter iii, Book III of Arnold Bennett's *The Old Wives' Tale* (1908), entitled 'An Ambition Satisfied'. This follows closely upon the elopement of Sophia, the more wilful and adventurous of the two sister-heroines, with Gerald Scales, a commercial traveller who has inherited a small fortune, and whose superficial sophistication has dazzled Sophia and blinded her to his essentially weak and coarse-grained character. Scales in fact intended to seduce Sophia and to take her to Paris as his mistress, but when Sophia, sensing danger, insists on being married before proceeding beyond London, Gerald capitulates. The couple spend their honeymoon in Paris and for a while all goes well: Gerald, who is familiar with the country and the language, enjoys showing the worldly, dazzling capital of Louis Napoleon to his innocent and provincial bride, buying her Parisian dresses and taking her to expensive restaurants patronized by the *demi-monde*. Sophia's disillusionment in her husband begins one night when he becomes involved in a drunken quarrel at the Restaurant Sylvain, causing her considerable embarrassment and anxiety (III, ii, 2). However, she rationalizes her criticisms of his conduct, and when the next day he announces his intention of satisfying 'a lifetime's ambition' by witnessing an execution, she agrees to accompany him and his friend Chirac.

> In five minutes it seemed to be the most natural and proper thing in the world that, on her honeymoon, she should be going with her husband to a particular town because a notorious murderer was about to be decapitated there in public. (III, iii, 1)[1].

The town is Auxerre and the condemned is a young man called Rivain, convicted of murdering his elderly mistress: the case had been eagerly discussed at the Restaurant Sylvain, where Gerald met Chirac.

For Sophia the experience is a deepening nightmare. At each stage of the journey she becomes more and more uncomfortably aware of the unpleasant emotion and excitement generated by the impending execution, and of the unsavoury character of those who are attracted by the spectacle. She is in fact being led unawares into a sadistic and sexual orgy. By a series of evasions and subterfuges, Gerald installs her not in the respectable hotel he had promised but in a seedy establishment overlooking the very square where the execution is to take place the next morning, paying for the dingy bedroom a grossly inflated price. (III, iii, 2) At supper that evening, Sophia is alarmed and repelled by the greedy, noisy and licentious behaviour of the company. 'All the faces, to the youngest, were brutalized, corrupt, and shameless.' (III, iii, 3) Gerald, eventually 'somewhat ashamed of having exposed his wife to the view of such an orgy', takes her to the bedroom and leaves her, explaining that he does not intend to go to bed. Sophia lies awake, depressed by the events of the day and disturbed by sounds reaching her from every part of the hotel, some of which are obviously sexual, though with sadistic connotations: 'long sighs suddenly stifled; mysterious groans as of torture, broken by a giggle ....' Suddenly she is startled by a noisy commotion in the square—the first signs of the crowd gathering to witness the execution. Against the promptings of her better self, she 'yielded to the fascination and went to the window'. It is dawn, and the windows of the other buildings around the square are already filled with spectators. 'On the red-tiled roofs, too, was a squatted population.' Down below the police are engaged in pushing back

> a packed, gesticulating, cursing crowd . . . as the spaces of the square were cleared they began to be dotted by privileged persons, journalists or law officers or their friends, who walked to and fro in conscious pride; among them Sophia descried Gerald and Chirac, strolling arm in arm and talking to two elaborately clad girls who were also arm in arm.
>
> Then she saw a red reflection coming from one of the side streets of which she had a vista.

This comes from a lantern on the wagon, drawn by a gaunt grey horse, that brings the components of the guillotine to the square. The crowd bursts into a ferocious chant as the 'red columns' of the guillotine are erected and its mechanism tested;

> *Le voila!*
> *Nicolas!*
> *Ah! Ah! Ah!*

('Nicolas' is evidently a familiar name for the guillotine deriving from its first victim, Nicolas Jacques Pelletier.) To Sophia's dismay the executioner's party retires to the hotel where she herself is situated, and occupies a room on the same floor. The excitement in the square increases.

> In a corner of the square she saw Gerald talking vivaciously alone with one of the two girls who had been together. She wondered vaguely how such a girl had been brought up, and what her parents thought—or knew! . . . Her eye caught the guillotine again, and was held by it. Guarded by gendarmes, that tall and simple object did most menacingly dominate the square with its crude red columns. Tools and a large open box lay on the ground beside it. (III, iii, 4)

She loses sight of Gerald and then, fearing that he might return to the room and find her at the window, she returns to bed, vowing that she will remain there until he comes back. She is awakened from a doze by

a tremendous shrieking, growling and yelling: a phenomenon of human bestiality that far surpassed Sophia's narrow experience. . . . 'I must stay where I am,' she murmured. And even while saying it she rose and went to the window again and peeped out. The torture involved was extreme, but she had not sufficient force within her to resist the fascination. She stared greedily into the bright square. The first thing she saw was Gerald coming out of a house opposite, followed after a few seconds by the girl with whom he had previously been talking. Gerald glanced hastily up at the facade of the hotel, and then approached as near as he could to the red columns . . . the racket beyond the square continued and even grew louder. But the couple of hundred persons within the cordons, and all the inhabitants of the windows, drunk and sober, gazed in a fixed and sinister enchantment at the region of the guillotine, as Sophia gazed. 'I cannot stand this!' she told herself in horror, but she could not move; she could not move even her eyes. . . . Then a gigantic passionate roar, the culmination of the mob's fierce savagery, crashed against the skies. The line of maddened horses swerved and reared, and seemed to fall on the furious multitude while the statue-like gendarmes rocked over them. It was a last effort to break the cordon and it failed.

From the little street at the rear of the guillotine appeared a priest, walking backwards and holding a crucifix high in his right hand, and behind him came the handsome hero, his body all crossed with cords, between two warders, who pressed against him and supported him on either side. He was certainly very young. He lifted his chin gallantly, but his face was incredibly white. Sophia discerned that the priest was trying to hide the sight of the guillotine from the prisoner with his body, just as in the story she had heard at dinner.

Except the voice of the priest, indistinctly rising and falling in the prayer for the dying, there was no sound in the square or its environs. The windows were now occupied by groups turned to stone with distended eyes fixed on the little procession. Sophia had a tightening of the throat, and the hand trembled by which she held the curtain. The central figure did not seem to her to be alive: but rather a doll, a marionette wound up to imitate the action of a tragedy. She saw the priest offer the crucifix to the mouth of the marionette, which with a clumsy unhuman shoving of its corded shoulders butted the thing away. And as the procession turned and stopped she could plainly see that the marionette's nape and shoulders were bare, his shirt having been slit. It was horrible. 'Why do I stay here?' she asked herself hysterically. But she did not stir. The victim had disappeared now in the midst of a group of men. Then she perceived him prone under the red column, between the grooves. The silence was now broken only by the tinkling of the horses' bits in the corners of the square. The line of gendarmes in front of the scaffold held their swords tightly and looked over their noses, ignoring the privileged groups that peered almost between their shoulders.

And Sophia waited, horror-struck. She saw nothing but the gleaming triangle of metal that was suspended high above the prone, attendant victim. She felt like a lost soul, torn too soon from shelter, and exposed for ever to the worst hazards of destiny. Why was she in this strange, incomprehensible town, foreign and inimical to her, watching with agonized glance this cruel, obscene spectacle? Her sensibilities were all a bleeding mass of wounds. Why? Only yesterday, and she had been an innocent, timid creature in Bursley, in Axe, a foolish creature who deemed the concealment of letters a supreme excitement. Either that day or this day was not real. Why was she imprisoned alone in that odious, indescribably odious hotel, with no one to soothe and comfort her, and carry her away?

The distant bell boomed once. Then a monosyllabic voice sounded sharp, low; she recognized the voice of the executioner, whose name she had heard but could not remember. There was a clicking noise. . . .

She shrank down to the floor in terror and loathing, and hid her face and shuddered. Shriek after shriek, from various windows, rang on her ears in a fusillade; and then the mad yell of the penned crowd, which, like herself, had not seen but had heard, extinguished all other noise. Justice was done. The great ambition of Gerald's life was at last satisfied. (III, iii, 4)

It might be felt that in the last paragraph but two in this extract, the one beginning 'And Sophia waited . . .', Bennett has to some extent spoiled his effect by spelling out explicitly and somewhat clumsily what has already been adequately implied. Certainly, any sensitive reader will have apprehended, either analytically or intuitively, that the execution at Auxerre is experienced by Sophia as a violation, both literal and symbolic, of her selfhood, and is therefore an 'objective correlative' for her disillusionment in Gerald as lover and husband. In its way the episode fills up a conspicuously vacant space in the narrative—the absence of any description of Sophia's initiation into sex. In the Restaurant Sylvain, Sophia's face is described as 'so candid, so charmingly conscious of its own pure beauty and of the fact that she was no longer a virgin, but the equal in knowledge of any woman alive'. But the context, contrasting Sophia's 'baby's bonnet' and 'huge bow of ribbon' with the 'violently red lips, powdered cheeks, cold, hard eyes, self-possessed arrogant faces, and insolent bosoms' of the Parisiennes (III, ii, 2) makes it clear that Sophia's 'knowledge' is of a very superficial or self-deceiving kind. Real knowledge comes later, at Auxerre. Or, to put it another way, the execution brings to a crisis Sophia's suppressed suspicions about her husband's weakness of character simultaneously with her suppressed feelings of having been sexually outraged by him. Of course it is not only Sophia who is suppressing these feelings but also Bennett. But it is obvious that if Bennett, in the manner of a present-day novelist, had described the sexual side of the honeymoon in detail, it would have been as trauma for Sophia: everything we are told about her and Scales compels this deduction. The reticence of Edwardian taste, or Bennett's own reticence, led him to transfer this trauma to the execution (though without leaving the bedroom). Possibly this was to the book's advantage.

The expedition to Auxerre is steeped in a thickening atmosphere of sexual licence and degradation from its genesis in the Restaurant Sylvain to its climax in the square, where Gerald is flagrantly unfaithful to his new bride under her very eyes (whether or not Sophia realizes, or allows herself to realize, the full implications of Gerald's emergence from the house opposite with the girl he has picked up in the square is not entirely clear—she reflects later on his 'fatuous vigil of unguessed licence' (III, iii, 5)—but she certainly feels betrayed). It is because she is herself emotionally alienated to an agonizing degree that Sophia is unable to achieve any sympathetic imaginative connection with the prisoner Rivain. Unlike the narrator of 'A Hanging', she is not struck by the poignant contrast between her own freedom and the prisoner's fate. On the contrary, she sees him as 'a doll, a marionette wound up to imitate the action of a tragedy' because she feels herself to be equally deprived of free will, unable (as that antepenultimate paragraph makes clear) to account for her own actions and her own situation. But this does not lead to anything like the penitent and therefore spiritually liberating identification with the condemned man claimed by the narrator of 'The Ballad of Reading Gaol':

> But there were those amongst us all
> Who walked with downcast head,
> And knew that, had each got his due,
> They should have died instead . . .

Interestingly, the colour red, which we traced in its various mutations through 'The Ballad of Reading Gaol' is also a recurrent motif in the Bennett text, though to very different effect. The references to the red rooftiles, the red lantern and the four references to the red columns of the guillotine have already been quoted. One might add that the furnishings of Sophia's hotel bedroom are 'crimson'. Although these references are entirely literal they acquire considerable connotative force, but it is semantically quite remote from Wilde's poem and more deeply buried. Clearly Bennett's 'red' has nothing to do with the redeeming blood of Christ any more than Rivain's 'incredibly white face' has anything to do with the 'white seal' of Christ. There is no possibility of transcendence in Bennett's materialist vision, either for Sophia or for Rivain—who butts the offered crucifix away with his head. Transcendence is hardly present even in a negative or demonic form: though the crowd's roar is 'devilish' we cannot say with much conviction that the red in this scene is the glow of hellfire.

Red is the colour of passion, of sexual love, of sexual sin (the courtesan in the Restaurant Sylvain wears a vermilion cloak in case there should be any doubt that she is a scarlet woman), the colour of blood (which is shed at deflowerings as well as beheadings) and of the erect male sexual organ. We need look no further to explain why Sophia's gaze keeps returning with horrified fascination to the 'red columns' of the guillotine which 'had risen upright from the ground' (as though by their own volition) and beside which she observes 'a large open box'—presumably a receptacle for the head, but also a classic female symbol in Freudian dream analysis. At the climax it is surely not only Rivain's head, but Sophia's maidenhead, and by extension her inviolate self, that lies 'prone under the red column' (*column* now significantly changed from the plural to the singular) 'between the grooves' (the analogy with female genitalia is striking) awaiting the brutal and irreversible stroke. Which she does not in fact see, does not need to see, before she 'shrank down to the floor in terror and loathing, and hid her face, and shuddered'. If there are any doubts about the validity of this reading they should be dispelled when we turn to the next section of the same chapter, where Gerald returns in a state of shock from the execution, and the contempt of Sophia, now beginning to rally, is expressed with veiled allusion to detumescence: 'Not long since he had been *proudly conversing* with impudent women. Now in *swift collapse*, he was as *flaccid* as a sick hound and as disgusting as an aged drunkard' (III, iii, 5, my italics; perhaps it is worth pointing out that 'proud' can mean swollen by sensual excitement and 'conversation' can refer to sexual intimacy).

The search for meaning, the process of interpretation, has taken us along the same path as before: identifying and relating recurrent items of the discourse. It has also led us, apparently, away from our ostensible topic, realism. Phallic guillotines are not the kind of thing we expect to find in realistic fiction, surely? But if there is any truth in the Freudian account of the mind, there is of course no reason why such things should not appear in the literary rendering of 'reality'. The point is simply that in realism we have to look very hard for them, we have to go down very deep to find them, because 'in reality' they are hidden, latent, suppressed. Sophia is not *conscious* of the full significance the 'red columns' have for her, and perhaps Bennett himself is not. Realism is a mode of writing derived from consciousness rather than the unconscious, the daylight rather than the nighttime world, the ego rather than the id: that is why it is such an excellent mode for *depicting* repression.

But in describing *The Old Wives' Tale* as a realistic novel we should be thinking in the first place of the justice it does to the individual experience of a common phenomenal world. In the chapter just reviewed we should be responding to the vivid evocation of the atmosphere in Auxerre on the eve of the execution, the graphic description of the events in the square, and the convincing portrayal of how a young, innocent, provincial English bride reacts to these things—always assuming we considered that Bennett had succeeded in doing what he was trying to do. 'Yes, that's what it would have been like—yes, that's how she would have behaved', is on one important level the kind of response Bennett is seeking to elicit from the reader. As Henry James put it, in discussing this novel:

> the canvas is covered, ever so closely and vividly covered, by the exhibition of innumerable small facts and aspects, at which we assist with the most

comfortable sense of their substantial truth. The sisters, and more particularly the less adventurous [Constance] are at home in their author's mind, they sit and move at their ease in the square chamber of his attention, to a degree beyond which the production of that ideal harmony between creature and creator could scarcely go, and all by an act of demonstration so familiar and so quiet that the truth and poetry, to use Goethe's distinction, melt utterly together and we see no difference between the subject of the show and the showman's feeling, let alone the showman's manner about it.[2]

In his preface to the novel Bennett makes an observation on the effect of authenticity in the Auxerre episode which bears interestingly on some of the questions raised in our enquiry:

It has been asserted that unless I had actually been present at a public execution, I could not have written the chapter in which Sophia was present at the Auxerre solemnity. I have not been present at a public execution, as the whole of my information about public executions was derived from a series of articles on them which I read in the Paris *Matin*. Mr Frank Harris, discussing my book in *Vanity Fair*, said it was clear I had not seen an execution (or words to that effect), and he proceeded to give his own description of an execution. It was a brief but terribly convincing bit of writing, quite characteristic and quite worthy of the author of *Montes the Matador* and of a man who has been almost everywhere and seen almost everything. I comprehended how far short I had fallen of the truth! I wrote to Mr Frank Harris, regretting that his description had not been printed before I wrote mine, as I should assuredly have utilized it, and, of course, I admitted that I had never witnessed an execution. He simply replied: 'Neither have I.' This detail is worth preserving, for it is a reproof to that large body of readers, who, when a novelist has really carried conviction to them, assert off hand: 'O, that must be autobiography!'

In this last remark we encounter a recognition of the realist's paradoxical situation: that one hundred per cent success in creating an illusion of reality is a kind of failure, in that it denies him a recognition of his artistry. But there is in fact some confusion of categories here. No one could suppose that the Auxerre chapter as presented was 'autobiographical' in the sense that 'A Hanging' might reasonably be supposed to be autobiographical, because this would imply that Bennett was a woman. For the chapter is not really about the execution of Rivain but about Sophia's experience of it, an experience which partly overlaps with the common experience of all those present (the guillotine was red, the gendarmes struggled to control the crowd, the crowd roared the chant about Nicholas, etc.) but is largely peculiar to Sophia, determined by her personality, her physical angle of vision and her emotional situation. In this latter aspect of the experience— what is peculiar to Sophia—we can discriminate between the conscious (e.g. her observation of Gerald's movements) and the unconscious (e.g. the sexual significance of the guillotine) but it is clear that they are connected. Even if Bennett had been present at a guillotining, then, he couldn't possibly have experienced it in the same way as Sophia; whereas it is easy to suppose that if Orwell had been present at a hanging he would have reacted much as the narrator of 'A Hanging'. If Bennett's rendering of Sophia's experience of the event 'carries conviction', therefore, it must be an imaginative achievement on his part. Only the 'public' part of the chapter could possibly be autobiographical—i.e., remembered rather than re-searched or invented. But there is no way in which a novelist like Bennett can reveal which of these methods he has used at a particular point, no way in which he can indicate the seams joining together recalled, researched and imagined material, without violating the conventions of his mode and destroying his 'realism'.

In the scene that immediately follows the execution, however, Bennett finds a way of drawing attention to the fictiveness of his narrative without violating the illusion of historical veracity he has created. Gerald is brought back to the bedroom by Chirac in a state of shock: 'his curiosity had proved itself stronger than his stomach'. The arrival of the landlady to collect the price of the room, even more inflated than Gerald had admitted, completes Sophia's disillusionment. Surveying Gerald's ignoble, prostrate and dormant figure, she reflects:

> Such was her brilliant and godlike husband, the man who had given her the right to call herself a married woman! He was a fool. With all her ignorance of the world she could see that nobody but an arrant imbecile could have brought her to her present pass.

Sophia's rage gives her the strength to act independently. From this moment begins her recovery from her disastrous elopement with Gerald (a heroic recovery, but also a tragic one, based on the acquisition of money and the denial of eros). She takes from Gerald's coat an envelope containing £200 in English banknotes and sews them into the lining of her skirt, reasoning that he will assume he has lost them.

> With precautions against noise, she tore the envelope and the letter and papers into small pieces, and then looked about for a place to hide them. A cupboard suggested itself. She got on a chair, and pushed the fragments out of sight on the topmost shelf, *where they may well be to this day*. (III, iii, 5, my italics)

What is the force of that last phrase? It seems to claim a kind of verifiability for the narrative which would be appropriate to 'Michael Lake Describes . . .' but which is quite inapplicable to a novel. Of course it is not a serious claim. Only a very naive and muddleheaded reader would have set off to Auxerre in 1908 with any hopes of finding fragments of Gerald's letter and envelope in a hotel room there. The novelist has deliberately overreached himself in his realistic enterprise. By the excessiveness of his claim that Sophia and Gerald belong to real history he reminds us that they belong to fiction. He thus makes explicit what is, according to Roland Barthes, always implicit in the realistic novel: 'giving to the imaginary the formal guarantee of the real, but while preserving in the sign the ambiguity of a double object, at once believable and false.'[3] This is very different from the mode of *non*-realism, which we may briefly illustrate with the 'Orgasm Death Gimmick' section of William Burroughs's *The Naked Lunch* (1959).

6   William Burroughs: 'The Naked Lunch'

Burroughs is obviously alluding to this scene* when he says in the Introduction to *The Naked Lunch*:

> Certain passages in the book that have been called pornographic were written as a tract against Capital Punishment in the manner of Jonathan Swift's *Modest Proposal*. These sections are intended to reveal capital punishment as the obscene, barbaric and disgusting anachronism that it is.[1]

I have expressed elsewhere some scepticism about this defence:

> It may be that the disgust Mr Burroughs feels for capital punishment has been transferred to the antics of his sexual perverts, but the reverse process which should occur for the reader is by no means to be relied upon. The power of Swift's piece inheres very largely in the tone of calm reasonableness with which the proposal is put forward, so that we feel obliged to supply the emotion which is missing. In *The Naked Lunch*, instead of this subtly controlled irony we have a kinetic narrative style which suspends rather than activates the reader's moral sense, and incites him to an imaginative collaboration in the orgy.[2]

Although I stand by this comment in general, I am not sure that the final point is entirely fair, and I would certainly acknowledge that Burroughs's writing here is not pornographic. Pornography I define as a type of discourse designed to be used as a substitute for or stimulus to erotic pleasure. (Needless to say, much discourse not so designed can be used for the same purpose.) Like other types of nonliterary discourse (advertising, polemic etc.) pornography can become literary if it responds successfully to a literary reading. What usually prevents it from doing so is that it is *un*realistic rather than nonrealistic: it pretends to a realism it cannot sustain. In its world men are improbably potent, women improbably voluptuous, perfect orgasms are achieved with improbable frequency and sexual encounters are always structured in an order of progressively mounting excitement, novelty and ecstasy. All this bears little resemblance to actual sexual

*See Appendix C.

experience, yet for pornography to be effective in its special function, the fantasy has to be sufficiently realistic for the reader to enter into it imaginatively. This no doubt explains why so many pornographic works from *Fanny Hill* onwards are cast in the form of confession or autobiography, the simplest and most obvious way of giving fiction an appearance of authenticity. If pornographic fiction does not invariably try to be realistic this is because some sexual deviations are inherently fantastic; or, more often, because the use of exotic or fantastic settings legitimizes the pornographic content for the consumer, and perhaps for the guardians of public morality, by providing an alternative, though spurious, focus of attention and by reducing the erotic charge of the action through distancing. The more permissive the moral climate, however, the more realistic pornography tends to be. The soft-core pornography published in contemporary girlie magazines of the *Penthouse* variety, for instance, shows a steady tendency towards pseudo-documentary: stories are illustrated by photographs rather than drawings or paintings, and much space is devoted to letters from readers recounting their sexual experiences, which, whether they come from *bona fide* readers or are in fact written by the magazine's staff, are in most cases fairly obviously erotic fantasies with a 'realistic' dressing. The realistic dressing does not merely contribute to pornography a general air of probability—it also constitutes the only element of variety in the genre, which is otherwise necessarily repetitive, condemned to rehearse again and again the same basic rhythm of excitement and release, the same limited repertoire of physical actions and reactions. This restriction, it should be observed, derives not merely from the sexual possibilities of the human body (e.g. its number of orifices) but also from the tastes of the pornographer's readers, who will usually accept only one particular type of sexual activity—heterosexual *or* homosexual *or* sado-masochistic *or* rubber fetichistic, etc. Only by varying the context of these actions through realistic specificity can the pornographer to some extent disguise their stereotyped character and introduce an element of unpredictability and spontaneity into his narrative, without which the reader could hardly get any satisfaction from it.*

By these criteria, *The Naked Lunch* is not pornographic. Though

*In this respect he is not, from a structuralist point of view, very differently situated from any other writer: 'the affectivity which is at the heart of all literature includes only an absurdly restricted number of functions; I desire, I suffer, I am angry, I contest, I love, I want to be loved, I am afraid to die—out of which we must make an infinite literature. Affectivity is banal, or, if you prefer, typical, and this circumstance governs the whole Being of literature; for if the desire to write is merely the constellation of several persistent figures, what is left to the writer is no more than an activity of variation and combination . . .' (Roland Barthes, *Critical Essays*, translated by Richard Howard (Evanston, 1972) pp. xvi–xvii). Arguably, however, pornography does not have the authentic (if banal) affectivity of literature: the pornographer says not, *I* lust, but *you shall* lust.

parts of the passage quoted in the Appendix do, I think, 'incite the reader to an imaginative participation in the orgy' the context is never stable enough for long enough to allow a steady build-up of erotic excitement. The sequence of actions becomes impossible to accept on any kind of 'realistic' level at three points in particular: when Mary eats the corpse of Johnny, when Mark 'turn[s] into Johnny' and when Mark/Johnny leaps out of the room into space. We note, too, that all kinds of sexual behaviour and perversion are mixed up together in this sequence, in defiance of the strict decorum of pornography, just as literary decorum is breached in the mixture of horrific and comic motifs.

The passage in question comes from a chapter entitled *a.j.'s annual party*, and is supposed to be part of a blue movie shown on this occasion. This in a sense 'explains' the non-realistic element in the narrative, since effects and sequences (like the transformation of Mark into Johnny, or the dive through the window into space) that are impossible in actuality can readily be contrived in film.* But such techniques are not generically characteristic of pornographic films, which are as wedded to a surface realism of treatment as pornographic literature, and for the same reasons. The movie in *The Naked Lunch* would be more appropriately described as 'surrealistic'—as is the whole novel. And perhaps here we find the reason why this passage, though not strictly pornographic, is difficult to defend on the grounds advanced by Burroughs himself.

It would seem to be a general rule that where one kind of aesthetic presentation is embedded in another, the 'reality' of the embedded form is weaker than that of the framing form. For instance the presentation of stage action in a film always seems (and is meant to seem) more artificial than the same action would seem as experienced in the theatre, and the same principle applies in reverse to the case of film projection used in a play, even when the film is documentary. The same rule applies when one kind of *writing* is embedded in another, and novelists have exploited this fact from the time of Cervantes. In *Don Quixote* the absurdity of the medieval romances which the hero reads guarantees the reality of the experience that consistently falsifies them, and Gothic romance serves much the same function in Jane Austen's *Northanger Abbey*. But the effect is not inevitably parodic. In *Ulysses*, for example, the surrealistic and dramatic 'Circe' episode is clearly not introduced to guarantee the reality of the framing narrative, but to add another dimension to that reality.

The system of conventions and contrasts between different conventions is much more confused in *The Naked Lunch*. The context in which the passage under discussion is embedded (both the local

---

*Cf. the hospital sequence in Lindsay Anderson's *O Lucky Man*, where the hero discovers another patient who has been surgically transformed into a sheep, and in nausea and horror hurls himself through a high plateglass window—and survives.

context and the whole book) is no more 'realistic' than the passage itself; indeed *it is in many ways less so*. That is to say, although the events reported in this passage are 'impossible', the style in which they are reported is clear, lucid and for the most part of the kind appropriate to descriptions of actuality. Most of *The Naked Lunch*, in contrast, is written in a fluid, fragmentary style of verbal montage, the reader never being quite sure what is happening, or where or when, or why. The justification for this surrealistic method is that the book expresses the consciousness of a drug addict, perhaps one undergoing the agonies of withdrawal; but it means that when we come to the Orgasm Death Gimmick, no norms have been established by which its nauseating grotesquerie can be measured and interpreted in the way intended by Burroughs. Deprived of our bearings in empirical reality, plunged into the ethically uncontrolled world of hallucination and dream, we are in no position to apply the episode (as we apply Swift's Modest Proposal) to the real world and draw an instructive moral.

7   The Realistic Tradition

In *The Old Wives' Tale* the imaginary and the historical, the public and the private, are blended together in a very stable mixture. This rendering of an individual's experience of a common phenomenal world, whereby we share the intimate thoughts of a single character while at the same time being aware of a reality, a history, that is larger and more complex than the individual in the midst of it can comprehend—this is the characteristic achievement of the nineteenth-century realistic novel—the novel of Scott, Jane Austen, Stendhal and Flaubert, to name but four of the novelists whose contribution to the tradition can be clearly discerned in Bennett's novel. From Scott derives the bold, confident handling of the crowd scenes in III, iii (one thinks especially of *The Heart of Midlothian*), the vividly evoked excitement and terror of being caught up in some great and violent public event. The difference between Scott and Bennett is of course that in the former the characters really *are* caught up in history—they are involved in it, made to choose and act in it—they are not (except for the minor characters) mere spectators of it. In the subsequent development of the nineteenth-century realistic novel the main characters are more alienated, their efforts to participate in history are mocked and frustrated (as in Stendhal) or else they are frankly helpless and terrified before it, as Sophia is before the execution of Rivain (she is incapable of mentally integrating her accustomed life in Bursley with her presence at the guillotining: 'either that day or this day was not real') or they are completely indifferent to it, as Sophia is later to the Seige of Paris ('Her ignorance of the military and political situation was complete; the situation did not interest her. What interested her was that she had three men to feed wholly or partially, and that the price of vegetables was rising.')*

The confrontation of private and public experience on the grand scale was beyond Jane Austen's reach and ambition, but she did treat with unsurpassed subtlety the disparities between the inner and the outer life, and the peculiar difficulties of moral judgment in an era of 'secularized spirituality',[1] when manners—the code of external behaviour—constitute a language that simultaneously discloses and disguises the 'reality' within. All the elaborate notation of dress and speech and personal conduct in Bennett's narrative—the *louche* elegance of the Restaurant Sylvain, the hectic, disorganized departure for Auxerre, the increasingly uncomfortable journey, Gerald's incompetent and dishonest management of the matter of hotels, the manners of the other diners at supper, the dress and deportment of the girls in the square—the whole accumulation of clues which gradually inform Sophia that she has been morally and socially compromised and sexually betrayed by her husband—all this is very reminiscent of Jane Austen. She was also perhaps the first novelist to master that judicious blend of authorial omniscience and limited view-point, sliding subtly between direct narrative and free indirect speech, that permits the novelist to command the simultaneous double perspective of public and private experience. It is of course a technique made for irony, for the destruction of illusions, and it is no coincidence that the climaxes of so many realistic novels are ironic discoveries, passages from innocence to experience, the abandonment of convenient fictions and the acknowledgement of harsh reality. This happens to Emma Woodhouse and several other heroines of Jane Austen. But the quality of Sophia's disillusionment, the collapse of all her romantic dreams, the grim irony of her elopement terminating in a sordid hotel room overlooking a public beheading, from which she, who was 'carried away' by Gerald Scales from her safe but dull provincial nest, now longs only to be carried away once more by some other, unspecified, impossible protector—this, and the cool, detached, almost pitiless stance of the implied narrator, remind one strongly of Stendhal and

*III, vi, 2. In the Preface, Bennett recalls asking his servant for information relevant to this part of his story. 'I said to the old man, "By the way, you went through the Siege of Paris, didn't you?" He turned to his old wife and said, uncertainly, "The Siege of Paris? Yes, we did, didn't we?" The Siege of Paris had been only one incident among many in their lives. Of course they remembered it well, though not vividly, and I gained much information from them. But the most useful thing which I gained from them was the perception, startling at first, that ordinary people went on living very ordinary lives in Paris during the siege, and that to the vast mass of the population the siege was not the dramatic, spectacular, thrilling, ecstatic affair that is described in history.'

above all Flaubert. The appropriate defence of the somewhat overblown rhetoric of the antepenultimate paragraph of this passage is, therefore, that it is *intended* to jar, to distance the reader, affectively, from Sophia at the very point when the writing, by modulating into free indirect speech ('Why was she in this strange, incomprehensible town . . . ?') penetrates most deeply into her consciousness. Compare *Madame Bovary*:

> What caused this inadequacy in her life? Why did everything she leaned on simultaneously decay? . . . Oh, if somewhere there were a being strong and handsome, a valiant heart, passionate and sensitive at once, a poet's spirit in an angel's form, a lyre with strings of steel, sounding sweet-sad epithalamiums to the heavens, then why should she not find that being?[2]

I am not suggesting that Bennett combined all the virtues of these great novelists—on the contrary, I think he is equal to none of them—but he is clearly writing at the end of a tradition of novel-writing to which they (and of course many others) contributed. It is a tradition which depends upon certain assumptions, especially the assumption that there is a common phenomenal world that may be reliably described by the methods of empirical history, located where the private worlds that each individual creates and inhabits partially overlap. Hence the typical narrative method for this kind of novel is the third-person, past-tense narrative in which, whether the narrator chooses to intervene rhetorically or not, the grammar is a constant sign of his presence, and hence of some context, some reality larger than that defined by the limits of any character's consciousness. As Barthes puts it: 'the discourse of the traditional novel . . . alternates the personal and the impersonal very rapidly, often even in the same sentence, so as to produce, if we can speak thus, a proprietary consciousness which retains the mastery of what it states without participating in it.'[3]

A similar effect can be obtained in first-person narration by opening up and making explicit the distance between the 'I' who narrates and the 'I' who is narrated, making the former supply all the contextual information of which the latter was ignorant or unheeding: but this has the disadvantage of dissipating the immediacy of the narrative preterite, the curious convention by which we experience the story not as a past, but as a continuous present, moving from one unpredictable moment to another into an open-ended future. To the extent that the novelist exploits the superior knowledge of the narrating 'I' over the narrated 'I', he will (as Tristram Shandy discovered) tend to make narration itself the real subject matter of his novel. In most first-person novels the problematical relationship between the two 'I's tends to be suppressed for precisely this reason, though it is apt to become abruptly and awkwardly visible at the very end of the narrative—for example at the end of *Huckleberry Finn*. Yet the first-person method continues to be favoured by realistic novelists throughout the twentieth century. This might be explained by reference to the collapse of confidence in history in our time—confidence in the onward march of progress, in the possibility of reconciling individual and collective aims, in the responsiveness of public events to private actions: a confidence which made possible the ambitious scope and panoramic method of the classic nineteenth-century novel. Total alienation from history leads to solipsism and, in literary terms, the abandonment of realism. 'History,' said Stephen Daedalus, 'is a nightmare from which I am trying to awake', and his creator woke eventually into the mythic dream-world of *Finnegans Wake*. But a less extreme alienation from history leads to the belief that in an absurd or threatening world what the individual sees and feels is real, is alone real: 'I was there.' A good deal of modern realistic fiction is founded on that postulate, on that model—imitating not so much historiography as the documentary sources of historiography: the confession, the traveller's log, the deposition, the case history. Immediately that is said, however, one sees the need to distinguish between writers who use the 'I' as an unqualified sign of authenticity, and those who (like James in 'The Turn of the Screw', Conrad in *Lord Jim*) bracket it within another 'I', and thus draw attention to the inherent ambiguity of all human report, and by inference, to the ultimate impossibility of 'realism'.

8 Two Kinds of Modern Fiction

The Old Wives' Tale was published in 1908. By that time Henry James had published (among other things) *The Ambassadors* (1903) and *The Golden Bowl* (1904), and Conrad *Heart of Darkness* (1902) and *Nostromo* (1904): works beside which, from our present literary vantage-point, Bennett's novel seems technically extraordinarily old-fashioned, so that it is difficult for us to understand James's deference to him in that article, 'The New Novel', from which I have already quoted. Of course, when that article is read in its entirety (it ends with a handsome tribute to Conrad) and read with the care appropriate to James's late style, it is clear that his reservations about Bennett (and Wells) were serious and damaging. Behind the polite compliments, swathed in the veils of James's allusive diction and intricate syntax, there is discernible a fundamental contempt for the way Bennett and Wells practiced the art of the novel. For several decades James had been preaching and striving to put into practice the ideal of organic form in prose fiction—the exquisite adjustment of means to end, without waste, without irrelevance, but with infinite sublety of nuance. Bennett and Wells fell far short of his exacting standards. Of *Clayhanger*, for instance, James says:

> This most monumental of Mr Arnold Bennett's recitals, taking it with its supplement *Hilda Lessways* ... is so describable through its being a monument exactly not to an idea, a pursued and captured meaning, or in short *to* anything whatever, but just simply *of* the quarried and gathered material it happens to contain, the stones and bricks and rubble and cement and promiscuous constituents of every sort that have been heaped in it and thanks to which it quite massively piles itself up. .... A huge and in its way a varied aggregation, without traceable lines, divinable direction, effect of composition. ....[1]

Essentially the same ironic judgment is passed on H. G. Wells:

> The more this author learns and learns, or at any rate knows and knows, however, the greater is this impression of his holding it good enough for us, such as we are, that he shall but turn out his mind and its contents upon us by any free familiar gesture and as from a high window forever open—an entertainment as copious surely as any occasion should demand, at least till we have more intelligibly expressed our title to a better.[2]

Why was James's attack so oblique and tentative? Partly, of course, because obliquity and tentativeness were in his nature. Partly because he was genuinely impressed by the extension of subject matter Bennett and Wells had achieved in their novels, and by their comparative freedom from the evasions of Victorian prudery and sentimentality.[3] But the most likely reason for his devious strategy in this essay is that at the time, early in 1914,[4] a direct attack by James on Bennett and Wells would have looked like an instance of sour grapes. James's own literary career was almost over, and it had brought him neither fame nor fortune on any really significant scale. Bennett and Wells were popular, successful and at the same time enjoyed the reputation of being serious artists, advanced thinkers. They were indeed, in James's sardonic but perceptibly envious phrase, 'chin-deep in trophies'.[5] This literary situation had been brought about by the suppression or retardation of the modern movement in England in the first decade of the century. Bennett was a self-conscious disciple of the French realists and naturalists like Zola, the Goncourts and De Maupassant, but he stopped well short of the point at which realism began to turn into symbolism (as it does in, say, *Heart of Darkness*, *The Golden Bowl* and *Dubliners*). The introduction of innovatory ideas from the Continent of Europe initiated by the English Decadents fizzled out in the Edwardian era—it has been suggested, indeed, that the trial of Oscar Wilde provoked a kind of philistine backlash in England against any kind of artistic avant-gardism.[6] Certainly the promise of an English development of *Symbolisme* in poetry was stifled by the supremacy of Kipling, Newbolt and Bridges. Even Yeats seemed discouraged and comparatively unproductive in this first decade of the century. In fiction, James and Conrad were persistently misunderstood, unappreciated and neglected, and Joyce couldn't find a publisher for his work.

When James wrote his article on 'The New Novel' in the *Times Literary Supplement*, this literary situation was about to change for two reasons. The first was Ezra Pound, whose personal mission to make London the centre of a new avant-garde was approaching fruition. It was in 1914 that he made contact with Joyce and met T. S. Eliot, and busied himself promoting their work. Eliot, he observed with awe, had 'modernized himself on his own'. Joyce's prose, he asserted, on the evidence of the first part of *A Portrait of the Artist as a Young Man*, was 'fine stuff, readable as no other recent English prose but James's, Hudson's* and some of Conrad's was readable'.[7] Pound's choice of paragons is interesting, as is his word of commendation: 'readable' was, to most people at the time, precisely what James and Conrad were not. The second reason was the Great War, which at first seemed likely to frustrate Pound's plans—distracting public attention from matters artistic, breaking up the coteries, dispersing the artists and poets, sending many to their deaths on the battlefield—but which eventually ensured the triumph of the modern movement by creating a climate of opinion receptive to artistic revolution. After the convulsion of the Great War the Edwardian certainties and complacencies were unable to reassert themselves, and the stage was set for that astonishing burgeoning of modernism in English literature which saw the appearance, within a few years of each other, of such masterpieces as *Hugh Selwyn Moberly* (1920), *Women in Love* (1920), *The Waste Land* (1922), *Ulysses* (1922), *A Passage to India* (1924) and *Mrs Dalloway* (1925): works beside which the novels of Bennett and Wells suddenly looked what in fact they had always been, distinctly conservative and old-fashioned in form.

Writing in the *TLS* in the spring of 1914, James of course had no knowledge of the war that was coming and the effects it would have on society and culture at large; nor, though he was acquainted with Pound, is it likely that he saw the February issue of a little magazine called *The Egoist* in which, through Pound's offices, the first chapter of *A Portrait of the Artist as a Young Man* appeared. And if he had seen it, would he have recognized its implications for the future of the novel? Probably not. He didn't, after all, appreciate the full significance of *Sons and Lovers*, classifying Lawrence with Compton Mackenzie in 'The New Novel' as a rather wild and undisciplined exponent of the

*William Henry Hudson, author of *Green Mansions* (1904). His reputation has not worn well, but he was highly regarded by the literary avant-garde in the early decades of this century. Virginia Woolf, for instance, commends him in her important 1919 essay, 'Modern Fiction'.

same kind of 'saturated' realism as was practised by Bennett and Wells: again, an understandable misjudgment, given the literary moment at which it was made. The whole essay on 'The New Novel' has the defensive, wistful, ironic, gently reproving tone of a master disappointed by the failure of his pupils to profit by his lessons, though compelled to acknowledge that they have achieved some worldly success in their own way. James obviously feels that he represents a certain attitude to the art of fiction—an attitude in which form is accorded maximum importance because 'Form alone *takes*, and holds and preserves, substance'[8]—but an attitude which is out of favour.

How different, how much more confident and aggressive, is the tone of Virginia Woolf's 1919 essay 'Modern Fiction'. Her arguments and her targets are essentially the same as James's in 'The New Novel', but unlike him she writes with buoyant confidence in a nascent literary avant-garde to which she herself and the future of the novel belong. Of Bennett, Wells, Galsworthy she says brusquely: 'the sooner English fiction turns its back on them, as politely as may be, and marches, if only into the desert, the better for its soul.'[9] At first her critique seems to be based on an appeal to content rather than form:

> If we fasten, then, one label on all these books, on which is one word, materialists, we mean by it that they write of unimportant things; that they spend immense skill and immense industry making the trivial and the transitory appear the true and enduring.

But it soon becomes evident that the form, the fictional technique, which Bennett, Wells and Galsworthy are using condemns them to the trivial and transitory content: 'So much of the enormous labour of proving the solidity, the likeness to life, of the story is not merely labour thrown away but labour misplaced to the extent of obscuring and blotting out the light of the conception.' (Compare James on Bennett: 'Yes, yes—but is this *all*? These are the circumstances of the interest—we see, we see; but where is the interest itself, where and what is its centre and how are we to measure it in relation to *that*?')[10] For 'reality', Virginia Woolf substitutes the word 'life'; and 'life', she asserts, is something that traditional realism cannot capture. 'We suspect a momentary doubt, a spasm of rebellion, as the pages fill themselves in the customary way. Is life like this? Must life be like this?' No, 'Life is not a series of gig-lamps symmetrically arranged: life is a luminous halo, a semi-transparent envelope surrounding us from the beginning of consciousness to the end. Is it not the task of the novelist to convey this varying, this unknown and uncircumscribed spirit, whatever aberration or complexity it may display . . .?' As an example of a contemporary novelist who has taken up the challenge she adduces (not without some prim reservations) James Joyce, whose *Ulysses* was then being serialized in the *Little Review*; and she suggests:

For the moderns . . . the point of interest lies very likely in the dark places of psychology. At once, therefore, the accent falls a little differently; the emphasis is upon something hitherto ignored; at once a different outline of form becomes necessary, difficult for us to grasp, incomprehensible to our predecessors . . . there is no limit to the horizon, and . . . nothing—no 'method', no experiment, even of the wildest—is forbidden, but only falsity and pretence.[11]

Virginia Woolf is using the word 'modern' here in a qualitative sense, denying it to novelists (like Bennett) who nevertheless go on writing in the 'modern' age. To distinguish between these two kinds of modern fiction, critics have added a syllable to one of them and called it *modernist*, thus drawing attention to its place in a cosmopolitan movement in all the arts. Modernist fiction is pioneered in England by James and Conrad. It reaches its fullest development in the work of Joyce. Virginia Woolf and Gertrude Stein display some of its most characteristic mannerisms. The late Forster and the early Hemingway, D. H. Lawrence and Ford Madox Ford connect tangentially with this movement. The relationships of alliance and hostility—the traditions which individual talents claimed as their own—were varied and complex. James admired Conrad but not Hardy. Virginia Woolf admired Conrad and Hardy. Lawrence admired Hardy and Conrad but with exasperated reservations; he seems to have had little interest in James and hated Joyce. Joyce hated Lawrence. Everyone except Lawrence seemed to have admired Flaubert. Forster was condescending about James, but admired Lawrence, and of course Virginia Woolf, but was cool about Joyce. Hemingway seems to have admired James, but learned more from Gertrude Stein. Ford collaborated with Conrad, obviously learned much from James, but was among the first to recognize the merit of Lawrence. And so on. Obviously there is no orthodoxy here, no single set of aesthetic assumptions or literary aims; but equally clearly there is a 'family resemblance' between the modernist novelists. There are features which we keep encountering in their work, though they are never found all together or in the same combinations. From these features we can compose a kind of identi-kit portrait of the modernist novel.

Modernist fiction, then, is experimental or innovatory in form, displaying marked deviations from preexisting modes of discourse, literary and non-literary. Modernist fiction is concerned with consciousness, and also with the subconscious and unconscious workings of the human mind. Hence the structure of external 'objective' events essential to traditional narrative art is diminished in scope and scale, or presented very selectively and obliquely, or is almost completely dissolved, in order to make room for introspection, analysis, reflection and reverie. A modernist novel has no real 'beginning', since it plunges us into a flowing stream of experience with which we gradually familiarize ourselves by a process of inference and association; and its ending is usually 'open' or ambiguous, leaving the reader in doubt as to the final destiny of the characters. To compensate for the diminution of narrative structure and unity, alternative methods of aesthetic ordering become more prominent, such as allusion to or imitation of literary models or mythical archetypes, and the repetition-with-variation of motifs, images, symbols—a technique variously described as 'rhythm', 'Leitmotif' and 'spatial form'.[12] Modernist fiction eschews the straight chronological ordering of its material, and the use of a reliable, omniscient and intrusive narrator. It employs, instead, either a single, limited point of view, or a method of multiple points of view, all more or less limited and fallible: and it tends towards a fluid or complex handling of time, involving much cross-reference backwards and forwards across the chronological span of the action.

We have no term for the kind of modern fiction that is not modernist except 'realistic' (sometimes qualified by 'traditionally' or 'conventionally' or 'social'). It makes a confusing and unsatisfactory antithesis to 'modernist' because the modernists often claimed to be representing 'reality' and indeed to be getting closer to it than the realists. Most of them in fact began working within the conventions of traditional realism, and some never made a decisive rupture with it. But the most representative modernist writers (e.g. Joyce, Woolf, Stein) in their pursuit of what they took to be the real found it necessary to distort the form of their discourse until it bore less and less resemblance to the historical description of reality—which, I suggested earlier, provides the principal nonliterary model for literary realism. It is because the norms of the historical description of reality have remained remarkably stable for the last two or three hundred years that I cannot accept the argument that 'realism' is a completely relativistic concept. We can see, for instance, that the characteristic writing of the 1930s in England, which challenged the modernist version of reality, did so *formally* by reverting to norms of nonliterary description of reality not very different from those observed by Bennett and Wells. Of course Orwell, Isherwood and Graham Greene (to name three representative writers of the 1930s) were affected by, and had learned from the modernists; of course they did not merely duplicate the art of the Edwardian realists. The 'materialist' ethos of Arnold Bennett deplored by Virginia Woolf—his acquiescence, one might say, in the values and assumptions of a capitalist class-society— is clearly not embraced by the 1930s novelists; and the informational 'saturation' of the Edwardian novel, wearily acknowledged by James, is replaced in the 1930s by a much more artfully selective use of documentary detail. But there is nevertheless a definable continuity in technique between these two groups of writers, which leads back eventually to classical nineteenth-century realism. The fiction of Orwell, Isherwood, Greene, like the fiction of Bennett, Wells and

Galsworthy, and the fiction of George Eliot, Scott and Jane Austen, is based on the assumption that there is a common phenomenal world that may be reliably described by the methods of empirical history—even if to the later writers in the tradition what this world *means* is much more problematical. From this assumption derives the kind of novel form we have already associated with realism: the blending of public and private experience, inner and outer history conveyed through a third-person past-tense authorial mode of narration or the autobiographical-confessional mode. The tradition continues in the work of many highly regarded English novelists in the next generation or two: Angus Wilson, C. P. Snow, Kingsley Amis, Anthony Powell, Alan Sillitoe, Margaret Drabble, and many others. The post-war period has, indeed, been dubbed an age of reaction against experiment in the English novel,[13] as though the reaction had not occurred much earlier. (Admittedly, there was an interregnum in the 1940s, when modernism enjoyed a qualified revival.)

The politically engagé writers of the 1930s—Auden, Isherwood, Spender, MacNeice, Day Lewis, Upward—criticized the modernist poets and novelists of the preceding generation for their elitist cultural assumptions, their failure or refusal to engage constructively with the great public issues of the time and to communicate to a wide audience. In his Introduction to the anthology *New Signatures* (1932) which launched the poetry of the Auden generation, Michael Roberts had this to say about the previous one:

> The poet, contemptuous of the society around him and yet having no firm belief, no basis for satire, became aloof from ordinary affairs and produced esoteric work which was frivolously decorative or elaborately erudite.[14]

'The poets of *New Signatures*', wrote Louis MacNeice in *Modern Poetry* (1938) 'have swung back to the Greek preference for information or statement. The first requirement is to have something to say, and after that you must say it as well as you can.'[15] In *Lions and Shadows* (1938), Christopher Isherwood described and disowned the artistic assumptions with which he composed his first novel, *All The Conspirators* (1928), when 'experiment' was still a fashionable slogan:

> I thought of the novel (as I hoped to learn to write it) essentially in terms of technique, of conjuring, of chess. The novelist, I said to myself, is playing a game with his reader; he must continually amaze and deceive him, with tricks, with traps, with extraordinary gambits, with sham climaxes, with false directions. I imagined a novel as a contraption—like a motor-bicycle, whose action depends upon the exactly co-ordinated working of all its interrelated parts; or like a conjuror's table, fitted with mirrors, concealed pockets and trapdoors. I saw it as something compact, and by the laws of its own nature, fairly short. In fact my models were not novels at all, but detective stories, and the plays of Ibsen and Tchekhov. *War and Peace*, which I read for the first time a few months later, disarranged and altered all my ideas.[16]

That Isherwood's conversion from this highly formalist view of the art of fiction should have been due to the influence of Tolstoy—that Tolstoy's realism still seemed valid and viable to a young writer in the 1930s—proves that there is consistency and continuity in the concept of literary realism in spite of those critics who consider it to be a totally relative concept.

Formalism is the logical aesthetic for modernist art, though not all modernist writers accepted or acknowledged this. From the position that art offers a privileged insight into reality there is a natural progression to the view that art creates its own reality and from there to the position that art is not concerned with reality at all but is an autonomous activity, a superior kind of game. Russian Formalism began as an attempt to explain and justify early modernist experiment in Russian writing, especially Futurist verse, and the view of the novel which Isherwood derisively summarizes is one that echoes many quite serious statements of the Formalists before Socialist Realism became the Soviet literary orthodoxy. George Orwell, though he dissociated himself from the Marxist or fellow-travelling writers of the 1930s and had little respect for their work, which he considered unlikely to last as well as *Ulysses* or *The Waste Land*, was nevertheless representative of his generation in deploring the indifference to contemporary reality displayed by the writers of the 1920s, and their obsession with form to the neglect of content.

> Our eyes are directed to Rome, to Byzantium, to Montparnasse, to Mexico, to the Etruscans, to the subconscious, to the solar plexus—to everywhere except the places where things are actually happening. When one looks back at the twenties, nothing is queerer than the way in which every important event in Europe escaped the notice of the English intelligentsia. . . . In 'cultured' circles art-for-art's sake extended practically to a worship of the meaningless. Literature was supposed to consist solely in the manipulation of words. To judge a book by its subject matter was the unforgivable sin, and even to be aware of its subject matter was looked on as a lapse of taste.[17]

Graham Greene had little in common ideologically with either the Auden-Isherwood group or with Orwell, but it seemed to John Lehmann, the literary historian of this period in *New Writing in Europe* (1940), that he belonged

> to the movement by reasons of his aims in style and the milieu he chooses . . . as emphatically as Pritchett or Isherwood he has pursued speed in dialogue, simplicity of prose structure, and colloquialism in his diction. He is thus extremely readable and has none of the airs and graces of what Cyril Connolly . . . has called the 'Mandarin style'. And he is as interested as any of the 'Birmingham School' in the ordinary urban and suburban scene of working lives. He has, in fact, exactly the same claim to be called a realist as they—and can make squalor smell as efficiently as Orwell. But *within* that world his preoccupations are entirely different.[18]

These 'preoccupations' were, of course, religious and spiritual—questions of good and evil, salvation and damnation, which are posed with such memorable intensity in relation to small-time gangsters in *Brighton Rock* and priests and peasants in the abandoned Mexico of *The Power and the Glory*. These very personal preoccupations drew Greene into an equally personal definition of the fictional traditions under discussion here. His 1945 essay on Francois Mauriac is particularly interesting in this respect, and worth quoting at length. He begins by recalling—and beautifully characterizing—that essay of Henry James's, 'The New Novel':

After the death of Henry James a disaster overtook the English novel: indeed long before his death one can picture that quiet, impressive, rather complacent figure, like the last survivor on a raft, gazing out over a sea scattered with wreckage. He even recorded his impressions in an article in *The Times Literary Supplement*, recorded his hope—but was it really hope or only a form of his unconquerable oriental politeness?—in such young novelists as Mr Compton Mackenzie and Mr David Herbert Lawrence, and we who have lived after the disaster can realize the futility of those hopes.

For with the death of James the religious sense was lost to the English novel, and with the religious sense went the sense of the importance of the human act. It was as if the world of fiction had lost a dimension: the characters of such distinguished writers as Mrs Virginia Woolf and Mr E. M. Forster wandered like cardboard symbols through a world that was paper-thin. Even in one of the most materialistic of our great novelists—Trollope—we are aware of another world against which the actions of the characters are thrown into relief. The ungainly clergyman picking his black-booted way through the mud, handling so awkwardly his umbrella, speaking of his miserable income and stumbling through a proposal of marriage, exists in a way that Mrs Woolf's Mr Ramsay never does, because we are aware that he exists not only to the woman he is addressing but also in a God's eye. His unimportance in the world of the senses is only matched by his enormous importance in another world.

The novelist, perhaps unconciously aware of his predicament, took refuge in the subjective novel. It was as if he thought that by mining into layers of personality hitherto untouched he could unearth the secret of 'importance', but in these mining operations he lost yet another dimension. The visible world for him ceased to exist as completely as the spiritual. Mrs Dalloway walking down Regent Street* was aware of the glitter of shop windows, the smooth passage of cars, the conversation of shoppers, but it was only a Regent Street seen by Mrs Dalloway that was conveyed to the reader: a charming whimsical rather sentimental prose poem was what Regent Street had become: a current of air, a touch of scent, a sparkle of glass. But, we protest, Regent Street too has a right to exist; it is more real than Mrs Dalloway, and we look back with nostalgia towards the chop houses, the mean courts, the still Sunday streets of Dickens. Dickens's characters were of immortal importance. . . . M. Mauriac's first importance to an English

*Actually, Bond Street.

C

reader, therefore, is that he belongs to the company of the great traditional novelists: he is a writer for whom the visible world has not ceased to exist, whose characters have the solidity and importance of men with souls to save or lose, and a writer who claims the traditional and essential right of the novelist, to comment, to express his views.[19]

It is not entirely clear whether Greene is presenting James as the last custodian of the religious sense in the English novel or as the novelist who finally killed it. The opening paragraphs (and Greene's essays on James[20]) seem to imply the former, but the passage quoted continues: 'For how tired we have become of the dogmatically 'pure' novel, the tradition founded by Flaubert and reaching its magnificent tortuous climax in England in the works of Henry James. . . . The exclusion of the author can go too far. Even the author, poor devil, has a right to exist and M. Mauriac reaffirms that right.' In fact neither Flaubert nor James excluded the author absolutely, while D. H. Lawrence and E. M. Forster, who exercised the privilege of authorial comment on a large scale in the post-Jamesian period, nevertheless fail to win Greene's approval.

The main source of confusion in this fascinating essay is that Greene has reacted against the modernist or symbolist mode of writing for two quite independent reasons, between which he has tried to establish a causal connection. One reason was literary and was shared in common by most writers of his generation: they deplored the emphasis on individual consciousness and sensibility in modernist writing because it seemed to dissolve and deny the empirical reality of 'the visible world'. ('But, we protest, Regent Street . . . is more real than Mrs Dalloway.' To which protest Virginia Woolf had, of course, already provided an answer in her 1924 essay 'Mr Bennett and Mrs Brown': 'But I ask myself, what is reality? And who are the judges of reality?'[21]). The other set of reasons was moral and religious and was largely peculiar to Greene (though Evelyn Waugh, another Catholic convert, shared them to some extent). He thought the methods of the modernist novel were incompatible with the expression of a Christian world-view. One can see why: Christianity is based on a linear concept of history extending from Genesis to the Last Day, and assumes the unique identity of the individual soul, as the realistic novel is based on the linear plot and the notion of autonomous 'character'; whereas modernist writing is strongly attracted to pagan or neo-Platonic forms of religion, cyclic theories of history and the idea of reincarnation. In fact, however, the realistic novel has much more in common with liberal humanism than it has with either Christian or pagan world views. Certainly there is no necessary connection between an empirical respect for the 'visible world' in literature and a belief in Christianity, though that is what Greene tries to assert.

The introductory part of his essay is designed to set up François Mauriac (and by implication Greene himself, since his technique at this period was similar) as a novelist who has reasserted the great tradition of realistic fiction, but it is a great tradition revised to admit the Christian eschatology which earlier practitioners had tended to exclude from it. It is a commonplace that the most striking thing about the clergymen of Trollope—and for that matter of Jane Austen—is their lack of interest in God; nor does the authorial commentary suggest that God is much interested in them. George Eliot, in that often quoted conversation with Myers in the Fellows' Garden at Trinity, pronounced God inconceivable, immortality unbelievable and only duty peremptory and absolute,[22] and orthodox religion functions in her fiction mainly as a covert metaphor for her own humanistic 'doctrine of sympathy'.[23] The parts of Dickens's novels which invoke a hereafter are the least convincing. In short, although the convention of the omniscient author may derive from the idea of an omniscient deity, and although this narrative method can be used to express a religious world-view, the connection is by no means invariable or even normative. In the realistic novel the third-person omniscient mode is more often used to assert or imply the existence of society, or of history, than of heaven and hell. Indeed, the further the premises of realism are pushed, the more evident becomes their inherent materialism, even atheism, as we see in the French and American naturalists. In England the true successors of Dickens and Trollope were Gissing, Bennett, Wells, and Galsworthy; just as the true successors of James were Virginia Woolf, Ford Madox Ford and E. M. Forster. Neither line of succession is Christian, but surely there is no doubt which of the two is the more 'religious'? The concept of sin is at the heart of Ford's best work; *A Passage to India* is full of the longing for transcendence even if it is ultimately unfulfilled; and was it not for their 'materialism' that Virginia Woolf condemned Bennett, Wells and Galsworthy?

A little later we find C. P. Snow, a novelist much more like Bennett in temper and interests, and certainly in no sense a Christian, taking up essentially the same stance towards the experimental novel as Greene's and forced into a like distortion of literary history:

> Looking back, we can see what an odd affair the 'experimental' novel was. To begin with, the 'experiment' stayed remarkably constant for thirty years. Miss Dorothy Richardson was a great pioneer; so were Virginia Woolf and Joyce: but between *Pointed Roofs* in 1915 and its successors, largely American, in 1945, there was no significant development. In fact there could not be; because this method, the essence of which was to represent brute experience through the moments of sensation, effectively cut out precisely those aspects of the novel where a living tradition can be handed on. Reflection had to be sacrificed; so did moral awareness; so did the investigatory intelligence. That was altogether too big a price to pay and hence the 'experimental' novel . . . died from starvation, because its intake of human stuff was so low.[24]

Twenty years on and we find B. S. Johnson, writing shortly before his untimely death, fulminating against writers (among whom Lord Snow would have to be numbered) who continue to practice 'the nineteenth-century novel' in the twentieth century: 'No matter how good the writers are who attempt it, it cannot be made to work for our time, and the writing of it is anachronistic, invalid, irrelevant and perverse.'[25] That sounds very like Virginia Woolf's comment on the Edwardian realists: 'But those tools are not our tools, and that business is not our business. For us those conventions are ruin, those tools are death.'[26] 'Life does not tell stories,' Johnson continues, 'Life is chaotic, fluid, random; it leaves myriads of ends untied, untidily.' Does this sound familiar? 'Life is not a series of gig-lamps symmetrically arranged. . . .'

Wherever we touch down in the twentieth century we seem to find the same argument about the novel going on. Clearly there is no foreseeable end to it, though we might suggest that the pendulum of fashion in its movement between realism and modernism has speeded up to the point where all possible modes of working between the two extremes are now simultaneously available to a single generation of writers (and poets, dramatists, filmmakers, even artists and sculptors, for the same basic issues are raised in all the arts with a mimetic potential). Some writers, perhaps most writers, are unhappy with a tolerant aesthetic pluralism and feel it necessary to take a stand on one side or the other. This is understandable, and perhaps a necessary way of generating creative energy. But there is surely no reason or excuse for literary critics to do the same. As Northrop Frye says, it is not legitimate for the critic 'to define as authentic art what he happens to like and to go on to assert that whatever he happens not to like is, in terms of that definition, not art'.[27] It is necessary, therefore, for criticism of the novel to come to terms with the continuing coexistence of two kinds of modern fiction, with their many sub-species and crossbreeds. But when we look at criticism of the novel we find, more often than not, a repetition of the same polemical and factional spirit as we have found in the *obiter dicta* of practising novelists: a literary politics of confrontation (and in France, lately, of terrorism).

What is needed is a single way of talking about novels, a critical methodology, a poetics or aesthetics of fiction, which can embrace descriptively all the varieties of this kind of writing. The main resistance to the achievement of this aim has been on the side of the realistic novel, which works by concealing the art by which it is produced, and invites discussion in terms of content rather than form, ethics and thematics rather than poetics and aesthetics.

9 Criticism and Realism

> The novel gives a familiar relation of such things as pass each day before our eyes, such as may happen to our friends or to ourselves, and the perfection of it is to represent every scene in so easy and natural a manner, and to make them appear so probable, as to deceive us with a persuasion (at least while we are reading) that all is real, until we are affected by the joys and distresses, of the persons in the story, as if they were our own.[1]

It would be idle to deny that something like the effect described by Clara Reeve in 1785 enters into most people's pleasure in reading realistic fiction, or to pretend that it is limited to the more naive kind of reader, such as the inhabitants of Slough who rang the church bells when the blacksmith's public reading of *Pamela* (1740) reached the heroine's wedding, or the friend of Jane Austen's niece Fanny who wrote of *Emma*: 'I am at Highbury all day, and can't help feeling I have just got into a new set of acquaintances.'[2] 'It is the *point* about the novel that it is interesting' declares the far from naive Professor John Bayley, 'that it is social intercourse by other means. Its unprecedented flux of words is concerned—as Tolstoy said—with questions of how men live and should live. . . . It is a sharing of the commonplace through the medium of the exceptional man, the medium of the artist-novelist.'[3] And a critic writing recently in an academic quarterly commented on *Middlemarch* in terms entirely comprehensible by Clara Reeve's Euphrasia or Fanny Knight's Mrs Cage: 'When we read about the problems of Lydgate's marriage, or about Casaubon's "inward trouble" or about Bulstrode's public fall, it doesn't occur to us that these are *imagined* realities.'[4]

'Speak for yourself,' we may be inclined to respond to Mr Calvin Bedient, who makes this assertion; and indeed all criticism which puts its money on the truthfulness or verisimilitude of fictions is vulnerable to such an objection—all the more because it has usually disarmed itself of any defence based on the formal properties of the fictions concerned. The article by John Bayley from which I quoted is called 'Against a New Formalism'. '*Middlemarch* is rich in reality,' says Mr Bedient, 'It is in effect all vehicle, all medium, all transparency: dead to itself. And this must be said in the face of the vast formal mining to which the novel has been subjected.'[5] The kind of 'formal mining' to which he alludes may be represented by Mark Schorer's analysis of patterns of imagery in *Middlemarch*:

> I should like to suggest a set of metaphorical qualities in *Middlemarch* which actually represents a series apparent in the thinking that underlies the dramatic structure ... metaphors of unification ... of antithesis ... metaphors which conceive things as progressive ... metaphors of shaping and making, of structure and creative purpose; finally there are metaphors of what I should call a 'muted' apocalypse.[6]

It is a common reproach against this kind of critical method that it neglects the human substance of realistic fiction. For example, Malcolm Bradbury complained in 1967,

> We are ... inclined to assume that if we can show that the imagery of cash and legality runs through a Jane Austen novel, or that a whiteness-blackness opposition runs through *Moby Dick*, we can show more about the real being of the book than by showing that it deals with a society, with dispositions of character and relationship, so as to create a coherent moral and social world and an attitude towards it.[7]

Bradbury presents Schorer's kind of approach as a fashionable orthodoxy, which perhaps it was in quarters dominated by the New Criticism in the 1950s and early 1960s; but when Schorer first applied it in the late 1940s he saw it as revolutionary, his task to

> overcome corrupted reading habits of long standing; for the novel, written in prose, bears an apparently closer resemblance to discursive form than it does to poetry, thus easily opening itself to first questions about philosophy or politics, and, traditionally a middle-class vehicle with a reflective social function, it bears an apparently more immediate relation to life than it does to art, thus easily opening itself to first questions about conduct. Yet a novel, like a poem, is not life, it is an image of life; and the critical problem is first of all to analyse the structure of the image.[8]

This of course simply reverses the priorities of Bayley's definition of the novel quoted above—or rather we should say, following chronology, that Bayley is reversing Schorer's priorities. Schorer himself was probably reacting against the vogue for naturalism in the American writing of the 1930s and early 1940s that paralleled developments in England at the same period and had similar sources in political and social consciousness. In 'Technique as Discovery', a companion essay to 'Fiction and the Analogical Matrix', he attacks the reputations of Farrell, Thomas Wolfe, William Saroyan and praises Faulkner, Wescott, and Katherine Ann Porter—inheritors of the modernist or symbolist tradition in fiction. The New Criticism, which was firmly established in America by the time Schorer wrote his article, was itself in large part a product of the modernist-symbolist movement, stemming from the cross-fertilization of the Eliot-Pound literary avant-garde and the Cambridge English School;[9] but the early

New Critics had not concerned themselves much with prose fiction. The originality of Schorer's work was to apply to the novel, and especially to the classic realistic novel (e.g. Jane Austen, George Eliot) critical tools honed and sharpened on poetic drama and lyric poetry. 'Modern criticism,' Schorer declared at the outset of 'Technique as Discovery', 'has shown us that to speak of content as such is not to speak of art at all, but of experience; and that it is only when we speak of the *achieved* content, the form, that we speak as critics. The difference between content, or experience, and achieved content, or art, is technique.'[10] 'It is art that *makes* life, makes interest, makes importance,' wrote Henry James to H. G. Wells, who in turn said (and is condemned by Schorer for saying) 'Literature is not jewellery, it has quite other aims than perfection, and the more one thinks of "how it is done" the less one gets it done. These critical indulgences lead along a fatal path, away from every natural interest towards a preposterous emptiness of technical effort, a monstrous egotism of artistry, of which the later work of Henry James is the monumental warning. "It" the subject, the thing or the thought, has long since disappeared in these amazing works; nothing remains but the way it has been manipulated.'[11]

It will be seen that we are riding the same switchback of attitudes towards the novel that we followed in the preceding chapter. We are also circling back towards the issues raised in the very first chapter. Professor Bayley, for instance, is clearly a 'message-plus' man in Stanley Fish's terms: the novel is 'social intercourse by other means', that is, life as we know it, but rendered more knowable by the mediation of the 'exceptional man', the 'artist-novelist'. Todorov accused modern critics of sliding between imitation and autonomy theories of literature, but Bayley has no hesitation in plumping for the former to the exclusion of the latter, and expressing his preference for writers of the same persuasion:

A writer like Tolstoy whose intention is solely to communicate, to infect us with what he thinks and feels, will be indifferent to any notion of autonomy; all his work will strike us as connected together like our own experience of life, and present us with a complex perspective into which we move as if it were life.[12]

In Henry James and Virginia Woolf, in contrast,

communication is synonymous with the exhibition of an aesthetic object. Their claim to autonomy and the claim to communication in fact coincide, presenting us with a somewhat uneasy amalgam of the two.[13]

The 'new formalists' whom Bayley declares himself 'against' in this essay are principally Frank Kermode and Susan Sontag. The former is reproved for 'attaching far greater weight to the manipulation of the knowingly fictive, the explored illusion, than to the possibility that experience in the novel or poem represents, and joins up with, experience in life. The most enlightened literary artist, according to Kermode, is the one who is most aware that the paradigms of his art are formal, not experiential, and assumes a valid and valuable acquiescence in the fictive, never an attempt at the truth.'[14] Actually this seems to me to misrepresent Kermode's argument in *The Sense of an Ending*.[15] Although Kermode certainly assumes a much less stable 'reality' than Bayley, this does not, as in earlier, more extreme versions of formalism, allow literature the luxury and perhaps irresponsibility of total autonomy, but implicates the writer in a universal human enterprise: understanding a problematical universe. Literature is not the only kind of fiction: history, theology and even. physics are also fictions, man-made structures of thought that inevitably distort or misrepresent the brute, irreducible, ineffable 'nature' they grapple with. Literary fictions are special only in being acknowledged as fictions from their inception, but all types of fiction, from predictions of the end of the world to the laws of physics, are subject to obsolescence and replacement. It is true that this theory predisposes Kermode to favour modern novelists who share it, or something like it, but it does not (as Bayley implies) automatically demote writers of the past with a more trusting faith in a stable and knowable reality. On the contrary, Kermode's explanation of the process by which the paradigms of literary fiction are constantly adjusted to take account of changes in public knowledge and consciousness is just about the best model we have to explain in large-scale terms the evolution of the novel, and especially the tendency of major novelists to assert the authenticity of their work by parodic or ironic allusion to the fictive stereotypes they have dispensed with.

Susan Sontag is chiefly interesting as an apologist for postmodernism, and her work need not detain us here. Bayley also glances at the pronouncements of the French *nouveaux romanciers*, like Alain Robbe-Grillet and Michel Butor. But behind the *nouveau roman*, and to some extent behind the criticism of Frank Kermode and Susan Sontag, there is a formidable body of literary theory which, originating in Russian Formalism and structuralist semiotics, has lately dominated literary criticism in France. Bayley does not explicitly refer to the *nouvelle critique* in his article, but it is there, if anywhere, that a 'new formalism' is to be found.

10 The Novel and the Nouvelle Critique

The French *nouvelle critique* has much in common with the Anglo-American New Criticism, and has certainly fought its opponents over many of the same battlefields; but it also has significant differences of origin, principle and practice. Both movements can be traced back to more or less the same source—the ferment of ideas about art and culture generated by early modernism; but whereas the New Criticism was fertilized by the literary avant-garde of Western Europe and America, especially the Pound-Eliot circle, the *nouvelle critique* traces its genealogy back to the creative interaction of Futurist poetry and Formalist poetics in Russia immediately before and after the Revolution. And whereas the New Criticism inherited a theory of language provided by C. K. Ogden and I. A. Richards, the *nouvelle critique* is based on the semiology of Ferdinand de Saussure and the structural linguistics of Roman Jakobson.

The linguistic theory of Ogden and Richards in fact turned out to be limited and incapable of convincing development, while the post-Bloomfieldian linguistics (also, confusingly, called 'structural') which came to dominate language study in the Anglo-American world had little to offer the literary critic. The New Critics—e.g. Empson and the young Leavis in England; Ransom, Tate, Brooks etc. in the United States—though committed in principle to a formalistic view of literature as an art of language, and in practice to the close analysis of texts, of 'the words on the page', had at their disposal a somewhat improvised set of tools with which to carry out their programme: Richards's categories of meaning, his distinction between emotive and referential language, a grammar generally regarded as obsolete by contemporary linguists, and a little traditional rhetoric. On the whole, the work of the New Critics is remarkable for how much they managed to achieve in terms of practical criticism with this limited apparatus, and in spite of (in some cases) a dogmatic hostility to linguistics as a discipline.

The structuralist linguistics of Saussure and the Russian and Czech linguistic circles, largely ignored or undervalued by the Anglo-American academic world until quite recently (Saussure's *Cours de Linguistique Général* (1916), for instance, was first published in an English translation in 1959) has proved immensely more powerful than the linguistic theory of Ogden and Richards who, as John Sturrock has observed,[1] fatefully dismissed Saussure early in *The Meaning of Meaning* (1923). The main puzzle is why the European structuralist tradition of thought about language and literature took so long to make itself felt in the Atlantic cultural hemisphere—for the *nouvelle critique* did not begin to emerge until the 1950s, and in turn made little impact on English and American criticism until the 1960s. Probably the turbulence of European political life in the 1930s and 1940s, which broke up the artistic and scholarly communities of Russia and Eastern Europe, and scattered their participants to the winds, had much to do with it. Many emigrated to America, where they were absorbed and assimilated into the domestic development of the New Criticism, while war-torn Europe itself was hardly a congenial climate in which to work out the implications of semiotic formalism. Although the *nouvelle critique* (unlike the New Criticism) has been associated with the political Left rather than the Right—and, in the case of the critics using the journal *Tel Quel* as their platform, notably Julia Kristeva and Philippe Sollers, with the extreme, Maoist Left—this was a relatively late development which has partly obscured the debt of the movement as a whole to Russian and Czech literary and linguistic theory. The *Tel Quel* group's effort to reconcile Marxism with structuralism has entailed significant revisions of both sides of the equation, and for all the dialectical ingenuity with which it has been pressed,* has met with considerable scepticism from both Left and Right. Certainly structuralism's essential claim would seem to be that it helps us to interpret the world rather than to change it, and initially the *nouvelle critique* (like the *nouveau roman* with which it often acted in partnership) was a schismatic breakaway from the politically committed existentialism of Sartre and Camus that dominated the French literary scene in the immediate post-war era.

The career of the most brilliant of the French new critics, Roland

---

*There seem to be two main lines of argument. One is that the myths about language which structuralist semiology exposes are bourgeois myths (even if unfortunately perpetuated by orthodox communist writers in the form of socialist realism) which must be eliminated before any authentic revolution can take place. The other is that although literature cannot contribute directly to the revolution, because it is an autonomous activity, the effort to establish this autonomy in the practice of writing is in its own terms radically revolutionary and therefore a model for political revolution. Lacan's structuralist reading of Freud is also invoked to forge a link between political revolution and literary innovation; the subject's experience of contradiction, questioning and crisis, leading to new practice, being seen as essential to psychological maturity, political progress and the production of authentic modern literature alike. See David Paul Funt, 'Newer Criticism and Revolution', *Hudson Review* XXII (1969) pp. 87–96 and Graham Dunstan Martin, 'Structures in Space: an account of *Tel Quel*'s Attitude to Meaning', *New Blackfriars*, III (1971) pp. 541–52; and for more sympathetic (indeed fully committed) accounts, Stephen Heath, *The Nouveau Roman* (1972) and John Ellis, 'Ideology and Subjectivity', *Working Papers in Cultural Studies* 9 (Spring 1976) pp. 205–19.

Barthes, shows a steady disengagement from, culminating in a virtual repudiation of, the views of Sartre. In *What is Literature?* Sartre took over Paul Valéry's symbolist distinction between poetry (which is like dancing, an autonomous activity) and prose (which is like walking, purposive and therefore without the grace of art) but reversed the priorities. The poet, locked in his private, magical, incantatory relationship with language is, according to Sartre, plainly incapable of 'engagement' and is therefore respectfully but firmly eliminated from the investigation of *What is Literature?* as early as page 13. 'The art of prose is employed in discourse; its substance is by nature significative; that is, the words are first of all not objects [as in poetry] but designations for objects. . . . In short it is a matter of knowing what one wants to write about, whether butterflies or the condition of the Jews. And when one knows, then it remains to determine how one will write about it.'[2] These assertions (which echo remarks of Orwell and MacNeice quoted earlier) are in due course denied by Barthes and other exponents of the *nouvelle critique*, who argue that what Valéry said about poetry must be true for all literature, and that the 'crisis of language' which Sartre claimed was peculiar to modern poetry, is in fact common to *all* writing in the modern period.

This was Barthes's starting point in *Writing Degree Zero* (1953). The crisis of language is dated somewhere in the middle of the nineteenth century when the failure of the 1848 revolution brought about 'the definitive ruin of liberal illusions',[3] confronting the bourgeois writer with the uncomfortable fact that he was no longer in accord with the inevitable march of history, and that his reality was no longer Reality. Hence the activity of writing, which had hitherto been seen simply as the process by which life was turned into literature through the medium of a classic style accepted and understood by all, now became highly problematical. To justify writing as an activity, it was made an infinitely difficult and complex craft: 'writing is now to be saved not by virtue of what it exists for, but thanks to the work it has cost.'[4] Hence the 'Flaubertization' of literature[5] of which Barthes is particularly contemptuous when it appears in modes of writing that attempt to deny their artificial status and continue to claim some purchase on the authentic 'real'—the naturalism of Zola, De Maupassant and Daudet, or the social realism of later communist writers. *Writing Degree Zero* is a somewhat bleakly determinist book, which appears to see no solution to the modern writer's dilemma apart from *either* ever more desperate experiments with an ostentatiously literary language in the manner of the symbolists and surrealists, leading eventually to incoherence and silence, *or* the effort to achieve a 'degree zero style', neutral, innocent and transparent, of the kind attempted by Camus in *The Outsider*—a Utopia of writing which is no sooner proposed than withdrawn:

> Unfortunately, nothing is more fickle than colourless writing; mechanical habits are developed in the very place where freedom existed, a network of

set forms hem in more and more the pristine freshness of discourse, a mode of writing appears afresh in lieu of an indefinite language. The writer, taking his place as a 'classic', becomes the slavish imitator of his original creation, society demotes his writing to a mere manner, and returns him a prisoner to his own formal myths.[6]

Despite its pessimism, *Writing Degree Zero* is sufficiently historicist in method and Marxist in sympathy to be precariously reconcilable with Sartre's argument in *What is Literature?* It was some time later that Barthes began explicitly to overturn the principles on which Sartre's book was based. In a 1966 paper significantly entitled, 'To Write: an intransitive Verb?' he asserts: 'language cannot be considered a simple instrument, whether utilitarian or decorative, of thought. Man does not exist prior to language, either as a species or as an individual. We never find a state where man is separated from language, which he then creates in order to "express" what is taking place within him: it is language which teaches the definition of man, not the reverse.'[7] The traditional realistic novel is criticized more for its falsification of the relationship between words and things than (as in *Writing Degree Zero*) for its social and political bad faith—politics is now a source of metaphor to describe how language works, rather than the other way round: 'these facts of language were not readily perceptible so long as literature pretended to be a transparent expression of either objective calendar time or of psychological subjectivity, that is to say, as long as literature maintained a totalitarian ideology of the referent, or more commonly speaking, as long as literature was realistic.'[8] The goal of zero degree writing has disappeared to be replaced by something which, though carefully discriminated from the old symbolist modernism diagnosed in *Writing Degree Zero* as suicidal, has obvious continuity with it, and includes several early modernists—Mallarmé, Proust, Joyce—among its exponents:

> modern literature is trying, through various experiments, to establish a new status in writing for the act of writing. The meaning or the goal of this effort is to substitute the instance of discourse for the instance of reality (or of the referent) which has been, and still is, a mythical 'alibi' dominating the idea of literature. The field of the writer is nothing but writing itself, not as the pure 'form' conceived by an aesthetic of art for art's sake, but, much more radically, as the only area [*espace*] for the one who writes.[9]

The distinction drawn in that last sentence would not perhaps be visible to a hostile eye. To George Orwell, one of the three genuinely funny jokes produced by *Punch* since the Great War was a cartoon of a literary youth crushing his aunt's innocent question by saying, 'My dear aunt, one doesn't write *about* anything, one just *writes*.'[10] What seemed self-evidently absurd and affected to Orwell, and emblematic of the experimental, aesthetic literary climate of the twenties, is a sign of coming-of-age to Barthes, 'the writer being no longer one who writes *something*, but one who writes, absolutely.'[11]

Barthes's development after *Writing Degree Zero* in the direction of a radical theory of literary autonomy was directly related to his immersion in Saussurian semiology or semiotics (as the 'science of signs' is variously called.) Saussure is fundamental not only to the *nouvelle critique* but to the whole interdisciplinary movement, loosely called structuralism, of which it is a part. In Saussure's semiology, language is taken to be the model for all systems of signs, and it has been used as such in the fields of anthropology, psychology and philosophy as well as literary criticism. The first major product of Barthes's interest in the method was in fact his studies of popular culture and the mass media collected in *Mythologies* (1957).

Saussure defined the verbal sign, or word, as the union of a signifier (i.e. an acoustic image, a sound or symbolization of a sound) and a signified (i.e. a concept) and the relationship between signifier and signified is an arbitrary one. That is, there is no natural or necessary reason why the acoustic image *cat* [kaet] should denote the furry, feline quadruped which it in fact denotes in the English language: it does so by cultural agreement. This nucleus of arbitrariness at the heart of language is an idea of the greatest importance because it implies that it is the relationship *between* words, which means in effect the differences between them, that allows them to communicate, rather than their individual relationships of reference to discrete objects or any (totally illusory) *resemblance* between words and things.* Indeed, in some extreme formulations of the principle, language is seen as only, as it were, accidentally communicative:

> As with most utterances it would seem that the writer's purpose is to communicate a message and make statements, 'to say something'. He tells a story, describes a situation, relates an event, yet, as we know, language communicates only because of a certain number of fundamental properties which make communication possible. Communication is not at the heart of the linguistic act but only an epiphenomenon . . . if literature tells a story, if the author has to use a reference, it is simply a consequence of the fact that he is manipulating a linguistic sign.[12]

The logic of this statement may seem somewhat perverse—why should

---

*This extreme view of the arbitrariness of language has been forcefully challenged by Roman Jakobson in his article 'Quest for the Essence of Language', *Diogenes* LI (1965) pp. 21–37. Drawing on the classification of signs by the pioneering American semiologist Charles Sanders Peirce into icons, indices and symbols, only the last of which are arbitrary, Jakobson argues, with a wide range of illustration, that there is an iconic, or more precisely a *diagrammatic* relationship of resemblance 'patent and compulsory in the entire syntactic and morphological pattern of language, yet latent and virtual in its lexical aspect [which] invalidates Saussure's dogma of arbitrariness'. For example 'in various Indo-European languages the positive, comparative and superlative degrees of adjectives show a gradual increase in the number of phonemes, e.g., *high, higher, highest, altus, altior, altissimus*. In this way the signantia reflect the gradation gamut of the signata'. (p. 29).

we not deduce that language has the 'fundamental properties' it has because it was evolved as a means of communication, and that writers use it because they wish to communicate? Going a stage further, the writers associated with *Tel Quel* have attempted to work out a whole poetics of non-communication, in which 'unreadable' becomes a term of the highest praise, and have themselves produced texts carefully designed to be unintelligible.[13]

It will be obvious how this view of language militates against any mimetic theory of literature and especially against the status of the most mimetic of all the genres, the realistic novel. Not only does semiotic formalism seek to abolish the referential function of language in literary texts, a function in ordinary language on which the novel has always modelled its discourse; it also denies the epistemological validity of empiricism and the concept of the unique, autonomous self-conscious individual, on both of which the novel has usually been seen as founded.[14] Primitive man, Peter Caws explains in a shrewd account of structuralist thinking, 'is in the fortunate position of not knowing that he has a self, and therefore of not being worried about it. And the structuralists have come to the conclusion that he is nearer the truth than we are, and that a good deal of our trouble arises out of the invention of the self *as an object of study*, from the belief that man has a special kind of being, in short from the emergence of humanism. Structuralism is not a humanism, because it refuses to grant man any special status in the world.'[15] But the traditional novel is nothing if not humanistic, and its subject is characteristically a man or a woman worrying like mad about his or her 'self'. In the psychology of Jacques Lacan, 'The subject is an activity, not a thing . . . the subject produces itself by reflecting on itself, but when it is engaged on some other object it has no being apart from the activity of being so engaged.'[16] Hardly the stuff of which 'character' is made.

This radical readjustment of the subject-object relation in structuralist thought does not merely subvert literature of a traditionally mimetic kind, but also the critical procedures which have developed alongside it. If there is no single Truth about the world for the writer to identify and transcribe, then neither is there a single Truth about a text for the critic to identify and transcribe. 'The critic experiences before the book the same linguistic conditions as does the writer before the world,' says Barthes.[17] The task of criticism 'is not to discover forms of truth, but forms of "validity" . . . if there is such a thing as critical proof, it lies not in the ability to *discover* the work under consideration but, on the contrary, to cover it as completely as possible with one's own language'.[18] This in turn leads to a blurring of the conventional distinction between the creative work and the critical commentary on it:

> instead what we have is language and the single problematic it imposes, namely that of interpretation. . . . If, as Derrida puts it, linguistic signs refer

themselves only to other linguistic signs, if the linguistic reference of words is words, if texts refer to nothing but other texts, then, in Foucault's words, 'If interpretation can never accomplish itself, it is simply because there is nothing to interpret.' There is nothing to interpret, for each sign is not itself the thing that offers itself to interpretation but the interpretation of other signs. . . . Interpretation is nothing but sedimenting one layer of language upon another to produce an illusory depth which gives us the temporary spectacle of things beyond words.[19]

As Edwards W. Said has observed, 'Nearly everyone of the structuralists acknowledges a tyrannical feedback system in which man is the speaking subject whose actions are always being converted into signs that signify him, which he uses in turn to signify other signs and so on into infinity',[20] (an impression fostered, one might add, by their habit of quoting each other's aphorisms to rephrase rather than advance the argument, and by their addiction to strings of 'if—' clauses).

All this is profoundly alien and disconcerting to the Anglo-American critical temperament, and is apt to send critics, who in their native intellectual milieu figure as rampant formalists, scurrying for cover behind an old-fashioned, commonsense belief in 'content'. This reaction can be observed in the proceedings of an international conference on the subject of Literary Style, at which Roland Barthes delivered a paper on 'Style and Its Image' that concluded with the following words:

> . . . if up until now we have looked at the text as a species of fruit with a kernel (an apricot, for example) the flesh being the form and the pit being the content, it would be better to see it as an onion, a construction of layers (or levels, or systems) whose body contains, finally, no heart, no kernel, no secret, no irreducible principle, nothing except the infinity of its own envelopes—which envelop nothing other than the unity of its own surfaces.[21]

The editor of the symposium, Seymour Chatman, reports:

> Barthes's final reduction of content to form raised some questions. It was argued that it is one thing to say that even the smallest details of a literary text have a structure, but quite another to say that is all there is, that there is nothing *but* structure. Surely there must be such a thing as the subject of a literary work; that is, it is a meaningful thing to say (for example) that the subject of a story by Hemingway is the sensations of a man returned from the war who finds that even a trout stream seems sinister to him. That is a subject, a choice among other things in the world to write about that Hemingway has made, that is, a content—what Hemingway does with it is the form. How can one reduce the substantive or contentual choice to 'form'? There must remain some pre-existent material which is irreducibly content or subject-matter. Barthes replied that for him 'subject' was an illusory notion. There is no subject expressed by an author; subject is a level in the hierarchy of interpretation.[22]

We observe here the collision of two quite different philosophical traditions, which may be called for the sake of convenience French rationalism and Anglo-Saxon empiricism, and it is difficult to see how the argument could be profitably continued without moving from the area of literature and criticism to that of philosophy. Not all the French new critics are quite so Calvinistically fierce in denouncing empiricism as Barthes. But much structuralist criticism on the typology of narrative in the tradition of Propp[23] leads away from the characteristic concern of Anglo-American criticism with texts. Following Saussure's notion of language as the model for all sign-systems, and his distinction between *langue* (the system, the field of linguistic possibility offered by a given language) and *parole* (the individual utterance, speech act or text) it is argued that there is a homology or fundamental likeness between the structure of sentences and the structure of narrative, so that you can analyse narrative as you can analyse sentences, and you can produce a grammar of narrative which, like ordinary grammar, would show what *paroles* are possible and not possible in the *langue* of narrative. Such criticism need not deal with actual texts at all—indeed Tzvetan Todorov has said, 'The nature of structural analysis will be essentially theoretical and non-descriptive; in other words, the aim of such a study will never be the description of a concrete work. The work will be considered as the manifestation of an abstract structure, merely one of its possible realizations. . . .'[24] This programme has much in common with the anthropology of Lévi-Strauss, for whom all that can be observed of actual societies is 'a series of expressions, each partial and incomplete, of the same underlying structure, which they reproduce in several copies without ever completely exhausting its reality,'[25] and whose work is as disconcerting and challenging to Anglo-American functional anthropology as the *nouvelle critique* is to Anglo-American criticism. Indeed, one of Lévi-Strauss's aphorisms might be nailed to the mast of the entire structuralist enterprise as a message and a warning to the rest of us: 'to reach reality we must first repudiate experience.'[26]

This is a slogan that looks to the novelist about as inviting as the skull-and-crossbones to one of Defoe's merchants. Yet the interesting thing about the *nouvelle critique* is that it has mainly concentrated on the novel—it has pressed its formalism upon precisely the kind of literature that seems most resistant to it. This is another of the significant differences between the *nouvelle critique* and the New Criticism. The latter, as observed earlier, was founded in the first place upon the study of lyric and dramatic poetry, and for a long time the novel was tacitly or explicitly excluded from the general neocritical creed that literary texts are verbal systems in which what is said is indistinguishable from the way it is said—indeed, in many ways it still is excluded, and it may be doubted whether Roland Barthes's paper 'Style and its Image' would have aroused such opposition among its auditors if it had been orientated towards poetry rather than towards prose, and had taken its examples from T. S. Eliot or Valéry rather than Balzac. It is surely significant that the text invoked on that occasion to assert the existence of a content or subject-matter prior to form was a short story by Hemingway ('Big Two-Hearted River', which Philip Young has very plausibly related to the trauma of Hemingway's war wound).[27] It would have been more difficult to make the same point using, say, *The Waste Land* or *Le Cimétier Marin* as examples.

I have no quarrel with the *nouvelle critique*'s insistence on the primacy of language in the creation and criticism of prose fiction, and find the vigour with which the point is pressed exhilarating. But I am less impressed by the polemic against realism that absorbs so much of its energy, since this seems to lead us into the same limiting dichotomy between two kinds of fiction, only one of which we are permitted to admire, that we have already traced in Anglo-American criticism. This tendency can be seen very clearly in one of the first books of criticism published in England to show the influence of the *nouvelle critique*, Gabriel Josipovici's *The World and the Book* (1971). The theory of literary history advanced by this impressively wide-ranging study is a variation on the idea of a Second Fall in consciousness, comparable to T. S. Eliot's idea of a dissociation of sensibility. For Josipovici, as for Eliot, the Second Fall, though long in preparation, occurred decisively round about the seventeenth century; and the dire consequence for literature was realism. It is from literary realism (and all the fallacies about art and reality on which it is, in Josipovici's view, based) that modern fiction has freed us, restoring to us—not the unified and divinely meaningful universe of medieval Christianity, for that is lost for ever, even to Christians—but something equivalently valuable and liberating for modern man: an understanding of the laws of existence, of the nature of human consciousness and human perception, of the inevitable gap between our desires and reality. It is for this reason that he begins with a chapter on Proust and in his second chapter goes back to Dante. For Proust is, in Josipovici's view, the exemplary modern novelist, who makes the uncovering of the 'laws of existence' the aim of his great novel, and Dante the supreme voice of the medieval Christian synthesis. Read correctly, a novel like *A la Recherche du Temps Perdu*

> draws the reader into tracing the contours of his own labyrinth and allows him to experience himself not as an object in the world but as the limits of his world. And, mysteriously, to recognize this is to be freed of these limits and to experience a joy as great as that which floods through us when, looking at long last, with Dante, into the eyes of God, we sense the entire universe bound up into one volume and understand what it is to be a man.[28]

The realistic novel is incapable of producing this liberating effect because while the reader 'is immersed in it . . . there is nothing . . . to falsify what the imagination creates.'[29] 'The act of perception or the act of consciousness is never a neutral one,' says Josipovici. 'Proust and Homer and Virginia Woolf are all aware of this, but the traditional novel appears to ignore it. As a result it implicitly assumes that the world and the world as we are made conscious of it are one.'[30] And: 'to imagine like the traditional novelist that one's work is an image of the real world, to imagine that one can communicate directly to the reader what it is that one uniquely feels, that is to fall into the real solipsism, which is, to paraphrase Kierkegaard on despair, not to know that one is in a state of solipsism.'[31] All this is very reminiscent of Barthes, though Josipovici's wistful and eloquent evocation of an 'unfallen' medieval culture in which the world and the book were one, is not.

Josipovici's discussion of the writers who illustrate his argument positively—Dante, Chaucer, Rabelais, Hawthorne, Proust—is perceptive and persuasive. But his overall thesis, as I have argued at greater length elsewhere,[32] leads to a very selective and narrow concept of the 'modern' and an absurdly reductive caricature of the realistic novel—which in the end Josipovici himself repudiates, citing Proust as follows:

> Genuine art, then, Proust argues, even when it appears to be purely naturalistic fiction, always contains references to that secret world which is the artist's alone and which is normally inaccessible to his or to another's consciousness. . . . This feeling does not attach itself to the overt content of the novel, and it can never be discovered by an analysis of the content, but only by a response to what Proust calls style. This style may be the recurrence of certain images, as in Hardy or Dostoevsky, but it may also manifest itself in the peculiar choice of verbal tense in which the narration is conducted, as Proust noted in Flaubert.[33]

Thus the realistic novel, excluded from the palace of art because of its naive pretensions to represent reality in its content, is finally admitted by the back door when it is acknowledged after all to have a form or 'style'. Something of the same ambiguous redemption of the realistic novel takes place in Roland Barthes's *S/Z* (1970), a line-by-line commentary on a story by Balzac, 'Sarrasine', interspersed with more general explorations of the theory of narrative.

Barthes begins by making a distinction between two kinds of text, that which is *lisible* ('readable') and that which is *scriptible* ('writable'). Richard Miller usefully brings out the meaning of these two terms by translating them as 'readerly' and 'writerly'. The readerly text is based on logical and temporal order; it communicates along a continuous line, we read it one word after another, we consume it, passively. This use of the term overlaps with the usual sense of 'readable' as a term of praise in critical discussion—for instance John Lehmann's description of Graham Greene as 'readable' (see p. 48 above); but when Ezra Pound praised Joyce and James and Conrad for being 'readable' (see p. 43 above) he was thinking of a quality closer to Barthes's *scriptible*. The writerly text makes us not consumers but producers, because we write ourselves into it, we construct meanings for it as we read it, and ideally these meanings are infinitely plural:

> this ideal text . . . is a galaxy of signifiers, not a structure of signifieds; it has no beginning; it is reversible. . . . Systems of meaning may take over this absolutely plural text, but their number is never closed, based as it is on the infinity of language . . . it is a question of asserting the very existence of plurality, which is not that of the true, the probable or even the possible.[34]

Modernist writing aspires to the condition of the *scriptible* (and perhaps in *Finnegans Wake* achieves it) but the classic text (like 'Sarrasine') is a 'multivalent but incompletely reversible system. What blocks its reversibility is just what limits the plural nature of the classic text. These blocks have names: on the one hand truth, on the other empiricism: against—or between them, the modern text comes into being.'[35]

All this seems intended to discredit the classic, realistic, readerly text; but the very extremism of the argument paradoxically works to the latter's advantage. The infinite plurality to which the writerly text aspires renders it ultimately unamenable to analysis, baffling criticism by the plethora of its possible meanings. Of the *scriptible* text, 'there may be nothing to say.'[36] The 'limited plurality' of the classic text is, however, accessible to criticism through the analysis of connotation: the process by which one signified serves as the signifier of something else. This is perhaps the most important single point made (and brilliantly demonstrated) in *S/Z*: that in the literary text, however realistic, nothing is ever merely referential; everything connotes something, and usually several things simultaneously. For example, at one point in 'Sarrasine' the aged Duenna escorts the eponymous hero to a rendezvous with the singer La Zambinella:

> *Elle entraîna le Français dans plusieurs petites rues et s'arrêta devant un palais d'assez belle apparence. Elle frappa. La porte s'ouvrit. Elle conduisit Sarrasine à travers un labyrinthe d'escaliers . . .* *

At first sight the two short sentences about knocking on the door seem banal, and, as far as the narrative is concerned, redundant, their function being merely to locate the story in a recognizable world in which houses have doors upon which visitors must knock for admittance. But as Barthes rightly insists, these sentences have literary meanings, 'first because every door is an object of some vague symbolism (a whole complex of death, pleasure, limit, secret, is bound up in it); and next because this door which opens (without a subject) connotes an atmosphere of mystery; last because the open door and the

---

*She led the Frenchman along several back streets and stopped before a rather handsome mansion. She knocked. The door opened. She led Sarrasine along a labyrinth of stairways . . .'

end of the route still remain uncertain, the suspense is prolonged, in other words heightened.'[37] Furthermore, this incident belongs to a series of 'door' motifs which punctuate the story—a story that is itself a delayed disclosure of a mystery, like the opening of a series of doors.

For La Zambinella is in fact a castrato, and Sarrasine the victim of a cruel deception. When he becomes ardent and carries her off to a boudoir, the singer draws a dagger.

> *L'Italienne était armée d'un poignard.—Si tu approches, dit-elle, je serai forcée de te plonger cette arme dans le coeur.* *

Barthes discriminates several different interwoven codes in this passage. On the actional or 'proairetic' level it is a recognized stage in the series 'Rape'—the victim's armed defence of her virtue. But since La Zambinella is in fact defending, not 'her' virtue, but a lie, by this gesture, on the hermeneutic level it is a deception—for Sarrasine, and, on first reading, for the reader. On yet another level, the symbolic, the dagger signifies castration, which is the hidden secret and thematic core of the whole tale.[38] When he flourished this example before the Literary Style symposium Barthes mentioned two more codes present in the passage: the French language and the rhetorical code.[39] The rhetorical code (apostrophe, the antonomasia of 'L'Italienne' and the interpolation of an *inquit* into direct speech) confers upon Balzac's use of the French language the status of an *écriture*. It also reinforces the actional code by the somewhat histrionic resonances it imparts to Zambinella's speech and gesture, and at the same time it collaborates with the hermeneutic code, for the use of an epithet, 'L'Italienne', instead of a proper name (like 'le Français' in the previous example) covertly underlines the importance of nationalities in the intrigue (Sarrasine, a recent visitor to Rome, does not know that female roles are always played by castrati in the Papal States at this period).

To Barthes, literature has its very being in this interweaving of multiple codes, none of which has precedence over the rest—certainly not the literal or referential code. 'The literality of the text is a system like any other . . . the meaning of a text can be nothing but the plurality of its systems, its infinite (circular) transcribability.'[40] The infinite transcribability (from one code into another) of the readerly text is presumably different from the infinite plurality of the writerly text; but here and elsewhere Barthes comes close to collapsing his own distinction between the *lisible* and the *scriptible*; and indeed one may wonder whether the distinction is not one of degree rather than essence. Certainly Barthes's commentary impresses one more with the plurality of meanings to be found in 'Sarrasine' than with the limits of that plurality, and thus, against the critic's apparent intention, constitutes a triumphant vindication of the classic text.

*The Italian woman was armed with a dagger, 'If you come any closer,' she said, 'I will be forced to plunge this weapon into your heart.'

Balzac himself, of course, was (to revert to the literary history of *Writing Degree Zero*) writing before the crisis of language hit the bourgeois writer: he was still in good faith in supposing he was describing a stable reality, and it seems that we may legitimately enjoy reading him as long as we do not fall into the same fallacy. The writer, Barthes insists, never applies language to a referent, even if that is what he thinks he is doing; he merely applies one code to another. When he describes a scene, he describes something already organized and framed pictorially.[41] And when he describes a voice, for example in 'Sarrasine'–

> —*Addio, Addio! disait-elle avec les inflexions les plus jolies de sa jeune voix. Elle ajouta même sur la dernière syllabe une roulade admirablement bien exécutée, mais à voix basse et comme pour peindre l'effusion de son coeur par une expression poétique**

Barthes asks:

> What would happen if one actually performed Marianina's '*addio*' as it is described in the discourse? Something incongruous, no doubt, extravagant, and not musical. More: is it really possible to perform the act described? This leads to two propositions. The first is that the discourse has no responsibility vis-à-vis the real: in the most realistic novel, the referent has no 'reality': suffice it to imagine the disorder the most orderly narrative would create were its descriptions taken at face value, converted into operative programmes and simply *executed*. In short (this is the second proposition) what we call 'real' (in the theory of the realistic text) is never more than a code of representation (of signification): it is never a code of execution: *the novelistic real is not operable*. To identify—as it would, after all, be 'realistic' enough to do—the real with the operable would be to subvert the novel at the limit of its genre (whence the inevitable destruction of novels when they are transferred from writing to film, from a system of meaning to an order of the operable).[42]

As so often in reading Barthes, a spasm of empirical doubt intrudes just as one is about to surrender to the energy and eloquence of the argument. Is it really true that novels are destroyed by transference to the cinema screen? One might be more impressed by how *readily* they transfer, compared to poems, plays or *scriptible* prose narratives like *Finnegans Wake*.

What is provocative overstatement in Barthes is apt to become intolerant dogma in his epigones, and this applies particularly to his critique of realism. He is absolutely right to affirm that realism, like any other mode of writing, like any product of culture (this is perhaps the most important single message of structuralism) is a human code, or tissue of codes, not a natural reflection of the Real. But we are not

---

*'Addio, addio,' she said, with the prettiest inflection in her youthful voice. She added to the final syllable a marvellously well-executed trill, but in a soft voice, as if to give poetic expression to the emotions in her heart.

bound to accept the historicist argument that realism ceased to be a valid literary mode by the middle of the nineteenth century. To hold that position entails unwriting (*i.e.* wishing unwritten) a large part of the imaginative effort of the last one hundred years.

11   Conclusion to Part One

In the preceding pages we have surveyed many different issues of literary theory and practice, and considered a variety of texts, writers and schools of criticism. But all of the attitudes and arguments we have reviewed could, I think, be divided into two large and opposing groups according to whether they give priority to content or to form, to the 'what' or the 'how' of literature.

The fundamental principle of one side is that art imitates life, and is therefore in the last analysis answerable to it: art must tell the truth about life and contribute to making it better, or at least more bearable. That is the classical definition and justification of art, which of course covers a considerable diversity and division of opinion about the manner of imitation that is most desirable—for instance whether art should imitate the actual or the ideal. It dominated Western aesthetics from the time of Plato and Aristotle until the beginning of the nineteenth century when it began to be challenged by Romantic theories of the imagination; and by the end of the century it had been turned on its head. 'Life imitates art', Oscar Wilde declared,[1] meaning (a structuralist *avant la lettre*) that we compose the reality we perceive by mental structures that are cultural not natural in origin, and that it is art which is most likely to change and renew those structures when they become tired and mechanical. ('Where, if not from the Impressionists, do we get those wonderful brown fogs that come creeping down our streets, blurring the gas-lamps and changing the houses into monstrous shadows?')[2] What, then, from this point of view does art imitate? The answer is, of course, other art, especially other art of the same kind. Poems are not made out of experience, they are made out of poetry—that is, the tradition of disposing the possibilities of language to poetic ends. T. S. Eliot's 'Tradition and the Individual Talent' is a classic exposition of the idea. It is not so often applied to prose fiction, but novels, too, are demonstrably made out of other novels, and nobody could write one without having read one first. In short, art is autonomous.

The trouble with these two theories of art is that they are equally plausible yet mutually contradictory. It is possible to believe each of them at different times—probably most of us do—but difficult to believe them both simultaneously. As soon as they are brought into the same conceptual space, a battle usually develops. It is a running battle, as I have tried to demonstrate in following the debate about the novel through the twentieth century, and makes a fascinating spectacle; but it does not seem to progress very much. In dialectical terms we observe the clash of thesis and antithesis with little prospect of a synthesis. Since art is supremely the province of forms, and since literature is an art of language, I believe such a synthesis can only be found in linguistic form. But the synthesis must be catholic: it must account for and be responsive to the kind of writing normally approached via content, via the concept of imitation, as well as to the kind of writing usually approached via form, via the concept of autonomy. In the next part of this book I describe a theory of language which offers, I believe, the basis for such a synthesis. It belongs to the European formalist/structuralist tradition, and has therefore entered into the vocabulary of the *nouvelle critique* (notably in the work of Gérard Genette), but as the basis for a poetics it resists the polemical tendency of Barthes and his followers to instate one kind of writing at the expense of another. Of course, the synthesis will only satisfy those who are sympathetic to formalism in the first place. There are an infinite number of possible contents, and many of them are mutually irreconcilable on the level of ethics, ideology, praxis. Content-based criticism cannot be all-embracing by its very nature. But structurally the forms of literature are finite in number. In fact, at a certain level, they can be reduced to two types. If this seems a drastic reduction, it must be remembered that most modern formalist criticism has endorsed only one type.

Part Two

Metaphor and Metonymy

1 Jakobson's Theory

The idea of a binary opposition between metaphor and metonymy can
be traced back to Russian Formalism. Erlich observes that Zirmunskij
'posited metaphor and metonymy as the chief earmarks of the
Romantic and classic styles respectively' in an essay of 1928.[1] Roman
Jakobson records that he 'ventured a few sketchy remarks on the
metonymical turn in verbal art' in articles on realism (1927) and
Pasternak (1935), and applied the idea to painting as early as 1919.[2]
Alluding briefly in their *Theory of Literature* (1948) to 'the notion that
metonymy and metaphor may be the characterizing structures of two
poetic types—poetry of association by contiguity, of movement within
a single world of discourse, and poetry of association by comparison,
joining a plurality of worlds', Wellek and Warren refer the reader to
Jakobson's essay on Pasternak, Karl Bühler's *Sprachtheorie* (1934) and
Stephen J. Brown's *The World of Imagery* (1927).[3] The most
systematic and comprehensive (though highly condensed) exposition
of the idea, however, and the source most often cited in modern
structuralist criticism, is Jakobson's essay 'Two Aspects of Language
and Two Types of Aphasic Disturbances', first published in
Fundamentals of Language (1956) by Jakobson and Morris Halle. In
his 'Closing Statement: Linguistics and Poetics' addressed to the 1958
Indiana Conference on Style in Language,[4] Jakobson referred to the
same distinction but in a less even-handed way, reinforcing that bias of
criticism towards the metaphoric at the expense of the metonymic
mode which he had himself diagnosed in the earlier paper. The later
one is, however, much better known to English and American critics
than the earlier. Perhaps the title, 'Two Aspects of Language and Two
Types of Aphasic Disturbances' has not seemed very inviting to
literary critics, and a quick glance at the contents of that essay might
well discourage further investigation. The seminal distinction
between the metaphoric and metonymic poles is compressed into half-
a-dozen pages, and seems almost an afterthought appended to a

specialized study of language disorders. The theory of language upon which the distinction rests is expounded in a highly condensed fashion, with few concessions to lay readers. In the account of this essay which follows I have tried to make its content and implications (as I understand them) clear by expansions and illustrations which may seem obvious or redundant to readers already familiar with structuralist thinking about language and literature.

Jakobson begins by formulating one of the basic principles of structural linguistics deriving from Saussure: that language, like other systems of signs, has a twofold character. Its use involves two operations—selection and combination:

> Speech implies a selection of certain linguistic· entities and their combination into linguistic units of a higher degree of complexity.[5]

This distinction between selection and combination corresponds to the binary oppositions between *langue* and *parole*, between *paradigm* (or *system*) and *syntagm*, between *code* and *message*, in structural linguistics and semiotics. It is perhaps most readily grasped in relation to concrete objects that function as signs, such as clothing, food and furniture. Roland Barthes gives useful illustrations of this kind in his *Elements of Semiology*. For example, to the garment *langue*/paradigm/system/code belongs the 'set of pieces, parts or details which cannot be worn at the same time on the same part of the body, and whose variation corresponds to a change in the meaning of the clothing', while the garment *parole*/syntagm/message is 'the juxtaposition in the same type of dress of different elements'.[6] Imagine a girl dressed in teeshirt, jeans and sandals: that is a message which tells you what kind of person she is, or what she is doing or what mood she is in, or all these things, depending on the context. She has selected these units of clothing and combined them into a garment unit 'of a higher degree of complexity'. She has selected the teeshirt from the set of clothes which cover the upper half of the body, jeans from the set of clothes which cover the lower half of the body and sandals from the set of footwear. The process of selection depends on her knowing what these sets are—on possessing a classification system of her wardrobe which groups teeshirt with, say, blouse and shirt as items which have the same function and only one of which she needs. The process of combination depends upon her knowing the rules by which garments are acceptably combined: that for instance sandals, not court shoes, go with jeans (though the rules of fashion are so volatile that one cannot be too dogmatic in these matters). The combination teeshirt-jeans-sandals is, in short, a kind of sentence.

Consider the sentence, 'Ships crossed the sea'. This has been constructed by selecting certain linguistic entities and combining them into a linguistic unit (syntagm) of a higher degree of complexity: selecting *ships* from the set (paradigm) of words with the same grammatical function (i.e. nouns) and belonging to the same semantic field (e.g. *craft, vessels, boats* etc.); selecting *crossed* from the set of verbs with the same general meaning (e.g. *went over, sailed across, traversed* etc.) and selecting *sea* from another set of nouns such as *ocean, water* etc. And having been selected, these verbal entities are then combined according to the rules of English grammar. To say 'The sea crossed the ships' would be nonsensical, equivalent to trying to wear jeans above the waist and a teeshirt below (both types of mistake commonly made by infants before they have mastered the basic rules of speech and dressing).

Selection involves the perception of similarity (to group the items of the system into sets) and it implies the possibility of substitution (*blouse* instead of *teeshirt, boats* instead of *ships*). It is therefore the process by which metaphor is generated, for metaphor is substitution based on a certain kind of similarity. If I change the sentence, 'Ships crossed the sea' to 'Ships *ploughed* the sea', I have substituted *ploughed* for *crossed*, having perceived a similarity between the movement of a plough through the earth and of a ship through the sea. Note, however, that the awareness of *difference* between ships and ploughs is not suppressed: it is indeed essential to the metaphor. As Stephen Ullmann observes: 'It is an essential feature of a metaphor that there must be a certain distance between tenor and vehicle.* Their similarity must be accompanied by a feeling of disparity; they must belong to different spheres of thought.'[7]

Metonymy is a much less familiar term than metaphor, at least in Anglo-American criticism, though it is quite as common a rhetorical device in speech and writing. The *Shorter Oxford English Dictionary* defines metonymy as 'a figure in which the name of an attribute or adjunct is substituted for that of the thing meant, e.g. *sceptre* for *authority*'. Richard A. Lanham gives a slightly different definition in his *A Handlist of Rhetorical Terms* 'Substitution of cause for effect or effect for cause, proper name for one of its qualities or vice versa: so the Wife of Bath is spoken of as half Venus and half Mars to denote her unique mixture of love and strife.' Metonymy is closely associated with synecdoche, defined by Lanham as 'the substitution of part for whole, genus for species or vice versa: "All hands on deck".'[8] The hackneyed lines, 'The hand that rocks the cradle/Is the hand that rules the world' include both tropes—the synecdoche 'hand' meaning 'person' (by inference, 'mother') and the metonymy 'cradle' meaning 'child'. In Jakobson's scheme, metonymy includes synecdoche.

Rhetoricians and critics from Aristotle to the present day have generally regarded metonymy and synecdoche as forms or subspecies

---

*Terms coined by I. A. Richards in *The Philosophy of Rhetoric* to distinguish the two elements in a metaphor or simile. In 'Ships ploughed the sea', 'Ships' movement' is the tenor and 'plough' the vehicle.

of metaphor, and it is easy to see why. Superficially they seem to be the same sort of thing—figurative transformations of literal statements. Metonymy and synecdoche seem to involve, like metaphor, the substitution of one term for another, and indeed the definitions quoted above use the word 'substitution'. Jakobson, however (and there is no more striking example of the advantages a structuralist approach may have over a commonsense empirical approach) argues that that metaphor and metonymy are *opposed*, because generated according to opposite principles.

Metaphor, as we have seen, belongs to the selection axis of language; metonymy and synecdoche belong to the combination axis of language. If we transform our model sentence into '*Keels* crossed the *deep*' we have used a synecdoche (*keels*) and a metonymy (*deep*) not on the basis of similarity but of contiguity. *Keel* may stand for *ship* not because it is similar to a ship but because it is part of a ship (it so happens that a keel is the same shape as a ship, but *sail*, which would be an alternative synecdoche, is not). *Deep* may stand for *sea* not because of any similarity between them but because depth is a property of the sea. It may be objected that these tropes are nevertheless formed by a process of substitution—*keels* for *ships*, *deep* for *sea*—and are not therefore fundamentally different from metaphor. To answer this objection we need to add an item to Jakobson's terminology. In his scheme selection is opposed to combination, and substitution is opposed to 'contexture'—the process by which 'any linguistic unit at one and the same time serves as a context for simpler units and/or finds its own context in a more complex linguistic unit.'[9] But 'contexture' is not an optional operation in quite the same way as 'substitution'—it is, rather, a law of language. I suggest that the term we need is *deletion*: deletion is to combination as substitution is to selection. Metonymies and synecdoches are *condensations* of contexture. The sentence, 'Keels crossed the deep' (a non-metaphorical but still figurative utterance) is a transformation of a notional sentence, *The keels of the ships crossed the deep sea* (itself a combination of simpler kernel sentences) by means of deletions. A rhetorical figure, rather than a précis, results because the items deleted are not those which seem logically the most dispensable. As the word *ship* includes the idea of keels, *keels* is logically redundant and would be the obvious candidate for omission in a more concise statement of the event, and the same applies to *deep*. Metonymy and synecdoche, in short, are produced by deleting one or more items from a natural combination, but not the items it would be most natural to omit: this illogicality is equivalent to the coexistence of similarity and dissimilarity in metaphor.

On a pragmatic level, of course, metonymy may still be seen as a process of substitution: we strike out *ships* in our manuscript and insert *keels*, without consciously going through the process of expansion and deletion described above. This does not affect the fundamental structural opposition of metaphor and metonymy, which rests on the basic opposition between selection and combination.

> Selection (and correspondingly substitution) deals with entities conjoined in the code, but not in the given message, whereas in the case of combination the entities are conjoined in both or only in the actual message.[10]

Ploughed has been selected in preference to, or substituted for, other verbs of movement and penetration (like *crossed, cut through, scored*) which are conjoined in the code of English (by belonging to a class of verbs with approximately similar meanings) but not conjoined in the message (because only one of them is required). *Keels*, on the other hand, is conjoined with *ships* both in the code (as nouns, as items in nautical vocabulary) and in the notional message, *The keels of the ships etc*. The contiguity of *keels* and *ships* in many possible messages as well as in the code reflects their actual existential contiguity in the world, in what linguistics calls 'context', whereas there is no such contiguity between ploughs and ships.

2 Two Types of Aphasia

Impressive evidence for Jakobson's argument that metaphor and metonymy are polar opposites corresponding to the selection and combination axes of language comes from the study of aphasia (severe speech disability). Traditionally aphasia has been studied under the two aspects of sending and receiving the verbal message. Jakobson, however makes his methodological 'cut' in a different dimension, along the line between selection and combination (and again the advantage of a structuralist over an empirical approach to the problem is striking):

> We distinguish two basic types of aphasia—depending on whether the major deficiency lies in selection or substitution, with relative stability of combination and contexture; or conversely, in combination and contexture, with relative retention of normal selection and substitution.[1]

Aphasics who have difficulty with the selection axis of language—who suffer, in Jakobson's terms from 'selection deficiency' or 'similarity disorder'—are heavily dependent on context, i.e. on contiguity, to sustain discourse.

> The more his utterances are dependent on the context, the better he copes with his verbal task. He feels unable to utter a sentence which responds

neither to the cue of his interlocutor nor to the actual situation. The sentence 'it rains' cannot be produced unless the utterer sees that it is actually raining.[2]

Even more striking: a patient asked to repeat the word 'no', replied, 'No, I can't do it'. Context enabled him to use the word that he could not consciously 'select' from an abstract paradigm. In this kind of aphasic speech the grammatical subject of the sentence tends to be vague (represented by 'thing' or 'it'), elliptical or non-existent, while words naturally combined with each other by grammatical agreement or government, and words with an inherent reference to the context, like pronouns and adverbs, tend to survive. Objects are defined by reference to their specific contextual variants rather than by a comprehensive generic term (one patient would never say *knife*, only *pencil-sharpener*, *apple-parer*, *bread knife*, *knife-and-fork*). And, most interesting of all, aphasics of this type make 'metonymic' mistakes by transferring figures of combination and deletion to the axis of selection and substitution:

> *Fork* is substituted for *knife*, *table* for *lamp*, *smoke* for *pipe*, *eat* for *toaster*. A typical case is reported by Head: 'When he failed to recall the name for "black" he described it as "What you do for the dead"; this he shortened to "dead".'
>
> Such metonymies may be characterized as projections from the line of a habitual context into the line of substitution and selection: a sign (e.g. *fork*) which usually occurs together with another sign (e.g. *knife*) may be used instead of this sign.[3]

In the opposite type of aphasia—'contexture deficiency' or 'contiguity disorder'—it is the combination of linguistic units into a higher degree of complexity that causes difficulty, and the features of similarity disorder are reversed. Word order becomes chaotic, words with a purely grammatical (i.e. connective) function like prepositions, conjunctions and pronouns, disappear, but the subject tends to remain, and in extreme cases each sentence consists of a single subject-word. These aphasics tend to make 'metaphorical' mistakes:

> 'To say what a thing is, is to say what a thing is like', Jackson notes. . . . The patient confined to the substitution set (once contexture is deficient) deals with similarities, and his approximate identifications are of a metaphoric nature. . . . *Spyglass* for *microscope*, or *fire* for *gaslight* are typical examples of such quasi-metaphoric expressions, as Jackson christened them, since in contradistinction to rhetoric or poetic metaphors, they present no deliberate transfer of meaning.[4]

This evidence from the clinical study of aphasia is not merely fascinating in its own right and persuasive support for Jakobson's general theory of language; it is, I believe, of direct relevance to the study of modern literature and its notorious 'obscurity'. If much modern literature is exceptionally difficult to understand, this can only be because of some dislocation or distortion of either the selection or the combination axes of language; and of some modern writing, e.g. the work of Gertrude Stein and Samuel Beckett, it is not an exaggeration to say that it aspires to the condition of aphasia. We shall investigate this further in due course; I proceed immediately to consider the final section of Jakobson's paper, 'The Metaphoric and Metonymic Poles', in which he applies his distinction to all discourse, and indeed to all culture.

3 The Metaphoric and Metonymic Poles

The development of a discourse may take place along two different semantic lines: one topic may lead to another either through their similarity or their contiguity. The metaphorical way would be the more appropriate term for the first case and the metonymic for the second, since they find their most condensed expression in metaphor and metonymy respectively. In aphasia one or other of these two processes is blocked. . . . In normal verbal behaviour both processes are continually operative, but careful observation will reveal that under the influence of a cultural pattern, personality, and verbal style, preference is given to one of the two processes over the other.[1]

Jakobson proceeds to classify a great variety of cultural phenomena according to this distinction. Thus, drama is basically metaphoric and film basically metonymic, but within the art of film the technique of montage is metaphoric, while the technique of close-up is synecdochic. In the Freudian interpretation of dreams, 'condensation and displacement' refer to metonymic aspects of the dreamwork, while 'identification and symbolism' are metaphoric.* In painting, cubism 'where the object is transformed into a set of synecdoches' is metonymic and surrealism metaphoric (presumably because it combines objects not contiguous in nature, and selects and substitutes

---

*These are the basic processes by which the latent content of the dream—the real anxieties or desires which motivate it—is translated into its manifest content, the dream itself. Condensation is the process by which the latent content of the dream is highly compressed, so that one item stands for many different dream thoughts, and displacement is the process by which dreams are often differently centred from the anxieties or guilts which trigger them off. Thus something trivial in a dream may have the significance of something important in actuality and the connection between the two can be traced along a line of contiguities by the technique of free association. Dream symbolism is the more familiar process by which, for instance, long pointed objects represent male sexuality and hollow round objects female sexuality.

visual/tactile values on the principle of similarity or contrast.* The two types of magic discriminated by Frazer in *The Golden Bough*, homeopathic or imitative magic based on similarity and contagious magic based on contact, correspond to the metaphor/metonymy distinction. In literature, Russian lyrical songs are metaphoric, heroic epics metonymic. Prose, which is 'forwarded essentially by contiguity' tends towards the metonymic pole, while poetry, which in its metrical patterning and use of rhyme and other phonological devices emphasizes similarity, tends towards the metaphoric pole. Romantic and symbolist writing is metaphoric, and realist writing is metonymic: 'following the path of contiguous relationships, the realistic author metonymically digresses from the plot to the atmosphere and from the characters to the setting in space and time. He is fond of synecdochic details. In the scene of Anna Karenina's suicide Tolstoy's artistic attention is focused on the heroine's handbag. . . .'[2]

'The dichotomy here discussed', says Jakobson, 'appears to be of primal significance and consequence for all verbal behaviour and for human behaviour in general'† and it may be asked whether anything that offers to explain so much can possibly be useful, even if true. I believe it can, for the reason that it is a binary system capable of being applied to data at different levels of generality, and because it is a theory of dominance of one quality over another, not of mutually exclusive qualities.‡ Thus the same distinction can serve to explain

*Cf. Max Ernst: 'One rainy day in 1919, finding myself in a village on the Rhine, I was struck with the obsession which held under my gaze the pages of an illustrated catalogue showing objects designed for anthropologic, microscopic, psychologic, mineralogic, and paleontologic demonstration. There I found brought together elements of figuration so remote that the sheer absurdity of that collection provoked a sudden intensification of the visionary faculties in me and brought forth an illusive succession of contradictory images, double, triple and multiple images, piling up on each other with the persistence and rapidity which are peculiar to love memories and visions of half-asleep.

'These visions called themselves new planes, because of their meeting in a new unknown (the plane of non-agreement).' *Beyond Painting* (New York, 1948), quoted in *The Modern Tradition* (New York, 1965) ed. Richard Ellmann and Charles Feidelson Jr. p. 163.

† And perhaps not only human behaviour. Recent experiments in America in teaching chimpanzees sign-language have made impressive progress. The chimps are able spontaneously to combine the signs they have learned to describe novel situations, and it is reported that one chimp, Washoe, referred to a duck as 'water-bird' and another, Lucy, referred to a melon as 'candy-drink'—metonymic and metaphoric expressions, respectively. 'The Signs of Washoe', *Horizon*, BBC 2, 4 November, 1974.

‡ I think Hayden White fails to appreciate this point about dominance when he describes the metaphor-metonymy distinction as 'dualistic' (*Metahistory*, p. 33n.) He himself follows a more traditional fourfold distinction between the 'master-tropes' of Metaphor, Metonymy, Synecdoche and Irony, which he ingeniously combines with other fourfold classifications of Argument (Formism, Organicism, Mechanism, Contextualism) Emplotment (Romance, Comedy, Tragedy, Satire) and Ideology (Anarchism, Conservatism, Radicalism, Liberalism) to establish a typology of historiography. The symmetry of this apparatus is not without its disadvantages; in

both the difference between category A and category B and the difference between item X and item Y in category A. To make this point clear it is necessary to look more closely at some of Jakobson's pairings of opposites, and to follow up what are no more than cryptic hints in his paper. But first, for convenience of reference, the main points of the paper may be summarized in a schematic fashion by two lists:

METAPHOR	METONYMY
Paradigm	Syntagm
Similarity	Contiguity
Selection	Combination
Substitution	[Deletion] Contexture
Contiguity Disorder	Similarity Disorder
Contexture Deficiency	Selection Deficiency
Drama	Film
Montage	Close-up
Dream symbolism	Dream Condensation & Displacement
Surrealism	Cubism
Imitative Magic	Contagious Magic
Poetry	Prose
Lyric	Epic
Romanticism & Symbolism	Realism

4 Drama and Film

When Jakobson says that drama is essentially 'metaphoric' he is clearly thinking of the generic character of dramatic art as it has manifested itself throughout the history of culture. Arising out of religious ritual (in which a symbolic sacrifice was *substituted* for a real one) drama is correctly interpreted by its audience as being analogous to rather than directly imitative of reality, and has attained its highest achievements (in classical Greece, in Elizabethan England, in neoclassical France) by being poetic, using a language with a built-in emphasis on patterns of similarity and contrast (contrast being a kind of negative similarity). The 'unities' of classical tragedy are not means of producing a realistic

---

particular it entails a strong contrast between synecdoche (seen as essentially integrative, relating part to whole, and thus allied to metaphor) and metonymy (seen as essentially reductive, relating effect to cause, and allied to irony) which tends to blur the meaning of all four terms and thus limit their explanatory power.

illusion, but of bringing into a single frame of reference a constellation of events (say, Oedipus's birth, his killing of an old man, solving of a riddle, marriage) that were not contiguous in space or time but combine on the level of similarity (the old man is the same as the father, the wife is the same as the mother, the son is the same as the husband) to form a message of tragic import. Elizabethan drama is more obviously narrative than Greek tragedy (that is, more linear or syntagmatic in its construction) but its most distinctive formal feature, the double plot, is a device of similarity and contrast. The two plots of *King Lear* and the complex pairing and contrasting and disguising of characters in that play is a classic example of such dramatic structure, which generally has the effect of retarding, or distracting attention from, the chronological sequence of events. In the storm scene of *Lear*, for instance—one of the peaks of Shakespeare's dramatic achievement—there is no linear progress: nothing happens, really, except that the characters juggle with similarities and contrasts: between the weather and human life, between appearances and realities. And it is not only in *Lear* that the chain of sequentiality and causality in Shakespearean tragedy proves under scrutiny to be curiously insubstantial. Stephen Booth has convincingly demonstrated how the opening of *Hamlet* plunges us immediately into a field of paradoxes and non-sequiturs which we struggle in vain to unite into a coherent pattern of cause and effect[1] (hence, perhaps, the ease with which Tom Stoppard grafted on to it his more explicitly absurdist and metaphorical *Rosencrantz and Guildenstern Are Dead*). It is demonstrable that the plot of *Othello* allows no time in which Desdemona could have committed adultery with Cassio—but that anomaly doesn't matter, and is indeed rarely noticed in the theatre: the play is built on contrasts—Othello's blackness with Desdemona's whiteness, his jealousy against her innocence, his naivety against Iago's cunning—not cause-and-effect. Othello's self-justifying soliloquy, 'It is the cause, it is the cause, my soul' (V, ii, 1) carries a bitter irony, for there is no cause: not only is Desdemona innocent, but Iago's malice has no real motive (that is why it is so effective).

The naturalistic 'fourth wall' plays which have dominated the commercial stage in our era must be seen as a 'metonymic' deviation from the metaphoric norm which the drama displays when viewed in deep historical perspective. In naturalistic drama every action is realistically motivated, dramatic time is almost indistinguishable from real time, ('deletions' from the chronological sequence being marked by act or scene divisions) and the characters are set in a contextual space bounded and filled with real (or *trompe l'oeil* imitations of) objects—doors, windows, curtains, sofas, rugs—all arranged in the same relations of contiguity with each other and with the actors as they would be in reality. Such naturalism is, arguably, unnatural in the theatre. In reaction against it, many modern playwrights have put an extreme stress on the metaphoric dimension of drama. In Beckett's plays for instance, there is no progress through time, no logic of cause and effect, and the chintz and upholstery of drawing-rooms has given way to bare, stark acting spaces, with perhaps a chair, a row of dustbins and a high window from which nothing is visible (*End Game*). These plays offer themselves overtly as metaphors for the human condition, for on the literal level they are scarcely intelligible. Yet arguably *any* play, however naturalistic in style, is essentially metaphorical in that it is recognized as a *performance*: i.e. our pleasure in the play depends on our continuous and conscious awareness that we are spectators not of reality but of a conventionalized model of reality, constructed before us by actors who speak words not their own but provided by an invisible dramatist. The curtain call at which the actor who died in the last act takes his smiling bow is the conventional sign of this separation between the actors and their roles, between life and art.

The experience of watching a film is entirely different, notwithstanding the superficial similarity of modern theatre and cinema auditoria. There is, for example, no cinematic curtain call. Credits scarcely serve the same function: being written signs in an essentially non-literary medium their impact is comparatively weak, and often considerable ingenuity is used to make it even weaker, distracting our attention from the information the credits convey and integrating them into the film 'discourse' itself (by, for instance, delaying their introduction and/or by superimposing the words on scenic establishing shots or even action shots). Some films do attempt something like a curtain call at the end when they present a series of stills of the main actors with their real names superimposed, but these are invariably stills taken from the film itself, portraying the actor 'in character'—in other words the gap between performance and reality is not exposed.

Of course it is always possible for the film-maker to expose the artificiality of his production—Lindsay Anderson's *O Lucky Man*, for instance, ends with a celebration party on the set for actors and technicians, and Fellini likes to incorporate his cameras and other equipment into his pictures—but this is a highly deviant gesture in film. It is a commonplace that film creates an 'illusion of life' much more readily than drama. We are more likely to feel strong physical symptoms of pity, fear, etc. in the cinema than in the theatre, and this has little to do with aesthetic values. Whereas the play is created before us at every performance, the film is more like a record of something that happened, or is happening, only once. The camera and the microphone are voyeuristic instruments: they spy on, eavesdrop on experience and they can in effect follow the characters anywhere—out into the wilderness or into bed—without betraying their presence, so that nothing is easier for the film-maker than to create the illusion of reality. Of course film is still a system of signs, a conventional language that has to be learned (films are more or less unintelligible to primitive people never exposed to them before).[2] The oblong frame around the image does not correspond to the field of human vision, and the repertoire of cinematic shots—long-shot, close-up, wide-angle, etc.—bears only a schematic resemblance to human optics. Nevertheless, once the language of film has been acquired it *seems* natural: hence the thudding hearts, the moist eyes, in the stalls. We tend to take the camera eye for granted, and to accept the 'truth' of what it shows us even though its perspective is never exactly the same as human vision.

This verisimilitude can be explained as a function of the metonymic character of the film medium. We move through time and space lineally and our sensory experience is a succession of contiguities. The basic units of the film, the shot and the scene, are composed along the same line of contiguity and combination, and the devices by which the one-damn-thing-after-another of experience is rendered more dramatic and meaningful are characteristically metonymic devices that operate along the same axis: the synecdochic close-up that represents the whole by the part, the slow-motion sequence that retards without rupturing the natural tempo of successiveness, the high or low angle shot that 'defamiliarizes', without departing from, the action it is focused on. Consciousness is not, of course, bound to the line of spatio-temporal contiguity, in the way that sensory experience is, but then film does not deal very much or very effectively with consciousness except insofar as it is manifested in behaviour and speech, or can be reflected in landscape through the pathetic fallacy, or suggested by music on the sound track.

This does not mean that film has no metaphoric devices, or that it may not be pushed in the direction of metaphorical structure. Jakobson categorizes montage as metaphoric, presumably because it juxtaposes images on the basis of their similarity (or contrast) rather than their contiguity in space-time. However, the fact that the techniques of cutting and splicing by which montage is achieved are also the techniques of all film editing, by which any film of the least degree of sophistication is composed, creates the possibility of confusion here. John Harrington, for example, in his *The Rhetoric of Film*, defines montage as

> a rhetorical arrangement of juxtaposed shots. The combination, or gestalt, produces an idea by combining the visual elements of two dissimilar images. A longing face, for instance, juxtaposed to a turkey dinner suggests hunger. Or the image of a fox following that of a man making a business deal would indicate slyness. Segments of film working together to create a single idea have no counterpart in nature; their juxtaposition occurs through the editor's imaginative yoke.[3]

The main drift of this definition confirms Jakobson's classification of montage as metaphorical, but the first of Harrington's examples is in fact metonymic or synecdochic in Jakobson's sense: longing faces and turkey dinners *are* found together in nature (i.e. real contexts) and all that has been done in this hypothetical montage is to delete some of the links (*e.g.* a window) in a chain of contiguities that would link the face with the turkey. The fox and the businessman, on the other hand, are not contiguous in nature, but are connected in the montage through a suggested similarity of behaviour, as in the verbal metaphor 'a foxy businessman'. Context is all-important. If the montage of longing face and turkey dinner described by Harrington were in a film adaptation of *A Christmas Carol*, we should interpret it metonymically; if it were interpolated in a documentary about starving animals, it would be metaphoric. Those favourite filmic metaphors for sexual intercourse in the pre-permissive cinema, skyrockets and waves pounding on the shore, could be disguised as metonymic background if the consummation were taking place on a beach on Independence Day, but would be perceived as overtly metaphorical if it were taking place on Christmas Eve in a city penthouse.

Eisenstein himself included in the concept of montage juxtapositions that are metonymic as well as metaphoric:

The juxtaposition of two separate shots by splicing them together resembles not so much a simple sum of one shot plus another shot—as it does a *creation* . . . each montage piece exists no longer as something unrelated, but as a given *particular representation* of the general theme that in equal measure penetrates all the shot-pieces. The juxtaposition of these partial details in a given montage construction calls to life and forces into the light that *general* quality in which each detail has participated and which binds together all the details into a whole, namely, into that generalized *image*, wherein the creator, followed by the spectator, experiences the theme. . . . What exactly is this process? A given order of hands on the dial of a clock invokes a host of representations associated with the time that corresponds to the given order. Suppose, for example, the given figure be five. Our imagination is trained to respond to this figure by calling to mind pictures of all sorts of events that occur at that hour. Perhaps tea, the end of the day's work, the beginning of rush hour on the subway, perhaps shops closing, or the peculiar late afternoon light. . . . In any case we will automatically recall a series of pictures (representations) of what happens at five o'clock. The image of five o'clock is compounded of all these individual pictures.[4]

Translated into film such a montage of 'five o'clock' would be metonymic or synecdochic rather than metaphorical, representing the whole by parts, parts which are contiguous (because they belong to a larger complex of phenomena taking place at the same time) rather than similar. This is confirmed by Eisenstein's use of the word 'condensation' a few lines later: 'There occurs "condensation" within the process above described: the chain of intervening links falls away, and there is produced instantaneous connection between the figure and our perception of the time to which it corresponds.'[5]

Condensation, it will be recalled, belongs to the metonymic axis in Jakobson's scheme.

Eisenstein was not so much concerned with the difference between metaphoric and metonymic montage as with the difference between montage in general, and what he calls 'representation'—the photographing of an action from a single set-up by a simple accumulation of 'one shot plus another shot'—the cinematic equivalent of non-rhetorical, referential language in verbal discourse. Though celebrated for his daring use of the overtly metaphorical montage (e.g. soldiers being gunned down juxtaposed to cattle being slaughtered, Kerensky juxtaposed with a peacock) Eisenstein was comparatively sparing in his use of the device[6] (*Battleship Potemkin*, for instance, has no fully metaphorical montage though, as Roy Armes points out, the juxtaposition of shots of the three lions, one lying, one sitting and one roaring in the Odessa Steps sequence, creates the impression of a lion coming to life and 'conveyed the idea of protest—with an emotional meaning something like "Even the very stones cried out"'[7]) for the simple reason that if it becomes the main principle of composition in a film, narrative is more or less impossible to sustain. 'Underground' movies define themselves as deviant by deliberately resisting the natural metonymic tendency of the medium, either by a total commitment to montage, bombarding us with images between which there are only paradigmatic relations of similarity and contrast, or by parodying and frustrating the syntagm, setting the naturally linear and 'moving' medium against an unmoving object—the Empire State Building, for instance, or a man sleeping. Poetic drama, as I suggested earlier, is also in a paradoxical sense unmoving, nonprogressive, more concerned with paradigmatic similarities and contrasts than with syntagmatic sequence and cause-and-effect. The peculiar resistance of Shakespearian drama to successful translation into film, despite its superficial abundance of cinematic assets (exotic settings, duels, battles, pageantry etc.) is notorious; and one may confidently assert that the same difficulty would be still more acutely felt in any attempt to film Beckett's plays.* Even modern naturalistic drama (e.g. Albee's *Who's Afraid of Virginia Woolf* or Neil Simon's *The Odd Couple*) seems slightly ill-at-ease in the film medium, and

---

*It is noteworthy that Beckett's one screenplay, for a short film entitled *Film*, made in 1964 with Buster Keaton in the main role, is quite different in structure from his plays, though just as 'experimental' and aesthetically self-conscious. There is plenty of action and no dialogue. Event succeeds event in a logical time/space continuum. The camera follows a man along a street and up some stairs to a room; whenever the camera eye threatens to get a view of the man's face he displays anxiety and takes evasive action. In the room he banishes or covers all objects with eyes—animals, pictures, etc. But while he is dozing the camera eye stealthily moves round to view his face. The man wakes and registers horror at being observed. A cinematic 'cut' identifies the observer as the man himself 'but with a very different expression, impossible to describe, neither severity nor benignity, but rather acute *intentness*'. (Samuel Beckett, *Film* (1972) p. 47.)

most obviously so when it deserts the economical single setting for which it was originally designed, to take advantage of the freedom of location afforded by film. The two media seem to pull against each other. The realistic novel, on the other hand, converts very easily into film—and novelists were in fact presenting action cinematically long before the invention of the moving-picture camera. Consider this passage from George Eliot's first published work of fiction, 'The Sad Misfortunes of Amos Barton':

> Look at him as he winds through the little churchyard! The silver light that falls aslant on church and tomb, enables you to see his slim, black figure, made all the slimmer by tight pantaloons, as it flits past the pale gravestones. He walks with a quick step, and is now rapping with sharp decision at the vicarage door. It is opened without delay by the nurse, cook and housemaid, all at once—that is to say by the robust maid of all work, Nanny; and as Mr Barton hangs up his hat in the passage, you see that a narrow face of no particular complexion—even the smallpox that has attacked it seems to have been of a mongrel, indefinite kind—with features of no particular shape, and an eye of no particular expression, is surmounted by a slope of baldness gently rising from brow to crown. You judge him, rightly, to be about forty. . . .[8]

The passage continues in the same style: Barton opens the sitting-room door and, looking over his shoulder as it were, we see his wife Milly pacing up and down by the light of the fire, comforting the baby. Change George Eliot's 'you' to 'we' and the passage would read not unlike a film scenario. The action certainly breaks down very readily into a sequence of 'shots': *high-angle crane shot of Barton walking through churchyard; cut to door of vicarage opened by Nanny; close-up of Barton's face as he hangs up his hat* . . . and so on. In one respect the passage requires the cinema for its full realization: the charmless, yet human, ordinariness of Barton's physiognomy—the ordinariness which is unloveable yet which (George Eliot insists) we must learn to love—is a quality the cinema can convey very powerfully and immediately, whereas George Eliot can only indicate it verbally by means of negations. There is little doubt, I think, that George Eliot would have been deeply interested in the possibilities offered by the motion-picture camera of capturing the human significance of the commonplace: as it was, she had to appeal, as a visual analogy for her art, to the static pictures of the Dutch painters.[9]

5 Poetry, Prose and the Poetic

Jakobson's characterization of prose as 'forwarded essentially by contiguity' is consistent with the commonsense view that prose is the appropriate medium with which to describe logical relationships between concepts or entities or events. The formal rules of poetry (i.e. verse)—metre, rhyme, stanzaic form etc.—are based upon relationships of *similarity* and cut across the logical progression of discourse. The physical appearance of prose and verse in print illustrates the distinction: the end of a line of prose is arbitrary and of zero significance—the line ends merely so that the text may be accommodated on the printed page (there is no reason other than convenience why prose should not be printed on a continuous strip of paper like ticker tape) and the justification of margins is a visible sign that we should ignore line length in reading prose. The important spaces in the printed prose text are those of punctuation, which are directly related to the sense of the discourse. In verse, on the other hand, the separation of one line from another, made visible on the printed page by the irregular right-hand margin and the capital at the commencement of each new line, is a crucially important component of the discourse, which may be exploited either to support or to contrast with the punctuation according to sense. Jonathan Culler points out that 'If one takes a piece of banal journalistic prose and sets it down on a page as a lyric poem, surrounded by intimidating margins of silence, the words remain the same but their effects for readers are substantially altered.'[1]

The elaborate phonological patterning of poetry, though not in itself semantically motivated, makes metaphor, as Jakobson puts it, 'the line of least resistance' for poetry. Rhyme illustrates the point most clearly, for effective rhyme in poetry, as W. K. Wimsatt observed, consists not in pairing words of similar sound and closely parallel meanings, but in pairing words of similar sound and widely divergent meanings, or with contrasting associations, or having different grammatical functions, e.g. Pope's:

> One speaks the glory of the British Queen,
> And one describes a charming Indian screen.

or

>What dire offence from am'rous causes springs,
>What mighty contests rise from trivial things.[2]

As Roland Barthes puts it: 'rhyming coincides with a transgression of the law of distance between the syntagm and the system (Trnka's law); it corresponds to a deliberately created tension between the congenial and the dissimilar, to a kind of structural scandal.'[3]

Rhyme, in its combination of similarity and dissimilarity, is thus equivalent to metaphor, and is often contrived *by* metaphor, i.e. the two rhyming words are combined through a metaphorical substitution. If we look at the compositional process we can see that the prose writer and the poet are quite differently situated. Both set out to tell a story or expound an argument (all writing must in a sense do one or both of these things) but the poet is constantly diverted from combining items in a natural, logical or temporal succession by the arbitrary demands of the metrical form he has elected to employ. Rhyme, especially, is apt to prevent the poet from saying what he originally intended to say, and to lead him to say something that he would not otherwise have thought of saying. This is well known to anyone who has ever tried to write regular verse, though it is rarely admitted, as though there were something vaguely shameful about it. Of course, if the sense is completely controlled by the exigences of metre and rhyme, doggerel and nonsense result. Successful poetry is that which manages to fulfil all the requirements of a complex, purely formal pattern of sound and at the same time to seem an utterly inevitable expression of its meaning:

>I said, 'A line will take us hours, maybe;
>Yet if it does not seem a moment's thought,
>Our stitching and unstitching has been naught'.[4]

Sometimes this process of stitching and unstitching will lead the poet so far from his original design that the final draft of the poem is unrecognizable from the first; invariably he will be obliged to follow his original line of argument or narrative in an oblique or convoluted fashion, deviating from it and returning to it via metaphorical digression:

>O Wild West Wind, thou breath of Autumn's being,
>Thou from whose unseen presence the leaves dead
>Are driven like ghosts from an enchanter fleeing,
>
>Yellow, and black, and pale and hectic red,
>Pestilence-stricken multitudes! O thou
>Who chariotest to their dark wintry bed
>
>The winged seeds, where they lie cold and low,
>Each like a corpse within its grave, until
>Thine azure sister of the Spring shall blow

Her clarion o'er the dreaming earth, and fill
(Driving sweet buds like flocks to feed in air)
With living hues and odours plain and hill;

Wild Spirit, which art moving everywhere;
Destroyer and preserver; hear, O hear!

Although rhyme is only one of the poetic devices involved here, it is surely doubtful that Shelley's apostrophe would have been so extended or so rich in imagery, or that it would have developed in precisely this way, if it had not been expressed in *terza rima*, in which the second line of each stanza dictates the rhyme of the first and third lines in the next stanza.

The progress and final shape of a prose composition is not necessarily more predictable—one always discovers what it is one has to say in the process of saying it—but this is because of the plurality of contiguities in any given context. In describing a given event (say, a hanging) we cannot record all the relationships between all the items in the context (the context being in any case theoretically infinite); we are obliged to choose at every stage of the discourse to report this detail rather than that, make this connection rather than that. But the combination of discrete items is almost completely under the writer's semantic control—it is not subject to arbitrary and complex phonological requirements as in verse. I say 'almost' because there is, clearly, such a thing as prose rhythm, however difficult to analyse, and other phonological values enter into prose composition and exert some influence over the choice and combination of words (e.g. the obligation to *avoid* rhyming); but it is an infinitely more flexible and less rigorous system of restraints than operates in poetry, where the natural impulse of discourse to thrust onwards and generate new sentences is checked and controlled by the obligation to *repeat* again and again a certain pattern of sounds, syllables, stresses and pauses. The 'poetic function [of language]' Jakobson stated in his paper 'Linguistics and Poetics', 'projects the principle of equivalence from the axis of selection into the axis of combination.'[5]

This is one of Jakobson's most celebrated and often-quoted pronouncements, but there is a difficulty about the word 'poetic' here which has not, I think, been generally recognized: in theory it embraces the whole of literature; in this paper, however, it is applied almost exclusively to verse composition. 'Poetics', Jakobson states at the beginning of his paper, 'deals primarily with the question, *What makes a verbal message a work of art?*' and his answer, already referred to in Part One, is that 'The set (*Einstellung*) towards the MESSAGE as such, focus on the message for its own sake, is the POETIC function of language.'[6] He is quick to point out (following Mukařovský on foregrounding) that the poetic function is not *peculiar* to poetic messages (it occurs in advertising, political slogans and ordinary speech) but is their 'dominant, determining function, whereas in all other verbal activities it acts as a subsidiary, accessory constituent.'[7] How does the poetic function focus attention on the message for its own sake? Jakobson answers with the formula just quoted: 'The poetic function projects the principle of equivalence from the axis of selection into the axis of combination.' He continues:

> Equivalence is promoted to the constitutive device of the sequence. In poetry one syllable is equalized with any other syllable of the same sequence; word stress is assumed to equal word stress, as unstress equals unstress; prosodic long is matched with long, and short with short; word boundary equals word boundary; no boundary equals no boundary; syntactic pause equals syntactic pause, no pause equals no pause. Syllables are converted into units of equal measure, and so are morae or stresses.[8]

While the paper sets out to define 'literariness' in general, this passage seems to identify 'poetry' with metrical composition. Certainly if literature (verbal message as work of art) is characterized by the dominance of the poetic function of language, and the poetic function is dominated by 'equivalence', the whole theory of what constitutes 'literariness' is heavily biased towards verse rather than prose literature. Not surprisingly most of Jakobson's article is taken up with (highly perceptive) analysis of verse writing, with particular attention to phonological patterning. Though he produces examples of the poetic function in nonliterary discourse (e.g. the complex paronomasia of *I like Ike*, and the principle of syllable gradation that makes us prefer 'Joan and Margery to Margery and Joan') he does not face the question of what makes the verbal message in prose a work of art until almost at the end of his paper:

> 'Verseless composition', as Hopkins calls the prose variety of verbal art— where parallelisms are not so strictly marked and strictly regular as 'continuous parallelism' and where there is no dominant figure of sound— presents more entangled problems for poetics, as does any transitional linguistic area. In this case the transition is between strictly poetic and strictly referential language. But Propp's pioneering monograph on the structure of the fairy tale shows us how a consistently syntactic approach may be of paramount help even in classifying the traditional plots and in tracing the puzzling laws that underlie their composition and selection. The new studies of Lévi-Strauss display a much deeper but essentially similar approach to the same constructional problem.
>
> It is no mere chance that metonymic structures are less explored than the field of metaphor. May I repeat my old observation that the study of poetic tropes has been directed mainly towards metaphor, and the so-called realistic literature, intimately tied with the metonymic principle, still defies interpretation, although the same linguistic methodology, which poetics uses when analysing the metaphorical style of romantic poetry, is entirely applicable to the metonymical texture of realistic prose.[9]

This is a puzzling and tantalizing passage. The reference to 'the entangled problems' presented by the 'transitional linguistic area' of prosaic verbal art may seem evasive—or patronizing towards such art. We do not, after all, feel any less confident of classifying *Middlemarch* as literature than *In Memoriam*, and a comprehensive poetics should be able to tell us why. The allusions to Propp and Lévi-Strauss are not really relevant to this problem because these analysts deal with narrative structures abstracted from any particular verbalization, whether in prose or verse. Jakobson seems to acknowledge this lacuna in his argument in the second paragraph, where he invokes his earlier distinction between metaphoric and metonymic writing, but it is a curiously cryptic acknowledgment. Why does realistic literature continue to 'defy interpretation' if metonymy is the key to it? Why doesn't Jakobson himself analyse some examples of this kind of writing in this paper? The answer to these questions is perhaps to be found in the discrepancy between 'Linguistics and Poetics' and the earlier paper on the two aspects of language, namely that the latter implied a concept of literariness ('poetry', verbal message as art) that included *both* metaphoric and metonymic types, but 'Linguistics and Poetics' identifies literariness with only *one* type, the metaphoric. The projection of 'the principle of equivalence from the axis of selection into the axis of combination', offered as a definition of the poetic function in 'Linguistics and Poetics', is in fact a definition of metaphorical substitution according to the linguistic theory of 'Two Aspects of Language'.

Jakobson is more explicit about the problem in the last paragraph of this earlier paper. There he points out that research into poetics has been biased towards metaphor for two reasons. First, the relationship between tenor and vehicle in metaphor is paralleled by the relationship between language and metalanguage, both operating on the basis of similarity. 'Consequently, when constructing a metalanguage to interpret tropes, the researcher possesses more homogeneous means to handle metaphor, whereas metonymy, based on a different principle, easily defies interpretation. Therefore nothing comparable to the rich literature on metaphor can be cited for the theory of metonymy.' The second reason is that 'since poetry is focused upon sign, and pragmatical prose mainly upon referent, tropes and figures were studied mainly as poetic devices' and poetry (i.e. verse) is innately metaphorical in structure. 'Consequently the study of poetical tropes is directed chiefly towards metaphor. The actual bipolarity has been artificially replaced in these studies by an amputated, unipolar scheme which, strikingly enough, coincides with one of the two aphasic patterns, namely with contiguity disorder.'[10] After this laconic observation, it is a little surprising that Jakobson should have perpetuated the 'amputated, unipolar' approach in his later paper on linguistics and poetics.

But one can appreciate the difficulties. To preserve the binary character of the general theory, there ought to be some formula parallel to 'the projection of the principle of equivalence from the axis of selection into the axis of combination' that would describe the *metonymic* aspect of the poetic function. Logically, this ought to be: 'the projection of the principle of contiguity from the axis of combination into the axis of selection'. But if we interpret this formula in the strong sense, as a deviant or foregrounded manoeuvre, we find that it applies to verbal errors characteristic of the similarity disorder, such as saying *fork* for *knife*, *table* for *lamp*, *smoke* for *pipe* etc., of which Jakobson observed, 'Such metonymies may be characterized as projections from the line of a habitual context into the line of substitution and selection.' And if we interpret the formula in the weak sense, to mean simply that contiguity, or context, controls the field of selection, then we have nothing more than a simple description of the way ordinary referential discourse works. This is in fact what we might expect, since literature written in the metonymic mode tends to disguise itself as nonliterature (cf. 'A Hanging') but it does not help us to accommodate such writing in a linguistically-based poetics. On the contrary it would licence us to discuss such literature entirely in terms of its content.

6   Types of Description

I suggested earlier (p. 76) that metonymy and synecdoche, considered as verbal tropes, are transformations of literal kernel statements produced by a process of combination and nonlogical deletion. This would seem to correspond to what we commonly refer to as a novelist's 'selection' of details in narrative description. Such details, E. B. Greenwood claims, 'are surrogates . . . for the mass of observed detail which would have been there in actuality.'* If, then, the appropriate critical response to the metaphoric text is to construct a metalanguage that will do justice to its system of equivalences, the appropriate response to the metonymic text would seem to be an attempt to restore the deleted detail, to put the text back into the total context from which it derives. And indeed the most familiar kind of criticism of the

---

*'Critical Forum', *Essays in Criticism* XII (July 1962) pp. 341–2. Greenwood was contributing to a discussion of F. W. Bateson's and B. Shakevitch's commentary, published in an earlier issue of the same journal, on a story by Katherine Mansfield. Greenwood actually applied the terms metonymy and synecdoche to descriptive detail in realistic fiction, without, it would appear, being aware of Jakobson's theory. I, certainly, was not when I quoted Greenwood's remark in *Language of Fiction* (pp. 43–4).

realistic novel follows precisely this path. The critical commentary is not so much an analysis of the novel's system as a witness to its truthfulness, or representativeness, its contribution to, and consistency with, the sum of human knowledge and human wisdom. Up to a point such a procedure is natural and indeed inevitable in discussing realistic fiction, and literary education in schools rightly begins by teaching students how to do criticism at this level. But such a procedure can never supply the basis for a 'poetics' of fiction because its essential orientation is towards content rather than form. At its worst it merely regurgitates what the novelist himself has expressed more eloquently and pointedly. Perhaps this is what Jakobson means when he says that realistic literature 'defies interpretation'.

Characterizing the realistic text as metonymic need not, however, lead us to adopt such a critical procedure if we remember that metonymy is a figure of *nonlogical* deletion. This is where we may locate a specifically literary motivation for the selection of detail. Since we cannot describe everything in a given context, we select certain items at the expense of not selecting others: this is true of all discourse. But in discourse with no 'poetic' coloration at all, (Jakobson's 'pragmatic prose') the selection of items is based on purely logical principles: what is present implies what is absent, the whole stands for the part, the thing for its attributes, unless the part or attribute is itself vital to the message, in which case it is brought into the message as a whole or thing in its own right. Here, for instance, is an American desk-encyclopaedia entry on the city of Birmingham, England:

BIRMINGHAM (bur'ming-um) second largest English city (pop. 1,112,340) Warwickshire; a great industrial centre. Covers 80 sq. mi. Has iron-and coal nearby and is noted for metal mfg. Most of Britain's brass and bronze coins minted here. Utilities and a bank are city owned. Has noted city orchestra. Site of Anglican and Roman Catholic cathedrals and Univ. of Birmingham. Heavily bombed World War II.[1]

In reference books of this type, space is at a premium, so abbreviations and elliptical syntax are used whenever words and letters can be omitted without causing confusion. This graphological and syntactical condensation is representative of the way the text is organized semantically. It does not, for instance, tell us that the skyline of Birmingham displays many factory chimneys—that is implied by 'great industrial centre'. 'Utilities' includes several agencies and services, but not banks, so the bank has to be mentioned separately. Birmingham is not noted for the arts generally, only for its orchestra, so the orchestra is specified; but we are not told anything about the orchestra and therefore infer that it is an ordinary symphony orchestra. In short, the general only yields to the particular when it does not adequately imply the particular, and the particular never represents the general—except insofar as the whole catalogue of facts collectively 'represents' the real city. The text is therefore metonymic only in the sense that it is not metaphoric. It has selected certain details rather than others and combined them together—but any text must do the same. The point is that there is nothing figurative or rhetorical in the mode of selection and combination corresponding to the actual tropes of metonymy and synecdoche. The article is not, of course, a neutral or objective account of Birmingham, just because it *is* selective. But the selection of information, it is safe to assume, is governed by the general conventions and utilitarian purpose of the encyclopaedia rather than by the particular interests and observations of the author, or any design upon the reader's emotions. As a message it is orientated almost entirely towards context; or, in other words, it is referential. Compare this:

> Most students who come to Birmingham are agreeably surprised by their first view of the campus. Steeled to expect an environment of unrelieved industrial sprawl and squalor, they find the University situated on a fine, spacious site, its oddly but interestingly assorted architecture not noticeably stained by soot, surrounded on most sides by the leafy residential roads and green spaces of Edgbaston, a rare example of an inner suburb that has kept its privacy in a modern city.
>
> On one side of the campus, however, the factory chimneys and mean terraced cottages of Selly Oak strike a note more characteristic of 'Brum'. At the Bournbrook gate, indeed, as if by symbolic intent, one small factory (which seems, on acoustic evidence, to be breaking rather than making things) edges right up against the University grounds. Overalled men, stunned by the din inside, emerge occasionally to breathe fresh air, draw on a fag, and stare quizzically at the scholars passing in and out of academe. Whatever illusions life at Birmingham University may foster, the ivory tower mentality is not likely to be one of them.[2]

These are the opening paragraphs of an article published in the *Guardian*, 9 October, 1967, in a series on British Universities entitled 'A Guide for the First Year Student'. It was orientated to a much more specific audience than the encyclopaedia article (not merely Birmingham University first-year students, of course, but *Guardian* readers in general, especially those interested in higher education). And although written by an anonymous 'correspondent', it obviously expressed a more individualized and personal point of view than the encyclopaedia article. Comparing the two texts, one immediately notices how much the *Guardian* article depends on metonymical devices of an overtly rhetorical kind—for example, synecdoche in, 'leafy residential roads and green spaces of Edgbaston' and 'the factory chimneys and mean terraced cottages of Selly Oak'. Parts stand for wholes in these formulations, and they do so with a certain affective and thematic intent. It would have been just as 'true' to the facts to have said, 'the silent streets and hushed houses of Edgbaston' and 'the busy pavements and snug back-to-backs of Selly Oak'; but that would not have served the writer's purpose, which was to set up an opposition between (A) suburban-pastoral and (B) urban-industrial environments. In the first paragraph, the expectation of B is corrected by the experience of A, and in the second paragraph this recognition is in turn corrected by the experience of B: a kind of double peripeteia. The passage reads more smoothly than the encyclopaedia article not simply because it eschews abbreviations and ellipses, but because it combines items in a sequence that both corresponds to their natural contiguity and supports the text's theme. The description in a sense imitates the physical process of exploring the campus, approaching it from the Edgbaston side, and finishing at its border with Selly Oak—where the implied explorer is himself, as it were, observed by the quizzical workers (synecdochically evoked by their overalls and fags). In comparison, the items in the encyclopaedia article are 'contiguous' only in the sense of being connected with the same place—Birmingham. At first unified by what one might call an 'industrial theme', that text quickly disintegrates into a series of heterogeneous facts.

These distinctions are not intended as comparative value-judgments. The two passages have quite different ends in view, and it may well be that the encyclopaedia article does its job better. But there is no doubt, I think, that the *Guardian* piece is more 'literary', and that this is directly traceable to the fact that it exploits metonymic form (both at and above the level of the sentence) for optional, expressive purposes, whereas the encyclopaedia article only uses metonymic procedures inasmuch as it has to, and because it has to.

Am I then claiming that the *Guardian* text is 'literature'? That question could only be answered by putting the passage back into its original context—the entire article, which in fact becomes much more like an encyclopaedia article as it goes on. So my answer would be, no. There is not the kind of systematic internal foregrounding through the whole text which would allow it to sustain a literary reading. Those first two paragraphs do, however, exhibit within themselves a systematic foregrounding of detail, and could conceivably be the opening of a novel, without any revision at all.*

Let us look now at a couple of classic fictional descriptions of cities. They both occur at the beginnings of their respective texts. The first is from E. M. Forster's *A Passage to India*.

> Except for the Marabar Caves—and they are twenty miles off—the city of Chandrapore presents nothing extraordinary. Edged rather than washed by the river Ganges, it trails for a couple of miles along the bank, scarcely

*The encyclopaedia article could of course also provide the opening to a novel—Kingsley Amis's *The Green Man* (1969) begins with a clever pastiche of an entry in the *Good Food Guide*—but such a novel could not possibly continue for long in the same mode: the encyclopaedia article could only serve as a prelude or foil to the main narrative.

distinguishable from the rubbish it deposits so freely. There are no bathing steps on the river-front, and bazaars shut out the wide and shifting panorama of the stream. The streets are mean, the temples ineffective, and though a few fine houses exist they are hidden away in gardens or down alleys whose filth deters all but the invited guest. Chandrapore was never large or beautiful, but two hundred years ago it lay on the road between Upper India, then imperial, and the sea, and the fine houses date from that period. The zest for decoration stopped in the eighteenth century, nor was it ever democratic. There is no painting and scarcely any carving in the bazaars. The very wood seems made of mud, the inhabitants of mud moving. So abased, so monotonous is everything that meets the eye, that when the Ganges comes down it might be expected to wash the excrescence back into the soil. Houses do fall, people are drowned and left rotting, but the general outline of the town persists, swelling here, shrinking there, like some low but indestructible form of life.[3]

A Passage to India might be described as a symbolist novel disguised as a realistic one, and realistic writing, as we have already seen, tends to disguise itself as nonliterary writing. This opening paragraph certainly achieves its effect of knowledgability and authenticity partly by skilfully imitating the tone and method of the guidebook or travel essay. Yet the passage mentions only three specific topographical items—the Marabar Caves (very deliberately nudged into the prime position by syntactical inversion), Chandrapore itself, and the Ganges. The other substantives are mostly vaguely generalized plurals—bazaars, temples, streets, alleys, fine houses, gardens. There are no overt metonymies and synecdoches of the kind commonly found in travel writing to evoke 'atmosphere' and local colour. The reason for this is obvious: Chandrapore (that is, the original, native city—for the second paragraph goes on to draw a contrasting picture of the suburbs dominated by the British civil station) *has* no local colour, no atmosphere, except that of neglect, monotony and dirt; and to have evoked these qualities by metonymy and synecdoche, to have made them concrete and sensible, would have been to risk making them positive and picturesque. The dominant note of the description is negativity and absence: *nothing extraordinary—scarcely distinguishable . . . no bathing steps . . . happens not to be holy . . . no river front . . . shut out . . . temples ineffective . . . deters . . . never large or beautiful . . . stopped . . . nor was it ever democratic . . . no painting and scarcely any carving . . .* The only overtly metaphorical expressions enforce the same theme: *The very wood seems made of mud, the inhabitants of mud moving . . . like some low but indestructible form of life.**

If the passage has no metonymic and few metaphorical tropes, what

*These are of course similes, not metaphors proper. Although Jakobson does not comment on simile as such it must belong on the metaphorical side of his bipolar scheme since it is generated by the perception of similarity, but it does not involve substitution in the same radical sense as metaphor. For this reason it is more easily assimilated into metonymic modes of writing. For a fuller discussion of this point see below pp. 112–13

is its rhetoric, and why does it remind us of guidebook writing? I think the answer is to be found in the schemes of repetition, balance and antithesis—especially isocolon (repetition of phrases of equal length and usually corresponding construction): *edged rather than washed . . . the streets are mean, the temples ineffective . . . no painting and scarcely any carving . . . The very wood seems made of mud, the inhabitants of mud moving. So abased, so monotonous . . . Houses do fall, people are drowned . . . swelling here, shrinking there . . .* These patterns of words and word order, and the rhythms and cadences they create, are very like the 'figures of sound' that Jakobson analyses in poetry, and they are perhaps the nearest thing in prose to 'the projection of the principle of equivalence from the axis of selection into the axis of combination'. Their familiarity in travelogue and guidebook writing is a good example of the appearance of the 'poetic function' in nonpoetic discourse. In such writing rhetorical patterning provides a certain aesthetic pleasure—the pleasure that inheres in all rhythm—which is supplementary to the interest of the information conveyed and separable from it—in Jakobson's phrase it 'acts as a subsidiary, accessory constituent'.[4] It has a general effect of humanizing the discourse by imparting to it a homogeneous tone of voice and of enabling graceful transitions between discrete facts, thus making the text generally more accessible and assimilable, or in common parlance more 'readable'. The encyclopaedia article on Birmingham could be recast in such a style without any significant modification of the information conveyed (and would indeed have to be so recast if it were an article of any length). But it would be quite impossible to recast Forster's description into the style of the encyclopaedia without loss or change of effect because his tone of voice is inextricably part of the paragraph's meaning. The elegant syntactical inversions, pointed antitheses, delicate cadences, artful repetitions, are not merely wrapping up the facts in a pleasing package, but are at every point organizing and presenting the 'facts' in a way which will emphasize the underlying theme of negativity and absence.

This is still not quite a case of 'projection of the principle of equivalence from the axis of selection into the axis of combination', however. The rhetorical paradigms do not actually intrude into, or divert or frustrate or cut across the syntagmatic continuity of the discourse (in the manner of stanzaic form in poetry)—they collaborate with it. With due respect to Pope, it is in prose not verse that the sound should be an echo to the sense. If this happens consistently in verse, a trite jingle results. Conversely, if phonological patterning is allowed to dominate sense in prose, as in Euphuistic writing, the result is freakish and ultimately self-defeating. Between these two extremes there is plenty of room for verse to shift in the direction of prose norms and vice versa; but the opening of *A Passage to India* is not 'poetic' prose. It is metonymic writing, not metaphoric, even though it contains a few metaphors and no metonymies; it is metonymic in structure, connecting topics on the basis of contiguity not similarity. The description of Chandrapore begins with the river Ganges, then proceeds to the river banks, then to the bazaars which are built along the river banks, then to the streets and alleys that lead away from the river, with the occasional fine houses and gardens. There the description pauses for a brief historical digression (temporal rather than spatial contiguities) before reversing itself and proceeding back from the houses to the bazaars and eventually to the river. Thus the whole paragraph is a kind of chiasmus pivoting on the historical digression, its symmetrical structure duplicating on a larger scale the dominant figures of repetition and balance within individual sentences. Ending, topographically, where it began, it mimics the defeat of the observer's quest for something 'extraordinary' in the city of Chandrapore.

Another example:

> London. Michaelmas Term lately over, and the Lord Chancellor sitting in Lincoln's Inn Hall. Implacable November weather. As much mud in the streets, as if the waters had but newly retired from the face of the earth, and it would not be wonderful to meet a Megalosaurus, forty feet long or so, waddling like an elephantine lizard up Holborn Hill. Smoke lowering down from chimneypots, making a soft black drizzle, with flakes of soot in it as big as full-grown snow-flakes—gone into mourning, one might imagine, for the death of the sun. Dogs, undistinguishable in mire. Horses, scarcely better; splashed to their very blinkers. Foot passengers, jostling one another's umbrellas, in a general infection of ill-temper, and losing their foothold at street corners, where tens of thousands of other foot-passengers have been slipping and sliding since the day broke (if this day ever broke) adding new deposits to the crust upon crust of mud, sticking at those points tenaciously to the pavement, and accumulating at compound interest.[5]

This is prose pushed much further towards the metaphoric pole than any of the other examples. The basic structure is a catalogue of contiguous items, but there is a marked tendency for the items to be elaborated metaphorically rather than represented metonymically. The text accelerates rapidly from brief, literal statements to the personification of the November weather ('implacable') then to the fantastic vision of the Megalosaurus and the apocalyptic vision of the death of the sun (metaphorical time-trips to the beginning and end of creation, respectively).* Then the paragraph, so to speak, comes down

---

*The reference to 'waters . . . newly retired from the face of the earth' is ambiguous in that it could allude either to the separation of the waters from the dry land at the Creation (*Genesis* i, 9–10) or to the aftermath of the Flood (*Genesis* viii, 7–17). Verbally the latter passage is more closely echoed, but thematically the other interpretation is more satisfying. In either reading the image yokes together Biblical and modern scientific versions of prehistory in a very striking way, as Mrs J. Politi has observed in a discussion of this passage (*The Novel and its Presuppositions*, Amsterdam, 1976, pp. 201–2). She points to a similar double perspective in the image of the death of the sun, which both echoes Biblical prophecy ('The sun shall be darkened in his going forth'—*Isaiah*, xiii,

to earth again, starts a new sequence of short, literal descriptive details (dogs, horses, umbrellas) but it is not long before the literal mud has generated a new metaphorical excursion. It is perhaps worth comparing this image of the mud 'accumulating at compound interest' with Forster's 'the very wood seems made of mud, the inhabitants of mud moving'. The metaphorical force of the latter is far more muted because of the contextual relationship between tenor and vehicle: with the Ganges present in the scene, mud does not seem an incongruous or unexpected source of analogy. The wood and the people are in fact in physical contact with (contiguous to) the mud with which they are compared. In Dickens, the mud is the tenor of the metaphor, and the vehicle, 'compound interest' has no such physical contiguity with it— and could not have since it is an abstraction. There *is*, however, a contextual relationship of a kind, and one that has been often pointed out; namely, that the setting is the City of London, dedicated to making money ('filthy lucre' in the proverbial phrase) and that the misery caused by the Court of Chancery, which is one of the main themes of the novel, derives from greed for money. Thus, through the conceit, 'accumulating at compound interest', the mud appears to be not merely an attribute of London in November, but an attribute of its institutions: it becomes a kind of metaphorical metonymy, or as we more commonly say, a symbol. The symbolic significance of the mud (as of the fog introduced in the next paragraph) is made explicit a little later in the chapter:

> Never can there come fog too thick, never can there come mud and mire too deep, to assort with the groping and floundering condition which this High Court of Chancery, most pestilent of hoary sinners, holds, this day, in the sight of heaven and earth.[6]

In this opening of *Bleak House*, then, 'the principle of equivalence' has projected into 'the axis of combination' on a considerable scale. Another indication that it belongs to or at least inclines to the metaphoric mode is that any attempt to translate it into film would inevitably rely on the technique of montage: a rapid sequence of juxtaposed shots—panorama of London, the Lord Chancellor in his hall, 'special effect' of a Megalosaurus, smoke lowering down from chimneys, dogs and horses splashed with mud, pedestrians colliding at a street-corner—making up what Eisenstein called a 'generalized *image*, wherein its creator, followed by the spectator, experiences the theme'. No doubt the omission of finite verbs, creating an impression

---

10, 'The sun became black as sackcloth of hair'—*Revelation*, vi, 12) and alludes to the modern geological theory of the gradual cooling of the sun. Mrs Politi plausibly traces the underlying pessimism of the authorial sections of *Bleak House* in part to the troubling impact of biological and geological science upon orthodox belief in the mid-nineteenth century.

of synchrony, the lack of smooth transitions between sentences, and the uniform syntactical structure of sentences, contribute to this montage effect. A film treatment of Forster's opening to *A Pasage to India*, on the other hand, or of the description of Birmingham University and environs, would use a much smoother and less noticeable cutting technique, aiming at a condensed version of a 'natural' visual survey or exploration of the scene. Dickens's verbal montage is, however, more boldly metaphorical than film montage can generally manage to be—and is not, in the last analysis, truly cinematic. The things it makes us 'see' most vividly aren't actually there at all; and what *is* there—muddy dogs and horses, ill-tempered pedestrians—are rather drably and vaguely described. The image of a Megalosaurus waddling down Holborn Hill would be quite difficult to interpret in a film, and might arouse expectations that we were about to see a science-fiction fantasy of the *King Kong* variety. The subtlety of the sootflakes and compound-interest metaphors would be more or less impossible to communicate visually. Quite simply, Dickens's paragraph is not so much a seeing as a saying. It approximates to drama rather than to film inasmuch as the narrator, instead of disguising himself as an eye, a lens, seems to address us as a voice, a histrionic voice (quite different from Forster's relaxed, ruminative voice): the voice of Chorus. He summons up by the power of his eloquence a vision of the familiar, prosaic capital (the technique could hardly work on an *un*familiar city like Chandrapore) strangely denatured and time-warped, fit setting for the tale of twisted motives and distorted values that is to follow. To literal-minded readers, the description will, of course, appear overdone or 'exaggerated'. 'I began and read the first number of *Bleak House*', Henry Crabb Robinson wrote in his diary on 19 March 1852. 'It opens with exaggerated and verbose description. London fog is disagreeable even in description and on the whole the first number does not promise much.'[7]

Bleak House, as Philip Collins observes, 'is a crucial item in the history of Dickens's reputation. For many critics in the 1850s, 1860s and 1870s, it began the drear decline of "the author of Pickwick, Chuzzlewit and Copperfield"; for many recent critics—anticipated by G. B. Shaw—it opened the greatest phase of his achievement.'[8] *Bleak House* marked Dickens's transition from being a humorous, cheerful, essentially reassuring entertainer, who deployed large casts of comic and melodramatic characters against realistic and recognizable backgrounds, to being an ironic and pessimistic critic of what he diagnosed as a sick society,* using symbolist techniques that impart to the physical world a sinister and almost surreal animation; or in our terms, it marked his shift from a metonymic to a metaphoric mode of

*H. M. Daleski has drawn attention to the submerged imagery of disease in the opening paragraphs of *Bleak House*: *infection, pollutions, pestilent*. *Dickens and the Art of Analogy* (1970), p. 169.

writing (as far as the authorial chapters are concerned, for Esther's narrative is essentially metonymic, contrasting in this, as in so many other ways, with the author's). The description of London at the beginning of *Bleak House* might be contrasted with the description of Jacob's Island and Folly Ditch in Chapter 50 of *Oliver Twist*, which begins:

> Near to that part of the Thames on which the church at Rotherhithe abuts, where the buildings on the banks are the dirtiest and the vessels on the river blackest with the dust of colliers and the smoke of close-built, low-roofed houses, there exists the filthiest, the strangest, the most extraordinary of the many localities that are hidden in London, wholly unknown, even by name, to the great mass of its inhabitants.[9]

Immediately one notices how much closer this is to the tone of the opening to *A Passage to India*. Like E. M. Forster, Dickens models his discourse on the guide-book: 'To reach this place the visitor has to penetrate through a maze of close narrow streets . . . he makes his way with difficulty . . . Arriving, at length, in streets remoter and less frequented than those through which he has passed. . . .' And so on. There is a profusion of synecdochic detail:

> he walks beneath tottering house-fronts projecting over the pavements, dismantled walls that seem to totter as he passes, chimneys half crushed, half hesitating to fall, windows guarded by rusty iron bars that time and dirt have almost eaten away, every imaginable sign of desolation and neglect.[10]

Although there are metaphorical expressions here (*tottering, hesitating, eaten away*) they are familiar, almost dead metaphors and their impact is relatively weak. Collectively their anthropomorphism invests the environment with a certain quality of menace, but more importantly these architectural details function as indices of (not metaphors for) desolation and neglect. The same strategy is repeated in the following paragraph, which describes the houses on and overlooking Jacob's Island:

> Crazy wooden galleries common to the backs of half-a-dozen houses, with holes from which to look upon the slime beneath; windows, broken and patched, with poles thrust out, on which to dry the linen that is never there; rooms so small, so filthy, so confined, that the air would seem too tainted even for the dirt and squalor which they shelter; wooden chambers thrusting themselves out above the mud, and threatening to fall into it—as some have done; dirt-besmeared walls and decaying foundations; every repulsive lineament of poverty, every loathesome indication of filth, rot, and garbage; all these ornament the banks of Folly Ditch.[11]

This description is clearly a more 'realistic' townscape than that which begins *Bleak House*—which is not to say that *Oliver Twist* as a whole is the more realistic novel. Indeed, one of the signs of its being a relatively immature piece of work is the distance or disparity between its fairy-tale-like plot and the topographical specificity of its London setting. Arguably, Dickens was never an essentially realistic novelist (as, say, George Eliot or Trollope were), and achieved his finest work when he allowed his novels to develop according to metaphorical principles. 'It is my infirmity', he wrote, 'to fancy or perceive relations in things which are not apparent generally.'[12]

These terms—metaphoric, metonymic—are however (it has to be emphasized) relative. Any prose narrative, however 'metaphorical', is likely to be more tied to metonymic organization than a lyric poem. To illustrate the point, and to complete our sample of urban descriptions, we might cite the 'Unreal city' sequence of *The Waste Land*, which, beginning with a deceptively metonymic description of London commuters, in which there is a submerged analogy with Dante's *Inferno*

> Under the brown fog of a winter dawn,
> A crowd flowed over London Bridge, so many
> I had not thought death had undone so many

suddenly explodes into metaphor:

>   'Stetson!
> 'You who were with us in the ships at Mylae!
> 'That corpse you planted last year in your garden
> 'Has it begun to sprout? Will it bloom this year?
> 'Or has the sudden frost disturbed its bed?'

There is no contextual support for these remarks, which would explain them or supply links between them. They are intelligible only as metaphorical articulations of motifs already introduced elsewhere in the poem (e.g. in the very first lines, with their allusions to the distressing burgeonings of spring). *The Waste Land* is indeed a prime example of metaphorical discourse, since it is structured almost exclusively on the principle of similarity and contrast, dislocating and rupturing relationships of contiguity and combination.

7   The Executions Revisited

If we arrange the texts discussed in the preceding section in a horizontal order, thus:

1	2	3	4	5
Encyclopaedia	*Guardian*	*Passage to India*	*Bleak House*	*The Waste Land*

we have a kind of spectrum of discourse extending from the metonymic to the metaphoric poles. Wherever we draw a vertical line between the numbered texts, those on the right of the line will be more 'metaphoric' than those on the left, and those on the left more 'metonymic' than those on the right. The line between literature and nonliterature would go straight through text no. 2, since that is the only one whose status is problematical in this respect.

A similar ordering is possible of the accounts of executions discussed in Part One, thus:

1	2	3	4	5
'Michael Lake Describes . . .'	'A Hanging'	*The Old Wives' Tale*	*The Naked Lunch*	'The Ballad of Reading Gaol'

The two sets do not correspond exactly. There is no equivalent to the encyclopaedia article in the second set, where the line between literature and nonliterature passes through text no. 1. But the comparison of the texts in left-to-right sequence reveals the same basic movement from metonymic to metaphoric dominance. It also confirms and clarifies the distinctions we made between the texts, on other grounds, in Part One; or, to put it another way, our critical reading of these texts confirms the soundness of Jakobson's distinction.

'The Ballad of Reading Gaol', for instance, fully supports the proposition that poetry (as compared to prose) is inherently metaphorical, not necessarily in the quantitative dominance of actual metaphors (though the 'Ballad' is full of them) but in the way the discourse is generated and maintained by 'the projection of the principle of equivalence from the axis of selection into the axis of combination'. Analysis of the complex but highly symmetrical patterning of the first stanza demonstrated this process at work in microscosm, while on the level of the poem's total structure we traced the dominant role, in the development of the poem, of certain thematic and symbolic similarities and contrasts: between human and divine justice, between the condemned man and Christ, between the various connotations of red and white, and so on. This emphasis on metaphorical or paradigmatic relationships in the discourse leads correspondingly to a weakening of metonymic or syntagmatic relationships—i.e. the relationships of contiguity in time and space, and of cause and effect. Whereas all the prose texts, even *The Naked Lunch* passage, keep to a chronological *sequence*, the 'Ballad' is strikingly ambiguous in its handling of time. As we observed, the central act of execution, which is the unique and irreversible climax of the texts by Lake, Orwell and Bennett, seems to occur not once but several times in the course of Wilde's poem—which is to say that it doesn't really 'occur' at all: it is anticipated, recalled and moralized upon, but never presented directly as a single, discrete happening. The structure of the poem is indeed not linear but centripetal—a system of looping digressions from and returns to the central symbolic-thematic core; the subject is not so much unfolded as *rotated* before us. As well as serving the poet's interest in parallels rather than contiguities, the deliberate ambiguity about time makes it difficult and indeed irrelevant to try and distinguish between the real and the imaginary in the poem, so that the question of 'realism' doesn't arise in connection with it.

The distinction is just as difficult to make, but perhaps not quite so irrelevant, in the passage from *The Naked Lunch*. Though this is structured as a sequence, a continuous syntagm, it is unintelligible as such because of logical contradictions between its component parts (e.g. Mark turns into Johnny whom Mary has just eaten). We therefore naturally look for some metaphorical meaning which would 'explain' this impossible combination of events, and Burroughs has told us what it is: the obscenity of capital punishment. If this meaning fails to emerge from the actual reading, it is, I suggested above, because the impossible events are narrated in a style that is more realistic (metonymic in Jakobson's terms) than the surrounding narrative; and it is significant that this style is borrowed from the film medium, which is also metonymic in Jakobson's scheme. The local metaphorical expressions in the Burroughs passage ('scream like a mandrake . . . sound like a stick broken in wet towels . . . one foot flutters like a trapped bird . . . pinwheel end over end and leap high in the air like great hooked fish . . .') do not contribute to the emergence of the moral theme concerning capital punishment, but tend rather to render the actions to which they are applied more physically immediate and credible. And these expressions mostly take the form of simile, which is precisely the form of metaphorical language most amenable to realism because least disturbing to syntagmatic continuity (see below p. 112). If, therefore, this text seems gratuitously obscene, it may be because it displays a fundamental confusion between the metaphoric and metonymic modes of writing: instead of cooperating, the two are pulling in opposite directions.

Jakobson's distinction also enables us to establish why the antepenultimate paragraph of *The Old Wives' Tale*, III, iii, 4, strikes a different note from the rest of the section, and a slightly false one:

> She felt like a lost soul, torn too soon from shelter, and exposed for ever to the worst hazards of destiny. Why was she in this strange, incomprehensible town, foreign and inimical to her, watching with agonized glance this cruel, obscene spectacle? Her sensibilities were all a bleeding mass of wounds. Why?

The metaphors here—vague, 'mixed', rather literary in their derivations—contrast with the essentially metonymic preceding account of the preparations for the execution, and seem comparatively inauthentic beside it. This is not a criticism of Bennett because, as I suggested earlier, he probably intends, in the manner of Flaubert, to hold us back from too ready an identification with Sophia at this point. The whole episode has been narrated from Sophia's point of view, limited to what she could observe from her hotel window, but with a certain detachment which is a function of the impersonal but everpresent narrator: we are always, so to speak, observing Sophia observing the events in the square. Her emotions and sensations are reported to us, or rendered through the convention of monologue (' "I cannot stand this!" she told herself in horror, but she could not move'). In the paragraph under discussion, however, Bennett uses free indirect speech to admit us directly to Sophia's consciousness as her experience reaches its climax. If, verbally, the paragraph seems an *anti*climax, this is appropriate inasmuch as she is unable to cope emotionally with the crisis.

It is noteworthy that the one term significantly absent from the account of the preparations for the execution, which is yet the key to the whole event—blood—finally makes its appearance in this paragraph in the metaphorical 'bleeding'. The guillotining is a ritual of blood: that is what the baying crowd has come to see and that is why the guillotine itself is painted red (though we are not told this and have to infer it). Sophia cannot acknowledge that blood is the source of her appalled fascination by the event, all the more because the shedding of Rivain's blood is identified with the loss of her own virginity. Emotionally paralysed by her unresolved and conflicting feelings about Gerald, she is incapable of a fully human response to the victim Rivain, and her metaphorical claim to be a 'bleeding mass of wounds' seems particularly self-dramatizing and self-pitying in the context of Rivain's literal decapitation.

In general *The Old Wives' Tale* fully exemplifies Jakobson's characterization of literary realism as a metonymic mode: 'following the path of contiguous relationships, the realistic author metonymically digresses from the plot to the atmosphere and from the characters to the setting in space and time. He is fond of synecdochic details.' From its origins in the Restaurant Sylvain to its climax in the hotel bedroom at Auxerre, the story of Sophia's final disillusionment with her husband is woven out of contiguities, which confer plausibility and meaning simultaneously upon the narrative. It is at the restaurant that Gerald first gets interested in the execution and meets Chirac, who offers to conduct him to it; at the same time the *louche* atmosphere of the restaurant (conveyed synecdochically in the 'violently red lips, powdered cheeks, cold, hard eyes, self-possessed arrogant faces and insolent bosoms' clustered about the tables) associates the expedition from its inception with moral corruption, specifically of a sexual character. The description of the journey to

Auxerre maintains the linear continuity of the story but also affords opportunities for thickening the atmosphere of moral and physical degradation: 'Although the sun was sinking the heat seemed not to abate. Attitudes grew more limp, more abandoned. Soot and prickly dust flew in unceasingly at the open window.' Gerald's sexual infidelity just before the execution is coded entirely in terms of contiguity: the presence of two young women in the square at such a time is a sign that they are not respectable; the fact that they are arm-in-arm and talking to Gerald and Chirac who are also arm-in-arm suggests the possibility of an alternative pairing-off, a suggestion which is fulfilled when Gerald is next sighted, 'talking vivaciously alone with one of the two girls who had been together'; and finally the sight of Gerald emerging from a house followed at an interval by the girl is a sign that she is a prostitute and that Gerald has just been her client. Gerald glances up at Sophia's hotel 'hastily'—which we interpret as 'guiltily'. Thus a message is conveyed to the reader through the observations of Sophia, who either does not understand the significance of what she sees, or does not want to understand it, and yet without Bennett's having to intervene as narrator to explain what is happening.

The way in which the guillotine itself is handled in this section is a classic example of how the realistic author can, by selection (or deletion) and repetition within a field of contiguities, construct a metonymic metaphor, or symbol, without disturbing the illusion of reality. The phallic significance of the guillotine is metaphorical, based on similarity, and corresponds directly to the metaphoric aspect of the dreamwork in Freudian analysis (see p. 79n. above). But whereas the mere appearance of a guillotine in a dream would itself in most cases be an enigma demanding interpretation, a vehicle for which we could not but seek a tenor, the appearance of the guillotine in *The Old Wives' Tale* is utterly predictable in context—it is indeed demanded by the context. What makes it capable of bearing a metaphorical meaning as well as taking its place in a natural sequence of contiguities is (a) the prominence it is given by repetition and (b) the synecdochic mode of its presentation, which focuses attention upon two of its properties: its columnar structure and its red colour. If the columns of the guillotine had been mentioned only once, or if the machine had been referred to several times but simply as 'the guillotine' or if it had been exhaustively described in every part and function in the style of Robbe-Grillet, the metaphorical meaning we have attributed to it could not have emerged.

One of the reasons why Orwell's 'A Hanging' reminds us of realistic fiction is the way the participants ('characters' one is inclined to call them) are established and identified by metonymy and synecdoche— e.g. the grotesque moustache of the prisoner, the contrasting toothbrush moustache and gruff voice of the prison superintendent, and the white suit, gold spectacles and black hand of the head jailer. The most interesting detail of this kind is the superintendent's stick, which both represents his authority and expresses his feelings as he manipulates it—moodily prodding the gravel in paragraph 3, slowly poking the ground as the prisoner calls on his god in paragraph 13, making the swift, decisive gesture of command in paragraph 14, poking the corpse in paragraph 16. Through this repetition the stick takes on, like the guillotine in Bennett, the function of a symbol. There is nothing like it in Michael Lake's report. His description of the hangman in paragraph 8 ('He wore a black broad-brimmed hat, a black trench coat, and heavy boots, and he was masked. Only the slit for his eyes and his white hands gleamed in the light') includes too many diverse details to be described as synecdochic, and—more important—none of these details is repeated or echoed subsequently in the text. Compared to 'A Hanging', 'Michael Lake Describes . . .' displays the metonymic mode in an inert, or rhetorically untransformed state. Like the encyclopaedia article on Birmingham (though not quite as starkly) it selects and deletes only because it must, and on pragmatic principles, without any discernible pattern developing through the discourse. The absence of significant repetition from this text is therefore closely related to the absence of any controlling idea comparable to Orwell's life-death-time matrix, and these absences prevent it from satisfying the demands of a 'literary' reading. This instance, at least, would seem to support Ruqaiya Hasan's notion of the kind of 'unity'—'the manifestation of some deep underlying principle'—that distinguishes the literary from the nonliterary text. The only deep underlying principle manifested by 'Michael Lake Describes . . .' is the professional code of the journalist: 'I report what I see, I tell it like it was.' And that is a principle that could be equally well expressed by a report of any event whatsoever. It is not that 'Michael Lake Describes . . .' fails to take up a moral attitude to the execution it describes (in which case it might have acquired the thematic unity of the Absurd). On the contrary it takes up explicit moral attitudes at several points; but these attitudes are not integrated with each other or with the other components of the discourse in any systematic way, such as 'A Hanging' displays under analysis.

8   The Metonymic Text as Metaphor

We observed earlier that even Jakobson himself seemed somewhat baffled by the problem of how to deal, analytically, with the metonymic mode of writing; and we traced the difficulty to the fact that in his scheme the POETIC (i.e. the literary) is homologous with the metaphoric mode, which in turn is opposed to the metonymic mode. How, then, can the metonymic be assimilated to the POETIC?

The solution would seem to lie in a recognition that, at the highest level of generality at which we can apply the metaphor/metonymy distinction, literature itself is metaphoric and nonliterature metonymic. The literary text is always metaphoric in the sense that when we interpret it, when we uncover its 'unity' in Ruqaiya Hasan's sense, we make it into a total metaphor: the text is the vehicle, the world is the tenor. Jakobson himself, as we have already noted, observes that metalanguage (which is what criticism is, language applied to an object language) is comparable to metaphor, and uses this fact to explain why criticism has given more attention to metaphorical than to metonymic tropes. Likewise, at the level of discourse, it is easier to see the entire text as a kind of metaphor applied to reality if it is written in the metaphorical mode than if it is written in the metonymic mode. We are not likely to interpret *King Lear* or *Paradise Lost* as literal reports of the real: at every point these works point to their own status as total metaphors. The human condition, Shakespeare is saying, 'is' *King Lear*; the human condition, Milton is saying, 'is' *Paradise Lost*. The metonymic text however—*Emma*, say, or *The Old Wives' Tale*—seems to offer itself to our regard not as a metaphor but as a synecdoche, not as a model of reality, but as a representative *bit* of reality. Human life 'is like' *Emma*, 'is like' *The Old Wives' Tale*, these authors seem to be saying—the phrase 'is like' denoting, here, a relationship of contiguity rather than similarity, for the writers create the illusion that their stories are or were part of real history, from which they have been cut out and of which they are representative. Taken a little further towards the metonymic pole, such fiction is often described as a 'slice of life'. Yet this phrase, which points to the synecdochic character of the realistic text, is itself a metaphor; and we know that it is not possible for the literary artist to limit himself to merely making a cut through reality, as one might cut through a cheese, exposing its structure and texture without altering it, for the simple reason that his medium is not reality itself but signs. For the same reason, although the metonymic text retards and resists the act of interpretation which will convert it into a total metaphor, it cannot postpone that act indefinitely. As Guy Rosolato puts it:

> The most descriptive or most realistic work culminates in a metaphor which it secretly sustains by the continuity of its narrative, and which is revealed at certain points, notably at its end: metaphor of a 'life', a 'reality', an 'object' thus put into the flow of the work defined by the limits of the book and by the break of its ending.[1]

The truth of this proposition is confirmed by that most characteristic of all gambits in the teaching and criticism of literature: the question, what is the text *about*? Ian Gregor has culled a nice quotation on this subject from Isherwood's novel *A Single Man* (1964) where George, an assistant professor of English at an American college, is discussing a novel by Huxley with his class:

> Before we can go any further, you've got to make up your minds what this novel actually *is* about. . . . At first, as always, there is a blank silence. The class sits staring, as it were, at the semantically prodigious word. *About. What* is it about? Well, what does George want them to say it's about? They'll say it's about anything he likes, anything at all. For nearly all of them, despite their academic training, deep deep down still regard this *about* business as a tiresomely sophisticated game. As for the minority, who have cultivated the *about* approach until it has become second nature, who dream of writing an *about* book of their own one day, on Faulkner, James or Conrad, proving definitively that all previous *about* books on that subject are about nothing—they aren't going to say anything yet awhile. They are waiting for the moment when they can come forward like star detectives with the solution to Huxley's crime. Meanwhile let the little ones flounder.[2]

Isherwood, like many creative writers, seems to be deeply suspicious of and hostile to academic criticism, and obviously intends the passage as satire on its procedures. Yet there is no alternative to the 'about game', unless we are to sit before works of literature in dumb silence (which might indicate either admiration or disgust). The most rudimentary exchange of information or opinion about a text ('This is a terrific book'—'Oh, what's it about?') involves the participants immediately in its preliminary moves, and with players of any sophistication the game moves inevitably from mere paraphrase into interpretation. This is just as true of the metonymic text as of the metaphoric. A typical professional critical essay on *Emma* begins:

> The subject of *Emma* is marriage. Put that way the statement seems ludicrously inadequate, for *Emma*—we instinctively feel—is not about anything that can be put into one word. And yet it is as well to begin by insisting that this novel does have a subject. . . .

> *Emma* is about marriage. It begins with one marriage, that of Mrs Taylor, ends with three more and considers two others by the way. The subject is marriage; but not marriage in the abstract. There is nothing of the moral fable here; indeed it is impossible to conceive of the subject except in its concrete expression, which is the plot.[3]

Arnold Kettle's repeated qualifications of his own original proposition indicate his respect for the metonymic structure and texture of the novel, and his anxiety to avoid a reductively 'metaphorical' reading of the text, that would neglect the density and subtlety of detail through which the theme of 'marriage' emerges. Nevertheless, some such reductiveness is inevitable if criticism is going to do more than merely repeat the words of the text. In the metalanguage of criticism, metonymy ultimately yields to metaphor—or is converted into it.

If it is asked why we should value literature written in the metonymic mode, since this mode appears to run against the grain of literature itself (a challenge that has often been directed at the realistic novel) we should probably answer that it is the very resistance which the metonymic mode offers to generalizing interpretation that makes the meaning we *do* finally extract from it seem valid and valuable. No message that is decoded without effort is likely to be valued, and the metaphoric mode has its own way of making interpretation fruitfully difficult: though it offers itself eagerly for interpretation, it bewilders us with a plethora of possible meanings. The metonymic text, in contrast, deluges us with a plethora of data, which we seek to unite into one meaning. Furthermore, it must always be remembered that we are not discussing a distinction between two mutually exclusive types of discourse, but a distinction based on dominance. The metaphoric work cannot totally neglect metonymic continuity if it is to be intelligible at all. Correspondingly, the metonymic text cannot eliminate all signs that it is available for metaphorical interpretation.

9 Metaphor and Context

Apart from the fact that the metonymic text must ultimately submit to a 'metaphoric' interpretation, most such texts, certainly most realistic fiction, contain a good deal of local metaphor, in the form both of overt tropes and of submerged symbolism. And it is not surprising that interpretative critics of a formalist bent (such as Mark Schorer) look with particular attentiveness at this level of the metonymic text. There are however certain controls on the use of metaphoric strategies in realistic fiction, which Jakobson's theory helps to make clear. The basic point is very simple, and has already been touched on in connection with film-montage: it is that, in the metonymic text, metaphorical substitution is in a highly sensitive relation to context or contiguity. The greater the distance (existentially, conceptually, affectively) between the tenor (which is part of the context) and the vehicle of the metaphor, the more powerful will be the semantic effect of the metaphor, but the greater, also, will be the disturbance to the relationships of contiguity between items in the discourse and therefore to realistic illusion. This disturbance can to some extent be muted by using simile rather than metaphor proper, for simile, although it creates a relationship of similarity between dissimilars, spreads itself along the line of combination which metaphor, by its radical strategy of substitution, tends to disrupt. Metaphor, it is sometimes said, asserts identity, simile merely likeness,[1] and perhaps on this account the former trope is usually considered the more 'poetic'.

Northrop Frye, indeed, offers the distinction between metaphor and simile in much the same way as Jakobson offers the distinction between metaphor and metonymy—as models of mythical and realistic literature respectively:

> Realism, or the art of verisimilitude, evokes the response 'How like that is to what we know!' When what is written is *like* what is known, we have an art of extended or implied simile. And as realism is an art of implicit simile, myth is an art of implicit metaphorical identity. The word 'sun-god' with a hyphen used instead of a predicate, is a pure ideogram, in Pound's terminology, or literal metaphor, in ours.[2]

'Like' is an ambiguous word because it can denote either a relationship of similarity between things otherwise dissimilar ('My love is like a red, red rose') or a quality of representativeness deriving from an original contiguity between part and whole or unit and set ('All the roses in the garden are like this one'). I argued in the preceding section that the response to realistic writing, 'How like that is to what we know' is nearer to the second use of *like* than the first; and that it suggests a relationship between the realistic novel and the world that is closer to synecdoche than to simile. This does not, however, entirely invalidate the suggestion that there is some kind of affinity between simile and realism. It is easy to see, for instance, that simile lends itself more readily than metaphor to the empiricist philosophical assumptions that historically underpin realism as a literary mode. When we say that A is like B, we do not confuse what is actually there with what is merely illustrative, but when we say that A in a sense *is* B, the possibility of such confusion is always present, as even the old school text-book examples, 'He fought like a lion' and 'He was a lion in the fight', demonstrate. Aristotle acutely described metaphor as 'midway between the unintelligible and the commonplace';[3]

simile is a little nearer the commonplace, and to common sense.

We may therefore suggest that the difference between metaphor and simile corresponds to the more comprehensive distinction between the metaphorical (which includes simile) and the metonymic poles of language. But two qualifications must be made. First, a writer does not always enjoy freedom of choice between expressing a perceived similarity through metaphor or simile because, as Winifred Nowottny has pointed out, very often the language he is using does not permit him to use the former trope.[4] Graham Greene, for instance, describes an African baby as 'smiling like an open piano',[5] and it is difficult to see how the analogy could be expressed in metaphor proper. Secondly, the factor of 'distance' between tenor and vehicle is more significant than the choice of metaphor or simile. Consider this passage from Virginia Woolf's *The Waves*:

> The sun fell in sharp wedges inside the room. Whatever the light touched became dowered with a fanatical existence. A plate was like a white lake. A knife looked like a dagger of ice. Suddenly tumblers revealed themselves upheld by streaks of light. Tables and chairs rose to the surface as if they had been sunk under water and rose, filmed with red, orange, purple like the bloom on the skin of ripe fruit. The veins of the glaze of the china, the grain of the wood, the fibres of the matting became more and more finely engraved. Everything was without shadow. A jar was so green that the eye seemed sucked up through a funnel by its intensity and stuck to it like a limpet.[6]

This is the metaphoric imagination running riot, and the fact that the vision is expressed sometimes through metaphor proper and sometimes through simile doesn't seem to make much difference.

To sum up the foregoing: we would expect the writer who is working in the metonymic mode to use metaphorical devices sparingly; to make them subject to the control of context—either by elaborating literal details of the context into symbols, or by drawing analogies from a semantic field associated with the context; and to incline towards simile rather than metaphor proper when drawing attention to similarity between things dissimilar. We can observe these principles operating in 'A Hanging', with regard to both symbolism and figurative language.

The superintendent's stick acquires symbolic force by its repeated appearance in the text, associated with a variety of gestures and postures. As an object it is entirely appropriate to its context, and indeed in context it already has a quasi-symbolic function, as a sign of the superintendent's authority. When the superintendent pokes the ground with his stick, and still more when he pokes the corpse of the prisoner, he goes beyond the strictly ritualistic use of his stick and thus reveals the psychological tensions and moral contradictions of his situation. But these violations of decorum are so slight that we scarcely register them as such and the symbolic effect of the stick is almost subliminal. If, however, Orwell's superintendent made much more play with his stick—did much more bizarre and eccentric things with it, e.g. holding it between his legs like a phallus, or aiming it at the prisoner like a gun, then it would become a metaphorical rather than a metonymic symbol. Or suppose Orwell gave the superintendent not a stick but a cricket bat, then the object would become completely metaphorical and not at all metonymic because a cricket bat would be quite out of place in this context. There being no natural contiguity in language or reality between cricket bats and prison superintendents (as there is between sticks and superintendents), we could only interpret the cricket bat on the basis of similarity: between, say, the British colonial prison system and the British public school system; and we should also observe a negative similarity, or contrast, between cricket and executions, generating an irony of a more extreme and overt kind than that which Orwell provides through the appearance of the playful dog. In other words such alterations would transform the text from the metonymic mode of realism or confessional documentary to the metaphoric mode of black comedy or satiric fantasy.

'A Hanging' doesn't use very many metaphors. There is the pathetic fallacy of the *sickly light* in paragraph 1, and the transferred epithet of *desolately thin* in paragraph 3. There are conventional, almost dead metaphors like *toothbrush moustache* and *volley of barks*; and a few other metaphorical expressions that are only a little removed from cliché: *puny wisp of a man* [1], *floated* [3], *gambolled* [8] and *in full tide* [10]. The most obviously metaphorical expressions (i.e. those which draw our conscious attention to a relationship of similarity between dissimilars) are in fact similes:*

Paragraph 1:   like yellow tinfoil
          1:   like small animal cages
          2:   like men handling a fish which is still alive and may jump back into the water
         12:   like the tolling of a bell
         13:   like bad coffee
         15:   dead as a stone

Of these images the most striking, the most 'poetic', is probably the fish simile, and it is also the one that relates most immediately to what I take to be the thematic core of the piece, the life/death/time matrix (because a fish out of water has a short, finite time to live). The comparison of the man to a fish has much more force than the comparison of the prisoners to animals in paragraph 1, implied in *like small animal cages* and reinforced by the reference to *brown silent men squatting*, which without being explicitly metaphorical, irresistibly

---

*I do not classify *not like a prayer or cry for help* [12] and *like a flour bag* [12] as similes, since the word *like* is used in each case not to draw attention to similarity between dissimilars, but to define what is distinctive about something which belongs to a set of things that are axiomatically similar—cries and bags.

evokes the image of animals in a zoo. There is not a great conceptual distance between a cage and a cell, and indeed 'cage' is sometimes used as a kind of dead metaphor in the vocabulary of prisons. Likewise there is an element of contextual appropriateness in the similes, *like the tolling of a bell* and *like bad coffee*: bells often toll to announce a death, and bad coffee is an analogy that comes naturally to mind in a prison at breakfast time. Even *like yellow tinfoil* is naturalized by coming immediately after the reference to Burma, which we associate with yellowish complexions and the saffron robes of Buddhist monks. (The simile would seem more fanciful, more 'poetic' if the text began, 'It was in Africa', or if the simile itself was 'like gold tinfoil'—which would convey the same visual impression.) The fish simile stands out in a way the other similes do not because *there is no sea in the context:* therefore all the semantic impact of the simile is centred on similarity, not contiguity. If there were a great many such similes in 'A Hanging', drawing analogies from sources far removed from the context, the quality of documentary authenticity which it possesses would be dissipated.

This rule does not apply only to writing of a decidedly metonymic bias, like 'A Hanging'. All prose fiction that aims at any degree of realistic illusion will tend to give context a good deal of control over metaphor. Gérard Genette has shown this very perceptively in discussing Proust. *The Remembrance of Things Past* is a book heavily biased towards metaphor: the action of involuntary memory, which is the prime moving force behind the narrative, is a linking of experiences on the basis of their similarity (an irregularity in the paving-stones of Paris, for instance, recalling to Marcel the floor of the baptistery of St Mark's in Venice). But, says Genette, if the initial trigger-mechanism of memory is metaphoric, the expansion and exploration of any given memory (though accomplished with a great display of local metaphor and simile) is essentially metonymic, because of Proust's characteristic tendency towards 'assimilation by proximity ... the projection of analogical affinity upon relationships of contiguity' and vice versa.[7] One of Genette's examples of this interpenetration of metaphor and metonymy is a comparison of two descriptions of pairs of church steeples. In the first, from *Swann's Way*, the narrator contemplates the plain of Méséglise:

> Sur la droite, on apercevait par-delà les blés les deux clochers ciselés et rustiques de Saint-André-des-Champs, eux-mêmes effilés, écailleux, imbriqués d'alvéoles, guillochés, jaunissants et grumeleux, comme deux épis.*

In the second passage, from *Sodom and Gomorrah*, Marcel, at Balbec, evokes the church of St Mars-le-Vêtu thus:

*'On the right one saw, beyond the corn fields, the two carved and rustic steeples of St André-des-Champs, themselves tapering, scaly, honeycombed, symmetrically patterned as though by an engraving tool, yellowing and rough textured like two ears of corn.'

Saint-Mars, dont, par ces temps ardents ou on ne pensait qu'au bain, les deux antiques clochers d'un rose saumon, aux tuiles en losange, légèrement infléchis et comme palpitants, avaient l'air de vieux poissons aigus, imbriqués d'écailles, moussus et roux, qui, sans avoir l'air de bouger, s'élevaient dans une eau transparente et bleue.*

Genette points out that the two pairs of steeples are clearly very similar in appearance, but that the basic analogies in each passage are quite different. Why does Proust compare the steeples in the first passage to ears of corn and those in the second passage to fish? Clearly because of the context of each perception—the cornfields of Méséglise and the sea and bathing of Balbec, respectively.[8]

Genette observes that 'resemblance in an analogy mattered less to Proust than its *authenticity*, its fidelity to relations of spatio-temporal proximity'.[9] In this respect there is a difference between Proust and Orwell. Resemblance *did* matter to the latter—indeed it was the only possible justification for using analogy at all—because his aim was to describe as vividly and accurately as possible some object or event in what he took to be a common phenomenal world. He was always aiming at a historical (or pseudo-historical) 'authenticity'. Proust, on the other hand, was concerned with the authenticity of subjective consciousness. Whereas Orwell's 'I was there' stance implies that if we had been 'there' we should have seen what he saw, Proust implies that no one ever sees the same thing as another: and if we feel that the analogies through which Marcel explores his spatio-temporal context are somewhat extravagant, or tenuous or idiosyncratic, this is entirely appropriate to the whole enterprise of *The Remembrance of Things Past*. The important point to emphasize, however, is that Proust displays the movements of the individual consciousness as it encounters a reality, a context, which is coherent and intelligible to the reader, which is the world that Proust and Marcel and the reader inhabit. This makes *The Remembrance of Things Past* an extension of rather than a deviation from the realistic novel tradition, and entails subordinating analogy to context in the manner analysed by Genette.†
Compare the use of analogy in another modern text concerned to display subjective consciousness:

> Let us go then, you and I,
> When the evening is spread out against the sky
> Like a patient etherized upon a table[10]

*"St Mars, whose two antique, salmon-pink steeples, covered with lozenge-shaped tiles, slightly curved and seemingly palpitating, looked, in this scorching weather when one thought only of bathing, like pointed fish of great age that, covered with overlapping scales, mossy and russet, without appearing to move, rose in blue and transparent water.'
† And it is worth noting that the memory-trigger which, in a sense, starts the whole book off, the taste of the madeleine described in the Overture to *Swann's Way*, is metonymic in its operation, recalling experience previously associated with that taste by contiguity.

There is not very much resemblance between an evening sky and a patient on an operating table, and the emotional and semantic distance between these two concepts is very great. The analogy therefore seems highly subjective. Yet we cannot say, as in Proust, that it is authenticated by context, because Prufrock has no associations with medicine, surgery etc., nor is there any other allusion to such things elsewhere in the text. In fact these lines, like so much of Eliot's early verse, turn upon a *violation* of context: an abrupt shift from association of items according to contiguity (first two lines) to association of items according to similarity, (third line) made all the more disconcerting because the perceived similarity is so eccentric and unexpected. The lines also violate poetic decorum in refusing the conventional response to the sunset as something sublime and harmoniously beautiful, and together these violations declare the poem as modernist. The opening lines are representative of the rest of the poem, in which we are given hints about the speaker's spatio-temporal context which we struggle to compose into a coherent 'history' (Prufrock is a middle-aged, middle-class bachelor with cultured and genteel female acquaintance, etc.) but from which the discourse is continually digressing via bizarre analogies ('When I am formulated, sprawling on a pin . . . I should have been a pair of ragged claws . . . though I have seen my head (grown slightly bald) brought in upon a platter . . .') which are far removed from this context.

Like most modernist verse, Eliot's pushes Jakobson's poetic principle to an extreme: substitution not merely projects into, but radically disrupts combination, and the similarities on which substitution is based are often strained or recondite—hence the obscurity of such writing, its (in some cases, to some readers) wilful unintelligibility. A classic instance of such a clash between poet and audience was recorded in the correspondence published in the magazine *Poetry* (Chicago) between the editor, Harriet Monroe, and Hart Crane, concerning one of the latter's poems, 'At Melville's Tomb'. 'Take me for a hardboiled unimaginative unpoetic reader,' Miss Monroe wrote,

> and tell me how *dice* can *bequeath an embassy* (or anything else); and how a calyx (of *death's bounty* or anything else) can give back a *scattered chapter*, *livid hieroglyph*; and how, if it does, such a *portent* can be *wound in corridors* (of shells or anything else).

The first of these queries referred to the lines

> The dice of drowned men's bones he saw bequeath
> An embassy.

Crane replied:

> Dice bequeath an embassy, in the first place, by being ground (in this connection only, of course) in little cubes from the bones of drowned men by the action of the sea, and are finally thrown up on the sand, having 'numbers' but no identification. These being the bones of dead men who never completed their voyage, it seems legitimate to refer to them as the only surviving evidence of certain messages undelivered, mute evidence of

certain things, experiences that dead mariners have had to deliver. Dice as a symbol of chance and circumstances is also implied.

There was more explanation of this kind, but Harriet Monroe was unappeased. 'I think that in your poem certain phrases carry to an excessive degree the "dynamics of metaphor" ' She wrote in her last letter:

> —they telescope three or four images together by mental leaps (I fear my own metaphors are getting mixed!) which the poet, knowing his ground, can take safely, but which the most sympathetic reader cannot take unless the poet leads him by the hand with some such explanation as I find in your letter.[11]

We need not here attempt to adjudicate between the correspondents. Both contributions show that the deviance of modernist poetry consists in emphasizing an existing bias in all poetry towards the metaphorical pole. A different kind of deviance results when the poet, especially the lyric poet, pushes his medium in the opposite direction—when he makes the metaphorical development of his topic subject to the kind of metonymic constraints that the realistic prose writer normally applies. This is a path likely to be followed by a poet reacting against what he feels to be a decadent metaphorical mode—for example, Wordsworth.

Romanticism as a literary movement is classified as 'metaphoric' by Jakobson in relation to realism, and by Zirmunskij in relation to classicism. But the first generation of English romantic poets, at least, thought of themselves as replacing one, inauthentic, kind of metaphorical writing (Coleridge's 'Fancy') with another, more powerful kind ('Imagination') which didn't necessarily express itself through a profusion of metaphorical figures. Certainly the specialized 'poetic diction' of eighteenth-century verse which Wordsworth deplored belonged to a type of poetic discourse that had become compulsive and mechanical in its metaphorizing.

> In vain to me the smiling mornings shine,
> And reddening Phoebus lifts his golden fire:
> The birds in vain their amorous descant join,
> And cheerful fields resume their green attire.[12]

The metaphors click into place as regularly and predictably as the rhymes. Wordsworth's effort to purify the language of English poetry entailed forcing it back towards the metonymic pole: hence his insistence in the Preface to *Lyrical Ballads* that there was no essential difference between poetry and prose, hence his shiftiness about the role of metre in poetry,* hence his determination to 'choose incidents

---

*First he suggests that metre 'superadds' a 'charm' to what otherwise might have been as well said in prose; then that metre makes painful subjects in literature less distressing because of 'the tendency of metre to divest language in a certain degree of its reality';

and situations from common life and to relate or describe them, throughout, as far as was possible in a selection of language really used by men',[13] which makes the preface sound more like the manifesto of a novelist than of a poet. Wordsworth was well aware that readers accustomed to a more ostentatiously metaphoric mode of verse-writing would 'look round for poetry and will be induced to inquire by what species of courtesy these attempts can be permitted to assume that title.'[14] Very little of the vast amount of criticism that has accumulated around Wordsworth's work since then would be of much assistance in answering that question. Wordsworth's greatness as a poet is widely acknowledged, and invoked to justify the detailed explication of his poetry by reference to his life and thought, but rarely demonstrated in formal terms. The reason would seem to be that, as Jakobson says, the verbal analysis of literature is biased towards the metaphoric pole and cannot deal easily with metonymic discourse—all the more when the latter takes the form of verse, where we expect 'equivalence' to dominate 'combination'. How, for instance, does one demonstrate that this is poetry of a high order?

> It is the first mild day of March:
> Each minute sweeter than before,
> The Red-breast sings from the tall Larch
> That stands beside our door.
>
> There is a blessing in the air,
> Which seems a sense of joy to yield
> To the bare trees and mountains bare,
> And grass in the green field.[15]

There doesn't seem to be much here for the usual tools of 'practical criticism' to get a purchase on. Some of the words are arguably metaphorical—*sweeter, blessing, yield*—but in such a weak, muted degree that we scarcely register them as such. Certainly we should be unlikely to praise these verses (as we might praise the opening of Shelley's *To The West Wind*) for their vivid and striking metaphors. In linking items according to contiguity rather than similarity, the verses conform to the metonymical mode, but they don't exploit the rhetorical figures proper to this mode very extensively either: 'the Red-breast' and 'the green field' are synecdoches even weaker than the weak metaphors just mentioned.

Invoking the theory of the Russian Formalists and Czech structuralists we can say that this extreme simplicity is aesthetically

---

finally he touches on the heart of the matter: 'the pleasure which the mind derives from the perception of similitude in dissimilitude. The principle is the great spring of the activity of our minds and their chief feeder. . . . It would not have been a useless employment to have applied this principle to the consideration of metre. . . .' But unfortunately he excuses himself from doing so.

powerful because it is 'foregrounded' against the background of the highly ornate and highly rhetorical poetic diction of the received poetic tradition, and this is obviously true. But there must be something more than mere abstention to Wordsworth's simplicity if its peculiar effectiveness is to be explained; there must be an art in his apparent artlessness (as in the parallel case of the early Hemingway) which prevents simplicity from degenerating into banality, and which allows us to re-read these lines without feeling that we exhausted their significance on the first reading. In short, he must be *doing something* with the axis of combination which he appears to follow in such a straightforward way. We can begin to see what he is doing by rearranging the words into prose and altering them when logic and clarity require it.

> It is the first mild day of March. The redbreast sings (more sweetly with each minute) from the tall Larch that stands beside our door. There is a blessing in the air which seems to yield a sense of joy to the bare trees and mountains and to the green grass in the field.

This exercise reveals nuances and ambiguities in the original text so slight and subtle as almost to be subliminal in their effects (as are many devices in realistic prose fiction). *Each minute sweeter than before,* though the punctuation indicates that it must describe the birdsong, is likely to be interpreted by the reader, before he gets to the 'Red-breast' as referring back to the March day, partly because of this ordering of information and partly because *sweeter* is more often an adjective than an adverb in English. Likewise the second line of the second stanza, *Which seems a sense of joy to yield* doesn't grammatically require an extension of its predicate, and the subsequent naming of a series of indirect objects to which the sense of joy is yielded comes as a slight surprise. This 'double-take' effect, by which an apparently completed statement turns out to have an unexpected further application is deeply characteristic of Wordsworth, especially in his blank verse poetry, and is usually produced by the subtle and deliberate placing of the line-break in relation to sense and syntax. Christopher Ricks has commented acutely on the importance of the line as a unit, and the relationships between lines, in Wordsworth's verse:

> Life necessitates transitions, indeed it lives on them, but a true transition is one which finds its spontaneity and its surprise somewhere other than in violence. Such transitions and transformations can be set by the poet before your very eyes; they can be the transitions and successions by which a line is taken up by a sequence of lines without being impaired, without ceasing to be itself. In [Donald] Davie's words, 'a little surprise, but a wholly fair one.'[16]

In the poem under discussion, we might suggest that these little surprises, these hesitations of sense between one line and another, contribute to the general idea of the diffusion of the spirit of spring through all creation which is overtly developed later ('Love, now a universal birth/From heart to heart is stealing'); and the same effect is perhaps conveyed by the repeated, redundant *bare* that links the *trees* with the *mountains*, and the displacement of *green* from *grass* (with which it logically belongs) to *field*. Though a Wordsworth poem characteristically follows a linear path (Ricks observes how often the words *line, lines* actually occur in his verse) the line of contiguities is always animated by these subtle readjustments of the prosaic syntagm.

In case it should seem that a slight minor poem is being made to bear too much weight in the argument, let us look briefly at a major one, 'Resolution and Independence', of which Coleridge said, 'This fine poem is *especially* characteristic of the author; there is scarce a defect or an excellence of his writings of which it would not present a specimen.'[17] It displays, I think, the characteristic tendencies of metonymic writing in relation to metaphor, summarized earlier: to use metaphorical devices sparingly, to make them subject to context, and to use simile rather than metaphor proper in drawing analogies. The analogies applied to the leech gatherer are all similes:

> As a huge stone is sometimes seen to lie
> Couched on the bald top of an eminence;
> Wonder to all who do the same espy,
> By what means it could thither come and whence;
> So that it seems a thing endued with sense:
> Like a sea-beast crawled forth, that on a shelf
> Of rock or sand reposeth, there to sun itself;
>
> Such seemed this man . . . .
>
> Motionless as a cloud the old man stood,
> That heareth not the loud winds when they call;
> And moveth all together, if it move at all. . . .
>
> But now his voice to me was like a stream
> Scarce heard; . . .

(There are also several comparative formulae which are not quite similes e.g. 'Like one whom I had met with in a dream;/Or like a man from some far region sent'.) Of the similes, the stone, the cloud and the stream are all vehicles taken from the poem's context—the open country. The sea-beast, indeed, is a more exotic analogy, but it is of course applied directly to the stone, and only indirectly to the leech gatherer. Wordsworth himself commented:

> The stone is endowed with something of the power of life to approximate it to the sea-beast; and the sea-beast stripped of some of its vital qualities to assimilate it to the stone; which intermediate image is thus treated for the purpose of bringing the original image, that of the stone, to a nearer resemblance to the figure and condition of the aged Man; who is divested of so much of the indication of life and motion as to bring him to the point where the two objects unite and coalesce in comparison.[18]

From another point of view, however, the *stone* is the intermediate image, since it is more likely to appear in the same context with either *Man* or *sea-beast* than these two things are to appear together in the same context.

It is worth comparing the similes in Lewis Carroll's celebrated parody. They come mainly in the last few lines:

> . . . that old man I used to know—
> Whose look was mild, whose speech was slow,
> Whose hair was whiter than the snow,
> Whose face was very like a crow,
> With eyes, like cinders, all aglow,
> Who seemed distracted with his woe,
> Who rocked his body to and fro,
> And muttered mumblingly and low,
> As if his mouth were full of dough,
> Who snorted like a buffalo—
> That summer evening long ago,
>   A-sitting on a gate.[19]

From *snow* and *crow*, which belong to the same kind of context as Wordsworth's poem, Carroll turns to analogies that are progressively more remote from the context and progressively more absurd. The absurdity is heightened by the repeated 'O' rhyme—a good example of how doggerel results from allowing equivalence (of sounds) to tyrannize over combination (of sense). Compare, also, Wordsworth's 'his voice to me was like a stream/Scarce heard' with Carroll's deliberately debased and domesticated version:

> And his answer trickled through my head
>   Like water through a sieve.

Carroll's poem is not strictly speaking a parody, but a travesty. It treats the same situation as Wordsworth's poem (the poet, burdened with his own anxieties, meets a solitary old man, asks him what he does for a living, only half-listens to the answer because of his own preoccupations, yet is in the end fortified by the encounter) but in a quite different style. In true parody, the style is the object of ridicule which is achieved by exaggerating the mannerisms of the original and/or applying them to incongruous subject-matter; in travesty a change of style is used to ridicule the original subject matter. In the 'White Knight's Song', Carroll systematically violates the metonymic decorum of 'Resolution and Independence'. Whereas Wordsworth's old man gathers leeches, and only leeches—that is why he is encountered beside a moorland pond—Carroll's old man collects (or claims to collect, for he is not likely to collect anything a-sitting on a gate) a preposterous, Dadaist variety of things, most of which do not belong in any way whatsoever to the moors or countryside:

He said 'I hunt for haddocks' eyes
   Among the heather bright,
And work them into waistcoat-buttons
   In the silent night.

'I sometimes dig for buttered rolls
   Or set limed twigs for crabs:
I sometimes search the grassy knolls
   For wheels of Hansom-cabs.'

The principal focus of Carroll's satire is the somewhat egotistical preoccupation of the poet in *Resolution and Independence* which seems to prevent him from listening to the answers to his own questions. But whereas Wordsworth's persona is thinking first about poets, who being naturally solitary have some kind of affinity with the leech-gatherer, thinking of them, moreover, sometimes in pastoral terms ('I thought of . . . Him who walked in glory and in joy following his plough, along the mountain side') and then thinking about the leech-gatherer himself ('In my mind's eye I seemed to see him pace about the weary moors continually'), Lewis's White Knight is thinking of subjects both absurd in themselves and absurdly unrelated to anything in the actual situation:

But I was thinking of a plan
   To dye one's whiskers green,
And always use so large a fan
   That they could not be seen.
So having no reply to give
   To what the old man said,
I cried 'Come, tell me how you live!'
   And thumped him on the head.

It's not so far removed from the inconsequential ruminations of Eliot's Prufrock:

Shall I part my hair behind? Do I dare to eat a peach?
I shall wear white flannel trousers, and walk upon the beach.

I have examined a variety of literary texts in an effort to display, within a brief compass, the possibilities offered by Jakobson's metaphor/metonymy distinction for answering the questions about the ontology and typology of literature raised in Part One. I hope to have indicated that the distinction provides a common descriptive terminology for classifying and analysing types of literary discourse usually seen as based on essentially different and incompatible principles. The theory has been illustrated by comparative analysis of short texts and extracts without much regard to their relative positions in time. It is now appropriate to examine the possibilities of the distinction when applied to more historical concerns of criticism—the discrimination of periods, schools and movements in literature, and the examination of an individual writer's development through his *oeuvre*. In particular we shall see whether Jakobson's scheme enables us to study the differences between modernist and other types of writing in the modern period without being obliged to adopt the partisan and sometimes obfuscating attitudes encountered in Part One.

Part Three

Modernists, Antimodernists and Postmodernists

1   James Joyce

Since orthodox literary history tells us that modernist fiction is in one way or another in reaction against nineteenth-century realism, and deeply influenced by symbolist poetry and poetics, we should expect to find it tending towards the metaphorical pole of Jakobson's scheme. The mere titles of the novels seem to confirm such a classification. The Victorian novelists, and the Edwardian realists who carried on their tradition, tended to use names of persons or places for titles (*David Copperfield, Middlemarch, Barchester Towers, Kipps, Riceyman Steps, The Forsyte Saga*) thus indicating a field or focus of contiguous phenomena as their subject matter. In contrast, the titles of novels in the modernist tradition tend to be metaphorical or quasi-metaphorical: *Heart of Darkness, The Shadow Line, The Wings of the Dove, The Golden Bowl, A Passage to India, The Rainbow, To the Lighthouse, Ulysses, Finnegans Wake . . .*

But not *Dubliners*. *Dubliners* is a synecdochic title implying that the book describes a representative cross-section or sample of the life of the Irish capital. *A Portrait of the Artist as a Young Man* is quasi-metaphorical in that it applies to a work of literature a description that properly belongs to painting, but the word 'portrait' is so common-place in literary discussion as to be an almost dead metaphor. The titles of Joyce's works of prose fiction thus mirror his artistic development from realism to mythopoeia, from (in our terms) metonymy to metaphor.

To be sure, *Dubliners* is not a work of wholly traditional nineteenth-century realism, for the stories do not quite satisfy the criteria of intelligibility and coherence normally demanded of the classic readerly text (as Barthes calls it). In this latter type of text, he observes, 'everything holds together'—every detail, gesture, utterance has several cooperative functions: to forward the action, to explain the action, to describe the setting, and so on—in general to establish the plausibility of the story and protect it from the reader's latent scepticism. 'The readerly is controlled by the principle of non-contradiction, but by multiplying solidarities, by stressing at every opportunity the *compatible* nature of circumstances, by attaching narrated events together with a kind of logical "paste", the discourse carries this principle to the point of obsession.'[1] There may, as in 'Sarrasine', be a mystery or enigma in the story, but the reader knows what the enigma is and confidently awaits its eventual solution. Because of this confidence, he takes pleasure in the delay of the solution (for without this delay there could be no story) and within certain limits will accept authorial evasions or disguisings of the truth to this end. ('The discourse is trying to lie as little as possible,' says Barthes at one point in his commentary, 'just what is required to ensure the interests of reading, that is, its own survival.')[2] The reader who approaches *Dubliners* with expectations derived from such writing is, however, likely to be disappointed and disconcerted. The stories look superficially as if they belong to the classic, readerly, realistic mode: they have the smooth, logical, homogeneous prose style which naturalizes meaning in the readerly text ('the text is replete with multiple, discontinuous, accumulated meanings, and yet burnished, smoothed by the 'natural' movement of its sentences: it is an egg text')[3] yet the reader is likely to find himself forced continually to revise his sense of what any particularly story is 'about'—uncertain therefore what revelation the story is moving towards, and apt to be taken by surprise when it finally comes. The climaxes (epiphanies) of *Dubliners* are mostly anticlimaxes by the criteria of the classic readerly text.

Consider, for example, the first story in the collection, 'The Sisters'. The very title is a stumbling block to the reader, since it suggests the story is going to be 'about' the two sisters, though it proves to be much more concerned with their brother, the old priest, and with the young boy who is the narrator. I say 'young boy' because, despite the maturity of the prose style, we do not have in this story the sense of an adult consciousness *recalling* a boyhood experience. From the very first sentence, with its deictic 'this' ('*There was no hope for him this time: it was the third stroke*') we are situated in the consciousness and time-plane of the young boy at the time the old priest dies. Perhaps this is what naturalizes the many unresolved enigmas in the narrative, for we experience the events through the consciousness of a young boy struggling to interpret events while being deprived of most of the relevant data by the evasions of the adult world and by his own immaturity. The presentation of action through this limited consciousness justifies (*i.e.* logically explains) the introduction of false clues into the story—for instance, the suggestion that the old priest is guilty of simony. Simony is associated with the old priest in the narrator's mind for purely private and gratuitous reasons:

> Every night as I gazed up at the window I said softly to myself the word paralysis. It had always sounded strangely in my ears like the word gnomon in the Euclid and the word simony in the Catechism.[4]

Later, some fragments of overheard adult conversation imply that there was something corrupt and corrupting about the old priest and this provokes a dream in which the figure of the priest tries to confess to the boy: 'I felt that I too was smiling feebly, as if to absolve the simoniac of his sin.'[5] In fact, as one of the sisters reveals at the end of the story, the dark secret of the priest's past is not simony, not indeed a 'sin' at all, but an accident with the chalice at mass that 'affected his mind': a typical anticlimax.* One night after this mishap he was discovered in his confessional, ' "Wide-awake and laughing to himself. . . . So then, of course, when they saw that, that made them think that there was something gone wrong with him. . . ." '

So the story ends, but the trail of dots must make us wonder whether we have been told the 'whole story' after all. Was it the accident with the chalice that turned the old priest's head, or was the accident itself a symptom of some more deep-seated disease of mind and body—say general paralysis of the insane, as Richard Ellmann hints?[6] Is it fortuitous that running the words *simony* and *paralysis* together produces something close to the word *syphilis*? If this were indeed the real or suspected cause of the priest's death it would explain some of the undertones of the story, the vague suggestions of corruption that are attributed to the priest. But we cannot be at all sure, such is the deliberate ambiguity of the text. It is not, in fact, an 'egg-text': there is a continual leakage of implication and suggestion from its unfinished sentences. The narrator speaks for the reader when he says, 'I puzzled my head to extract meaning from [old Cotter's] unfinished sentences,'—sentences which first introduce the note of mystery and suspicion concerning the old priest:

> 'I think it was one of those . . . peculiar cases. . . . But it's hard to say. . . .'
> 'My idea is: let a young lad run about and play with young lads of his own age and not be. . . . Am I right, Jack?
> 'When children see things like that, you know, it has an effect. . . .'[7]

Cotter is not the only character whose speech has these suggestive lacunae (known to classical rhetoricians as 'aposiopesis'):

> My aunt fingered the stem of her wine-glass before sipping a little.
> 'Did he . . . peacefully?' she asked.
> 'Oh quite peacefully, ma'am,' said Eliza. You couldn't tell when the breath went out of him. He had a beautiful death, God be praised.'
> 'And everything . . .?'[8]

These gaps, however, are easy enough to fill, and exemplify a familiar feature of ordinary speech. Mukařovský observes that the automatization of language permits us to communicate in unfinished sentences because it enables us to predict or supply the missing

---

*I do not underestimate the almost superstitious fear and guilt that was attached to any mishap with the consecrated elements in a Catholic culture that took the doctrine of transubstantiation very literally; but it is obviously less serious and less culpable than the selling of sacred offices and objects for gain.

elements. Such fragmentary communication is normal in casual conversation, and a person who always speaks in perfectly formed sentences will in fact be calling aesthetic attention to his speech by foregrounding syntax. In the literary rendering of speech, however—at least in the 'readerly' tradition—the reverse, by convention, is true: characters generally speak in well-formed sentences, and any deviation from *this* norm is foregrounded—for example Miss Bates in *Emma* or Mr Jingle in *Pickwick Papers*. In 'The Sisters' the noncompletion of sentences is not confined (as in Jane Austen and Dickens) to one character, but is common to all the adult characters. It thus tends to be perceived as a general feature of the story, foregrounded against the norm of the tradition (the tradition represented by Jane Austen and Dickens among others), marking an advance towards a greater realism in the literary representation of speech. In fact, as we have just seen, the thematically more significant pattern is the foregrounding of the adults' incomplete sentences against the background of the youthful narrator's completed ones. Aposiopesis is thus disguised as mimesis. One kind of foregrounding (associated with realism) acts as a cover for another kind (associated with thematic patterning).

This was a favourite tactic of those early modernist writers who were concerned to steer naturalistic fiction in the direction of symbolism. We see another example of its operation in the way in which the motif of the Sacrament is cunningly hidden in the realistic texture of 'The Sisters', as in those children's picture-puzzles where the shapes of incongruous objects are hidden in the lines of, for example, wood grain and foliage. For instance, the name of the snuff that the narrator's aunt gives him to take to the priest, 'High Toast', is certainly an irreverent metaphor for (and pun on) 'Host', and the priest's clumsy way of handling it is strikingly parallel to his crucial accident at mass.

> It was always I who emptied the packet into his black snuff-box, for his hands trembled too much to allow him to do this without spilling half the snuff about the floor. Even as he raised his large trembling hands to his nose little clouds of snuff dribbled through his fingers over the front of his coat. It may have been these constant showers of snuff which gave his ancient priestly garments their green faded look, for the red handkerchief, blackened, as it always was, with the snuff grains of a week, with which he tried to brush away the fallen grains, was quite inefficacious.[9]

The gesture of the priest raising his large trembling hands, the decidedly ritualistic associations of the phrase 'ancient priestly garments', help to evoke subliminally the image of the priest celebrating mass, the narrator performing the office of acolyte. 'Inefficacious' is another interesting word, slightly foregrounded because its polysyllabic solemnity seems unwarranted by the comparatively trivial gesture to which it is applied. It is in fact a word favoured by Catholic theological manuals of the relevant period to describe the withholding of sacramental grace due to some irregularity in the administration or reception of the sacraments. The sacrament of penance, for instance, would be 'inefficacious' if the penitent concealed some grave sin from his confessor; and the Eucharist would be inefficacious if received in a state of mortal sin. These are the two sacraments which are central to the story. 'The duties of the priest towards the Eucharist and towards the secrecy of the confessional seemed so grave to me that I wondered how anybody had ever found in himself the courage to undertake them'[10] the narrator reflected after his conversations with the priest; and later Eliza recalls, with reference to her brother, 'The duties of the priesthood was too much for him. And then his life was, you might say, crossed.'[11] This last remark seems to be an allusion to the priest's accident with the chalice (Eucharist) which leads to his being discovered wide-awake and laughing in his confessional (Penance). The anecdote itself is told in the context of a kind of parody Eucharist of sherry and biscuits, served by the two sisters to the narrator and his aunt.

> A silence took possession of the little room and, under cover of it, I approached the table and tasted my sherry and then returned quietly to my chair in the corner.[12]

'Approached' is another slightly foregrounded word which has been transferred from the liturgical language of the day (in which communicants always 'approached the altar') to a secular social context. Certainly the parallel between the boy's comportment and that of a communicant in church is very close.

What is the meaning of these and other parallels and allusions to the sacraments? Some are clearly proleptic—like the priest's clumsiness with the High Toast, or the fact that he is seen laid out, 'vested as though for the altar, his large hands *loosely* retaining a chalice'[13] (my italics)—anticipating the revelation of Eliza on the last page. Others can be explained in thematic terms. The parody Eucharist of sherry and biscuits, for instance, might be interpreted as contributing to the theme of failed religion, spiritual paralysis, letter without spirit, ritual without efficacy, which Joyce generally attributed to Irish Catholicism, and of which the priest, last pictured with an 'idle chalice' on his breast, is a personification. The story is, to that extent, precariously contained within the readerly tradition in which 'everything hangs together'. Yet the patterning is in the last analysis in excess of any wholly logical interpretation, and looks forward to the more abundant and playful parallelisms and leitmotifs of *Ulysses* and *Finnegans Wake*, where the perception of similarity is overtly exploited as a comic or magical principle by which the anarchic flux of experience can be ordered and made tolerable. In the remorselessly drab, unredeemed world of *Dubliners* metaphorical similarity is still subordinated to metonymic contiguity: the Eucharist is so plausibly disguised as snuff or sherry and biscuits as scarcely to be perceptible at all, and a story like 'The Sisters' is more likely to be read as a realistic sketch or slice of life than as a symbolist composition of subtly interwoven leitmotifs.

What makes the former response more likely, as I remarked earlier, is the homogeneous 'readerly' prose style, that 'style of scrupulous meanness' as Joyce himself described it, in which all the stories, with the exception of the end of 'The Dead', are written. It was this that made possible the original publication of the 'The Sisters' and two of the other stories in such a middlebrow journal as *The Irish Homestead*; even if the scrupulous meanness of Joyce's observation eventually provoked a backlash from the readership that compelled the editor to ask Joyce not to submit any more, the point is that the subversiveness and originality of the stories was not *immediately* apparent from their verbal form. With *A Portrait of the Artist as a Young Man*, in which Joyce varied his style to imitate various phases of his hero's development, he declared his secession from the fully readerly mode of narrative, and began his career as a fully-fledged modernist writer. Metaphoric similarity is now at certain points given priority over the realistic decorum of metonymic contiguities—in for instance the hero's symbolically appropriate but ethnographically anomalous surname, Dedalus; and although the basic structure of the narrative is linear and chronological, there are gaping holes in the account of Stephen's life, which the discourse makes no attempt to bridge with summary or retrospect, and a corresponding emphasis on thematic echoes and parallels between the different episodes.

The break with the mode of *Dubliners* is not, however, radical. The art of the Christmas Dinner scene, for instance, is entirely continuous with the art of the short stories: here, as in 'The Sisters', we have to make an effort not to be completely hypnotized by the utterly convincing realism of the narration (a fully 'performable' realism, this, even if Balzac's is not) in order to draw out the wealth of connotation buried in the text. Consider, for example, the apparently 'innocent' referential sentence with which this scene begins:

> A great fire, banked high and red, flamed in the grate and under the ivytwined branches of the chandelier the Christmas table was spread.[14]

The sentence has a subtle cadence, characteristic of Joyce's writing, which has been produced by a slight modification of the most natural word order, which would have been:

> A great fire, banked high and red, flamed in the grate and the Christmas dinner was spread under the ivytwined branches of the chandelier.

That is a straightforward compound sentence formed by linking two parallel subject-predicate clauses; its structure makes clear spatial distinctions between the objects referred to. By rearranging the word order of the second clause Joyce has deliberately created a certain spatial confusion in the reader's mind, and, as it were, pushed the ivytwined branches of the chandelier into closer proximity to the fire. In fact when we read Joyce's sentence we probably run the first clause into the beginning of the second, because the adverbial phrase concerning the chandelier could grammatically qualify *flamed*, thus:

A great fire, banked high and red, flamed in the grate and under the ivytwined branches of the chandelier.

What is the expressive function of Joyce's syntactical shuffling? It brings into closer juxtaposition the fire (which is red) and the ivy (which is green), and thus strikes a thematic chord which has already been sounded several times in the book, and which is to dominate the scene which follows. The red and the green symbolize the union of socialist and nationalist aspirations in the political movement for Irish independence. On the first page of *A Portrait of the Artist as a Young Man* we learn that:

Dante had two brushes in her press. The brush with the maroon velvet back was for Michael Davitt and the brush with the green velvet back was for Parnell.[15]

(Michael Davitt was the Catholic leader of the socialist Irish Land League and Parnell, a Protestant, the leader of the Irish Nationalists in Parliament.) The picture of the earth, 'a big ball in the middle of clouds' on the first page of Stephen's geography textbook, has been coloured by another boy, the previous owner, with crayons, 'the earth green and the clouds maroon.' Later Dante tears the backing off her green brush, an incident that marks, domestically, the split in the Irish nationalist movement that occurred when Parnell was cited as co-respondent in a divorce case. Pressure from Davitt 'and the Catholic bishops wrested political leadership from Parnell and he died, a broken man, in 1891. These events are the main subject of conversation at the Christmas dinner in *A Portrait*, effectively destroying any spirit of Christian fellowship and charity on this occasion—indeed leading to outbursts of violent hatred and anti-Christian sentiment. (That the divorce petition in which Parnell was involved was originally filed on Christmas Eve, 1889, made it perhaps more likely that the wound would be re-opened at this season). Red and green are of course colours traditionally associated with Christmas as well as with Irish political life, so the first sentence of this chapter encapsulates the ironic conflict of political and religious attitudes that is to erupt in the course of the meal. 'Ivy' is particularly notable for a double connotation, being the emblem of the Parnellites (cf. 'Ivy Day in the Committee Room' in *Dubliners*) as well as an evergreen traditionally associated with Christmas (cf. the carol, 'The Holly and the Ivy'). All this weight of suggestion is packed into the sentence without any overt metaphorizing, and with only the subtlest readjustment, through syntax, of the chain of natural contiguities: fire—chandelier—ivy—table.

Later in the novel, in accord with the development of Stephen's romantic, egocentric and literary sensibility, the prose becomes much more 'poetic': metaphor is overt, and the progress of the syntagm is deliberately impeded by repetition of key words and elaborate rhythmical patterning, which together impart a spiralling, rather than a linear movement to the prose, in, for example, the often quoted passage about the girl wading:

> Her bosom was as a bird's soft and slight, slight and soft as the breast of some darkplumaged dove. But her long fair hair was girlish: and girlish, and touched with the wonder of mortal beauty, her face.[16]

or Stephen's reverie about an imagined incestuous love affair:

> The park trees were heavy in the rain and rain fell still and ever in the lake, lying grey like a shield. A game of swans flew there and the water and the shore beneath were fouled by the greenwhite slime. They embraced softly, impelled by the grey rainy light, the wet silent trees, the shieldlike witnessing lake, the swans.[17]

Writing about the composition of *Finnegans Wake*, Richard Ellmann remarks of Joyce: 'He had begun his writing by asserting his differences from other men, and now increasingly he recognized his similarity to them.'[18]

Linguistically, 'difference' belongs to the axis of combination. It is the differences between words that enable them to be combined into syntagms that communicate meaning. One could conceive of a language that consisted of only two words (say, *yes* and *no*) but hardly of a language that consisted of only one. Homophones and homonyms are apt to cause confusion in speech or writing, because they violate this rule of difference. Writing that *emphasizes* the differences between things in the world, that emphasizes the uniqueness of individuals, places, objects, feelings, situations, will tend to operate mainly along the axis of combination or contiguity, in Jakobson's terminology: experience is pictured as an endless mesh of links extending in time and space, each link of which is slightly different from the others; or as a strip of moving-picture film, each frame of which is continuous with yet slightly different from the ones before and after. This way of representing reality can be rhetorically heightened by metonymic devices which delete or rearrange contiguous items, and this is the method of realism, or of symbolism operating under the constraints of realism, as in 'The Sisters' or in the Christmas Dinner scene in *A Portrait*.

Joyce's writing, however, developed steadily in the direction of emphasizing similarity rather than difference—not only psychologically and thematically, but structurally and stylistically. With *Finnegans Wake*, Joyce reached the logical terminus of this artistic development, where similarity is allowed almost total control over the discourse—and thus removed his writing beyond the reach of any criticism oriented to the novel, however elastically conceived. The novel, according to Ian Watt, is well named because of its commitment to imitating individual experience, 'which is always unique and therefore new'.[19] *Finnegans Wake*, however, as Ellmann says,

> is based on the premise that there is nothing new under the sun. . . . In all his books up to *Finnegans Wake* Joyce sought to reveal the coincidence of the present with the past. Only in *Finnegans Wake* was he to carry his conviction to its furthest reaches, by implying that there is no present and no past, that there are no dates, that time—and language which is time's expression—is a series of coincidences which are general all over humanity.* Words move into words, people into people, incidents into incidents, like the ambiguities of a pun, or a dream.[20]

The pun, which is the staple rhetorical device of *Finnegans Wake*, thrives on the abolition of difference and the exploitation of similarity. It seizes on homophones and homonyms, or generates new ones by telescoping two or more different words together. The pun may be considered a special form of metaphor. Metaphor, as we saw in Part Two, consists in substituting for one term another that is grammatically similar and semantically both similar and dissimilar, as when we say 'the ships *ploughed* the sea'. The pun *fuses* two terms that are phonologically or visually similar, but different in meaning, to create a new word in which the two different meanings are present at the same time—as, for instance, the anagrammatic word *cropse* in *Finnegans Wake* which includes *corpse* and *crops*, death and (re)birth; or a context is created in which the double meaning of a word is released, instead of being closed off, as in the very title of Joyce's work, where *Finnegan* contains the double echo of 'finish again' and 'begin again', and *Wake* signifies both death (as a noun) and awakening (as verb).

The ostensible justification of writing in this mode is that *Finnegans Wake* is the account of a dream; but if so, it is humanity that is dreaming. The dreamer in *Finnegans Wake*, Mr Porter, is so heavily disguised by his dreamself, Humphrey Chimpden Earwicker, and *his* innumerable incarnations, (not for nothing do his initials stand for 'Here Comes Everybody') as to be almost invisible. For this reason the metonymic devices of the dreamwork described by Freud are in *Finnegans Wake* thoroughly subordinated to the metaphoric. The suggestion of *earwig* in the name Earwicker, it has been plausibly argued,[21] derives

---

*A sly allusion to the famous last paragraph of 'The Dead', in which the snow that is 'general all over Ireland' is a metonymic symbol for the universality of death.

from a displacement of the taboo word *incest* into *insect*; but the text invites us to take this as a clue not so much to the relationship between Mr Porter and his daughter as to the relationship of all fathers to all daughters. In Freudian theory condensation and displacement operate on a chain of contiguities in the dreamer's experience, and their meaning is recoverable by the dreamer or his analyst by questioning and free association, which reconstitute the original chain (essentially the technique of Sherlock Holmes in dealing with clues). Since we know nothing about Porter except the distorted evidence of the dream itself, this is not a possible way of reading *Finnegans Wake*. We must interpret its condensations and displacements by reference to the history and mythology of the whole human race, which provide a circular field of similarities for Joyce's punning discourse to feed on, 'rounding up lost histereve'.

> Wharnow are alle her childer, say? In kingdome gone or power to come or gloria to be them farther? Allalivial, allalluvial! Some here, more no more, more again lost alla stranger. I've heard tell that same brooch of the Shannons was married into a family in Spain. And all the Dunders de Dunnes in Markland's Vineland beyond Brendan's herring pool take number nine in yangsee's hats, And one of Biddy's beads went bobbing till she rounded up lost histereve with a marigold and a cobbler's candle in a side strain of a main drain of a manzinahurries off Bachelor's Walk.[22]

This meditation on Irish emigration comes from the famous Anna Livia Plurabelle section in which, carrying to its limit the metaphorical principle that one river (the Liffey) stands for/evokes/may be replaced by, all other rivers, some five hundred river names are punningly buried in the discourse (e.g. *yangsee* [yankee] and *manzinahurries* [Manzaranes] in the quotation above) with a distorting and obscuring effect on the syntagmatic sense that has been found by many readers disproportionate to the expressive gain.[23] *Finnegans Wake* is not, indeed, a readerly text. Though short quotations may give delight (who could resist, from 'Anna Livia', 'It's that irrawaddyng I've stoke in my aars. It all but husheth the lethest zswound'?) few have been able to read the book through from beginning to end. Not that it *has* a beginning a middle or an end: the unfinished last sentence joins up with the truncated first sentence—and there you have the problem (for the reader) in a nutshell.

The axis of combination is not wholly neglected in *Finnegans Wake*—if it were, it would be truly unintelligible. Grammar—the code of combination—is still largely intact. If number and concord are not always strictly correct, word-order (the most important single feature of English syntax) is generally regular, as the quotation above shows. But semantically the discourse is developed with scarcely any observance of natural contiguities, of contextual coherence and continuity. As the grammar moves forwards to form predictable combinations of parts of speech the sense jumps sideways or backwards, by means of the pun, in quite *un*predictable ways, to the confusion of the reader who is trying to locate himself on some single narrative line. Narrative depends upon the notion of discrete figures whose fortunes are extended in time. As readers we form certain hypotheses about the future of the plot based on its past and present, and the characteristic affects aroused by narrative—concern, suspense, amusement, wonder, etc.—are achieved by the ways in which these hypotheses or expectations are fulfilled or falsified. But in *Finnegans Wake* the figures are unstable, constantly metamorphosing into each other, or substituted for each other, and the action has no past, present or future, since all events are simultaneously present. The result is a systematic deconstruction of that orthodox historical consciousness on which fictional realism is based, an enterprise strikingly similar to Nietzsche's heretical philosophy of history, characterized by Hayden White as 'metaphorical historiography':

> Just as poetry is itself the means by which the rules of language are transcended, so, too, Metaphorical historiography is the means by which the conventional rules of historical explanation and emplotment are abolished. Only the lexical elements of the field remain, to be done with as the historian, now governed by the 'spirit of music', desires. . . . The historian is liberated from having to say anything *about* the past; the past is only an occasion for his invention of ingenious 'melodies'. Historical representation becomes once more all *story*, no plot, no explanation, no ideological implication at all—that is to say, 'myth' in its original meaning as Neitzsche understood it, 'fabulation'.[24]

Perhaps 'chords' or 'harmonies' would be more appropriate musical terms than 'melodies' to describe Joyce's creative play with the data of history:

> riverrun, past Eve and Adam's [Dublin church on banks of Liffey/Garden of Eden], from swerve of shore to bend of bay, brings us by a commodius [Commodus, Roman Emperor] vicus [Latin, street/Vico, whose cyclic philosophy of history partly inspired *FW*/Vico Rd, Dalkey] of recirculation back to Howth Castle and Environs [HCE].
> Sir Tristram [Tristan and Isolde/Tristram Shandy, hero of another comic experimental novel] violer d'amores [violator/viola] fr'over [rover] the short sea, had passencore [passenger/Fr. *pas encore* = not yet] rearrived from North Amorica on this side the scraggy isthmus of Europe Minor to wielderfight [Germ. *wieder* = again] his penisolate [pen/penis/peninsular] war: nor had topsawyer's [Tom Sawyer's] rocks by the stream Oconee [river in Laurens County, Georgia, USA, on which there is a town called Dublin] exaggerated themselse to Laurens [Cf. Laurence Sterne, author of *Tristram Shandy*] County's gorgios [Romany, *youngsters*] while they went doublin[Dublin/doubling] their mumper all the time: nor avoice from afire bellowsed mishe mishe [Erse, *I am*] to tauftauf [Germ. *taufen* = baptize]thuartpeatrick [Thou art Peter/Patrick/peatrick]: not yet,

though venissoon [venison/very soon/Vanessa, friend of Swift, Dean of St Patrick's Dublin] after, had a kidscad [cadet = younger son = Jacob, disguised in kidskin] buttended a bland old isaac [Isaac, blind father of Jacob/Isaac Butt, ousted from leadership of Irish National Party by Parnell]: not yet, though all's fair in vanessy [Vanessa/Inverness] were sosie sesthers wroth [Susannah, Esther and Ruth/three weird sisters in *Macbeth*] with twone nathandjoe [Jonathan (Swift)/Nathan and Joseph]. Rot a peck of pa's malt had Jhem or Shen [Noah's sons Ham, Shem and Japhet, who saw their father drunk] brewed by arclight and rory end to the regginbrow was to be seen ringsome on the aquaface.[23]

Ulysses, which was originally conceived as a story for *Dubliners*, is situated halfway between the formal extremes represented by that book and *Finnegans Wake*. The title itself is of course metaphoric, pointing to a similarity between dissimilars: Bloom and Odysseus, Stephen and Telemachus, Molly and Penelope, modern Dublin and the Mediterranean of the ancient world. And this is a structural (not a merely decorative) metaphor, in that *it exerts control over the development of the narrative*. Once Bloom has been cast as Odysseus, Stephen as Telemachus and Molly as Penelope, then the story must end with Bloom and Stephen united (however briefly and casually) with Bloom returned (however ingloriously) to his wife (however unfaithful she may have been in his absence). And it is a reasonable assumption that many of the episodes in *Ulysses* were generated by the Homeric model rather than by the modern setting or the psychologies and interrelationships of the modern characters. Bloom's attendance at a funeral was probably suggested to Joyce by the felt obligation to have some contact with the Underworld in his modern epic; the barmaids at the Ormond Hotel, Miss Douce and Miss Kennedy, were no doubt summoned into literary existence by the wish to find some substitute for the Sirens in Bloom's modern Odyssey, and so on.

Joyce did not of course bind himself to a slavish imitation of his Homeric model. Some of the more artificial episodes, like the Oxen of the Sun, are only perfunctorily related to Homer, and, more importantly, a good deal of the material in the book derives from Joyce's own observation and experience, and a felt need to do literary justice to that observation and experience: Joyce's sense of his own youthful self and mature self: his sense of Dublin as a place and as a community; his recollection of that place and community as it was at a particular point in historical time. *Ulysses* thus combines two quite different and (in theory) opposed compositional principles: the realistic and the mythopoeic. On the one hand it is the supreme achievement of the realistic novel tradition. We know these characters with a convincing fullness, an intimacy, an utter candour that was unprecedented in literature before its publication and arguably has never been equalled since. And the milieu in which they move is established with equivalent concreteness and authenticity, achieved, as we know, by amazing feats of recall and patient research. It is all there: the names on the shopfronts, the name of the winner in the day's big race, the architecture of the Bloom's house at 6 Eccles Street. The Dublin of 16 June 1904 lives for ever in the pages of *Ulysses*, immortal and unchanged, consistent with historical fact in almost every detail, and the fictional characters are inserted into it so skilfully that the joins scarcely show: truly a novel that is, in the Goncourts' phrase, 'history as it might have happened.'

And yet: *Ulysses*. We have become so accustomed to that title as to forget its challenging strangeness inscribed above what purports to be a story of Dublin folk one summer day at the beginning of the twentieth century, their trivial, banal, unheroic doings: eating, drinking, excreting, masturbating, copulating, singing, talking, walking, thinking. Without that title, after all, it would be possible (though impoverishing) to read the whole book without realizing that there was a second, mythical dimension to the narrative,* that the actions of Bloom, Stephen and Molly are not merely consistent with and expressive of their individual characters and historical situation, but re-enact (or travesty or parody) the wanderings of Odysseus and the actions of *his* family and acquaintance. And not merely Odysseus, of course: there are many other similarities in the text—Stephen as Hamlet, for instance, or Bloom as 'Ben Bloom Elijah'. The adoption of an overarching metaphorical structure for the book licenses a plurality of other, local substitutions.

Joyce's method of 'manipulating a continuous parallel between contemporaneity and antiquity'[26] greatly excited T. S. Eliot, and probably influenced *The Waste Land*, which was being composed at the time when *Ulysses* was appearing in serial form. When it was complete and published as a book, Eliot saluted Joyce's achievement thus:

> Instead of the narrative method, we may now use the mythical method. It is, I seriously believe, a step toward making the modern world possible for art . . .[27]

What Eliot meant by 'the narrative method' was the method of the classic 'readerly' text: the story that turns upon the solution of an enigma, the disentanglement of an intrigue, or an instructive change of fortune, the story in which 'everything hangs together' in a very obvious way—causality, moralizing, verisimilitude and narrative interest all working together in harness. In the latter part of the nineteenth century, starting perhaps with Flaubert ('The novel ended with Flaubert and with James', Eliot remarked in that same essay on *Ulysses*) this stable synthesis began to show cracks, as a conflict of

---

*Originally, in the serial publication of the novel, Joyce gave to each of the episodes a title drawn from the *Odyssey* (Telemachus, Nestor, Proteus etc.) by which they are still referred to in critical commentary; but he deleted these headings from the text when it was published in book form.

interest between its various elements became evident. For example, the more 'true to life' fiction became, the less likely it was to observe the conventions of the readerly plot. It was the staple complaint of the early modernists against the Edwardian realists that they had not absorbed this lesson, and that their painstaking accumulation of realistic detail was therefore fatally compromised, deprived of authentic 'life'. 'The writer', Virginia Woolf complained in 1919 'seems constrained, not by his own free will, but by some powerful and unscrupulous tyrant who has him in thrall, to provide a plot, to provide comedy, tragedy, love interest, and an air of probability embalming the whole. . . . Is life like this? Must novels be like this?'[28] The modernists found the modes of late Victorian and Edwardian poetry similarly inauthentic in clinging to the myth of a universe that was intelligible and expressible within the conventions of a smoothly homogeneous lyrical idiom. 'We can only say,' T. S. Eliot declared in 1921, 'that it appears likely that poets in our civilization, as it exists at present, must be *difficult*. Our civilization comprehends great variety and complexity, and this variety and complexity, playing upon a refined sensibility, must produce various and complex results. The poet must become more and more comprehensive, more allusive, more indirect, in order to force, to dislocate, if necessary, language into his meaning.'[29]

The modernist enterprise, however, had its dangers and its problems. The logical terminus of their fictional realism was the plotless 'slice of life' or the plotless 'stream of consciousness', and plotlessness could easily become shapelessness, or randomness. 'Difficulty' in poetry could easily become a cover for self-indulgent incoherence. The post-impressionist painters faced the same problem. Glossing Cézanne's celebrated remark that he wanted to paint 'Poussin from nature', E. H. Gombrich says:

> The Impressionists were true masters in painting 'nature'. But was that really enough? Where was that striving for an harmonious design, the achievement of solid simplicity and perfect balance which had marked the greatest paintings of the past? The test was to paint 'from nature', to make use of the discoveries of the Impressionist masters, and yet to recapture the sense of order and necessity that distinguishes the art of Poussin.[30]

Hence the attraction, to Eliot, of Joyce's mythical method, which, so to speak, 'painted Homer from nature'. Eliot's essay is called ' "Ulysses", *Order* and Myth' (my italics) and is concerned to rebut the accusation of Richard Aldington that *Ulysses* was a chaotic, Dadaist work. On the contrary, 'It is . . . a step towards making the modern world possible for art, toward that order and form which Mr Aldington so earnestly desires.'[31] Modern experience, 'the immense panorama of futility and anarchy which is contemporary history'[32] is represented in all its triviality, aimlessness, sordidness, absurdity and contingency, without apparently being tampered with in the interests of plot; yet the representation proves after all to have a structure, a principle of aesthetic order derived from a quite different source (Homer). The representation of a demythologized world, a world 'fallen into the quotidian' (Heidegger's phrase) is thus ingeniously redeemed by allusion to the lost mythical world—aesthetically redeemed by our perception of the structure, and spiritually redeemed by our perception of human continuity between the two worlds.

Ulysses, then, is a realistic or metonymic fiction, (about Bloom, Stephen and Molly) with a mythopoeic or metaphorical structure. As Walton A. Litz has shown in his study of the various drafts of the novel,[33] metaphorical procedures came to predominate as the novel progressed and was progressively revised. The Homeric parallel was of course present from its inception, but the idea of each episode having its own set of leitmotifs—its special art, colour, organ, symbol, 'technic', etc.—was decided at a late stage and the earlier episodes were revised to make them consistent with the later ones. This feature of *Ulysses* must be described as metaphoric in our terms, since it entailed the insertion into the discourse of items on a basis of similarity not contiguity—for instance, allusions to horses, the 'symbol' of 'Nestor', in that episode, or the references to 'heart', the 'organ' of 'Hades', in that episode. These elaborate systems of leitmotifs reinforce the general tendency of *Ulysses* towards an encyclopaedic allembracingness, away from that concern with individual experience that is typical of the realistic novel. If they do not seem intrusively metaphorical—if, indeed, they are seldom consciously perceived by readers without the help of commentators like Stuart Gilbert[34]—it is because what could hardly be contiguous in time or space can very easily be contiguous in a person's 'stream of consciousness'. As Lawrence Sterne had demonstrated in the eighteenth century, the process of association in human consciousness seldom works in a logical, linear fashion, but is characterized by idiosyncratic twists and turns and jumps: the moment of Tristram Shandy's conception was disturbed by Mrs Shandy's untimely enquiry about winding up the clock, 'an unhappy association of ideas which have no connection in nature'.[35] Therefore, under cover of plausibly rendering 'the atoms as they fall upon the mind in the order in which they fall . . . [tracing] the pattern, however disconnected in appearance, which each sight or incident scores upon the consciousness'[36] (as Virginia Woolf put it) Joyce could smuggle into his discourse items drawn from the most heterogeneous contexts to make up other, quite artificial patterns, unrelated to the individual psychologies of his characters. Ignoring the signal of the title, it is possible to read the first few episodes of *Ulysses* (up to and including 'Hades') merely as realistic fiction equipped with psychological hi-fi. It is only with the pastiche headlines of 'Aeolus' that the discourse openly, verbally, displays its plurality of reference (in this case to journalism as an institution as well as to the Dublin *Evening Telegraph*). As the novel progresses, the use of parody and pastiche, which place the discourse at some aesthetic distance from the material it is mediating, becomes more and more pronounced, culminating in the virtuoso feats of 'The Oxen of the Sun' (based on a metaphorical equation between the evolution of English prose and the development of the foetus in the womb) and Circe (with its profusion of surrealistic substitutions and transformations). Joyce can afford these metaphoric flights because the metonymic base of his work is so secure; and in the closing episodes he returns us to that base. In *Ulysses*, the metonymic mode is transformed and enriched but not (as in *Finnegans Wake*) obliterated by the metaphoric.

One of the great achievements of this novel, unmatched by other exponents of the stream of consciousness technique, is the way Joyce discriminates stylistically between the consciousnesses of his main characters. It is noteworthy that this, too, is achieved by varying the proximity of the discourse to the metaphoric and metonymic poles. Stephen's consciousness is essentially metaphoric—he is constantly transforming what he perceives, the world of contiguities, of *nacheinander* (one thing after another) and *nebeneinander* (one thing next to another)[37] into other images and concepts drawn from his reading, on the basis of some perceived similarity or ironic contrast. The more insistently he does this—the more substitutions he makes— the weaker becomes the chain of combination and the more difficult it is for the reader to follow the discourse. Thus 'Proteus', in which Stephen is actively pondering the metaphorical processes of the mind (and stepping up their power artificially by closing his eyes and shutting off one sensory channel to the world of contiguities) is the most 'difficult' of the first three episodes. And all these episodes are more difficult than any of the episodes pertaining to Bloom.

For Bloom's stream of consciousness is by comparison essentially metonymic. We are always much more aware of what he is doing— where he is situated in time and space—because there is a more direct connection between what he is thinking and what he is doing. When his consciousness digresses from what he is doing, his associations still connect items that are contiguous rather than similar. The difference between Stephen and Bloom in this respect may be illustrated by comparing the responses of each to the perception of a female figure. This is Stephen, on Sandymount strand, catching sight of the midwife, Mrs Florence MacCabe:

> Mrs Florence MacCabe, relict of the late Patk MacCabe, deeply lamented, of Bride Street. One of her sisterhood lugged me squealing into life. Creation from nothing. What has she in the bag? A misbirth with a trailing navelcord, hushed in ruddy wool. The cords of all link back, strandentwining cable of all flesh. That is why mystic monks. Will you be as

gods? Gaze in your ómphalos. Hello. Kinch here. Put me on to Edenville.
Aleph, alpha: nought, nought, one.

Spouse and helpmate of Admon Kadmon: Heva, naked Eve. She had no
navel. Gaze. Belly without blemish, bulging big, a buckler of taut vellum,
no, whiteheaped corn, orient and immortal, standing from everlasting to
everlasting. Womb of sin.[38]

What is significant here is not the mere profusion of metaphors
('hushed', 'cable of all flesh', 'buckler', 'whiteheaped corn' etc.) but
that the interior monologue *proceeds* by a series of perceived
similarities and substitutions. It is the perception of similarity between
a telephone cable and the umbilical cord that leads Stephen's thought
from the midwife to Eve, from his own birth to the birth of the race,
drawing in other similarities and contrasts: the cords that monks wear
around their waists (symbols of chastity and also of being joined
together in the Mystical Body of Christ) the navels contemplated by
oriental mystics, the navelless belly of Eve which reminds Stephen of
the 'whiteheaped' bosses (*omphaloi*, the same word meaning 'navels'
also) on the Achaean shields in the *Iliad*, of the Song of Songs ('Thy
belly is like a heap of wheat set about with lilies' vii, 2) and of Thomas
Traherne's vision of Paradise ('The corn was orient and immortal
wheat, which never should be reaped, nor was ever sown. I thought it
had stood from everlasting to everlasting').[39]

Compare Bloom, also looking at a woman: his neighbour's servant
girl, who is just ahead of him at the counter of the pork butcher:

A kidney oozed bloodgouts on the willowpatterned dish: the last. He stood
by the nextdoor girl at the counter. Would she buy it too, calling the items
from a slip in her hand. Chapped: washing soda. And a pound and a half of
Denny's sausages. His eyes rested on her vigorous hips. Woods his name is.
Wonder what he does. Wife is oldish. New blood. No followers allowed.
Strong pair of arms. Whacking a carpet on the clothes line. She does whack
it, by George. The way her crooked skirt swings at eàch whack.

The ferreteyed porkbutcher folded the sausages he had snipped off with
blotchy fingers, sausagepink. Sound meat there like a stallfed heifer.[40]

Bloom's perception of the girl herself is very strikingly synecdochic—
he sees her in terms of her chapped hands, vigorous hips, strong arms
and skirt: parts standing for the whole. Also his thought *proceeds* by
associating items that are contiguous rather than (as in the case of
Stephen) similar. The girl is linked with her master (Woods), the
master with the mistress, the age of the mistress with the youth of the
girl, the youth of the girl with the jealousy and repressiveness of the
mistress who forbids her to have male visitors. In the second
paragraph we appear to have metaphor rather than metonymy:
ferreteyed, sausagepink, like a stallfed heifer. But is is significant how
heavily these similitudes depend upon contiguity and context. The
physical juxtaposition of the butcher's fingers and the sausages he is
handling provides Bloom with the readymade metaphor *sausagepink.*

The comparison of the butcher to a stallfed heifer makes a substitution from the same vocabulary area of meat, butchery etc., and even *ferret* is associated with the killing of animals for human consumption. These are all, in fact, weakish metaphors or similes precisely because, in each case, the two terms of the figure, the tenor and the vehicle, are drawn from essentially the same context, not from 'different spheres of thought', in Ullmann's phrase,[41] as are, for instance, the umbilical cord and the telephone cable in the passage just quoted from 'Proteus'.

Molly Bloom's stream of consciousness is still more 'metonymic' than her husband's, inasmuch as she seldom makes *any* metaphorical connections between items. Such metaphors and similes as occur in her discourse are rarely coined by her, but are colloquial or proverbial clichés. She is very literalminded, pragmatic, down-to-earth. Bloom's speculative, whimsical thought is as far removed from hers as Stephen's complex, ironic and cultured intelligence is from Bloom's. Molly is always asking Bloom to explain words to her, but is dissatisfied with his answers because they refer the question of meaning to the system of language rather than to reality.

—Metempsychosis?
—Yes. Who's he when he's at home?
—Metempsychosis, he said, frowning. It's Greek: from the Greek. That means the transmigration of souls.
—O, rocks! she said. Tell us in plain words.[42]

This exchange in 'Calypso' is recalled in Molly's soliloquy at the end of the novel:

Arsenic she put in his tea off flypaper wasnt it I wonder why they call it that if I asked him he'd say its from the Greek leave us as wise as we were before[43]

She is correspondingly contemptuous of the prurient periphrases of the priest hearing her youthful confession of petting:

he touched me father and what harm if he did where and I said on the canal bank like a fool but whereabouts on your person my child on the leg behind high up was it yes rather high up was it where you sit down yes O Lord couldn't he say bottom right out and have done with it[44]

'Bottom', as Stuart Gilbert has pointed out, is one of the keywords of the 'Penelope' episode, which mark transitions in Molly's consciousness from one train of thought to another.

The movements of Molly Bloom's thoughts in this episode appear, at first sight, capricious and subject to no law. But a close examination shows that there are certain words which, whenever they recur, seem to shift the trend of her musings, and might be called the 'wobbling points' of her monologue. Such words are 'woman', 'bottom', 'he', 'men'; after each of these there is a divigation in her thoughts, which, as a general rule, revolve about herself.[45]

Gilbert ingeniously compares this process to the movement of the earth through space. Molly (an Earth-mother figure) revolves on her own egocentric axis, but is subject to other forces in the planetary system to which she belongs. Another way of putting it would be to compare Molly's monologue to a long-playing gramophone record to which we, as readers, are listening, each track or band of which is concerned with a particular phase of her life and usually with a particular man. There is the track about the young Leopold and his courtship of her, the track about their married life, the track about her youth in Gibraltar and her lover Lieutenant Gardiner, and the more recently recorded tracks concerning her sexual encounter with Blazes Boylan the previous afternoon and Leopold's behaviour since returning to the house with Stephen in the early hours of the morning. The stylus or pick-up arm of Molly's consciousness, as she lies half-awake in bed, does not follow these tracks in chronological order, but jumps backwards and forwards across the surface of the disc. It will be following one track and then provoked by some psychic vibration (usually marked by one of the key words) suddenly 'skate' across to settle in the grooves of another track. When we first tune into her thoughts she is thinking about Bloom's behaviour on coming to bed, asking to have his breakfast in bed the next morning:

> Yes because he never did a thing like that before as ask to get his breakfast in bed with a couple of eggs

As becomes clear later, Molly suspects that Leopold has had some sexual encounter during the day which has given him an appetite (hence the 'Yes because') but the image of Bloom having breakfast in bed jogs the pick-up and sends it skipping back to an episode much earlier in their married life:

> since the *City Arms* hotel when he used to be pretending to be laid up with a sick voice doing his highness to make himself interesting to that old faggot Mrs Riordan that he thought he had a great leg of and she never left us a farthing all for masses for herself and her soul greatest miser ever was actually

The transition of thought here from the present to the past is triggered by a perceived similarity between Bloom having breakfast in bed the next morning and Bloom having breakfast in bed in the past, but this is not a metaphorical kind of similarity. The two events belong to the same order of reality, the married life of the Blooms; one occasion on which Bloom orders breakfast in bed reminds Molly of another. That is in fact all the events have in common, since the earlier breakfast in bed had nothing to do with sexuality at all. Molly's 'because' in the first line of her monologue is therefore characteristically lacking in any real logical force. Her memory plays over Mrs Riordan's character, but always egocentrically:

> she had too much old chat in her about politics and earthquakes and the end of the world let us have a bit of fun first God help the world if all the women were her sort down on bathingsuits and lownecks of course nobody wanted her to wear I suppose she was pious because no man would look at her twice I hope I'll never be like her a wonder she didn't want us to cover our faces but she was a well educated woman certainly and her gabby talk about Mr Riordan here and Mr Riordan there I suppose he was glad to get shut of her and her dog smelling my fur and always edging to get up under my petticoats especially then still I like that in him polite to old women like that[46]

The recollection of Bloom 'pretending to be laid up with a sick voice' leads to rumination on his tendency, representative of his sex, to make a great fuss when ill:

> when he cut his toe with the razor paring his corns afraid hed get blood poisoning but if it was a thing I was sick then wed see what attention only of course the woman hides it not to give all the trouble they do

and the word 'woman' jolts the pick-up again:

> yes he came somewhere Im sure by his appetite anyway love its not or hed be off his feed thinking of her . . ..[47]

Which is 'where we came in.'

2   Gertrude Stein

Our examination of Joyce's work, particularly of *Ulysses*, shows that, while the general tendency of modernist writing is towards metaphoric structure and texture, there are modernist versions of the metonymic mode: the interior monologues of Bloom and Molly are almost as 'modernist' in verbal form (i.e. as strikingly foregrounded against the norms of the fictional tradition) as that of Stephen. The most obviously foregrounded feature is the incompletion of sentences (given additional emphasis by the elimination of punctuation in the case of Molly)—a kind of grammatical synecdoche by which the rapid and erratic shifts of consciousness from one topic to another are imitated. This suggests that modernist prose writing may be characterized by a radical shift towards the metonymic pole of language to which prose naturally inclines anyway, as well as by a displacement towards the metaphoric pole. In this connection it is interesting to look at the work of Gertrude Stein, for her writing oscillated violently between the metonymic and metaphoric poles, pushing out in each direction to points where she began to exhibit symptoms of Jakobson's two types of aphasia.

It is not surprising that most readers find Gertrude Stein's work (apart from the relatively readerly *Autobiography of Alice B. Toklas* [1932]) intolerably monotonous and/or impenetrably obscure. She was one of those rare artists whose work was 'experimental' in a sense genuinely analogous to scientific experiment: a series of artificial and deliberate experiments designed to test some hypothesis about language, or perception, or reality, or about the relations between these things. Its interest and value is therefore largely theoretical, rather than particular and concrete, and can best be appreciated in the context of her own theoretical glosses upon it, in essays and lectures. Not that Gertrude Stein herself would have accepted this limiting definition of her artistic endeavours. She thought of herself, like other early modernists, as an artist who was adapting her medium, literary language, to communicate a new perception of reality, a personal vision of the world which was yet publicly valid, if only the public would wake up and recognize that perception and experience had changed.

> The only thing that is different from one time to another is what is seen and what is seen depends upon how everybody is doing everything. This makes the thing we are looking at very different and this makes what those describe it make of it, it makes a composition, it confuses, it shows, it is, it looks, it likes it as it is, and this makes what is seen as it is seen.[1]

Gertrude Stein's own view of reality and our experience of it has been traced back, in part, to the philosophy of William James, who was her tutor at Harvard, and of Henri Bergson, whom James acknowledged as an independent precursor of his own 'radical empiricism'. Certainly John Passmore's summary of salient points in the thought of these two philosophers, though written without any regard to Gertrude Stein, seems acutely relevant to her work:

> Bergson . . . contrasts time as we think about it and time as we experience it. Conceptually considered, he says, time is assimilated to space, depicted as a straight line with 'moments' as its points, whereas experienced time is *duration*, not a succession of moments—it flows in an invisible continuity. This flowing quality, according to Bergson, is characteristic of all our experience: our experience is not a set of 'conscious states' clearly demarcated. Its phases 'melt into one another and form an organic whole'. . . . Our language consists of distinct words with well-defined outlines; this same distinctiveness we are misled into ascribing to the world we symbolize in language. . . . This is extraordinarily similar to James's account of experience in his *Principles of Psychology* (1890) as a 'stream of consciousness'. James there drew attention to what he took to be the central error of traditional empiricism—that, for it, experience consists of isolated 'impressions' or 'sensations'. 'Consciousness does not appear to itself chopped up into bits,' he protested, 'it is nothing jointed, it flows.' From the beginning, according to James, our experience is of the related—a fact

which escapes our notice only because for practical reasons we have so strong a tendency to seize upon the 'substantative' parts of our experience at the expense of the 'transitive parts'.[2]

The first thing that happens when these ideas (which appealed to a great many writers besides Gertrude Stein) are applied to literature, is the diminution and eventual disappearance of story, for story depends upon the conventional 'spatial' conception of time as a series of discrete moments. 'A thing you all know is that the three novels written in this generation that are important things written in this generation, there is, in none of them a story,' Gertrude Stein declared. 'There is none in Proust in *The Making of Americans* or in *Ulysses*.'[3] This is an overstatement, of course, but less so with respect to Gertrude Stein's own book than in relation to the others.

To be sure, *The Making of Americans* (composed 1906–8) looks superficially like a story, a family saga, an ambitious extension of the classic realistic novel of the nineteenth century—truer, more historical:

> not just an ordinary kind of novel with a plot and conversations to amuse you, but a record of a decent family progress decently lived by us . . . and so listen while I tell you all about us, and wait while I hasten slowly forwards, and love, please, this history of this decent family's progress.[4]

'History' is constantly appealed to as the aim of the writing:

> some time there will be a history of every kind and every one of such of them . . .[5]
> Some time then there will be a history of all women and all men . . .[6]
> Some time then there will be every kind of a history of everyone who ever can or is was or will be living.[7]

The Making of Americans, then, seems to be offered as a fragment of some huge universal history or chronicle. Starting with the Hersland family, it aims to fan out and describe all the ramifications of their relationships—not merely their marriages into other families but the governesses and seamstresses they employed and *their* families and marriages—and then move out further to cover the whole field of human contiguities that makes up recorded history:

> Sometime there will be written a long book that is a real history of everyone who ever was or are or will be living from their beginning to their ending.[8]

Yet the discourse is very unlike what we expect from history or chronicle, still less from the realistic novel. To begin with, there are almost no events, and such events as are described are fairly trivial, e.g. the episode of Martha and the umbrella:

> This one, and the one I am now beginning describing is Martha Hersland, and this is a little story of the acting in her of her being in her very young

living, this one was a very little one then and she was running and she was in the street and it was a muddy one and she had an umbrella that she was dragging and she was crying. 'I will throw the umbrella in the mud,' she was saying, she was very little then, she was just beginning her schooling, 'I will throw the umbrella in the mud,' she said and no one was near her and she was dragging the umbrella and bitterness possessed her, 'I will throw the umbrella in the mud,' she was saying and nobody heard her, the others had run ahead to get home and they had left her, 'I will throw the umbrella in the mud', and there was desperate anger in her; 'I have throwed the umbrella in the mud,' burst from her, she had thrown the umbrella in the mud and that was the end of it all in her. She had thrown the umbrella in the mud and no one heard her as it burst from her, 'I have throwed the umbrella in the mud,' it was the end of all that to her.[9]

This is vivid and expressive, but instead of describing other such events Gertrude Stein repeats this one several times, with additions and variations of detail. Such episodes are in any case few and far between, and the text consists mainly of discourse about the processes of composition and the nature of psychological being.

In 'Portraits and Repetition' Gertrude Stein remarks:

I said in the beginning of saying this thing that if it were possible that a movement were lively enough it would exist so completely that it would not be necessary to see it moving against anything to know that it is moving. This is what we mean by life and in my way I have tried to make portraits of this thing have tried always may try to make portraits of this thing.[10]

In orthodox narrative, events are the points of reference by which we register that the story is 'moving', they correspond to the points on a line in the conventional conceptualization of time as characterized by Bergson. Gertrude Stein virtually eliminated events from *The Making of Americans* because she was more interested in capturing the Bergsonian *durée*, ('not a succession of moments, it flows in an invisible continuity') or what she herself called 'a continuous present':

A continuous present is a continuous present. I made almost a thousand pages of a continuous present. Continuous present is one thing and beginning again and again is another thing. These are both things. And then there is using everything.[11]

These are the three staple devices of Gertrude Stein's early narrative work, *Three Lives* (composed 1903–4), *The Making of Americans* and *A Long Gay Book* (composed 1909–12). 'Using everything' is the ostensible aim of writing a history of everybody; 'beginning again and again' is the device of reverting to the same episode (such as Martha and the umbrella) instead of describing fresh ones: and the 'continuous present' is the evocation of a sense of movement that is not measured on an orthodox chronological scale. These three interrelated devices are all experiments along the metonymic axis of discourse. 'Using everything', the megalomaniac desire to cover, eventually, the whole field of human contiguities with language, defies the practical necessity to *select*, and insists on the essential uniqueness or 'difference' of each human being underlying their superficial similarity or 'resemblance' to each other. Since the enterprise of using everything is actually impossible, Gertrude Stein doesn't actually attempt it; she merely *promises* it, while in fact 'beginning again and again'. As readers we are tantalized by a story that is always being promised but never actually materializes and teased into attending to another kind of movement that is not progressive in the same way as a story: the 'continuous present' of existence.

Stylistically, the continuous present is characterized above all by the domination of verbs and gerunds over nouns, of the 'transitive' over the 'substantive' in William James's terminology. This is a marked deviation from the stylistic norm of nineteenth-century realistic fiction, which was generally notable for nominalization, the appropriate vehicle of its heavy freight of specificity and local colour.[12] But it is not (as in most early modernist writing) a deviation away from the metonymic pole towards the metaphoric. The concrete nouns, the substantives, are not, as in Henry James for example, removed from the descriptions of external reality merely to reappear in metaphorical rendering of inner psychological processes:[13] they simply, in Gertrude Stein, *disappear*. In this, and in some other respects, the style of *The Making of Americans* corresponds to the speech of aphasics suffering from what Jakobson calls similarity disorder or selection deficiency, which he places on the metonymic side of his linguistic scheme. This type of aphasic, it will be recalled, has great difficulty in naming things. Shown a pencil, for instance, he is likely to define it metonymically by reference to its use: 'to write'. In his speech main clauses disappear before subordinate clauses, subjects are dropped or replaced by a repeated all-purpose substitute word (like *one*, *it*, or *thing*) while the words 'with an inherent reference to the context, like pronouns, pronominal adverbs, words serving merely to construct the context, such as connectives and auxiliaries, are particularly prone to survive.'[14] Compare Gertrude Stein in 'Poetry and Grammar':

> A noun is the name of anything, why after a thing is named write about it. A name is adequate or it is not. If it is adequate then why go on calling it, if it is not then calling it by its name does no good. . . . Adjectives are not really and truly interesting . . . because after all adjectives affect nouns. . . . Verbs and adverbs are more interesting. In the first place they have one very nice quality and that is they can be so mistaken. It is wonderful the number of mistakes a verb can make and that is equally true of its adverbs. . . . Then comes the thing that can of all things be most mistaken and they are prepositions. Prepositions can live one long life being really nothing but mistaken and that makes them irritating if you feel that way about mistakes but certainly something that you can be continuously using and everlastingly enjoying. I like prepositions the best of all. . . . Then there are

articles. . . . They are interesting because they do what a noun might do if a noun were not so unfortunately so completely unfortunately the name of something. . . . Beside that there are conjunctions, and a conjunction is not varied but it has a force that need not make anyone feel that they are dull. Conjunctions have made themselves live by their work. . . . So you see why I like to write with prepositions and conjunctions and articles and verbs and adverbs but not with nouns and adjectives. If you read my writing you will see what I mean.[15]

Thus Gertrude Stein's refusal to use nouns, her deliberate preference for those parts of speech most likely to generate 'mistakes', results in a style that has much in common with aphasics who make mistakes involuntarily because they *cannot* use nouns. This sort of style:

Each one is mostly all his living all her living, a young one, an older one, one in middle living, an old one to themselves, to any one, to some one. That is to say not any one is all his living all her living to anyone, that is to say not any one, that is to say not any one hardly is feeling another one being a young one and then an older one and then an old one. It is a very strange thing this thing and an interesting thing that almost not any one is to any one is to themselves inside them one having been in all parts of being living.[16]

It is difficult to convey by quotation the effect of this kind of writing sustained over 'a thousand pages'. To many readers it will seem—has seemed—merely perverse, yet behind it there was a thoroughly coherent and consistent artistic and epistemological theory. Gertrude Stein was seeking 'to make a whole present of something that it had taken a great deal of time to find out'—that is, to capture the living quality of a character or an experience that she had observed or brooded on for a long period, but without giving the impression of *remembering* it and thus destroying its existential presentness:

We in this period have not lived in remembering, we have living in moving being necessarily so intense that existing is indeed something, is indeed the thing that we are doing.[17]

Gertrude Stein described her literary development as a process of liberating herself from 'remembering' in order to capture the quality of existing:

When I first began writing although I felt very strongly that something that made that some one be some one was something that I must use as being them, I naturally began to describe them as they were doing anything. In short I wrote a story as a story, that is the way I began, and slowly I realized this confusion, a real confusion, that in writing a story one had to be remembering, and that novels are soothing because so many people one may say everybody can remember almost anything. It is this element of remembering that makes novels so soothing. But that was the thing that I was gradually finding out listening and talking at the same time that is realizing the existence of living being actually existing did not have in it any element of remembering and so the time of existing was not the same as in the novels that were soothing. . . . I wondered is there any way of making what I know come out not as remembering. I found this very exciting. And I began to make portraits.[18]

The Making of Americans is a text which purports to be a story but turns into a series of portraits, and these portraits are composed not, like traditional 'character-sketches', out of details but out of inner rhythms. 'I conceived what I at that time called the rhythm of anybody's personality,'[19] she said in 'Portraits and Repetition', and this was how she described her method in *The Making of Americans* itself:

> Some slowly come to be repeating louder and more clearly the bottom being that makes them. Listening to repeating, knowing being in every one who ever was or is or will be living slowly came to be in me a louder and louder pounding. Now I have it to my feeling to feel all living, to be always listening to the slightest changing, to have each one come to be a whole one to me from the repeating in each one that sometime I come to be understanding.[20]

The technique, then, entailed a close attention to repetition in others, and an elaborate use of repetition in verbal description. Yet Gertrude Stein later denied that it *was* repetition, strictly speaking, because of the 'slightest changing' that was always involved. Interestingly, she compared her technique to the (metonymic) technique of film, then in its infancy as a medium:

> Funnily enough the cinema has offered a solution of this thing. By a continuously moving picture of any one there is no memory of any other thing and there is that thing existing. . . . I was doing what the cinema was doing, I was making a continuous succession of the statement of what that person was until I had not many things but one thing. . . . In a cinema picture no two pictures are exactly alike each one is just that much different from the one before, and so in those early portraits there was . . . as there was in *The Making of Americans* no repetition . . . anything one is remembering is a repetition, but existing as a human being, that is being listening and hearing is never repetition. It is not repetition if it is that which you are actually doing because naturally each time the emphasis is different just as the cinema has each time a slightly different thing to make it all be moving.[21]

Gertrude Stein abandoned *A Long Gay Book* (the sequel to *The Making of Americans*), in which she intended to 'go on describing everything',[22] when she realized that the logic of her literary development made it necessary to dispense with even the pretence of story. She turned to the writing of portraits detached from any narrative context, for example the 'Picasso' of 1909, which begins:

> One whom some were certainly following was one who was completely charming. One whom some were certainly following was one who was charming. One whom some were following was one who was completely charming. One whom some were following was one who was certainly completely charming[23]

and continues in the same style of repetition with minimal variation. The next stage in Gertrude Stein's development was to eliminate the human altogether, because the human carried with it ineradicable vestiges of time as a continuum rather than as a continuous present:

> in regard to human beings looking inevitably carries in its train realizing movements and expression and as such forced me into recognizing resemblances, and so forced remembering and in forcing remembering caused confusion of present with past and future time.[24]

Gertrude Stein thus followed the aesthetic path later traced by Ortega y Gasset in *The Dehumanization of Art* (1948) with an unflinching resolve only equalled by the post-impressionist painters whose work she collected. The next stage was in fact to make portraits of inanimate objects that have been compared to the 'still-lives' of Picasso and Matisse.

> I began to make portraits of things and enclosures that is rooms and places because I needed to completely face the difficulty of how to include what is seen with hearing and listening and at first if I were to include a complicated listening and talking it would be too difficult to do. That is why painters paint still lives.[25]

But this phase in her development led to a radical reversal of direction in her verbal style.

The discourse of *The Making of Americans* was essentially an *extended* discourse: length and continuity were of the essence, for only in this way could Gertrude Stein's conception of human existence as an un-segmented flow, a play of secret rhythms, be rendered. Like the selection-deficiency aphasic, the narrator of her book does not readily switch from one topic to another, or stop and start a fresh line of discourse. New paragraphs frequently begin with the self-cueing phrase, 'as I was saying' which keeps the discourse tied to the same context for page after page. Punctuation which would disturb and interrupt the continuous present is avoided:

> When I first began writing, I felt that writing should go on, I still do feel that it should go on but when I first began writing I was completely possessed by the necessity that writing should go on and if writing should go on what had colons and semi-colons to do with it, what had commas to do with it, what had periods to do with it what had small letters and capitals to do with it to do with writing going on . . .[26]

The same contempt was extended to question marks and inverted commas to indicate direct speech. The only punctuation Gertrude Stein was prepared to admit at this stage were the full stop and the paragraph break—the sentence and the paragraph constituting in her mind natural units in prose writing (corresponding roughly, one might say, to the shot and the scene in cinematic discourse). In the transition from human portraits to still lives, however, she switched from length to brevity, from verbs to nouns, from prose to poetry and (in our terms) from metonymic to metaphoric experiment.

> But after I had gone as far as I could in these long sentences and paragraphs that had come to do something else I then began very short things and in doing very short things I resolutely realized nouns and decided not to get around them but to meet them, to handle, in short to refuse them by using them and in that way my real acquaintance with poetry was begun.[27]

The reference here is to the short prose-poems describing objects, food and rooms, collected in *Tender Buttons* (1911). Some examples:

A CARAFE, THAT IS A BLIND GLASS

A kind in glass and a cousin, a spectacle and nothing strange a single hurt colour and an arrangement in a system to pointing. All this and not ordinary, not unadorned in not resembling. The difference is spreading.

A BOX

Out of kindness comes redness and out of rudeness comes rapid same question, out of an eye comes research, out of selection comes painful cattle. So then the order is that a white way of being round is something suggesting a pin and it is disappointing, it is not, it is so rudimentary to be analysed and see a fine substance strangely, it is so earnest to have a green point not to red but to point again.

A CUTLET

A blind agitation is manly and uttermost.

A COLD CLIMATE

A season in yellow sold extra strings makes lying places.

APPLE

Apple plum, carpet steak, seed clam, coloured wine, calm seen, cold cream, best shake, potato, potato and no gold work with pet, a green seen is called bake and change sweet is bready, a little piece a little piece please. A little piece please. Cane again to the presupposed and ready eucalyptus tree, count out sherry and ripe plates and little corners of a kind of ham. This is use.[28]

This mode of writing, following the lead of Gertrude Stein herself, has been called the literary equivalent of cubism in painting. But it is in fact much closer to surrealism than to cubism, since it does not confine itself to merely changing the relationships of contiguous planes and of parts to wholes as they are in nature (as does for instance the Picasso 'Woman in an Armchair' that decorates the cover of the Penguin selection of Gertrude Stein) but presents an object in terms of other objects often far removed from it and from each other in context. The very title *Tender Buttons* is a surrealist metaphor, reminding one of the soft treatment of hard objects (melting watches etc.) in the painting of

Salvador Dali. Since buttons cannot be literally tender, 'Tender Buttons' must be a metaphor. For what? Nipples have been suggested, but without a context there is in fact no way of knowing what an expression like 'tender buttons' might mean, and this is generally true of the whole collection.

In 'Portraits and Repetition', Gertrude Stein described how, at this stage in her development, she was excited by the discovery that the words that made 'what I looked at be itself' were not the words that belonged to conventional description, that made the object merely 'look like itself'.[29] In 'Poetry and Grammar' she described her technique in *Tender Buttons* as 'looking at anything until something that was not the name of that thing but was in a way that actual thing would come to be written.'[30] *Tender Buttons* she described as 'poetry', and 'Poetry is concerned with using with abusing, with losing with wanting, with denying with avoiding with adoring with *replacing* the noun.'[31] (my italics). This is clearly a type of metaphorical writing based on radical substitution (or replacement) of referential nouns. But the perception of similarity on which metaphor depends is in this case private and idiosyncratic to a degree that creates almost insuperable obstacles to understanding.* Correspondingly, the axis of combination which should link the various substitutions together into an intelligible chain, is radically disturbed and dislocated. The result is a kind of discourse that has something in common with the speech of aphasics suffering from contiguity disorder or contextual deficiency, in which Jakobson says:

> The syntactical rules organizing words into a higher unit are lost; this loss, called agramatism, causes the degeneration of the sentence into a mere 'word-heap'. . . . Word order becomes chaotic, the ties of grammatical coordination and subordination whether concord or government, are dissolved. As might be expected, words endowed with purely grammatical functions, like conjunctions, prepositions, pronouns and articles, disappear first, giving rise to the so-called 'telegraphic style'. . . .[32]

The analogy is not exact. Word order, for instance, is still basically regular in *Tender Buttons*, and it is possible to construct perfectly intelligible sentences on the model of, for example 'A season in yellow sold extra strings makes lying places' e.g. 'A backstreet in the city, given appropiate markings, provides parking places')—the problem with the original sentence here is not so much syntactical as lexical or semantic. But there are some items (e.g. 'APPLE') where grammar has disintegrated to the point where 'word-heap' seems an appropiate description of the end result.

Superficially, Gertrude Stein's writing in *Tender Buttons* resembles the experiments of the Dadaists and their successors in aleatory art.

---

*See Allegra Stewart's heroic effort to explicate 'A CARAFE' in *Gertrude Stein and the Present* (Cambridge, Mass., 1967) p. 87ff.

Tristan Tzara composed poems by shredding his own writing and other miscellaneous texts, shaking up the pieces in a bag, and transcribing them in the order in which he plucked them out, one by one. William Burroughs has used a similar technique in some of his novels, cutting up and splicing together heterogeneous texts on an (allegedly) random basis. *Tender Buttons* looks as if it might have been composed in the same way. But whereas the aim of these other writers has been to affront human rationality and/or to demonstrate the capacity of nature (represented by the word-heap) to generate its own meanings independently of human intervention—essentially a postmodernist enterprise—Gertrude Stein maintained the traditional stance of the artist as one who by the exercise of a special gift or skill was seeking to bring her medium into closer and closer proximity to her perceptions. She would have heartily endorsed Ortega's words:

> There is no difficulty in painting or saying things which make no sense whatever, which are unintelligible and therefore nothing. One only needs to assemble unconnected words or draw random lines. But to construct something that is not a copy of 'nature' and yet possesses substance of its own is a feat which presupposes nothing less than genius[33]

This was precisely what Gertrude Stein admired in Picasso and Matisse, and what she aimed at in her own work. If *Tender Buttons* fails it is perhaps because it attempts something that violates the very essence of her medium, language: the combination axis of language cannot be so brutally dislocated without defeating the system's inherently communicative function. *Tender Buttons* is a feat of *de*creation: the familiar tired habits of ordinary discourse are shaken off by 'jolting words and phrases out of their expected contexts'[34] and this is certainly exhilarating, but the treatment is so drastic that it kills the patient. A new creation does not transpire. But it is important to recognize that Gertrude Stein hoped it would. She was a modernist, not a postmodernist* 'I had to feel anything and everything that for me was existing so intensely that I could put it down in writing as a thing in itself without at all necessarily using its name.' This is essentially the Symbolist poetic, expounded by Mallarmé in terms of evocation and suggestion:

> It is not description which can unveil the efficacy and beauty of monuments, seas or the human face in all their maturity and native state, but rather evocation, allusion, suggestion . . . out of a number of words, poetry

*Since writing this I have come across Neil Schmitz's article 'Gertrude Stein as a Post-Modernist: The Rhetoric of *Tender Buttons*' (*Journal of Modern Literature* III (1974) pp. 1203–1218), which contains some ingenious readings of *Tender Buttons* but does not convince me that the aesthetic principles on which that work was based were postmodernist. But there is, of course, some continuity between modernism and postmodernism, and I would not deny that it is particularly visible in the work of Gertrude Stein.

fashions a single new word which is total in itself and foreign to the language—a kind of incantation[35]

by Ezra Pound in terms of the image:

An 'Image' is that which presents an intellectual and emotional complex in an instant of time[36]

and by Eliot in terms of the 'objective correlative' and his catalytic model of poetic composition.[37] These were all poets speaking of poetry, or poetic drama, and Gertrude Stein herself regarded *Tender Buttons* as poetry. Yet the general aim behind all her writing is the same: to render the elusive quality of 'existence' as it is truly perceived when we shed the habits of an obsolete epistemology. In most of the early modernists this enterprise entailed a radical questioning of the conventional notion of time in relation to experience: a conversion of the dynamic or kinetic into the static, of the temporal into the spatial, of successiveness into simultaneity;[38] and on the whole this process could be taken furthest in lyric poetry, with its natural emphasis on paradigmatic similarity rather than in prose with its natural emphasis on syntagmatic continuity. Yet in her experimental metonymic writing, like *The Making of Americans*, Gertrude Stein showed how far prose might go in the same direction, by the artful use of repetition with variation; and it was this aspect of her work, rather than her experiments in the metaphoric mode, that had the most creative influence on other writers, in particular Ernest Hemingway.

3 Ernest Hemingway

Hemingway met Gertrude Stein in the early 1920s when he was living in Paris and struggling to establish himself as a writer. He became well acquainted with her work, especially *The Making of Americans*, which he persuaded Ford Madox Ford to print in the *Transatlantic Review* and which he proofread for the author. The friendship was always precariously dependent upon Hemingway's willingness to play the part of pupil to master, and in due course the inevitable breach occurred; but looking back on that period of his life in *A Moveable Feast* (1964), Hemingway acknowledged her importance as a literary innovator: 'She had . . . discovered many truths about rhythms and the use of words in repetition that were valid and valuable and she talked well about them.'[1]

Hemingway wanted to be both a realist and a modernist: the ambition is implicit in his trinity of 'good' American writers—Mark

Twain, Stephen Crane and Henry James.[2] A newspaper reporter himself, he was seeking to combine the truthfulness of good journalism with the intensity and permanence of great imaginative writing. Speaking of the time when he knew Gertrude Stein, Hemingway recalled:

> I was trying to write then and I found the greatest difficulty, aside from knowing what you truly felt, rather than what you were supposed to feel, and had been taught to feel, was to put down what really happened in action: what the actual things were which produced the emotion that you experienced. In writing for a newspaper you told what happened and, with one trick and another, you communicated the emotion aided by the element of timeliness which gives a certain emotion to any account of something that has happened on that day; but the real thing, the sequence of motion and fact which made the emotion and which would be valid in a year or in ten years, or, with luck and if you stated it purely enough, always, was beyond me and I was working very hard to try and get it.[3]

It was essentially a problem of style, though Hemingway tended to formulate it in terms of existential authenticity (the passage quoted is part of an explanation of why he studied bullfighting). Hemingway's vision of life, tempered by the experience of war, was bleakly materialistic, in the philosophical sense: positivist, anti-metaphysical, stoical; though by temperament he was highly sensitive, superstitious and sentimental. It is the tension between these two sets of qualities— the latter battened down under a style derived from the former—that accounts for the extraordinary power of his best work.

The logical medium for Hemingway's materialism was a style scrupulously restricted to denotation, as he himself suggested in one of the most celebrated passages of *A Farewell to Arms*:

> There were many words that you could not stand to hear and finally only the names of places had dignity. Certain numbers were the same way and certain dates and these with the names of the places were all you could say and have them mean anything. Abstract words such as glory, honour, courage or hallow were obscene beside the concrete names of villages, the numbers of roads, the names of rivers, the numbers of regiments and the dates.[4]

The banishment of abstraction is of course a rhetorical illusion: 'dignity' is allowed to stand in this passage and is indeed a concept absolutely central to Hemingway's vision of life. In the same way he purged his style of metaphor but contrived to retain in it the emotive resonance of metaphorical writing.

Overt metaphor, in the earlier (and better) Hemingway is invariably a sign of falsity and illusion. The story 'Hills Like White Elephants' is worth glancing at in this connection since its title draws ironic attention to the one overtly metaphorical expression in the text. The story begins in Hemingway's characteristic denotative mode: 'The hills across the valley of the Evro were long and white.' A young man and woman are sitting on a railway platform facing the hills, drinking and bickering as they wait for a train. They quarrel about the girl's observation that the hills 'look like white elephants'. Gradually it becomes clear to the reader that the man is trying to persuade the girl to have an abortion. Through trivial, banal, repetitious talk—the story consists almost entirely of dialogue—Hemingway communicates with wonderful exactness the feeling of a relationship that has reached that stage where the two people involved are disenchanted with each other yet frightened at the prospect of a crisis and separation. The action is minimal: they order drinks, get up, walk about, sit down. The conversation builds small reconciliations which immediately break down. The last words of the story are the girl's: 'I feel fine.' But we don't believe her. The white hills, fancifully transformed by the girl's simile, stand for impossibility: the recovery of innocence and the first careless rapture of love, freedom from the contingencies of the flesh. (In its French translation the story is entitled '*Paradis Perdu*'.) 'If I do it,' says the girl, referring to the abortion, 'then it will be nice again if I say things like white elephants and you'll like it?' 'I'll love it,' he replies. 'I love it now but I just can't think about it.'[5]

By denying himself metaphor, Hemingway was of course deliberately cutting himself off from the symbolist tradition which directly or indirectly nourished most of the early modernist prose writers—James, Conrad, Ford, Joyce, Virginia Woolf. Most of these authors shared the view that God (at least the God of orthodox Christianity) was dead and that the world was a wasteland, a place of meaningless suffering, unsuccessful communication and shattered illusions. Hemingway had no quarrel with them there. But in the exercise of their craft, which they invested with a quasi-religious solemnity, these writers found some relief or release from a nihilistic *Weltanschauung*. Writing itself, especially through metaphorical devices, turned life into art, made art into an alternative reality, luminous, harmonious, immutable and transcendent, and this was often accomplished by the invocation and reworking of old myths. Hemingway wanted nothing of that kind; yet he shared the same basic ambition of the modernists: to translate raw experience into immortal form by renewing the means of expression. It could only be done, therefore, by working on the metonymic axis of his medium, and this was where the precept and example of Gertrude Stein was probably crucial, in showing what might be done in prose by rhythm and repetition.

Repetition is a characteristic of vernacular speech, because most speakers of any language use a very limited vocabulary, and because speech (compared to writing) encourages a good deal of redundancy in the interests of communication (too high a ratio of information to lexical units puts great strain on the receiver of the message and makes the message vulnerable to interruption or interference from other sources). Now the characteristic mode of American realistic fiction is a narrative voice based on the vernacular. It was because Mark Twain showed how this could be done that Hemingway accorded him a prime place in American literary history ('All modern American literature comes from one book by Mark Twain called *Huckleberry Finn*'[6]). Hemingway had absorbed this lesson long before he met Gertrude Stein. A story written when he was seventeen includes the following paragraph:

> Yes, he was a bad Indian. Up on the upper peninsular he couldn't get drunk. He used to drink all day—everything. But he couldn't get drunk. Then he would go crazy; but he wasn't drunk. He was crazy because he couldn't get drunk.[7]

Here we see in embryo some of the characteristic devices of Hemingway's mature style: the short simple sentences, the refusal to avoid an awkward echo (*up on the upper*), the repetition and permutation of word and phrase, eschewing elegant variation. By conventional literary standards this is clumsy and tautologous writing, but it expresses quite powerfully a baffled and desperate state of mind. It hasn't, however, got much resonance, it is not particularly haunting or memorable, it doesn't have the purity of expression Hemingway described as his aim in the passage quoted earlier from *Death in the Afternoon*. It's the kind of thing Sherwood Anderson did well, but that was so far from (or so dangerously near to) what Hemingway was aiming at that he had to exorcise Anderson's influence in *The Torrents of Spring* (1926). What Hemingway learned from his exposure to modernist literary theory and practice and from his own trials and errors in the crucial Paris years, was to refine and complicate the basic devices of vernacular narration so as to give his writing something of the magical, incantatory quality of symbolist poetry, without losing the effect of sincerity, of authenticity, of 'the way it was'—in short to combine realism and modernism in a single style. Consider the opening paragraph of his story 'In Another Country':

> In the fall the war was always there, but we did not go to it any more. It was cold in the fall in Milan and the dark came very early. Then the electric lights came on, and it was pleasant along the streets looking in the windows. There was much game hanging outside the shops and the snow powdered in the fur of the foxes and the wind blew their tails. The deer hung stiff and heavy and empty, and small birds blew in the wind and the wind turned their feathers. It was a cold fall and the wind came down from the mountains.[8]

This perfectly illustrates Jakobson's account of the realistic author's metonymic method: 'Following the path of contiguous relationships, the realist author metonymically digresses from the plot to the atmosphere and from the characters to the setting in space and time.

He is fond of synecdochic details.' Hemingway's narrator digresses from the 'plot' (the situation of wounded soldiers receiving treatment—though the fact that the digression occurs so soon, before the situation has been properly explained, is of course a deviation from the procedures of classical realism) to the atmosphere (the cold autumn evenings) and the setting, Milan, which is presented synecdochically (the city represented by its shops, the shops by the game shops, the game by certain animals, and the animals by certain parts of their bodies—fur, tails, feathers). In this way the paragraph moves along a straight line of contiguity. But there is another system of relationships at work in the writing based on the repetition of certain words and grammatical structures and rhythmical patterns, which has the opposite effect, drawing our attention (if only subliminally) to similarities rather than contiguities, keeping certain words and concepts echoing in our ears even as our eyes move forward to register new facts. In particular the reader will be affected by the repetition of the words *fall*, *cold* and *wind*. Though *fall* and *cold* are paired together in the second sentence, all three words are combined together only once, in the last sentence—which is why it has a finality and resonance not easy to account for in logical or semantic terms. This last sentence clinches a network of association between the season and the emotions of the wounded soldiers. As the carefully arranged words of the opening sentence intimate, and the story goes on to make explicit, the war is always with the soldiers, in their minds and in their wounds (those who are cured will be returned to the front to face violent death again, and those who will not go to war again will not have lives worth living). The war is going on in the mountains; the wind comes from the mountains; *cold* and *fall* are connected obviously enough with death. In the context of these reverberating repetitions, the synecdochic details of the game hanging outside the shops inevitably function as symbols of death and destruction, though there is nothing figurative about the manner of their description, just as there is no pathetic fallacy in the description of the weather. In this way—by carefully disguising the 'projection of the principle of equivalence from the axis of selection into the axis of combination'—an apparently metonymic style is made to serve the purposes of metaphor.

4 D. H. Lawrence

Like Hemingway, D. H. Lawrence was obliquely connected to the modernist movement, sharing some of its aims and assumptions (e.g. the need to innovate, to revolutionize the traditional forms) but rejecting others (e.g. the tendency inherited from Symbolism to set art against life as an alternative and superior kind of order). Both Lawrence and Hemingway believed strongly in maintaining a vital connection between art and experience—but of course for very different reasons and to very different literary effects. Where Hemingway worked hard to disguise his artfulness as naive truthtelling, and strove for economy and understatement, Lawrence wrote throughout his career with unrestrained (and often uncontrolled) lyrical or prophetic exuberance, and responded with notable enthusiasm to those early American writers whom Hemingway rejected because of their artificial literary language.[1] Where Hemingway's style abstained as far as possible from abstraction and metaphor, Lawrence's revelled in both. Yet Lawrence cannot be classified, any more than Hemingway, as a 'metaphoric' writer in the same sense as we have applied that term to Joyce or T. S. Eliot. Similarity (and contrast) never, in Lawrence, control the development of the discourse as in the 'mythical method' of *Ulysses* or *The Waste Land*. Continuity was more important to Lawrence than irony. 'Flow' was one of his favourite words to express the quality he looked for in authentic living and authentic writing:

> It is the way our sympathy flows and recoils that really determines our lives. And here lies the vast importance of the novel, properly handled. It can inform and lead into new places the flow of our sympathetic consciousness, and it can lead our sympathy away from things gone dead.[2].

It is consistent with this concern for 'flow' that Lawrence rarely indulges in those deviations from chronological sequence that are generally typical of the modernist novel (though he is, significantly, vaguer about *dates* than the traditional realistic novelist*). And his

---

*Frank Kermode has commented on this feature of *Women in Love*, comparing it to George Eliot's *Middlemarch*, in 'D. H. Lawrence and the Apocalyptic Types', *Continuities* (1968), p. 149.

narrative voice, however much it varies in tone, from the shrewdly down-to-earth to the lyrically rhapsodic, and whatever character's consciousness it is rendering, is always basically the same, unmistakeably Lawrentian. Not for him the mimicry, the pastiche, the rapid shifts of voice and linguistic register, that we encounter in Joyce and Eliot. What we know about the compositional habits of these writers confirms the distinction. Joyce revised his work by making innumerable insertions and substitutions, often as late as proof stage. Lawrence, as is well known, to revise a novel had to write it all out from the beginning; he had to reactivate the basic continuity and rhythm of the discourse in order to make any changes in it. Whereas Joyce (and perhaps Eliot, if we judge by the evidence of *The Waste Land* manuscript) saw the text as a kind of *space*, a verbal object the components of which might be juggled about, replaced, added to and subtracted from, Lawrence seems to have regarded it as a *sound*, a 'tremulation on the ether' to use his own phrase:[3] an utterance that, like the oral epic, could only be modified in the act of recitation.

This concern for flow, for continuity, meant that Lawrence's style had to be essentially metonymic in structure, forwarded by contiguity, though the meanings he groped after could only be expressed metaphorically. As in Hemingway, therefore, though to totally different effect, repetition both rhythmical and lexical is exploited to shift an ostensibly metonymic style in the direction of metaphor. Here is a typical passage from *Women in Love*, just after Gudrun and Ursula have witnessed Gerald Crich ruthlessly subduing his horse which is panic-stricken by the passing of a colliery train:

> The man [i.e. the gatekeeper of the level-crossing] went in to drink his can of tea, the girls went on down the lane, that was deep in soft black dust. Gudrun was as if numbed in her mind by the sense of the indomitable soft weight of the man bearing down into the living body of the horse: the strong, indomitable thighs of the blond man clenching the palpitating body of the mare into pure control: a sort of soft white magnetic domination from the loins and thighs and calves, enclosing and encompassing the mare heavily into unutterable subordination, soft-blood-subordination, terrible.[4]

In this short, two-sentence paragraph there is a remarkable amount of repetition—lexical repetition (*soft, indomitable, man, body, thighs, mare, subordination*) and rhythmical repetition, produced by syntactical parallelism. The long second sentence consists of a main clause ('Gudrun was as if numbed in her mind by the sense of . . .') followed by three participial phrases, each of which is an expansion of the preceding one. The parallelism of syntactical structure can be shown by laying out the three phrases in columns, thus:

| 1 | the indomitable soft weight of the man | bearing down into the living body of the horse |

2 the strong indomitable thighs   clenching the palpitating body of
   of the blond man   the mare

3 a sort of soft white magnetic   enclosing and encompassing the
   domination from the loins and   mare heavily into unutterable
   thighs and calves   subordination,   soft-blood-
                                    subordination, terrible.

Of particular interest in this paragraph is the behaviour of the word
soft. 'Soft black dust' in the first sentence is a straightforward
referential use of the adjective. 'Soft weight' in the next sentence is
foregrounded by being a little paradoxical. It is not quite an oxymoron,
for some things can be heavy *and* soft, but it doesn't seem to be
particularly appropiate, in the circumstances, to Gerald, whose
physical contact with the horse seems rather to be 'hard'. One might
almost suspect that Lawrence lazily wrote '*soft* weight' simply because
he had just written '*soft* black dust' and the word was in his head. Yet
'soft weight' does, of course, make a kind of metaphorical sense,
because Gerald, the colliery owner, is associated with the soft black
dust that covers the countryside, and this chapter is in fact called
'Coal-Dust'. A kind of equation is implied—Gerald:mare as
colliery:countryside. The next use of *soft* is explicitly metaphorical: 'a
sort of soft white magnetic domination' (a phrase that echoes an earlier
description of Gerald on the horse: 'Gerald was heavy on the mare, and
forced her back. It seemed as if he sank into her magnetically, and
could thrust her back against herself.'[5]). Again, *soft* seems to be used
here more as a purely formal repetition rather than for any descriptive
aptness, but again under examination the word proves to contribute a
new meaning. For the repetition of *soft* is now linked with the
inversion of *white* (for *black*) and Gerald is, of course, associated
throughout the novel with whiteness as well as blackness in his fair
physique (here indicated by *blond*) and in the 'soft white' snow in
which he meets his death. 'Soft-blood-subordination', in which *soft*
appears for the fourth and last time in this paragraph, is another
mysteriously metaphorical expression, with yet another shade of
meaning. Exactly what meaning it is not possible to say with any
precision. We are told elsewhere in *Women in Love* that 'words
themselves do not convey meaning, that they are but gestures we make,
a dumb show like any other,'[6] and the passage under discussion
contains its own reminder to this effect in 'unutterable'. But clearly the
fourth use of *soft* would be quite incomprehensible without the other
three. We can in fact say with reasonable confidence that the whole
passage is a premonition of the ultimately destructive sexual
relationship that is to develop between Gerald and Gudrun. That
Gerald's horse is a mare rather than a stallion is not, of course,
fortuitous. Gudrun sees in his domination of the mare a type of sexual
possession which both appalls and fascinates her. Certainly much of

the language, from 'the soft weight of the man' to 'soft-blood-subordination', which seems odd as a description of a man trying to control a horse, becomes more intelligible when applied to a man making love to a woman or (to be more exact) when applied to a woman's imagining what it would be like to be made love to by a certain type of man. In short, the passage would seem to conform, at its deepest level of meaning, to Jakobson's metaphoric category, in that it turns on Gudrun's perception of a similarity between herself and the mare, and an emotional substitution of herself for the mare. Yet this substitution is never made explicit: it emerges out of an intense dwelling on the literal event.

Lawrence's writing in this passage appears to be 'forwarded by contiguity' in the sense that each clause or phrase takes its impetus from an item in the preceding one, the repeated words knitting the units together on the pattern of Ab Bc Cd De etc. Yet the effect of progression and continuity this produces is a kind of illusion: the discourse is not really moving forward to encompass new facts, but unfolding the deeper significance of the same facts. The passage develops a more and more psychological, a less and less referential, presentation of the event by a gradual accretion of vague metaphorical meaning, which does not interrupt or break the continuity of the discourse. In this process the repetition of *soft* plays a crucial role, for it is a metonymic attribute of the context at the beginning of the passage and a metaphorical vehicle for the sexual mysticism at its conclusion. In this respect the passage is a kind of microcosm of the process by which *Women in Love* as a whole grew out of the *ur*-novel 'The Sisters' and separated itself from *The Rainbow*; and a microcosm, too, of the way *The Rainbow* developed from its family-saga beginning to its visionary conclusion, and of the way Lawrence developed, in the writing of these paired novels, away from the more conventional realistic fiction of *Sons and Lovers*.

The same tendency may be observed in the three versions of *Lady Chatterley's Lover*[7] through which Lawrence's revisions transformed an initially realistic love story (in which an idyllic love affair between an aristocratic lady and her gamekeeper is tested against the harsh realities of a society in which class-differences and class-antagonisms threaten the permanence of the relationship) into a didactic pastoral romance in which the love idyll is allowed an easy victory over circumstances and offered as a type of redemption from the sickness of modern society. Pastoral is, in our terms, a 'metaphorical' genre: it does not pretend to describe agrarian society realistically, but offers an imaginative model of, or metaphor for, the good life. In literary tradition it often involves educated, genteel characters pretending, voluntarily or by force of circumstances, to be unsophisticated country folk. Lawrence's Connie and Mellors are both refugees from a corrupt and decadent world of civilization, from a countryside ravaged by industry, from a social and cultural life eaten away by greed, pseudo-sophistication and class antagonism; they plunge into the woods, throw off their clothes, decorate each other's bodies with flowers, use rude and dialect words (a feature of pastoral as far back as Theocritus) and make uninhibited love in the open air. It is true that pastoral elements were present in *The First Lady Chatterley*, but they were very much subdued in comparison with *John Thomas and Lady Jane* and *Lady Chatterley's Lover*. In these two revisions Lawrence made a crucial readjustment of the structural balance of the story: in the first version the love affair begins early in the narrative and dominates the first half of the book; the second half is concerned with the problems of fitting this relationship into society. In the second and third versions the initial meeting between Connie and Mellors is much delayed to allow an extensive treatment of Connie's sexual repression and alienation from her social milieu. The love affair, with its greatly expanded descriptions of sexual intercourse, thus dominates the *second* half of the final *Lady Chatterley's Lover*, and this has the effect of making it seem a solution to the problems raised in the first half. It is quite consistent with this move towards a more schematic pastoral treatment of the story that Mellors should be more educated (an ex-officer who can speak standard English if he wants to) than his precursor Parkin. Lawrence did not, however, solve all the problems of reader-response raised by his revisions, and left the final version vulnerable to complaints that it is often absurd, unconvincing and doctrinaire. *The First Lady Chatterley* is certainly the most aesthetically unified version of the three, but it is the least ambitious—almost a throwback to the Lawrence of *Sons and Lovers*.

To examine the dynamics of Lawrence's writing in some detail, especially the way in which he seems, as it were, to feed metaphorically upon his own metonymies, working himself up from shrewd observation of social and environmental realities into a poetic, prophetic mode of utterance, it is more convenient to look at one of his short stories than at the long, complex novels. 'England, my England' is not perhaps among his greatest stories, but it is a very powerful one, and belongs to the most important phase of his literary career. First written in the crucial year of 1915, when *The Rainbow* was completed and *Women in Love* begun, it was substantially revised and expanded in 1921, by which time Lawrence had not only made considerable progress in working out his 'metaphysic' but also achieved greater poise and confidence in expressing his ideas through narrative. He evidently considered the revised version of 'England, My England' to be important enough to stand as the title-story of a collection he published in 1922.

The second version of the story, in bare outline, is as follows: Egbert and Winifred are a young married couple, passionately in love, who occupy an old cottage on the edge of a common in Hampshire. The cottage is a gift from Winifred's father, Godfrey Marshall, a strong-willed, self-made man, who has settled several of his children in the same way on his estate. Egbert is handsome, charming, well-bred, but without a profession or ambitions, so the young couple are increasingly dependent upon the largesse of the father when they start a family. This dependence begins to come between them. Their eldest child cuts her leg on a sickle left lying in the garden by Egbert and, due to the incompetence of the local doctor, is eventually crippled by the accident. Winifred's response to this crisis, conditioned by her religious upbringing (the Marshalls are Catholics), is a deliberate frigidity towards her husband. The First World War begins and Egbert, who is unaffected by vulgar patriotism, hesitates about enlisting. He asks his wife's advice and she refers him to her father. Marshall advises him to join up. Egbert does so, and after some months' service is killed by a German shell. The last few pages of the story, describing this incident, contain heavy hints that Egbert expected, and in a sense willed, this death.

The first, much shorter version of the story has essentially the same narrative line, with the following important exceptions: the main character (called Evelyn) is in no way responsible for the accident to his daughter, and, at the end of the story, in his mortally wounded state he manages to shoot three German soldiers dead before he is killed and horribly mutilated by a fourth. (This version was never reprinted after its appearance in *The English Review*, October 1915, and is little known.)

In both versions the story poses obvious problems of interpretation. Egbert's death is presented not, as in most modern war literature (Hemingway's, for example) as something absurd and pitiful in its randomness and pointlessness, but as something profoundly meaningful and indeed inevitable, an appropiate termination of a futile life. But who, or what, is responsible for the futility? Is it Egbert himself, because of his fundamental decadence and lack of purpose? Is it his father-in-law who patronized him? Is it his wife who deliberately denied him her love? Or senseless circumstance that crippled his daughter and thus made him an outcast from his own family? Like so much of Lawrence's writing, 'England, My England' was partly inspired by real people and events, and it is tempting to look to these sources for a key to its enigmas, as does Harry T. Moore in his biography, *The Intelligent Heart*. In the first half of 1915, Lawrence and Frieda were loaned Viola Meynell's cottage on the family estate of Wilfred Meynell at Greatham, Sussex. Another cottage belonged to Wilfred Meynell's daughter Madeline and her husband Percy Lucas, brother of the man-of-letters E. V. Lucas. The Percy Lucases had three daughters, the eldest of whom, Sylvia, was crippled as the result of an injury to her leg caused by a sickle carelessly left lying in the grass outside the cottage (though *not* by her father). According to Moore,

Lawrence tutored this little girl for a while, but took a dislike to her father:

> he saw Percy Lucas as a loafer, dependent upon the bounty of Wilfred Meynell and leaning for spiritual support upon Madeline; these things Lawrence put into the cruel portrait of Percy, as Egbert, parasitic dweller at Godfrey Marshall's family colony at Crockham in 'England, My England'. Yet, for all its meanness, the portrait did not completely lack sympathy: the Egbert of the story was really a victim of the ostensibly benevolent paternalism that dominated the colony.[8]

Moore's account has been challenged on a number of points by Percy Lucas's daughter Barbara.[9] She states that Lawrence did not tutor Sylvia, but a cousin of hers, and that Sylvia, her mother and her sisters were in London throughout the Lawrence's stay at Greatham, except for a short visit in the Easter holidays; while Percy, who had volunteered for military service in 1914, would necessarily have been absent from the estate at this period except for the occasional brief leave. Barbara Lucas believes that Lawrence and the Lucas family met, in fact, on only one occasion, during those Easter holidays of 1915.[10] Lawrence's correspondence, however, suggests a closer acquaintance than that.

The story written in 1915 and published in October of the same year in *The English Review* proved cruelly prophetic when Percy Lucas died of wounds received in the battle of the Somme in July 1916. Even Lawrence, never overscrupulous about using friends and acquaintances as models for his characters, felt a pang of remorse. He wrote to Catherine Carswell on 16 July 1916:

> It upsets me very much to hear of Percy Lucas. I did not know he was dead. I wish that story at the bottom of the sea, before ever it had been printed. Yet, it seems to me, man must find a new expression, give a new value to life, or his women will reject him, and he must die. I liked Madeline Lucas the best of the Meynells really. She was the one who was capable of honest love: she and Monica. Lucas was, somehow, a spiritual coward. But who isn't?
>
> I ought never, never to have gone to live at Greatham. Perhaps Madeline won't be hurt by that wretched story—that is all that matters. If it was a true story, it shouldn't really damage.[11]

After continuing the letter on other topics, Lawrence added a characteristic postscript:

> No, I don't wish I had never written that story. It should do good in the long run.

It is not clear whether by 'true story' Lawrence meant, true to the facts of the Lucas marriage, or true in some wider, more representative sense. As Emile Delavenay has pointed out[12], the second version of the story is in several respects much more faithful to its sources in real life than the first version. For example, Godfrey Marshall, a Quaker in the first version, is made a Catholic in the second, (Meynell himself was a Catholic convert who had originally been a Quaker); and the whole account of the cottage and the 'Crockham' estate (unnamed in the first version) seems, to judge by Barbara Lucas's evidence, much more specifically evocative of Greatham in the second version. This seems a somewhat callous proceeding on Lawrence's part in view of his earlier misgivings about Madeline's possible response, unless he thought that by making the story more literally true to the facts he would make it somehow more acceptable. But in that case, why did he deliberately depart from the facts by making Egbert responsible for the accident—a suggestion that could only cause offence to the dead man's family? My own opinion is that by the time he came to revise the story, living in Sicily, far away from England, Lawrence was no longer interested in or bothered by the possible private repercussions of the story and that the specific details about Greatham came into the story almost accidentally, along with a great deal of 'doctrine' that has little to do with Greatham, in the process of revision, as Lawrence strove to give the story more depth and concreteness. Moore's description of 'England, My England' as a 'story *à clef*' is not only limiting, but misleading, based on a reading of the second version of the text in the light of Lawrence's comments on the first. Even of this first version Lawrence, describing it, at the time of publication. as 'a story about the Lucases', immediately went on to say, 'The story is the story of most men and women who are married today—of most men at the War, and wives at home.'[13] To Catherine Carswell the following year he was more specific about the theme: 'a man must find a new expression, give a new value to life, or his women will reject him and he must die.' And behind that theme is a still larger one: the idea that death and dissolution may be the route to a new creation, and that there may be a kind of heroism in following it, even at the cost of one's own extinction. I shall try to show how these ideas find expression in a mode of writing that is continually turning its realistic particulars into symbols and its descriptive metaphors into thematic ones. This process is observable both in the differences between the two versions and in the development of the second version itself. The evolution of the story, in short, was always in the direction of the metaphorical pole.

I observed above that Lawrence's novels are invariably chronological in structure, but the compression required by the short-story form sometimes led him to depart from this norm, as in 'England, My England'. The first version of the story is in the form of an extended retrospect in the hero's mind at the time of his mortal wounding. The second version begins on the day of the accident to the daughter, then looks back on the history of the marriage, then returns to the time of the opening paragraphs to describe the accident; the remainder of the narrative proceeds chronologically. The opening pages describe Egbert working, rather unsuccessfully, on the edge of

the common, extending the garden path that leads from his
'Hampshire cottage that crouched near the earth amid flowers
blossoming in the bit of shaggy wilderness round about.'[14] In the
opening description of the setting a long historical perspective is
introduced:

> The sunlight blazed down upon the earth, there was a vividness of flamy
> vegetation, of fierce seclusion amid the savage peace of the commons.
> Strange how the savage England lingers in patches: as here, amid these
> shaggy gorse commons, and marshy, snake infested places near the foot of
> the south downs. The spirit of place lingering on primeval, as when the
> Saxons came, so long ago. Ah, how he had loved it! The green garden paths,
> the tufts of flowers, purple and white columbines, and great oriental red
> poppies with their black chaps and mulleins tall and yellow, this flamy
> garden which had been a garden for a thousand years, scooped out in the
> little hollow among the snake infested commons. He had made it flame with
> flowers, in a sun-cup under its hedges and trees . . .. The timbered cottage
> . . . belonged to the old England of hamlets and yeomen . . . it had never
> known the world of today. Not till Egbert came with his bride. And he had
> come to fill it with flowers.[15]

The corresponding passage in the first version is as follows:

> The sunlight blazed down on the earth; there was a vividness of flamy
> vegetation and flowers, of tense seclusion amid the peace of the commons.
> The cottage with its great sloping roofs slept in the for-ever sunny hollow,
> hidden, eternal. And here he lived, in this ancient, changeless hollow of
> flowers and sunshine and the sloping-roofed house. It was balanced like a
> nest in a bank, this hollow home, always full of peace, always under heaven
> only. It had no context, no relation with the world; it held its cup under
> heaven alone, and was filled for ever with peace and sunshine and loveliness.
>   The shaggy, ancient heath that rose on either side, the downs that were pale
> against the sky in the distance, these were the extreme rims of the cup. It was
> held up only to heaven; the world entered in not at all.[16]

The timelessness of the cottage's setting, here associated with a
vaguely Christian 'eternity', is in the second version given a distinctly
primitive or 'savage' note, further emphasized by the mention of
snakes (which are wholly absent from the first version). The
description of the flowers in the second version is more detailed and
more lyrical, and they are associated metonymically with Egbert
because he planted and tended them. As the second version continues,
Winifred and her family are associated metaphorically with bushes
and trees, especially the hawthorn:

> She moved with a slow grace of energy like a blossoming, red-flowered bush
> in motion. She, too, seemed to come out of the old England, ruddy, strong,
> with a certain crude, passionate quiescence and a hawthorn robustness.[17]

The image is reiterated after the introduction of Godfrey Marshall, and the association of Egbert with flowers shifts from the metonymic to the metaphoric:

> The girls and the father were strong-limbed, thick-blooded people, true English, as holly-trees and hawthorn are English. Their culture [*i.e.* their high cultural interests] was grafted on to them as one might perhaps graft a common pink rose on to a thorn-stem. It flowered oddly enough, but it did not alter their blood. And Egbert was a born rose.[18]

Apart from a comparison of Winifred to 'a blossoming tree in motion' in the first version[19], all these metaphors of vegetation were added in the second version.

At first the marriage is a success, based on strong physical passion. 'Ah, that it might never end, this passion, this marriage! The flame of their two bodies burnt again in that old cottage, that was haunted already by so much by-gone, physical desire. . . . They too felt that they did not belong to the London world any more.'[20] But this feeling of having dropped out of the modern world is an illusion paid for by Godfrey Marshall's fortune, made in the industrial North and maintained in the City of London.

> They drew the sustenance for their fire of passion from him, from the old man. It was he who fed their flame. He triumphed secretly in the thought. And it was to her father that Winifred still turned, as the one source of all security and support. . . . For Egbert had no ambition whatsoever. . . .[21]

Then the first child is born. A fair, delicate-limbed child, Joyce takes after her father and is thus associated like him with flowers—'a wild little daisy-spirit . . . this light little cowslip child.'[22] But Joyce requires a Nanny and this entails further financial dependence on Godfrey. Furthermore, maternity makes sexual love less important to Winifred and cements her bond to the real provider and protector of her offspring.

> Her child seemed to link her up again in a circuit with her own family. Her father and mother, herself, and her child, that was the human trinity for her. Her husband? Yes, she loved him still. But that was like play. Till she married, her first human duty had been towards her father: he was the pillar, the source of life, the everlasting support. Now another link was added to the chain of duty: her father, herself, her child.[23]

The image of the father as a pillar is given an interesting Biblical association a little later:

> She began to resent her own passion for Egbert . . . he was charming, he was lovable, he was terribly desirable. But—but—oh, the awful looming cloud of that *but!*—he did not stand firm in the landscape of her life like a tower of strength, like a great pillar of significance.[24]

The close juxtaposition of *cloud* and *pillar*, though they are in fact metaphors applied to different things, evokes the image of the pillar of the cloud in Exodus, in which the patriarchal God of the Old Testament hid himself. And the image of Egbert as a flower also acquires Biblical associations:

> What did she want—what did she want? Her mother once said to her, with that characteristic touch of irony: 'Well, dear, if it is your fate to consider the lilies, that toil not, neither do they spin, that is one destiny among others, and perhaps not so unpleasant as most.' . . . Winifred was only more confused. It was not a question of lilies. At least, if it were a question of lilies, then her children were the little blossoms. They at least *grew* . . . as for that other tall, handsome flower of a father of theirs, he was full grown already, so she did not want to spend her life considering him in the flower of his days.[25]

The pillar-image returns in the form of a modified cliché: 'Why wasn't he like Winifred's father, a pillar of society, even if a slender, exquisite column?'[26]

Thus the marriage approaches deadlock. Egbert's basic desire was to 'hold aloof' from the world, but Winifred 'was not made to endure aloof. Her family tree was a robust vegetation that had to be stirring and believing.'[27] The dead metaphor 'family tree' is thus revived, and developed further in the next paragraph in respect of Marshall: 'In a dark and unquestioning way, he had a sort of faith: an acrid faith like the sap of some not-to-be-exterminated tree.'[28] This leads, *via* the repetition of 'acrid', into a disquisition on Marshall's potency as an Old Testament father-figure:

> He had a certain acrid courage, and a certain will-to-power . . . he had kept, and all honour to him, a certain primitive dominion over the souls of his children, the old, almost magic prestige of paternity. There it was, still burning in him, the old smoky torch of paternal godhead . . .. Here was a man who had kept alive the old red flame of fatherhood that had even the right to sacrifice the child to God, like Isaac.[29]

The association of Marshall with the God of the Old Testament, only hinted subliminally in the juxtaposition of *cloud* and *pillar*, now becomes more explicit. And the potent image of 'flame', originally attributed to the relationship between Egbert and Winifred, is now transferred to her father, its red glow contrasted with the 'hard white light of our fatherless world'.[30] Having 'once known the glow of male power [Winifred] would not easily turn to the hard white light of feminine independence,'[31] but her attempts to bring up her own children 'with the old dark magic of paternal authority' are neutralized by Egbert's passivity.[32]

With this passage, in which Lawrence's own voice, and opinions, dominate the discourse, (and which belongs exclusively to the second version) the long retrospect ends; and the story proceeds to narrate, in a vivid, dramatic style, the accident to Joyce and its painful aftermath. When Joyce proves to be irremediably crippled Winifred interprets the tragedy as a judgment on her own sensual indulgence, and becomes frigid towards her husband. Medical treatment for the child requires a move to London, but Egbert, driven away 'like Ishmael'[33] by self-reproach and his wife's hostility, spends much time alone in the cottage:

> with the empty house all around him at night, all the empty rooms, he felt his heart go wicked. The sense of frustration and futility, like some slow, torpid snake, slowly bit right through his heart. Futility, futility: the horrible marsh-poison went through his veins and killed him. . . .
>
> He was alone. He himself cleaned the cottage and made his bed. But his mending he did not do. His shirts were slit on the shoulders, when he had been working, and the white flesh showed through. He would feel the air and the spots of rain on his exposed flesh. And he would look again across the common, where the dark, tufted gorse was dying to seed, and the bits of cat-heather were coming pink in tufts, like a sprinkling of sacrificial blood.
>
> His heart went back to the savage old spirit of the place: the desire for old gods, old, lost passions, the passion of cold-blooded, darting snakes that hissed and shot away from him, the mystery of blood sacrifices, all the lost, intense sensations of the primeval people of the place, whose passions seethed in the air still, from those long days before the Romans came. The seethe of a lost, dark passion in the air. The presence of unseen snakes.[34]

This is an obscure passage, partly because the connotations of 'snakes' are so ambiguous. There are no references to snakes in the first version, but several in the second. On the first page the already isolated and resentful Egbert, working on the edge of the common, hears his children's voices from the cottage:

> high, childish voices, slightly didactic and tinged with domineering: 'If you don't come quick, nurse, I shall run out there to where there are snakes.' And nobody had the *sangfroid* to reply: 'Run then, little fool.' It was always, 'No darling. Very well, darling. In a moment, darling. Darling, you *must* be patient.'[35]

It is hard to say whether this is the author's reflection, or the character's. But if the latter's it certainly seems to have the author's support. Graham Hough, quoting this passage, comments:

> Only a fragment, and a fragment chosen probably in resentment at the contrast between this kind of childhood and [Lawrence's] own; yet a sharp, prying little searchlight on to a whole ethos.[36]

Fair enough. But the fragment is not merely a bit of shrewd social observation. The child's threat of running out 'to where there are snakes' is repeated some fifteen pages later as a cue to the reader that the narrative, after the long retrospect, has returned to the opening scene. After a brief silence Egbert hears a shriek: Joyce has run into the garden and cut her leg on a sickle that Egbert has carelessly left lying on the grass. Does that imply that he, in effect, willed the accident ('Run then, little fool'), his sickle substituted for the snake? We may be reminded of a strange episode in the preceding account of the early days of the marriage:

> One day Winifred heard the strangest scream from the flower-bed under the window of the living room: ah, the strangest scream, like the very soul of the dark past crying aloud. She ran out and saw a long brown snake on the flower-bed, and in its flat mouth the one hind leg of a frog was striving to escape, and screaming its strange, tiny, bellowing scream. She looked at the snake, and from its sullen, flat head it looked at her, obstinately. She gave a cry and it released the frog and slid angrily away.[37]

Is this a proleptic allegory of Winifred's child being injured in the leg through an accident caused by Egbert's carelessness, the 'obstinate' Egbert whom she finally drives away, Egbert who planted the flower bed? If not, it is hard to see what the episode means and why it is given such prominence. Much later in the story Egbert is indeed compared to a snake, but a harmless one:

> As soon as sympathy, like a soft hand, was reached out to touch him, away he swerved, instinctively, as a harmless snake swerves and swerves and swerves away from an outstretched hand.[38]

And in the passage I started with, in this survey of the snake motif, Egbert is the *victim* of a metaphorical snake-bite.

As Frank Kermode has observed[39], the snake was for Lawrence an emblem of corruption—a vital, possibly redemptive corruption. In *The Crown*, that strange, prophetic Bestiary written in the same year as the first 'England, My England', the snake is described as 'the spirit of the great corruptive principle, the festering cold of the marsh. This is how he seems, as we look back. We revolt from him, but we share the same life and tide of life as he.'[40] In the same place we find the identical story of the screaming frog discovered in the jaws of a snake on a flower-bed outside a cottage—obviously the incident had happened to the Lawrences at Greatham. Afterwards, Lawrence says, when the snake had slipped 'sullenly' away:

> We were all white with fear. But why? In the world of twilight as the world of light, one beast shall devour another. The world of corruption has its stages, where the lower shall devour the higher, *ad infinitum*.[41]

Lawrence is saying that we should try to overcome the natural revulsion we feel for the snake and recognize the promise of new life that is in him: 'under the low skies of the far past aeons, he emerged a king out of chaos, a long beam of new life.'[42] In the beast-symbolism of *The Crown* he is contrasted with the vulture, who represents a static, negative kind of corruption. Lawrence was brooding, at this time, on the idea that corruption carried to extremes, the vital kind of corruption represented by the snake, might be the only way for both the individual and civilization at large to achieve rebirth and renewal. 'In the soft and shiny voluptuousness of decay, in the marshy chill heat of reptiles, there is the sign of the Godhead . . . decay, corruption, destruction, breaking down, is the opposite equivalent of creation.'[43] The idea is discussed at some length by Birkin and Ursula in the 'Water-Party' chapter of *Women in Love*, where, as Kermode points out, the same emblems, including the snake and the marsh, are invoked.

It is difficult to see how the uninstructed reader could perceive all this occult doctrine in 'England, My England', but it is perhaps clear enough that Egbert's longing to seek relief or release from his intolerable marital situation in some kind of primitive, instinctual blood-letting is expressed symbolically by associating him with the snakes on the common before it is fulfilled literally by his participation in the Great War. In the corresponding scene in the first version, war has already been declared, there are no references to snakes or the primeval past, and Egbert's motivation is more obvious: 'Egbert as he worked in the garden . . . felt the seethe of the war was with him'[44] rather than feeling 'the seethe of a lost, dark passion in the air.' And in the second version Egbert is much more hesitant about joining in the war when it is declared—a point made by reverting to the flower-metaphor:

> He was a pure-blooded Englishman, perfect in his race, and when he was truly himself he could no more have been aggressive on the score of his Englishness than a rose can be aggressive on the score of its rosiness.[45]

The question for Egbert is not (as it was for most of his generation) one of patriotic duty, but of whether or not to seek his own annihilation:

> And yet, war! Just war! Not right or wrong, but just war itself. Should he join? Should he give himself over to war? The question was in his mind for some weeks. Not because he thought England was right and Germany wrong. Probably Germany was wrong, but he refused to make a choice. Not because he felt inspired. No. But just—war.[46]

We are told that 'What Egbert felt subtly and without question, his father-in-law felt also in a rough, more combative way. Different as the two men were, they were two real Englishmen, and their instincts were almost the same.'[47] Lawrence adds, a little inconsistently, that Godfrey Marshall supported English 'industrialism' against German 'militarism' as the lesser of two evils; but the point has been made that both men dissociated themselves from the patriotic emotion evoked by the title:

> What have I done for you,
>   England my England?
> What is there I would not do,
>   England my own?

> . . . .

> Ever the faith endures,
> England, my England:—
>
> Take and break us: we are yours,
> England my own![48]

'England, my England' was a phrase Lawrence was to invoke again in a famous elegiac passage in *Lady Chatterley's Lover*, where Connie drives through a Midlands landscape, the pastoral beauty and historical landmarks of which have been horribly disfigured by the ugly encroachments of modern industrial 'civilization'. Perhaps this association has encouraged critics to interpret the short story as also being an elegy for England—for example Stephen Spender:

> 'England, My England' is Lawrence's English elegy. Not that he sympathizes much with Egbert. Let the dead bury their dead, is his motto. For probably England is dead. Sometimes Lawrence thinks he is the only Englishman alive. But Egbert is nobler than the other characters in this story because, like Mrs Wilcox in *Howards End*, he lives and dies for a past which he symbolizes. And like Forster's heroine he does not resist death. It is the realization in him of the fate of English consciousness.[49]

This reading has elements of truth, but ignores the narrator's insistence throughout the story that there is something dilettante and superficial about Egbert's cult of the English past ('his old folk songs and Morris dances'[50]); and ignores, also, the very considerable respect that is accorded to Godfrey Marshall, in whom an equally authentic Englishness is combined with an ability to survive in the modern world (the flower/tree imagery enforces this distinction). In familial relationships Godfrey exerts far more power (a power specifically invested with ancient, primitive associations) than Egbert, who is defeated in his marriage long before he falls in battle. So far from being an admirable trait, Egbert's nostalgic cult of 'old England' (which should not be confused with the 'savage', 'primeval' snake-infested common) is a sign of his decadence and impotence. 'A man must find a new expression, give a new value to life, or his women will reject him and he will die,' Lawrence wrote to Catherine Carswell; and his writing of the war-time and post-war period, both fictional and non-fictional, shows him obsessed with these two, linked ideas: the definition of a healthy relationship between the sexes and the apocalyptic-utopian idea of a brave new world being born out of the painful dissolution of the old. Egbert, having (unlike, say, Birkin) no new value to offer, is rejected by Winifred and must die in the Great War which Lawrence was inclined to see as the death-throes of an exhausted culture, and perhaps the birth-pangs of a new one. 'The war is one bout in the terrific, horrible labour, our civilization labouring in child-birth and unable to bring forth.'[51]

Only in this way can we account for the curious tone of the ending of the story—especially the disconcerting lack of pity (conventional emotion of elegy) in the powerful description of Egbert's death—and for the apocalyptic imagery that permeates it. Egbert is doomed as soon as he enlists. 'At the end of the summer he went to Flanders, into action. He seemed already to have gone out of life, beyond the pale of life. He hardly remembered his life any more, being like a man who is going to take a jump from a height, and is only looking to where he must land.'[52] The story moves quickly to its dénouement. Egbert is manning one of three 'machine-guns' (so called by Lawrence, though they appear to be field-guns), behind the front line. 'The country was all pleasant, war had not yet trampled it. Only the air seemed shattered and the land awaiting death.'[53] Mention of gorse, and of Egbert's shirt slit on the shoulders, reminds us of him working at Crockham and brooding on primitive blood-sacrifice, but Egbert's own mind is almost blank: 'So many things go out of consciousness before we come to the end of consciousness.'[54] He mans the guns with brisk efficiency: 'Pure mechanical action at the guns. It left the soul unburdened, brooding in dark nakedness. In the end, the soul is alone. brooding on the face of the uncreated flux, as a bird on a dark sea.'[55]

This last image is very striking because it is not, like the imagery of flowers and trees and snakes, drawn from the realistic context, nor is it, like the earlier Biblical imagery, developed gradually through puns, clichés and progressive shifts of meaning. The image of a bird on a dark sea is remote from the context of an artillery battle, and signals the movement of the discourse into a new register, the extension of the author's imagination into a realm beyond the reach of empirical experience: death itself. Not that Lawrence dispenses with symbolism drawn from the context. Apocalyptic motifs are, for instance, neatly camouflaged in the next paragraph of description:

> Nothing could be seen but the road, and a crucifix knocked slanting and the dark autumnal fields and woods. There appeared three horsemen on a little eminence, very small, on the crest of a ploughed field. They were our own men. Of the enemy, nothing.[56]

The three horsemen presumably correspond to those seen by the author of Revelation before the appearance of the fourth horse, the pale horse with the rider that is Death;[57] for when Egbert finally dies on the last page of the story it is described as a hallucinatory vision of a mounted German soldier: 'What was that? A light! A terrible light! Was it figures? Was it the legs of a horse colossal—colossal above him: huge, huge?'[58]

To return to the earlier point in the story: a shell falls and the explosion makes a 'twig of holly with red berries fall like a gift on to the road below'—a poignant reminder of Egbert's severance from the Marshall family, and of the domestic fate that has brought him to this situation. Two more shells fall and then a third, which mortally wounds Egbert. This shell, by a now familiar rhetorical device, is metaphorically fused with the soul as bird:

into the silence, into the suspense where the soul brooded, finally crashed a
noise and a darkness and a moment's flaming agony and horror. Ah, he had
seen the dark bird flying towards him, flying home this time. In one instant
life and eternity went up in a conflagration of agony, then there was a weight
of darkness.

When faintly something began to struggle in the darkness, a
consciousness of himself, he was aware of a great load and a changing sound.
To have known the moment of death! and to be forced, before dying, to
review it. So, fate, even in death.[59]

In Egbert's last agony his own longing for oblivion is developed into
an apocalyptic vision of civilization itself desperately seeking its own
dissolution; and there can be no doubt that as a character he has been
deprived of all conventional, *dulce-et-decorum-est-pro-patria-mori*
motivation so that he may witness more effectively to the truth of
Lawrence's prophecies:

Death, oh, death! The world all blood, and the blood all writhing with
death. The soul like the tiniest little light out on a dark sea, the sea of blood.
And the light guttering, beating, pulsing in a windless storm, wishing it
could go out, yet unable.

There had been life. There had been Winifred and his children. But the
frail death-agony effort to catch at straws of memory, straws of life from the
past, brought on too great a nausea. No, No! No Winifred, no children. No
world, no people. Better the agony of dissolution ahead than the nausea of
the effort backwards. Better the terrible work should go forward, the
dissolving into the black sea of death, in the extremity of dissolution, than
that there should be any reaching back towards life. To forget! To forget!
Utterly, utterly to forget, in the great forgetting of death. To break the core
and the unit of life, and to lapse out on the great darkness. Only that. To
break the clue and mingle and commingle with the one darkness, without
afterwards or forwards. Let the black sea of death itself solve the problem of
futurity. Let the will of man break and give up.[60]

As Lawrence wrote in *The Crown*: 'the act of death may itself be a
consummation and life may be a state of negation.'[61] In his recognition
of that Egbert achieves a kind of heroism of the spirit, which we feel the
more strongly in the second version of the story because he does not
perform the superficially heroic action of the first (killing the three
German soldiers).

5 Virginia Woolf

In the modernist writers discussed so far we have observed a general tendency to develop (either within the individual work, or from one work to another) from a metonymic (realistic) to a metaphoric (symbolist or mythopoeic) representation of experience. Virginia Woolf exemplifies this tendency very clearly. The essential line of her literary development may be traced through the following novels: *The Voyage Out* (1915), *Jacob's Room* (1922), *Mrs Dalloway* (1925), *To The Lighthouse* (1927) and *The Waves* (1931) (her other books being, most critics agree, diversions, digressions or regressions from this line). And surveying these five novels rapidly in the order in which they were written, flicking the pages, as it were, rapidly before our eyes so that the changes in narrative form are speeded up and 'animated' in the fashion of a child's cartoon book, it is obvious how the structure of the traditional novel, with its rounded characters, logically articulated plot, and solidly specified setting, melts away; how the climaxes of plot are progressively pushed to the margins of the discourse, mentioned in asides and parentheses; how the author's voice, narrating, explaining, guaranteeing, fades away as the discourse locates itself in the minds of characters with limited knowledge and understanding; how the unity and coherence of the narratives comes increasingly to inhere in the repetition of motifs and symbols, while the local texture of the writing becomes more and more densely embroidered with metaphor and simile. The distance in technique between *The Voyage Out* and *The Waves* is almost as great as that between *Dubliners* and *Finnegans Wake*. But although the two writers travelled, formally, in the same general direction, they were driven by very different sensibilities working on very different experience, and Virginia Woolf's metaphorical mode is correspondingly different from Joyce's. It might be said that whereas his writing aspired to the condition of myth, hers aspired to the condition of lyrical poetry.

Essentially her writing does not so much imitate experience as question it. It is no exaggeration to say that all her important books are concerned with the question that opens the third section of *To The Lighthouse*: 'What does it mean, then, what can it all mean?'[1] 'It', of course, is life. And the question of the meaning of life is intimately tied up with the fact of death. For if life is, in itself, held to be good, it is always threatened by death and is therefore (if, like Virginia Woolf, you are an agnostic with no faith in an afterlife) tragic. On the other hand, if life is not held to be good, there is no point in living it and one might as well kill oneself. We hardly commit a critical indecorum by invoking biographical data at this point and remarking that Virginia Woolf's early life was darkened by a series of deaths in her immediate family, especially by the unexpected and premature deaths of her mother, her half-sister Stella and her brother Thoby; that immediately after her mother's death, and intermittently throughout her life, Virginia suffered acutely from depressive mental illness, and that eventually she committed suicide. A shrewd psychoanalyst might deduce as much from an examination of the novels listed above, for they are all explicitly concerned with the question of the 'meaning of life', and all involve the sudden, premature deaths of one or more of the major characters: Rachel Vinrace in *The Voyage Out*, Jacob in *Jacob's Room*, Septimus Smith in *Mrs Dalloway*, Mrs Ramsay and her children Andrew and Prue in *To The Lighthouse*, Percival and Rhoda in *The Waves*.

Either life is meaningless, or death makes it so: Virginia Woolf's fiction is the trace of her efforts to extricate herself from that existential double-bind, to affirm the value of life in the teeth of disappointment and death. Her answer, fragile enough, but delivered with eloquent intensity, was to invoke those privileged moments in personal, subjective experience when the world seems charged with goodness and joy—harmonious, unified and complete. Here is Mrs Ramsay at such a moment, presiding over her dinner table, and planning a match between Lily Briscoe and William Bankes:

> Foolishly, she had set them opposite each other. That could be remedied tomorrow. If it were fine, they should go for a picnic. Everything seemed possible. Everything seemed right. Just now (but this cannot last, she thought, dissociating herself from the moment while they were all talking about boots) just now she had reached security; she hovered like a hawk suspended; like a flag floated in an element of joy which filled every nerve of her body fully and sweetly, not noisily, solemnly rather, for it arose, she thought, looking at them all eating there, from husband and children and friends; all of which rising in this profound stillness (she was helping William Bankes to one very small piece more and peered into the depths of the earthenware pot) seemed now for no special reason to stay there like a smoke, like a fume rising upwards, holding them safe together. Nothing need be said, nothing could be said. There it was all around them. It partook, she felt, carefully helping Mr Bankes to an especially tender piece, of eternity; as she had already felt about something different once before that afternoon; there is a coherence in things, a stability; something, she meant, is immune from change, and shines out (she glanced at the window with its ripple of reflected lights) in the face of the flowing, the fleeting, the spectral, like a ruby; so that again tonight she had the feeling she had had

once today already, of peace, of rest. Of such moments, she thought, the thing is made that remains for ever after. This would remain.[2]

The experience described here has something in common with Joyce's 'epiphanies' ('the sudden "revelation of the whatness of a thing", the moment in which "the soul of the commonest object . . . seems to us radiant" ')[3], with Yeats's images of 'unity of being' and with T. S. Eliot's 'still points' redeemed from time in *Four Quartets*. But in Virginia Woolf the moment is not, as in Joyce, a kind of sacramental transubstantiation of the commonplace achieved by art: though sought by artists in her fiction, the privileged moment is not exclusive to them, and their attempts to fix it in words or paint are generally unsuccessful. Nor is it, as in Yeats and Eliot, attached to a particular metaphysic, guaranteed by Revelation, orthodox or heterodox. Lily Briscoe undoubtedly speaks for the author when she reflects: 'The great revelation had never come. The great revelation perhaps never did come. Instead there were little daily miracles, illuminations, matches struck unexpectedly in the dark.'[4] The privileged moment is, then, transitory and recognized as such by those that experience it ('this cannot last, she thought'), and yet it transcends time: 'It partook . . . of eternity . . . of such moments, she thought, the thing is made that remains for ever after.'

Thus a kind of immortality is asserted and death apparently defeated. But what kind of immortality? What is 'the thing that remains for ever after'? When Mrs Ramsay dies, the memory of this moment dies with her; for although she is as a person remembered with love and sympathy by her family and friends, they do not remember the particular moments that meant so much to her. In fact, at the very instant when Mrs Ramsay is looking fondly at Lily Briscoe and planning to marry her to William Bankes, Lily is consumed with a hopeless passion for Paul Rayley who has just engaged himself to Minta Doyle; and looking back on this meal many years later she remembers only the pain of Paul's rebuff, and the folly of Mrs Ramsay's matchmaking plans. The privileged moment Lily recalls in Part III in connection with Mrs Ramsay, 'which survived, after all these years, complete, so that she dipped into it to refashion her memory of her, and it stayed in the mind almost like a work of art', occurred on the beach with the usually unamiable Charles Tansley— 'Mrs Ramsay bringing them together; Mrs Ramsay saying, "Life, stand still here"; Mrs Ramsay making of the moment something permanent'[5]—a 'little miracle' of which Mrs Ramsay herself was quite unconscious. In short, Virginia Woolf's modernist insistence on the relativity and subjectivity of experience undermines the redeeming power of the privileged moment, because the moment is never shared.

As an answer to the fundamental problems of life and death, then, the privileged moment does not stand up to very close logical scrutiny; but it is intimated, and celebrated, in a cunningly woven web of verbal nuances which deliberately keeps the reader's analytical intelligence at bay. The long quotation above shows the different ways in which the writing accomplishes this feat: the paratactic syntax, adding clause to clause in the loosest fashion, seems perpetually to postpone the moment when the sentence will commit itself to something final (note the preference for semi-colons over full-stops). The parenthetic references to banal events outside consciousness ('It partook, she felt, carefully helping Mr Bankes to a specially tender piece, of eternity') break into the stream of reflection, mitigate the tendency to metaphysical pretentiousness and make the point that the miraculous joy of the moment arises out of the commonplace, not from some transcendental source. And the figurative expressions are dealt out in such profusion, withdrawn and substituted with such rapidity ('like a hawk... like a flag... like a smoke... like a fume... like a ruby') that we take from the passage a hazy, synaesthetic impression rather than any precise image.

Virginia Woolf's mature novels—*Mrs Dalloway, To The Lighthouse* and *The Waves*—are all about sensitive people living from one privileged moment to the next, passing through intervening periods of dissatisfaction, depression and doubt. For this reason, they are essentially plotless. Their endings are false endings, or non-endings, which leave the characters exactly where they have always been, living inside their heads, doomed to oscillate between joy and despair until they die. Virginia Woolf closes each book on an affirmative up-beat— 'For there she was', 'I have had my vision', 'Against you I will fling myself, unvanquished and unyielding, O Death!'—but the cut-off point is essentially arbitrary, and it is clear that if the text were to continue another down-beat must inevitably follow. It is not fortuitous that the presiding symbols of the two later novels—the lighthouse with its pulsing beam, and the waves breaking on the shore—have this same regular, oscillating rhythm, and are susceptible of bearing multiple and contradictory meanings. Arguably this oscillating psychological rhythm makes Virginia Woolf's work ultimately unsatisfying because the affirmation of the value of life so often uttered is never really made to stick. It certainly makes her writing liable to seem monotonous, especially in *The Waves*, where there is no variety in the verbal texture either—each character's consciousness being rendered in interior monologues of uniform style. It is this drastic subordination of *difference* to *similarity* in *The Waves* that makes it the most 'poetic' (or in our terms, metaphoric) of Virginia Woolf's novels. As in *Finnegans Wake*, the boundaries of individual character are dissolved, though it is a mystical impersonality rather than Joyce's mythic polysemy that dissolves them. 'And now I ask, "Who am I?"' Bernard says, in his long, remarkable final monologue:

'I have been talking of Bernard, Neville, Jinny, Susan, Rhoda and Louis. Am I all of them? Am I one and distinct? I do not know. We sat here together. But now Percival is dead, and Rhoda is dead; we are divided; we are not here. Yet I cannot find any obstacle separating us. There is no division between me and them. As I talked I felt "I am you". This difference we make so much of, this identity we so feverishly cherish, was overcome.'[6]

Although *The Waves* was the logical terminus of Virginia Woolf's artistic development, most readers will probably prefer *To The Lighthouse* or *Mrs Dalloway* (as they prefer *Ulysses* to *Finnegans Wake*)—novels in which lyrical intensity is combined with a lively, though distinctively modernist, mimesis of social and personal life.

I propose to examine in more detail the stages by which Virginia Woolf detached her writing from the formal constraints of the traditional novel, up to and including the writing of *Mrs Dalloway*. Her thematic preoccupation with the meaning of life and death was of course there from the beginning. 'And life, what was that?' wonders Rachel Vinrace, the heroine of *The Voyage Out*. 'It was only a light passing over the surface and vanishing as in time she would vanish, though the furniture would remain.'[7] And much later, looking at her fiancé reading as she writes letters, and struck by her ignorance of what is passing through his head and by the gap between her perceptions and what she is writing, she asks herself: 'Would there ever be a time when the world was one and indivisible?'[8]. Just when it looks as if there might be, for her, in her marriage, she is struck down by a fatal illness. The suddenness, the cruel arbitrariness of this death is very powerfully conveyed (it surely had its source in the death of Thoby Stephen) and implies that no affirmation of the value of life that is projected into future time is to be relied upon, because it is at the mercy of death. This ending inverts (as the match between Susan Warrington and Arthur Venning parodies) the endings of nineteenth-century novels in which the union of hero and heroine is an assurance of the possibility of a happy life extended in time and lived out in a world of meaningful social relationships. Indeed, *A Voyage Out* in many ways resembles a well-built Victorian novel the foundations of which are sinking into the morass of modern scepticism, causing the fabric to warp, crack and in places collapse. It has a huge cast of characters, most of them hit off with admirable wit and perception; but whereas the classic nineteenth-century novel accounted for all its characters (however implausibly) in terms of the plot, thus conveying the sense of society as something that was, however corrupt, ultimately intelligible and therefore redeemable, most of Virginia Woolf's characters drift in and out of focus in a curiously random way, and the plot that might unite them into a single pattern never transpires. Since the action takes place on a cruise and in a South American resort town, the random collision of disparate characters is 'realistic' enough, but what they are all doing in the book, apart from demonstrating the infinite variety of human nature, is not easy to say, since for a large part of the time they are not even under the observation of the heroine whose quest for the meaning of life is the ostensible subject of the novel. Chapter Nine, set in the hotel at San Marina, comes I think as a surprise to the reader, introducing, as it does, a whole crowd of new characters at a fairly late stage of the novel; and the manner of their introduction is interesting. The authorial narrator moves invisibly from one room to the next, fascinated by the contiguity of their forty or fifty varied inhabitants, whose interests, desires, and fears are totally disparate. Terence Hewet, Rachel's fiancé and an aspirant novelist, is similarly fascinated and baffled by the same phenomenon: 'I've often walked along the streets where people live all in a row, and one house is exactly like another house, and wondered what on earth the women were doing inside.'[9] The narrative of *The Voyage Out*, then, is forwarded by contiguity in the sense that it pursues a chain of events, a series of encounters between people brought into chance contact, but for the most part these contiguities resist any attempt at integration into a world 'one and indivisible'.

Virginia Woolf's critics usually describe *Jacob's Room* as her first truly experimental novel, which it was. They also describe it as experimenting with the stream of consciousness, which it hardly does to any significant extent, most of the text being authorial narration or dramatic presentation. Virginia Woolf left a vivid record of the book's genesis in her diary:

> . . . having this afternoon arrived at some idea of a new form for a new novel. Suppose one thing should open out of another—as in an unwritten novel—only not for 10 pages but 200 or so—doesn't that give the looseness and lightness I want; doesn't that get closer and yet keep form and speed, and enclose everything, everything? My doubt is how far it will enclose the human heart—Am I sufficiently mistress of my dialogue to net it there? For I figure that the approach will be entirely different this time: no scaffolding; scarcely a brick to be seen; all crepuscular, but the heart, the passion, humour, everything as bright as fire in the mist.[10]

The phrase 'an unwritten novel' refers to a short story of that title first published in *The London Mercury* in July of the same year (1920). In it, the narrator scrutinizes a woman seated opposite her in a railway carriage and tries to compose a novel about her, struggling to extract an imaginative truth from the clues of her appearance and deportment (the metonymic or synecdochic indices of character in realistic fiction). At the end of the journey the woman, whom the narrator has cast as a repressed spinster, is met by her son, and the fiction collapses:

> Well, my world's done for! What do I stand on? What do I know? That's not Minnie. There never was Moggridge. Who am I? Life's bare as a bone.[11]

This metafictional vein is continued, less archly, in *Jacob's Room*. The novel is really about the difficulty of writing a novel, of truly representing a person in the written word: 'It is thus that we live, they say, driven by an unseizable force. They say that novelists never catch it.'[12] Virginia Woolf does not deny the failure, but affirms the novelist's compulsion to keep trying:

> But though all this may very well be true—so Jacob thought and spoke—so he crossed his legs—filled his pipe—sipped his whisky, and once looked at his pocket-book, rumpling his hair as he did so, there remains over something which can never be conveyed to a second person save by Jacob himself. Moreover, part of this is not Jacob but Richard Bonamy—the room; the market carts; the hour; the very moment of history. . . . Even the exact words get the wrong accent on them. But something is always impelling one to hum vibrating, like the hawk moth, at the mouth of the cavern of mystery, endowing Jacob Flanders with all sorts of qualities he had not got at all—for though, certainly, he sat talking to Bonamy, half of what he said was too dull to repeat; much unintelligible (about unknown people and Parliament); what remains is mostly a matter of guess work. Yet over him we hang vibrating.[13]

The author's omniscience is, then, strictly limited. She rarely enters Jacob's mind to report what he is thinking, and when she does so her interpretation of his thoughts is uncertain. In interpreting his external behaviour she is little wiser than his friends and family: 'But whether this is the right interpretation of Jacob's gloom as he sat naked, in the sun, looking at the Land's End, it is impossible to say; for he never spoke a word. Timmy sometimes wondered (only for a second) whether his people bothered him. . . .'[14] Although, as always with Virginia Woolf, there is a great deal of metaphor and simile in the local texture of the writing, structurally *Jacob's Room* belongs in the metonymic category. Its experimentalism is all performed on the chain of combination—the chain of contiguous events that is Jacob's life—and consists mainly in cutting away huge sections of this chain and viewing the remainder from odd angles and perspectives. As readers we are rushed from one brief, fragmentary scene to the next ('one thing open[ing] out of another', as Virginia Woolf noted in her diary) without explanation or preparation. We come into ongoing coversations, hear a few scraps of dialogue and try to guess what is being talked about, before we are whisked on to another scene. Essentially *Jacob's Room* is a conventional *Bildungsroman* speeded up and subjected to drastic 'cutting' of a cinematic kind. Its experimentalism is a technique of radical and stylish *deletion* ('no scaffolding, scarcely a brick to be seen'), and deletion, as I argued earlier, is the operation by which metonymic devices are produced. The most daring deletion of all is Jacob's death in the Great War. This death, which is proleptically figured in his surname, Flanders (a metaphoric device, this, a kind of pun, but a discreet one) is crucial to *Jacob's Room* because it invests with a deep pathos the self-confessed failure of the novelist (and of the other characters) to understand Jacob or penetrate the mystery of his being, expressing the baffled grief of all those whose sons, brothers and lovers were killed before they were really known. Yet this death is not described, or even referred to directly. It is represented in the most oblique way, by metonymy and synecdoche—the sound of guns across the sea[15] and Jacob's empty room and empty shoes:

> Listless is the air in an empty room, just swelling the curtains; the flowers in the jar shift. One fibre in the wicker armchair creaks, though no one sits there.
>
> Bonamy crossed to the window, Pickford's van swung down the street. The omnibuses were locked together at Mudie's corner. Engines throbbed, and carters, jamming the brakes down, pulled their horses up sharp. A harsh and unhappy voice cried something unintelligible. And then suddenly all the leaves seemed to raise themselves.
>
> 'Jacob! Jacob!' cried Bonamy, standing by the window. The leaves sank down again.
>
> 'Such confusion everywhere!' exclaimed Betty Flanders, bursting open the bedroom door.
>
> Bonamy turned away from the window.
>
> 'What am I to do with these, Mr Bonamy?'
>
> She held out a pair of Jacob's old shoes.[16]

This is a beautifully judged conclusion, poignant, without the least sentimentality. But one can't help feeling that elsewhere in the novel Virginia Woolf used the technique of deletion as a means of evasion as well as expression—evasion of things she couldn't really handle. Sex, for instance: the stylish indirection with which Jacob's sexual life is represented doesn't quite conceal the essentially sentimental stereotypes to which it conforms. And the 'new form' she heralded in her diary did not take her any further than the form of *The Voyage Out* in vindicating life against death. The next, decisive step was taken with *Mrs Dalloway*.

Virginia Woolf had an interesting correspondence about aesthetics with the painter Jacques Raverat at the time when she was working on this novel. He suggested that writing, as an artistic medium, was limited by being 'essentially linear', unable therefore to render the complex multiplicity of a mental event, which he compared to a pebble cast into a pond, 'splashes in the outer air in every direction. and under the surface waves that follow one another into forgotten corners.'[17] Virginia Woolf replied that it was precisely her aim to go beyond 'the formal railway line of the sentence' and to disregard the 'falsity of the past (by which I mean Bennett, Galsworthy and so on) . . . people don't and never did think or feel in that way; but all over the place, in your way.'[18] As Quentin Bell remarks, 'it is possible to find in *Mrs Dalloway* an attempt of this nature.'[19] In our terms, the novel marks the transition in Virginia Woolf's writing from the metonymic to the metaphoric mode. Instead of lineality, simultaneity ('If *Jacob's Room* shows cinematic cutting and fading, *Mrs Dalloway* borrows from montage and superimposed frames,' Carl Woodring has shrewdly commented[20]). Instead of different people in the same place at the same time (e.g. the hotel at Santa Marina) different people in different places at the same time, (time marked by the chimes of Big Ben) perhaps looking at the same thing (the aeroplane in the sky). Instead of a life, or a voyage, a single day. Instead of authorial narration, the stream of consciousness in which events (i.e. thoughts) follow each other on the principle of similarity as much as contiguity—a June morning in Westminster, for instance, reminding Clarissa of mornings in her youth because a simile of children on a beach seems to her equally applicable to both:

> And then, thought Clarissa Dalloway, what a morning—fresh as if issued to children on a beach.
>   What a lark! What a plunge! For so it had always seemed to her when, with a little squeak of the hinges, which she could hear now, she had burst open the French windows and plunged at Bourton into the open air. How fresh, how calm, stiller than this of course, the air was in the early morning; like the flap of a wave; the kiss of a wave; . .[21]

Joyce, no doubt, had shown Virginia Woolf the way, though, as I observed earlier, there is no equivalent in *Mrs Dalloway* to the mythical subtext of *Ulysses*. Structurally, Virginia Woolf's novel resembles the 'Wandering Rocks' episode of *Ulysses*, in which a variety of Dublin characters are observed perambulating the city at the same time, thinking their own thoughts, crossing each other's paths, or linked by the throwaway leaflet, 'Elijah Comes' that is floating past them down the Liffey.

Virginia Woolf's abandonment of a linear narrative structure and her plunge into the stream of consciousness can be related readily enough to the avant-garde *Zeitgeist*. But it was also related to her personal concern with testing the meaning of life against the fact of death; for the privileged moment which she was to offer as a kind of answer to the problem could be only given proper emphasis in a novel of the new kind, in which the causal or chronological ordering of events was subordinated to rendering the impression they made on the individual consciousness, showing, in Lily Briscoe's words, 'how life, from being made up of separate little incidents which one lived one by one, became curled and whole like a wave which bore one up with it and threw one down with it, there, with a dash on the beach.'[22] Going out to order flowers for her party, Mrs Dalloway feels that life is good. She loves 'life; London; this moment of June'.[23] Walking towards Bond Street she is troubled by the thought of death: 'did it matter that she must inevitably cease completely: all this must go on without her;'[24] but consoles herself with a vague myth of immortality: 'somehow in the streets of London, on the ebb and flow of things, here, there, she survived, Peter survived, lived in each other, she being part, she was positive, of the trees at home;. . . part of people she had never

met; being laid out like a mist between the people she knew best . . .'[25]
In fact, it is not so much the prospect of her own physical death that
disturbs Clarissa as the death-in-life that overcomes her at moments of
negativity, hatred and self-loathing, and that (we infer later) has
tempted her to suicide. These moments are antithetical to the
privileged moments of joy and love by which she lives, and both can be
provoked by the most trivial stimuli. Coming back to her house from
shopping, for instance, she feels blessed:

> It was her life, and, bending her head over the hall table, she bowed beneath
> the influence, felt blessed and purified, saying to herself, as she took the pad
> with the telephone message on it, how moments like this are buds on the tree
> of life . . .[26]

But when the message proves to be one that injures her vanity and
separates her from her husband (Lady Bruton has asked him to lunch
without her) her love of life drains away and she feels herself 'suddenly
shrivelled, aged, breastless'.[27] She goes up to her room ('There was an
emptiness about the heart; an attic room') where she usually sleeps (or
rather reads, late into the night) apart from her husband. This leads to
a depressed meditation on her sexual frigidity which in turn yields to a
reviving memory of privileged moments when, through intimacy with
other women, she obtained an insight into erotic rapture:

> Only for a moment; but it was enough. It was a sudden revelation, a tinge
> like a blush which one tried to check and then, as it spread, one yielded to its
> expansion, and rushed to the farthest verge and there quivered and felt the
> world come closer, swollen with some astonishing significance, some
> pressure of rapture, which split its thin skin and gushed and poured with an
> extraordinary alleviation over the cracks and sores. Then for that moment,
> she had seen an illumination; a match burning in a crocus; an inner meaning
> almost expressed. But the close withdrew; the hard softened. It was over—
> the moment.[28]

The psychological rhythm of Peter Walsh is very similar, alternating
between love and aggression, optimism and pessimism, life and death.

> As a cloud crosses the sun, silence falls on London; and falls on the mind.
> Effort ceases, time flaps on the mast. There we stop; there we stand. Rigid,
> the skeleton of habit alone upholds the human frame. Where there is
> nothing, Peter Walsh said to himself; feeling hollowed out, utterly empty
> within. Clarissa refused me, he thought. He stood there thinking, Clarissa
> refused me.
>
> Ah, said St Margaret's, like a hostess who comes into her drawing room
> on the very stroke of the hour and finds her guests there already. I am not
> late . . .—like Clarissa herself, thought Peter Walsh, coming downstairs on
> the stroke of the hour in white. It is Clarissa herself, he thought, with a
> deep emotion, and an extraordinary clear, yet puzzling recollection
> of her, as if this bell had come into the room years ago, where they sat

at some moment of great intimacy, and had gone from one to the other and had left, like a bee with honey, laden with the moment. But what room? What moment? And why had he been so profoundly happy when the clock was striking? Then, as the sound of St Margaret's languished, he thought, she had been ill, and the sound expressed languor and suffering. It was her heart, he remembered; and the sudden loudness of the final stroke tolled for death that surprised in the midst of life, Clarissa falling where she stood, in her drawing room. No! No! he cried. She is not dead! I am not old, he cried, and marched up Whitehall, as if there rolled down to him, vigorous, unending, his future.[29]

Septimus Smith, however, has decided that life is not worth living. Traumatized by the horrors of the Great War, he sees the world as an evil place from which he is anxious to escape, and he does so by committing suicide. Through the coincidence of his consultant Sir William Bradshaw's being a guest at Clarissa's party that evening (it is the only vestige of 'plot' in the novel), this stranger's death comes to her attention:

> A young man had killed himself. And they talked of it at her party—the Bradshaws talked of death. He had killed himself—but how? . . . He had thrown himself from a window . . . She had once flung a shilling into the Serpentine, never anything more. But he had flung it away. They went on living . . . They (all day she had been thinking of Bourton, of Peter, of Sally), they would grow old. A thing there was that mattered; a thing, wreathed about with chatter, defaced, obscured in her own life, let drop every day in corruption, lies, chatter. This he had preserved. Death was defiance. Death was an attempt to communicate, people feeling the impossibility of reaching the centre which, mystically, evaded them; closeness drew apart; rapture faded; one was alone. There was an embrace in death.
>
> But this young man who had killed himself—had he plunged holding his treasure? 'If it were now to die, 'twere now to be most happy,' she had said to herself once, coming down, in white.[30]

It will be noted that this passage echoes words and ideas in the two long quotations preceding: the moments of 'close' intimacy, of rapture, that Clarissa has fleetingly experienced with other women, and Peter's memory of Clarissa coming downstairs in a white dress. Peter had then a vision of Clarissa 'falling dead where she stood in her drawing room'. But it is Septimus who, in a sense, dies in her drawing room ('"A young man had killed himself." Oh! thought Clarissa, in the middle of my party, here's death')[31] And Clarissa feels that Septimus has in a sense *died in her place*. For she has felt the same terror of life ('She had felt it only this morning . . . the terror; the overwhelming incapacity, one's parents giving it into one's hands, this life, to be lived to the end . . . there was in the depths of her heart an awful fear . . .') but she has been sufficiently protected, especially by her husband, from seeking the final remedy. 'She had escaped. But that young man had killed himself.' Paradoxically she feels her survival as 'Somehow . . . her disaster—her disgrace. It was her punishment to see sink here a man, there a woman, in this profound darkness, and she forced to stand here in her evening dress. She had schemed, she had pilfered. She was never wholly admirable.'[32] Thus Clarissa accepts her own failure, and acquires a new tranquility and peace. 'Odd, incredible, she had never been so happy. Nothing could be slow enough, nothing last too long.'[33] Yet at the same time 'she felt somehow very like him—the young man who had killed himself. She felt glad that he had done it, thrown it away while they went on living.'[34] This is the real climax of the novel: a moment of perceived similarity and spiritual substitution. And, as we know, it had an exact analogue in the genesis of the novel, for in Virginia Woolf's original design there was no Septimus character, and Clarissa was 'to kill herself, or perhaps merely to die at the end of the party'.[35]

6   In the Thirties

He went out into Oxford Street: there was no hurry now: nothing to be done until he saw Lord Benditch. He walked, enjoying the sense of unreality—the shop windows full of goods, no ruined houses anywhere, women going into Buzzard's for coffee. It was like one of his own dreams of peace. He stopped in front of a bookshop and stared in—people had time to read books—new books. There was one called *A Lady-in-Waiting at the Court of King Edward*, with a photograph on the paper jacket of a stout woman in white silk with ostrich feathers. It was incredible. And there was *Safari Days*, with a man in a sun helmet standing on a dead lioness. What a country, he thought again with affection. He went on. He couldn't help noticing how well clothed everybody was. A pale winter sun shone and the scarlet buses stood motionless all down Oxford Street: there was a traffic block. What a mark, he thought, for enemy planes. It was always about this time that they came over. But the sky was empty—or nearly empty. One winking, glittering little plane turned and dived on the pale clear sky, drawing in little puffy clouds, a slogan: 'Keep warm with Ovo.' He reached Bloomsbury—it occurred to him that he had spent a very quiet morning: it was almost as if his infection had met a match in this peaceful and preoccupied city.[1]

This passage from Graham Greene's *The Confidential Agent* (1939) contains within it a parodic allusion to Virginia Woolf. The traffic jam in the West End, the sky-writing aeroplane, are details taken from *Mrs Dalloway*, and the very structure of some sentences imitates Virginia Woolf's characteristic cadences ('What a mark, he thought, for enemy planes.'). But the centre of consciousness in Greene's passage is a visitor from a European country (not named, but obviously modelled on Spain) in the throes of civil war, and what seemed reassuringly normal in the London scene to Clarissa Dalloway seems to him extraordinary. Looked at in the perspective that he is familiar with, the red buses are potential bombing targets, and the single aeroplane in the sky is chiefly notable for its innocuousness. England seemed sunk in a bourgeois dream of peacefulness and stability. The character, 'D', feels its appeal, but judges it to be ultimately a dangerous illusion, hiding political tensions and injustices that are being openly fought over in his own country. The Bloomsbury he is walking towards is not Virginia Woolf's home ground, a region of high culture and discreetly unconventional *mores*, but a Bloomsbury of disconsolate foreigners and seedy hotels, in one of which D's political collaborators are planning to double-cross him, and where his only ally is the pathetic fourteen-year-old chambermaid, Else, whose best prospect of escape from drudgery is to become a prostitute's maid:

> Fourteen was a dreadfully early age at which to know so much and be so powerless. If this was civilization—the crowded prosperous streets, the women trooping in for coffee at Buzzards, the lady-in-waiting at King Edward's court, and the sinking, drowning child—he preferred barbarity, the bombed streets and the food queues: a child there had nothing worse to look forward to than death.[2]

The preference expressed here for 'barbarity' over 'civilization' strikes a characteristically Greeneian note of gloomy antihumanism, one which he sounded most emphatically in his African travel book *Journey Without Maps* (1936). But Greene was certainly not alone in thinking that there was something unreal about the surface tranquillity of English life in the 1930s. Reality, the young writers of the period felt, was elsewhere—especially in Germany or Spain—and was creeping upon England in the form of impending war. George Orwell's heroes can imagine as easily as D the English sky filled with bombing planes—and do so with a certain apocalyptic relish, a disgust with a modern 'civilization' and its fruits, which is not so very different from Greene's. Consider Gordon Comstock, for instance, in *Keep the Aspidistra Flying* (1936), enraged and nauseated by advertisements, especially one for Bovex ('Corner Table enjoys his meal with Bovex'):

> The sense of disintegration, of decay, that is endemic in our time, was strong upon him. Somehow it was mixed up with the ad-posters opposite. He looked now with more seeing eyes at those grinning yard-wide faces. After all, there was more there than mere silliness, greed and vulgarity. Corner Table grins at you, seemingly optimistic, with a flash of false teeth. But what is behind the grin? Desolation, emptiness, prophecies of doom. For can you not see, if you know how to look, that behind that slick self-satisfaction, that tittering, fat-bellied triviality, there is nothing but a frightful emptiness, a secret despair? The great death wish of the modern world. Suicide pacts.

Heads stuck in gas ovens in lonely maisonettes. French letters and Amen pills. And the reverberations of future wars. Enemy aeroplanes flying over London; the deep threatening hum of the propellers, the shattering thunder of bombs. It is all written in Corner Table's face.[3]

Although Orwell, consistent with his own humanist convictions, makes his hero ultimately renounce this alienated state of mind, the conversion is unconvincing and certainly lacks the rhetorical force of the earlier despair. A later hero, George Bowling, maintains his pessimism to the end:

It's all going to happen. All the things you've got at the back of your mind, the things you're terrified of, the things that you tell yourself are just a nightmare or only happen in foreign countries. The bombs, the food-queues, the rubber truncheons, the barbed wire, the coloured shirts, the slogans, the enormous faces, the machine-guns squirting out of bedroom windows.[4]

We have already glanced, in Part One, at the shift in literary taste and literary aims that characterized the new writers of the 1930s: their attacks on the obscurity, allusiveness and élitism of the modernist-symbolist tradition, and their call for a more politically aware and openly communicative approach to the practice of writing. 'Realism' came back into favour. Stephen Spender published a pamphlet called *The New Realism* in 1939, in which he said that:

there is a tendency for artists today to turn outwards to reality, because the phase of experimenting in form has proved sterile. If you like, the artist is simply in search of inspiration, having discovered that inspiration depends on there being some common ground of understanding between him and his audience about the nature of reality, and on a demand from that audience for what he creates.[5]

The reversal of modernist assumptions about art could scarcely be more clearly stated. In 1937 Spender, with Storm Jameson and Arthur Calder-Marshall, had founded a left-wing monthly review called *Fact*. It was short lived, but the title was symptomatic of a general appetite for and reliance upon empirical fact among literary intellectuals in the 1930s. It was the decade of the Left Book Club ('built on documents and the proposition that facts were knowledge'[6]) and of Mass Observation, an experiment in amateur sociology which had thousands of people all over the country writing reports of everything they saw and experienced in their ordinary lives on one day in every month (Graham Greene ingeniously introduces a Mass Observer into *The Confidential Agent* to incriminate the murderers of Else). History was no longer a nightmare from which the writer was struggling to awake but an enterprise in which he was keen to participate ('history forming in our hands' as John Cornford wrote)[7] and imaginative literature tended to model itself on historical types of discourse—the autobiography, the eye-witness account, the journal. *Journey to a War, Letters from Iceland, The Road to Wigan Pier, Journey Without Maps, Autumn Journal*, 'Berlin Diary', are some characteristic titles of the period. The result was the formation of a very distinctive and homogeneous period-style, or *écriture*, underlying the surface idiosyncracies of personal styles. In our terms there was a pronounced swing back from the metaphoric to the metonymic pole of literary discourse. One obvious trace of this can be seen in the quotations from Greene and Orwell above: the use of synecdochic detail to evoke a scene and to symbolise an abstraction at the same time. In the second quotation from *The Confidential Agent* Greene recapitulates in a condensed form details from his own previous descriptions—details which are now made to 'stand for' two contrasting cultural and political situations. Orwell uses a similar technique: 'Corner Table' (itself a metonymic expression) stands for a whole debased universe of discourse, the money-world of a capitalist class-society—and triggers in the observer's imagination a montage of images of modern death, spiritual and physical. The montage is metonymic, not metaphorical, for the various items in it belong to the same general context of modern urban life. The same is true of George Bowling's prophecy of totalitarian terror engulfing England: it is like a newsreel, cutting from one representative scene or close-up to another.

It is interesting to compare *Coming Up For Air* with *A la Recherche du Temps Perdu*. George Bowling's reminiscent evocation of his past is triggered (as Marcel's memory is often triggered) by a chance similarity: a newspaper headline, 'KING ZOG'S WEDDING POSTPONED' revives an echo of Og the king of Bashar in the psalm and transports George mentally back to the church services he attended as a child. But whereas Proust's evocations of the past are drenched in metaphor, George's are catalogues of literal facts, with little or no figurative elaboration:

> How it came back to me! That peculiar feeling—it was only a feeling, you couldn't describe it as an activity—that we used to call 'Church'. The sweet corpsy smell, the rustle of Sunday dresses, the wheeze of the organ and the roaring voices, the spot of light from the hole in the window creeping slowly up the nave.[8]

The same metonymic technique is used throughout the book. Boyhood, for instance, is evoked thus:

> It's a kind of strong, rank feeling, a feeling of knowing everything and fearing nothing, and it's all bound up with breaking rules and killing things. The white dusty roads, the hot sweaty feeling of one's clothes, the smell of fennel and wild peppermint, the dirty words, the sour stink of the rubbish dump, the taste of fizzy lemonade and the gas that made one belch, the stamping on the young birds, the feel of the fish straining on the line—it was all part of it.[9]

Obviously one of the reasons for Orwell's avoidance of metaphor is that he is using as his narrator an 'ordinary' sort of man to whom any fine writing of the Proustian kind would be quite inappropriate—'It's not that I'm trying to put across any of that poetry of childhood stuff' George assures us, 'I know that's all baloney.'[10] The choice of such a narrator, and the deliberate acceptance of the stylistic limitations entailed, is deeply characteristic of the period.

There *is* in fact a mythopoeic, metaphorical level in *Coming Up For Air*, but it is very thoroughly buried under the ordinary prosaic surface. As a child, George tells us, he had a passion for fishing, a pursuit which for him symbolizes the healthier state of culture and society in those pre-World-War-I days: 'fishing is somehow typical of that civilization'[11]. In the neglected garden of the local mansion, Binfield House, the young George discovered a pool filled with carp of prodigious size:

> It was a wonderful secret for a boy to have. There was the dark pool hidden away in the woods and the monstrous fish sailing round it—fish that had never been fished for and would grab the first bait you offered them. . . . But as it happened I never went back. One never does go back. . . . Almost immediately afterwards something turned up to prevent me, but if it hadn't been that it would have been something else. It's the way things happen.[12]

'The way things happen' sums up the rueful, shrugging, stoical pessimism of George Bowling's (and Orwell's?) attitude to life, one that the realistic novel is well adapted to express: life as a sequence of accidents, a plot without a Providence directing it, a chain of local cause-and-effect, the general pattern of which can only be seen in retrospect, when it is too late to do anything about it. Four years later George takes his girl friend into the grounds of Binfield House:

> Now I was so near, it seemed a pity not to go down to the other pool and have a look at the big carp. I felt I'd kick myself afterwards if I missed the chance, in fact I couldn't think why I hadn't been back before. I actually started wandering along the bank in that direction, and then when I'd gone about ten yards I turned back. It meant crashing your way through a kind of jungle of brambles and rotten brushwood, and I was dressed up in my Sunday best. Dark-grey suit, bowler hat, button boots, and a collar that almost cut my ears off. That was how people dressed for Sunday afternoon walks in those days. And I wanted Elsie very badly.[13]

George returns to Elsie and they have sex for the first time. 'So that was that. The big carp faded out of my mind again, and in fact for years afterwards I hardly thought about them.' When he goes back to Lower Binfield some twenty-five years later, hopefully carrying a newly purchased fishing rod, he finds that the grounds of the old house have been turned into a middle-class housing estate and that the carp pond has become a rubbish tip. 'I'd learned the lesson all right. Fat men of forty-five can't go fishing. That kind of fishing doesn't happen any longer, it's just a dream, there'll be no more fishing this side of the grave.'[14]

Behind this story there is detectable the faint outline of the Edenic myth: the carp-filled pool in the heart of the wilderness is a kind of Paradise, sacred and innocent, from which the hero is expelled by a double fall into social conformity (the Sunday best) and sexuality (Elsie), a Paradise which (since there is no Redemption in the Orwellian world) he is unable to regain. But the magical-mythical associations of fish and fishing (which Eliot, for example, exploits in 'The Waste Land') are not invoked. On the contrary, George attributes historical, not mythical connotations to fishing—'the very idea of sitting all day under a willow tree beside a quiet pool . . . belongs to the time before the war, before the radio, before aeroplanes, before Hitler'—and finds his poetry in the mere denotative names of fish:

> There's a kind of peacefulness even in the names of English coarse fish. Roach, rudd, dace, bleak, barbel, bream, gudgeon, pike, chub, tench. They're solid kind of names.[15]

I compared George Bowling's nightmare visions of the totalitarian future to a newsreel. Film (a metonymic mode in Jakobson's scheme) was a major source of inspiration for many of the 1930s writers. It was a period in which British documentary film-makers achieved great distinction, notably in the work of John Grierson's GPO Film Unit, and in an issue of *Fact* devoted to the theory of revolutionary writing, Storm Jameson explicitly recommended documentary writers to study the film medium:

> Perhaps the nearest equivalent of what is wanted exists already in another form in the documentary film. As the photographer does, so must the writer keep himself out of the picture while working ceaselessly to present the *fact* from a striking (poignant, ironic, penetrating, significant) angle.[16]

Perhaps Christopher Isherwood was thinking of snapshots rather than moving pictures when he compared his stance as narrator to a camera—'I am a camera with its shutter open, quite passive, recording, not thinking'—[17] but in his lightly fictionalized autobiography, *Lions and Shadows* (1938), he makes quite clear how deeply influenced he was, as a writer, by film—and incidentally confirms the close affinity between cinematic and literary realism:

> I had always been fascinated by films . . . I was a born film fan. Chalmers [Edward Upward] was inclined to laugh at my indiscriminate appetite for anything and everything shown on a screen. . . . I was, and still am, end-lessly interested in the outward appearance of people, their infinitely various ways of eating a sausage, opening a paper parcel, lighting a cigarette. The cinema puts people under a microscope. You can stare at them, you can examine them as though they were insects. . . . Viewed from this standpoint, the

stupidest film may be full of interesting revelations about the tempo and dynamics of everyday life: you see how actions look in relation to each other; how much space they occupy and how much time . . . if you are a novelist and want to watch your scene taking place visibly before you, it is simplest to project it on to an imaginary screen. A practised cinema-goer will be able to do this quite easily.[18]

There are two aspects to the connection Isherwood makes here between film and novel. One is the use of metonymic and synecdochic detail (detail of appearance, behaviour, dress, possessions etc.) as a way of identifying and defining character. One thinks, for instance, in Isherwood's own work, of Mr Norris's wig in *Mr Norris Changes Trains* (1935) and Sally Bowles's green-painted finger-nails ('a colour unfortunately chosen, for it called attention to her hands, which were much stained by cigarette smoking and dirty as a little girl's').[19] This kind of selective detail is, as we have seen, a staple device of realism and predates the motion-picture camera, but it is used by the writers of the 1930s with an economy and visual flair developed by their acquaintance with the cinema—and perhaps by the decade's enthusiasm for sociological rapportage. When Graham Greene's D evades pursuit by breaking into a basement flat in central London, his eyes pan round the room to note the furnishings from which the character of the occupier is confidently deduced:

> a divan covered with an art needlework counterpane; blue-and-orange cushions; a gas fire. He took it quickly in to the home-made watercolours on the walls and the radio set by the dressing-table. It spoke to him of an unmarried ageing woman with few interests.[20]

This woman never appears in the novel, but her character, and the context of furnishings from which it is inferred, contribute to the subsequent development of the story in a way which, if we follow it, illustrates the second aspect of Isherwood's comment—the cinematic construction of scene.

D breaks into the flat a second time, bringing with him, at gunpoint, the agent K who has double-crossed him and who has been partly responsible for the murder of Else. D intends to execute summary justice by shooting K, but has some difficulty in screwing himself up to do the deed. K frantically appeals to context:

> 'This is England!' the little man shrieked as if he wanted to convince himself. . . . Certainly it was England—England was the divan, the waste paper basket made out of old flower prints, the framed Speed map and the cushions: the alien atmosphere plucked at D's sleeve, urged him to desist. He said furiously, 'Get off that divan.'[21]

D forces K into the bathroom, shuts his eyes and pulls the trigger, missing his target by a foot. There is a ring at the front door, D shuts the bathroom door and goes to answer the bell. On the previous occasion when he broke into the flat a policeman had called, so we expect that the caller at this inopportune moment is another policeman. It is in fact D's girl, Rose: he had given her the address of his hideaway, but forgotten that he had done so (so have we). D tells Rose that he tried to shoot K but failed. When he opens the bathroom door, however, K pitches forward into the room—dead from heart failure. They lay him out on the divan and there is another knock on the door. This time it is a young man called Fortescue, a neighbour. D and Rose pretend that they are friends of the flat's rightful occupier, a Miss Glover, who has loaned them the place for a party and that K is drunk. Given the character of Miss Glover and the absence of any signs of a party such as bottles and glasses, this is a highly implausible story, but Fortescue, though puzzled, is too innocent to guess the truth. 'His young-old face was like a wide white screen on which you could project only selected and well-censored films for the family circle. . . . They watched him climbing up the area steps into the safe familiar reassuring dark. At the top he turned and waved his hand to them, tentatively.'[22] This sequence, as they say in the trade, 'shoots itself'. All the dynamics of its narrative interest—the suspense, the surprise, the irony—are highly cinematic, generated and expressed through contiguities of space and time: doors opening on the unexpected, crisis following crisis without respite or relaxation.

Graham Greene was himself a professional film critic in the 1930s, and the cinematic quality of his writing has often been commented upon. Richard Hoggart, for instance, observes of *The Power and the Glory*:

> Throughout, the eye shifts constantly, without explanatory links. In the first paragraph the solitary figure of Mr Tench is picked up crossing the hot deserted square; a few vultures look down at him; he tosses something off the road at them and one rises; with it goes the camera and introduces us to the town, the river, the sea.[23]

There are, of course, purely verbal ironies in the opening paragraph of *The Power and the Glory* (e.g. 'over the tiny plaza, over the bust of an ex-president, ex-general, ex-human being') for which it would be difficult to find visual equivalents. But the general strategy of the description, the kind of spatial relationships it establishes between the human figure and his environment, and in particular the way the focus of the description, following the flight of the vulture, pulls up and away to widen our perspective, is indeed all very cinematic in feeling. As Hoggart observes, 'Greene can assume an audience familiar with unusual camera angles and quick fadings in and out, and uses both with great skill.'[24]

Verse in the 1930s exhibited the same tendency as narrative prose to rely heavily on metonymic and synecdochic devices. The structure of

Auden's 'Spain', for example, a classic example of its period, is composed of three contrasting catalogues representing, respectively, the historical past in which civilization painfully evolved:

> Yesterday the assessment of insurance by cards
> The divination of water; yesterday the invention
>   Of cartwheels and clocks, the taming of
> Horses. Yesterday the bustling world of the navigators

—the utopian future that will follow a successful revolution:

> Tomorrow the rediscovery of romantic love
> The photographing of ravens; all the fun under
>   Liberty's masterful shadow;
> Tomorrow the hour of the pageant-master and the musician

—and the present, with its commitment to 'struggle'

> Today the deliberate increase in the chances of death,
> The conscious acceptance of guilt in the necessary murder;
>   Today the expending of powers
> On the flat ephemeral pamphlet and the boring meeting.[25]

This last stanza provoked a famous attack from George Orwell:

> The. . . . stanza is intended as a sort of thumbnail sketch of a day in the life of a 'good party man'. In the morning a couple of political murders, a ten-minute interlude to stifle 'bourgeois' remorse, and then a hurried luncheon and a busy afternoon and evening chalking walls and distributing leaflets. All very edifying. But notice the phrase 'necessary murder'. It could only be written by someone to whom murder is at most a *word*. Personally I would not speak so lightly of murder. It so happens that I have seen the bodies of a number of murdered men. . . . Therefore I have some conception of what murder means—the terror, the hatred, the howling relatives, the post-mortems, the blood, the smells.[26]

Orwell's rebuke was deserved and Auden acknowledged as much by subsequently revising the stanza (to read, 'the *inevitable* increase in the chances of death' and 'the *fact* of murder') and eventually repudiated the entire poem. What is interesting from our point of view, however, is that Orwell turns against Auden the very same 'thumbnail sketch' technique that the poet himself had used, filling out the abstract concept of 'murder' with a catalogue of metonymic and synecdochic details, just as Auden had filled out the abstract concept of the revolutionary struggle.

The prevalence of the definite article in 1930s verse, statistically measured by G. Rostrevor Hamilton in *The Tell-tale Article* (1949) and recently discussed by Bernard Bergonzi in an article on 'Auden and the Audenesque'[27] is a natural concomitant of this metonymic technique. In itself it is not of course peculiar to 1930s verse—as Hamilton discovered, the ratio of definite articles tends to be as high in descriptive poetry of the eighteenth century—but in 1930s verse it is often further emphasized by the deletion of finite verbs. This is the case in 'Spain'; and also in Geoffrey Grigson's poem 'The Non-Interveners', written in the same year (1937) as Auden's, and based on essentially the same antithesis as *The Confidential Agent*:

> In England the handsome Minister with the second
> and a half chin and his heart-shaped mind
> hanging on his thin watch-chain, the Minister
> with gout who shaves low on his holly-stem neck.
>
> In Spain still the brown and gilt and the twisted
> pillar, still the olives, and in the mountains
> the chocolate trunks of cork trees bare from
> the knee, . . .
> . . . and also the black slime under
> the bullet-pocked wall, also the arterial blood
> squirting into the curious future, . . .[28]

Louis MacNeice remembered Spain in the same fashion, as a collection of verbal snapshots:

> With writings on the walls—
>   Hammer and sickle, Boicot, Viva, Muerra;
> With *café au lait* brimming the waterfalls,
>   With sherry, shellfish, omelettes.
> With fretted stone the Moor
>   Had chiselled for effects of sun and shadow;
> With shadows of the poor,
>   The begging cripples and the children begging.[29]

Deletion or avoidance of finite verbs is the main deviation from conventional grammar in 1930s verse, and it is not, of course, one that causes much difficulty for the reader. On the whole, 1930s writing in verse and prose emphasized syntagmatic connections between verbal items, reflecting grammatically the empirical connections between entities in the observable world. The complex, self-embedding syntax of James and Conrad was as unfashionable as the fragmentary, dislocated, allusive language of Eliot, Pound, and Joyce, the mystical metaphorical flights of Lawrence, or Virginia Woolf's paratactic lyricism. Sentences in 1930s verse, like the plots of 1930s novels, have a clearly recognizable and intelligible structure. The tone of Audenesque lyric poetry is either hortatory:

And throw away
beginning from today
the eau de Cologne which disguised you, the stick which propped,
the tennis racquet, the blazer of the First Fifteen[30]

—or conversationally relaxed:

> About suffering they were never wrong,
> The Old Masters: how well they understood
> Its human position: how it takes place
> While someone else is eating or opening a window
> or just walking dully along;[31]

This last, much anthologized poem, Auden's 'Musée des Beaux Arts', is not topically political in theme, but it belongs to the 1930s and it is, significantly, an explicit inquiry into, and celebration of, the aesthetics of realism, emphasizing the cardinal importance of contingent contiguity in such art:

> How, when the ages are reverently, passionately waiting
> For the miraculous birth, there must always be
> Children who did not specially want it to happen, skating
> On a pond at the edge of a wood.[32]

'In general', Bernard Bergonzi writes in the article mentioned above, 'the characteristics of the Audenesque in syntax and diction seem to me to be ... copious use of the definite article, unusual adjectives and adjectival phrases, and surprising similes, which have a reductive or trivializing effect; and personified abstractions.'[33] The prevalence of the definite article we have already accounted for as an inevitable feature of a nominalizing style, and the other features are obvious ways of rhetorically heightening and varying such a style, preventing it from degenerating into mere catalogues of data. If a style emphasizes nouns, particularity must be conveyed through adjectives, or adjectival phrases, or through analogies, as the language of nineteenth-century realistic fiction shows. The use of personified abstractions is more distinctive, and no doubt derives from the writers' sense of being caught up in the tide of history, having important moral and political messages to deliver. 'History', indeed, was itself one of their favourite abstract words. Samuel Hynes remarks that Auden revised the line, 'And called out of tideless peace by a living sun' in the 'Prologue' of 1933 to read, in 1936, 'And out of the future into actual history.'[34] Bergonzi quotes the famous conclusion to 'Spain':

> History to the defeated
> May say alas but cannot help or pardon

and juxtaposes a passage from Edward Upward's story 'Sunday' in which the same abstraction is tied to a typical synecdochic catalogue:

History is here in the park, in the town. It is in the offices, the duplicators, the traffic, the nursemaids wheeling prams, the airmen, the aviary, the new viaduct over the valley. It was once in the castle on the cliff, in the sooty churches, in your mind; but it is abandoning them, leaving with them only the failing energy of desperation, going to live elsewhere.[35]

As Bergonzi remarks, the Marxist implications in this invocation of 'History' are obvious enough; but the peculiar stylistic *frisson* which the writers of the 1930s derived from clamping together huge abstractions with particular concrete details of ordinary life was not confined to Party members or to fellow-travellers. Graham Greene does the same with metaphysical and theological concepts like good, evil, faith:

> It isn't a gain to have turned the witch or the masked secret dancer, the sense of supernatural evil, into the small human viciousness of the distinguished military grey head in Kensington Gardens with the soft lips and the eye which dwelt with dull lustre on girls and boys of a certain age.[36]

> Good and evil lived in the same country, came together like old friends, feeling the same completion, touching hands beside the iron bedstead.[37]

> He was aware of faith dying out between the bed and the door.[38]

I have already commented, especially in connection with Orwell's 'A Hanging', on the preference of the realistic writer for simile rather than metaphor and his tendency to draw the vehicles of such similes from the literal context of the narrative. I commented in the same place on the ambivalence of the word *like*, which may indicate a synechochic relationship derived from contiguity as well as a relationship based on similarity. Both these points are well illustrated by the opening of Christopher Isherwood's 'A Berlin Diary (Autumn 1930)' in *Goodbye to Berlin* (1939):

> From my window, the deep solemn massive street. Cellarshops where the lamps burn all day, under the shadow of topheavy balconied facades, dirty plaster frontages embossed with scroll-work and heraldic devices. The whole district is like this: street leading into street of houses like shabby monumental safes crammed with the tarnished valuables and second-hand furniture of a bankrupt middle class.[39]

The first two sentences present the scene as a catalogue of selected details and attributes, the main verbs of these sentences being characteristically deleted. The third sentence uses the word *like* to stress the synecdochic character of the street: all streets in the district are like this one. Then *like* is used again to construct a simile: 'houses like monumental safes'. But the vehicle of this simile is taken from the context, and thus serves to reinforce our sense of the context rather than to introduce some other, quite different field of reference. For these houses almost certainly *contain* safes, safes very probably crammed with tarnished valuables (it was a period of chronic inflation and financial instability). That, at least, is the impression the sentence leaves us with—the simile is, as it were, simultaneously a synecdoche.

On the next page of the same text Isherwood describes the interior of his lodgings:

> The extraordinary smell in this room when the stove is lighted and the

window shut; not altogether unpleasant, a mixture of incense and stale buns. The tall, tiled stove, gorgeously coloured, like an altar. The washstand like a Gothic shrine. The cupboard also is Gothic, with carved cathedral windows: Bismark faces the king of Prussia in stained glass. My best chair would do for a bishop's throne. In the corner, three sham medieval halberds (from a theatrical touring company?) are fastened together to form a hatstand. Frl. Schroeder unscrews the heads of the halberds and polishes them from time to time. They are heavy and sharp enough to kill.

Everything in the room is like that: unnecessarily solid, abnormally heavy and dangerously sharp. Here, at the writing table, I am confronted by a phalanx of metal objects—a pair of candlesticks shaped like entwined serpents, an ashtray from which emerges the head of a crocodile, a paperknife copied from a Florentine dagger, a brass dolphin holding on the end of its tail a small broken clock. What becomes of such things? How could they ever be destroyed? They will probably remain intact for thousands of years: people will treasure them in Museums. Or perhaps they will merely be melted down for munitions in a war. Every morning, Frl. Schroeder arranges them very carefully in certain unvarying positions: there they stand, like an uncompromising statement of her views on Capital and Society, Religion and Sex.[40]

Here the similes, 'like an altar', 'like a Gothic shrine' introduce a different context, but they do so reductively, to ironic effect. The anticlimactic collocation 'incense and stale buns' ensures that no transcendental glamour will attach itself to the ecclesiastical look of the furniture. The simile construction, pivoting on the word *like*, maintains a clear distinction between what these things are and what they suggest, and the gap between the two serves as an index of bourgeois pretentiousness. When the narrator says that everything in the room was 'like' the mock halberds, 'unnecessarily solid, abnormally heavy and dangerously sharp', he uses the word *like* differently, to establish a 'real', i.e. synecdochic, relationship between the halberds and the other furnishings. The bric à brac described in the second paragraph of the passage is mocked for its iconic metaphorizing, the surrealism of *kitsch* (the serpentine candlesticks, crocodile ashtray etc.). The last use of *like* in this paragraph is particularly interesting. Although it seems to connect two parts of a simile, there is in fact no *similarity* between tenor and vehicle. There is no such thing as a statement of Frl. Schroeder's views on Capital and Society, Religion and Sex—and if there were, it would in no sense *resemble* a pair of candlesticks, an ashtray, a paperknife and a broken clock, however fantastically ornamented these things may be. One might say that the possession of these objects is congruous with the possession of those views, or even that in some sense the possession of those views *caused* the acquisition of these objects. Thus a synecdochic or metonymic relationship has been presented as if it were metaphorical.

Graham Greene uses simile in a similar, but more flamboyant way:

1 Congratulate me, he seemed to be saying, and his humorous friendly shifty eyes raked her like the headlamps of a second-hand car which had been painted and polished to deceive.[41]
2 Virginity straightened in him like sex.[42]
3 He felt anger grinding at his guts like the tide at the piles below.[43]
4 Evil ran like malaria in his veins.[44]
5 She carried her responsibilities carefully like crockery across the hot yard.[45]
6 He drank the brandy down like damnation.[46]

The analogy in (1) tells us little about the appearance of Anthony Farrant's eyes, but it reinforces the moral judgment of his character as 'shifty' by evoking the social context to which he belongs—one in which the buying and selling of deceptively shiny secondhand cars would be not uncommon. The similes in (3), (4) and (5) are all drawn from the character's immediate context—the sea and Brighton pier in (3), the disease-ridden Mexican climate in (4) and Coral's domestic role in (5). All yoke abstract and concrete violently together in a way that (as Richard Hoggart has observed)[47] is very characteristic of Graham Greene, but which is also, as we have seen, a common feature of 1930s writing generally. The contextual appropriateness of these similes helps to accommodate their abrupt leaps from abstract to concrete within a generally realistic or prosaic account of experience. Examples (2) and (6) also depend upon a kind of fusion, or confusion, of metaphorical similarity with metonymic contiguity. 'Virginity' and 'sex' are existentially, physiologically connected: this simile is not so much a comparison between two different but similar things as a comparison between the positive and negative sides of the same thing. Brandy is not 'like' damnation in any definable sense, but the priest is thinking about his own unworthiness for salvation while drinking brandy, and bargaining for some bottles of the liquor which he will pay for with the hard-won offerings of the pious peasantry who want their children baptized. His addiction to brandy, in short, brings him close to committing the sin of simony, and brandy could therefore be said to be his 'damnation' (as gin is jocularly and proverbially said to be 'mother's ruin') by a metonymic substitution of effect for cause.

I alluded briefly in Part One to Christopher Isherwood's account, in *Lions and Shadows*, of his early literary development—of how he weaned himself, partly under the influence of Tolstoy's realism, from what he came to regard as a shallow and trivializing experimentalism in his first attempts at writing fiction. He also describes in the same book the parallel case of his friend Edward Upward (referred to as 'Alan Chalmers'), a case that, traced through Upward's own early writings,[48] throws vivid light upon the motivation of that generation of writers in their quest for a more realistic and historically responsible *écriture* than that of the modernist tradition, and upon the kind of stylistic choices and sacrifices this quest entailed. The characteristic trend of formal development in the major modernist writers, as we have seen, was from a metonymic type of writing in their early work to a metaphorical mode in their mature and late work. Upward's development was exactly the reverse. And it should be remembered that although he now seems a comparatively minor figure, he enjoyed a legendary reputation in left-wing literary circles in the 1930s, and exerted a powerful influence on writers who became more famous than himself—not only Isherwood, but Auden and Stephen Spender among others.[49] For these reasons I propose to examine Upward's early writing in some detail.

Isherwood's relationship with Upward began at school: 'Never in my life have I been so strongly and immediately attracted to any personality, before or since. Everything about him appealed to me. He was a born anarchist, a born romantic revolutionary.'[50] The two youths went up together to Cambridge, where, as a form of escape from, or defence against, the various psychological pressures commonly experienced by clever, rebellious undergraduates, they began to invent a fictitious, surrealistic alternative world, known at first as the 'Old Town'. Isherwood describes a typical moment in the formation of this fantasy:

> One evening, I happened to read aloud the name under a fluttering gas-lamp: 'Garret Hostel Bridge'. 'The Rats' Hostel!' Chalmers suddenly exclaimed. We often conversed in surrealist phrases of this kind. Now we both became abnormally excited: it seemed to us that an all-important statement had been made. At last, by pure accident, we had stumbled upon the key-words which expressed the inmost nature of the Other Town.[51]

Later the Other Town was displaced by a mythical village called Mortmere, which the two young men gradually populated with a large cast of characters. From merely talking about it, they progressed to writing about it—Upward in particular seems to have written a great many Mortmere stories. Only the last of these survives: 'The Railway Accident', written in 1928, after Upward had left the University. Isherwood describes it as 'a farewell to Mortmere which left Chalmers free to develop his extraordinary technique in other, more fruitful directions. Nevertheless, Mortmere was the mad nursery in which Chalmers grew up as a writer.'[52] Comparison with the Angria and Gondol sagas of the Brontë children is irresistible. Like the Brontës, Upward and Isherwood came to see that they must disengage themselves from the mythology of their immature work in order to develop as artists. But in Upward's case, at least, the imaginative cost of the renunciation was great, and it is open to question whether the promise of 'The Railway Accident' was ever fulfilled.

This story begins with the narrator, Hearn, being seen off by the officious Gunball from an unidentified railway terminus on a journey to Mortmere. As the train leaves, he is joined by Gustave Shreeve, also bound for Mortmere, where both are to participate in a Treasure Hunt organized by the vicar, the Rev. Welken. Shreeve's remarks (disturbed by terrific noise emanating from a party of territorial soldiers in an adjoining carriage) recall a railway accident on the route to Mortmere caused by a collapsing tunnel, and hint that the accident may recur. The train indeed swerves on to the branch line that leads to the blocked and disused tunnel. Hearn and Shreeve manage to jump clear, but an express train follows closely behind at high speed with catastrophic results. The scene shifts to Mortmere and the Treasure Hunt, which ends in angry accusations of cheating and a duel fought with pea-shooting pistols. One of the pistols proves to be loaded with real ammunition and wounds one of the duellists. The story ends with the news that Harold Wrygrave, the Mortmere architect and builder of the tunnel, has been arrested on a charge of trainwrecking.

The mode of 'The Railway Accident' is best described as surrealistic. When Isherwood applies this term in *Lions and Shadows* to his and Upward's fantasy world he comments: 'I use the term "surrealism" simply for the purpose of explanation: we had, of course, no idea that a surrealist movement already existed on the Continent.'[53] Surrealism did not really make a full impact upon the English cultural scene until the International Surrealist Exhibition of 1936, but its roots were in the modernist 1920s. The first Surrealist Manifesto was published in 1924, and André Breton defined the period of 1912–1923 as 'the heroic epoch of surrealism'.[54] As the European literary and artistic *avant garde* became more politically conscious, some attempt was made by Breton and others at a synthesis of surrealism and Marxism on the flimsy ground that both were revolutionary movements, but by the time of the London Surrealist Exhibition the idea was beginning to look increasingly implausible. A writer in the *Left Review* at the time summed up the attitude of politically orthodox literary intellectuals: 'Surrealism is not revolutionary, because its lyricism is socially irresponsible. . . . Surrealism is a particularly subtle form of fake revolution.'[55] It is indeed difficult to see how the principles and methodology of Marxist-Leninism could be reconciled with Breton's definition of surrealism as 'Pure psychic automatism through which one seeks to express . . . the absolute functioning of thought . . . in the absence of all rational control and apart from any ethical or moral considerations . . . a belief in the supreme quality of certain forms of association heretofore neglected: in the omnipotence of dream, in the disinterested play of thought.'[56] The influence of surrealism on the writing of the 1930s was therefore either superficial or confined to writers who were not representative of the main literary current of the period, especially the poets sometimes referred to as the New Apocalypse school—David Gascoyne, George Barker, Dylan Thomas and others. Certainly by 1936, the year of the Surrealist

Exhibition, Upward and Isherwood had already weaned themselves from their own privately generated surrealistic world of Mortmere.

Surrealist painting, it will be recalled, is classified as metaphoric by Jakobson, and opposed to the metonymically experimental art of cubism. Surrealism is in fact a particularly radical metaphorical mode, the force of which is as much negative as positive. By this I mean that what strikes one about the juxtaposition of items in surrealist art (visual, or verbal) is in the first place not so much any similarity between them as their incongruity—the violation of natural relationships of contiguity entailed in the juxtaposition. The shock to the perceiver's expectations and habits, derived from the rational, empirical world-view of common sense, frees his mind and sensibility to play over the juxtaposition, and perhaps discover metaphorical meanings in it. The point may be illustrated from Magritte's painting 'Time Transfixed' which most appropriately decorates the cover of the Penguin edition of *The Railway Accident*. This interior, painted with Magritte's characteristic hardedged naturalism, depicts a fireplace with marble mantelpiece bearing a clock and two candlesticks and surmounted by a large mirror. The fireplace is boarded or walled up and from a point in this vertical plane, just under the mantelshelf, in the position where one might expect a stove to be connected by a flue to the chimney, there projects into the room a steam locomotive with smoke issuing from its funnel, drastically reduced in scale, though perceptively larger than the usual model train. The scale is very important: if the locomotive were big enough to fill the fireplace we would have an obvious and quickly exhausted visual joke based on the similarity between a tunnel and a fireplace (a kind of pictorial equivalent to the comic song, 'The railroad came through the middle of the house'). If the scale were smaller it would suggest a toy which had been eccentrically mounted in this position. But as it is, the locomotive looks like a real locomotive which has been subjected to some strange enchantment, shrunk in size, its weight still more drastically reduced (it gives the impression of floating two or three feet above the ground rather than being supported by a bracket) and its movement (the smoke is streaming backwards, indicating speed) frozen. In short, there is no possible logical, rational explanation for the contiguity of the engine and the fireplace, though the scrupulous naturalism of the treatment teasingly invites us to seek one. Defeated in our attempt to interpret the picture according to contiguity, we are, in our contemplation of it, led eventually to perceive various relationships of similarity, both visual and semantic, among its components. The lines of the floorboards look like railway lines, and are the right 'gauge' to accommodate the locomotive. Both a fireplace and an engine burn coal.[57] The circular face of the locomotive's boiler is the same size as the clock-face, and the reflection of the clock in the mirror, lengthening its shape by replication, emphasizes the formal symmetry between these two objects, both of which are in the centre of the picture, and project forward from the predominantly vertical planes of the wall, mantelpiece and mirror. The clock face shows the time as seventeen minutes to one. The hands of the clock may be moving, but there is no way of showing this in a painting: in the painting the time is always seventeen minutes to one. To paint a clock *is* to 'transfix time', but without the locomotive we should not be aware of this—we should interpret the clock face as a synecdoche for the progress of time. Unlike a clock, a locomotive can be painted in motion (by the treatment of the smoke). Because the locomotive in the picture is so obviously and strangely arrested in full career—spellbound, one might say—we are made to appreciate that the clock's movement is also spellbound by pictorial representation.

The railway train, it may be suggested, is an inherently metonymic product of technology. In form it is a kind of syntagm, a combination of units (locomotive, carriages, guard's van) in a prescribed order. Its progression is linear, unidirectional and highly predictable, like orthodox prose (we recall Virginia Woolf's wish to go beyond 'the formal railway line of the sentence'). Ships and aeroplanes lend themselves readily to metaphorical transformation, but trains, except in the rather strained anthropomorphism of children's stories, are likely to become realistic 'symbols' rather than metaphors: symbols of Progress, Energy, Industrialism, or whatever. Thus any radically metaphorical treatment of the railway train, any striking disturbance of its contextual norms, is likely to make a strong impact—as we see in 'The Railway Accident'.

At the beginning of the story, Hearn, waiting for his train to depart, is puzzled by the appearance of another train drawn up on the other side of the platform:

> My impression of most details in the design of this train were that they were unnecessary or, if necessary, belonging to a world in which I should have felt as wholly disorientated as though, suffering from amnesia after an accident, I had found myself among hoardings bearing futurist German advertisements.[58]

In fact, this *is* exactly how Hearn (and the reader) feels as the story develops. Gunball, who is seeing him off, disconcerts him by remarking:

> 'So I suppose this one will go there too . . .
> 'Where? Which one?'
> 'The train you're leaning out of at this moment. To Mortmere. But I was just saying I'd noticed that the other one certainly does.'[59]

It is too late for Hearn to change trains. Gunball shouts, 'Anyway, your train will arrive somewhere'—a patently absurd remark, since railway journeys are always made with a specific destination in view—and the train pulls out of the station. 'The first gasometers, restful, solemn, like stumps of semi-amputated breasts, curved past the window in frost-bright air. . . . Now for many months of complete summer I should idle in gardens warm with croquet and the tinkling of spoons. . . .'[60] The grotesquely vivid simile of the semi-amputated breasts is typically surrealistic (they *displace* rather than define the gasometers in our mind's eye) as is the impossible confusion of seasons. The railway accident itself is described with a fine profusion of varied metaphors and similes:

> Coaches mounted like viciously copulating bulls, telescoped like ventilator hatches. Nostril gaps in a tunnel clogged with wreckage instantly flamed. A faint jet of blood sprayed from a vacant window. Frog-sprawling bodies fumed in blazing reeds. The architrave of the tunnel crested with daffodils fell compact as hinged scenery. Tall rag-feathered birds with corrugated red wattles limped from holes among the reeds.[61]

W. H. Sellers seems to me wrong in suggesting that 'what gives the story its bizarre quality is that, from beginning to end, the incidents that occur do so only in the deranged mind of the narrator'.[62] On the contrary, the story is bizarre precisely because the text contains no normative reality against which we can measure Hearn's perceptions and declare them deranged. It is dreamlike, but he (and we) do not awake from the dream. The dream is, to quote André Breton, 'omnipotent'.

But Upward—and Isherwood—eventually came to feel that they must awake from the dream of Mortmere. By 1928, Isherwood comments,

> Mortmere seemed to have brought us to a dead end. The cult of romantic strangeness, we both knew, was a luxury for the comfortable University fireside; it could not save you from the drab realities of cheap lodgings and a dull underpaid job. . . . Chalmers . . . was to spend the next three years in desperate and bitter struggles to relate Mortmere to the real world of the jobs and the lodging houses; to find the formula which would transform our private fantasies and amusing freaks and bogies into valid symbols of the ills of society and the toils and aspirations of our daily lives. . . . And Chalmers did at last find it . . . quite clearly set down, for everybody to read, in the pages of Lenin and of Marx.[63]

Upward represented this quest in his novella *Journey to the Border* (1938), a work in which we can see the metaphorical mode of 'The Railway Accident' being subordinated to an allegorical purpose and finally crushed. Allegory is a metaphorical device, of course, but its exploitation of similarity is very rigidly controlled in the interests of a didactic message and it can be easily combined with an essentially metonymic type of narrative. For example, George Orwell's *Animal Farm* is based on a system of similarities between the story of the animals and the history of the Russian Revolution, but the narrative is quite intelligible without the application of this code, and is enjoyed as such by children. When the 1930s writers did not use documentary or realistic modes of writing, when they wrote in an overtly fictive, metaphorical mode, it was usually in forms of allegory—sometimes referred to, in the criticism of the period as 'fable', 'myth' and 'parable'.[64] Reviewing the Auden–Isherwood play, *The Ascent of F6*, and the first issue of *New Writing*, Stephen Spender noted in the former, 'the rhythmic contrast which the writers maintain between two entirely different methods of presentation: firstly, realistic scenes of political reportage; secondly fables'; and of the latter he observed: 'the best stories in the volume are either very realistic fragments of actual life ... or they are allegories.'[65] Other examples of the allegorical mode in the period would be the early poetic works of Auden and Day Lewis—*The Witnesses, The Orators, The Magnetic Mountain*—and the novels of Rex Warner—*The Professor, The Aerodrome*. It must always be remembered that these writers had grown up under the influence of the modernist movement of Eliot, Pound and Joyce, and never entirely repudiated its aesthetics even if they rejected its politics and philosophy. Most of them hoped that writing could continue to be 'modern' while at the same time being committed, and the allegorized myth or fantasy was one appealing way of making the metaphorical imagination historically responsible. In practice, the most successful efforts in this direction were ideologically ambiguous, while the felt obligation to deliver a politically 'orthodox' message was apt to deprive the fable of imaginative life. This was very much the problem that preoccupied Edward Upward, for of the Auden group he was the only one who could be said to be a fully committed Marxist, but it can hardly be said that he solved it. *Journey to the Border* is an allegory the message of which leads ultimately to a renunciation of its own imaginative devices.

The hero, referred to throughout, with the anonymity typical of allegory, as 'the tutor', is employed by a wealthy businessman (representing Capitalism) to coach his son. The action takes place on a day when the tutor is compelled against his inclinations to accompany father and son to a horse-race meeting. During the day, the tutor, who is in a state of barely controlled hysteria, undergoes various trials and temptations. His grip upon reality is insecure, and at the racecourse he is subject to strange visions and hallucinations, centering on a large marquee. When he first glances inside this erection he has an impression of luxury which he recalls with disgust 'tempered by a certain ... half-ashamed desire' as a profusion of surrealistically incongruous objects.[66] But when he eventually enters the marquee,

> The scene was reassuringly normal. Small tables covered with white cloths and surrounded by green iron chairs occupied the central area of uncarpeted grass, and he saw no Nubian statue, no chenille-hung buffalo head.[67]

Journey to the Border thus differs crucially from 'The Railway Accident' in that the hero's subjective distortion of reality is explicitly revealed and framed by a 'normal' version of the same objects and events. What is interesting from our point of view is that illusion and reality are explicitly equated with the metaphorical and metonymic modes, respectively. For example:

> Why shouldn't he dare to give free play, within sane limits, to a happiness which was no longer based on fantasies but on the actual possibilities of his real surroundings? . . . The marquee was not like a racing yacht in full sail, it was not like a white-walled aerodrome from which he could instantly fly to any part of the world, it was not like a crowded flutter of girls' frocks along the esplanade, was not like a mansion with circular mansard windows and broad white pillars and porticoes and gilded urns, not like a cool place for the protection of art and learning, not like a white balcony from which he could look at mountains through a powerful brass telescope. It was like an ordinary marquee, white and rather large. It was like the actual destination towards which a slowly moving car was taking the tutor.[68]

This destination *is* the marquee, so the opposition between similarity and contiguity could scarcely be more emphatic. However it must be pointed out that the tutor's rejection, here, of fanciful imagery is compromised by the fact that the 'actuality' he seeks to embrace is politically corrupt. Inside the marquee all his fear and loathing erupt again in a conversation with a sadistic young colonial administrator. The tutor proves susceptible to the indoctrination of a psychologist called Mavors who preaches a gospel of instinctual liberation and unreason. He lapses back into the language of surrealistic free association, and a seductive girl reminds him of a romantic encounter they had at Cambridge: 'You talked about pergolas and about fountains. I had never heard that sort of language before, but I knew at once that I had always wanted to hear it. I remember one phrase especially: "Rubber statuary in gardens of ice-cream roses'. "[69] Erotically excited, the tutor proposes to elope with her, but the frightening spectacle of a kind of fascist rally in the marquee forestalls him and he runs off in a panic.

The tutor's problem is explained to him by another girl (his 'good angel') Ann: 'you see quite clearly what is wrong with the system in which you are living. . . . But you take no action. You are content to hate and despise your life.'[70] Alienated from the real world, but unwilling to transform it morally by political action, he falls back upon private, surrealistic transformations of the world which correspond to the clinical symptoms of schizophrenia. The solution is therefore twofold: first he must abandon illusion and recognize reality. Then he must commit himself to changing reality. All this is explained in a long dialogue between the tutor and his own political conscience. Again it is fascinating to see how the argument conforms to the rhetorical opposition between metaphor and metonymy. The tutor defends his fantasies as having some basis in reality: 'even the maddest fantasies must fetch their materials from real life'. But his *alter ego* retorts:

> 'How far do your thoughts give a true picture of the relations actually existing among things? You might think of a man with wings. The man might be real, a friend of yours, and the wings might have belonged to a real swan you had seen in a public park, but the combination in your mind would be nothing more than a contemptible fantasy, a myth.'[71]

Whether intentionally or not, there is a fitting irony in the fact that the metaphorical birdman, the myth so contemptuously dismissed here, is the Icarus figure central to the imagination of the greatest modernist writer, James Joyce. The *alter ego* relentlessly orders the tutor to 'Look around you. Become aware of your real situation . . . what do you think you will see next?'

> 'The races will come to an end. People will begin to disperse. Some of them will go towards the car park. That's where I shall go. I shall see the car which brought me here. I shall see Mr Parkin and the boy.'
> 'Fine. Now you're facing it. And the next?'
> 'The return. The house with the four lawns. Bed. Tomorrow. The window and the treetops. Rooks. Beer. Latin and Scripture. The day after tomorrow and the days after that.'
> 'That's your real situation.'[72]

The world is thus reduced to chronological sequence, spatial contiguities, synecdochic detail. But the tutor protests that he cannot 'stand' this world—he would rather return to his delusions. *The alter ego* says that there is 'another way . . . the way of the workers. You must get in touch with the workers' movement'.[73]

This answer may seem rather facile, and hardly acquires more plausibility in the sequel, when the tutor hesitatingly strikes up acquaintance with a 'worker' on the racecourse—a naively handled episode in which a politically motivated encounter is invested with all the emotion of a sexual adventure ('Already the tutor had begun to feel interested and a little excited. A worker was looking at him. The tutor was pleasantly excited. Stop it at once. Try to feel indifferent').[74] But that is the didactic conclusion of the story. It is *Journey to the Border* rather than 'The Railway Accident' that was Upward's 'farewell to Mortmere', for the fantasies that the tutor tries unsuccessfully to defend against the criticism of his *alter ego* clearly recall the myth of Mortmere. 'Dreams of escape. Twisted fantasies. Unhealthy substitutes for the action you ought to have taken,' the *alter ego* calls them.

> 'Quite true. But they were something more than that. They may have been a substitute for action, but at the same time they were themselves a form of action. They may have been fantastic but at the same time they contained within them elements of something other than fantasy. . . . They were my attempts to find a significance in the life I was leading, to build up my experiences into a coherent, a satisfying pattern.[75]

H

In spite of this eloquent defence of imagination, the *alter ego* wins the debate, and the tutor, having resolved to join the workers' movement, rejoices, in the last lines of the story, at having 'come out of the cloud of his cowardly fantasies'.[76] Reading this dialogue of the mind with itself I was strongly reminded of Keats's *The Dream of Hyperion*, in which the poet first defends himself against, and then finally pleads guilty to, Moneta's accusation that he is 'a dreaming thing' incapable of benefiting 'the great world'. More ominously one may be reminded of the Moscow Trials which were taking place at about the time *Journey to the Border* was being written, and of the 'confessions' that were extracted from the accused on those occasions.

Edward Upward himself joined the Communist Party, and became one of the most uncompromising Marxist literary intellectuals of the 1930s. George Orwell quotes him, in 'Inside the Whale', as stating flatly that 'no book written *at the present time* can be "good" unless it is written from a Marxist or near-Marxist viewpoint'.[77] Upward's own career, however, seems to confirm Orwell's judgment that total commitment to any ideological orthodoxy is inimical to literary creation. Upward published only one short piece after *Journey to the Border* appeared in 1938, and from 1942 onwards he was totally silent. In 1948 he left the Party, and has since published two novels, conventionally realistic in technique, about the internal conflicts in the British Communist Party: *In the Thirties* (1962) and *The Rotten Elements* (1969).

In this chapter I have used the terms 'writers of the 1930s', '1930s writing', in a sense quite familiar to literary historians. It is not implied that *every* writer of that time shared the same aims and technical predilections; but looking back on the period we are probably more struck by the homogeniety than by the variety of its literary output. There is, I think, only one indisputably major writer belonging to that generation (the generation, roughly speaking, who were still at school when World War I ended) who has not been mentioned so far, and that is Evelyn Waugh. There are several reasons why his work does not fit neatly into the general characterization I have attempted of the *écriture* of the 1930s. Politically, he was a kind of conservative anarchist, and more sympathetic, therefore, than his left wing contemporaries to the pessimism, and despair of secular 'progress', that underlay so much modernist writing. I have attempted to show elsewhere how potent in Waugh's work was the 'myth of decline' which Northrop Frye has identified as central to T. S. Eliot's imagination.[78] Where Waugh parted company with the great modernists was in renouncing their 'subjectivity'—which as far as prose fiction was concerned meant renouncing the limited point of view or the stream of consciousness technique. His model was not Henry James or James Joyce, but Ronald Firbank.[79] The disorderliness, the contingency, the collapse of value and meaning in contemporary life, are rendered dramatically through conversational nuances and ironic juxtapositions; narratively through the elimination or parody of cause-and-effect. But the implied author mediating this vision of comical anarchy, this farcical Wasteland, remains objective—morally, emotionally and stylistically. He does not, except in passages of obvious pastiche, bend his verbal medium to fit the contours of his characters' sensibilities, nor dissolve the structure of formal English prose to imitate subconscious or unconscious processes of the mind. He retains always a classical detachment, lucidity and poise, and often makes his authorial presence felt as much by his abstention from comment as by what he actually says. This is the source of Evelyn Waugh's distinctive tone, and of his most characteristic comic effects; it is also what has troubled critics who accuse him of being cruel, snobbish and nihilistic. In the 1930s, when compassion, moral indignation and democratic sentiment were at a premium in the literary world, he was an isolated figure.

Nevertheless his style of writing was, in its own way, as 'readerly' as the other 1930s writing we have looked at; and although it seems misleading to describe Waugh as a 'realist' in the same sense as Isherwood, Greene and Orwell, because of the element of extravagant farce and caricature in his work, there is no doubt about his interest in and feeling for the signs and indices of social class, status and style in speech, dress and behaviour. In this regard he made extensive use of metonymic and synecdochic detail (consider, for example, the important function of architecture, furnishings and fittings in *A Handful of Dust* (1935)), while being very sparing of metaphorical figures.[80] It is vital to the effect of Waugh's novels that the absurd and outrageous is presented very literally. One might say that the technique of the early novels is metonymic in an experimental way—like Virginia Woolf's *Jacob's Room*, but applying the method she used to the purposes of comedy. Waugh deletes from and rearranges the contiguous elements of his subject to produce absurd and ironic incongruities—Agatha Runcible coming down to breakfast at No. 10 Downing St. dressed in a Hawaiian grass skirt, for instance; or Basil Seal unwittingly eating his girlfriend Prudence at a cannibal feast; or Tony Last reading Dickens aloud at gun-point in the depths of the South American jungle. But the imaginative idea which lies behind and unifies the narrative is often quasi-metaphorical in a way that reminds us of modernist writing. The title *Decline and Fall* (1928) hints at an analogy between modern Western society and the late Roman Empire; *Black Mischief* (1932), *A Handful of Dust* and *Scoop* (1938) all turn upon ironic parallels between civilization and barbarism—the social jungle of London compared with the real jungle of South America or tropical Africa. Ironic comparisons and cross-references between these different milieux are accomplished by a cinematic technique of cross-cutting between short scenes often occurring simultaneously in different places—like Greene and Isherwood, Waugh was deeply influenced by the cinema.[81]

In *Work Suspended* (1942), and still more obviously in *Brideshead Revisited* (1945), Waugh made a radical change in his technique. His style became heavily metaphorical, given to long, elaborate analogies, but at the same time the narrative itself became more conventional in structure, following the fortunes of a group of interrelated characters as they unfolded in time and space. The resemblance to Proust suggested by the retrospective stance of the narrator, and by the lush nostalgia of his reminiscence, is only skin deep: there is no questioning of the nature of perception and consciousness such as we find in *La Recherche du Temps Perdu*. Later, in the *Sword of Honour* trilogy, Waugh trimmed the self-indulgent metaphorizing from his writing and returned to a modified form of his earlier technique, with happy results. But his efforts to revise *Brideshead Revisited* (1960) in the same spirit were less successful: it was too much a product of its period, of the partial, somewhat phoney revival of modernism in the 1940s.

7 Philip Larkin

1930s writing was, characteristically, antimodernist, realistic, readerly and metonymic. In the 1940s the pendulum of literary fashion swung back again—not fully, but to a perceptible degree—towards the pole we have designated as modernist, symbolist, writerly and metaphoric. Sooner or later the leading writers of the 1930s became disillusioned with politics, lost faith in Soviet Russia, took up religion, emigrated to America or fell silent. Christianity, in a very uncompromising, antihumanist, theologically 'high' form, became a force in literature (the later Eliot, the Charles Williams–C. S. Lewis circle, the 'Catholic novel' of Greene and Waugh). Bourgeois writers no longer felt obliged to identify with the proletariat. Bohemian, patrician, cosmopolitan attitudes and life-styles became once more acceptable in the literary world. To say that the English novel resumed experimentalism would be an overstatement; but 'fine writing' certainly returned and an interest in rendering the refinements of individual sensibility rather than collective experience. There was a revival of Henry James, and many people saw Charles Morgan as his modern successor. Fantasy such as Upward and Isherwood had felt obliged to purge from their work was luxuriated in by Mervyn Peake. There was great excitement at an apparent revival of verse drama, principally in the work of T. S. Eliot and Christopher Fry. Perhaps the movement of the pendulum was most evident in the field of poetry. The reputations of Eliot and Yeats triumphantly survived the attacks launched against them in the 1930s, and the most enthusiastically acclaimed younger poet was Dylan Thomas, a 'metaphoric' writer if ever there was one.

In the middle of the 1950s, a new generation of writers began to exert an opposite pressure on the pendulum. They were sometimes referred to as 'The Movement' (mainly in the context of poetry) and sometimes, more journalistically, as the 'Angry Young Men' (mainly in the context of fiction and drama). Some of the key figures in these partially overlapping groups were: Kingsley Amis, Philip Larkin, John Wain, D. J. Enright, Thom Gunn, Donald Davie, Alan Sillitoe, John Osborne, Arnold Wesker. Others who shared the same general aims and assumptions as these writers, or contributed to the formation of a distinctively 1950s *écriture*, were William Cooper, C. P. Snow and his wife Pamela Hansford Johnson, Colin McInnes, Angus Wilson, John Braine, Stan Barstow, Thomas Hinde, Keith Waterhouse, David Storey and, in precept if not in practice, Iris Murdoch.* The 1950s writers were suspicious of, and often positively hostile to the modernist movement and certainly opposed to any further efforts at 'experimental' writing. Dylan Thomas epitomized everything they detested: verbal obscurity, metaphysical pretentiousness, self-indulgent romanticism, compulsive metaphorizing were his alleged faults. They themselves aimed to communicate clearly and honestly their perceptions of the world as it was. They were empiricists, influenced by logical positivism and 'ordinary language' philosophy. The writer of the previous generation they most respected was probably George Orwell.† Technically, the novelists were content to use, with only slight modifications, the conventions of 1930s and Edwardian realism. Their originality was largely a matter of tone and attitude and subject matter, reflecting changes in English culture and society brought about by the convulsion of World War II—roughly speaking, the supersession of a bourgeois-dominated class-society by a more meritocratic and opportunistic social system. The poets dealt with ordinary prosaic experience in dry, disciplined, slightly depressive verse. In short, they were antimodernist, readerly, and realistic, and belong on the metonymic side of our bi-polar scheme.

The most representative writers of this generation were Kingsley Amis and Philip Larkin (significantly they were close friends at Oxford). I have written elsewhere of Amis's work and its relation to modernist writing,[1] so I shall confine myself here to Philip Larkin. That he is an antimodernist scarcely needs demonstration. To find his

*See her essay 'Against Dryness', *Encounter* XVI (January 1961, pp. 16–20).
†In his introduction to the first important Movement anthology, *New Lines* (1956) Robert Conquest named Orwell as a major influence on these poets. Orwell's influence is even more evident in the fiction and criticism of the 1950s writers, especially John Wain's.

own poetic voice he had to shake off the influence of Yeats that pervades his first volume of poems *The North Ship* (1945); and he has made no secret of his distaste for the poetics of T. S. Eliot which underpins so much verse in the modernist tradition. 'I . . . have no belief in "tradition" or a common myth-kitty, or casual allusions in poems to other poems or poets,' he has written;[2] and, 'Separating the man who suffers from the man who creates is all right—we separate the petrol from the engine—but the dependence of the second on the first is complete.'[3] Like Orwell (see p. 21 above) Larkin believes that the task of the writer is to communicate as accurately as he can in words experience which is initially non-verbal: poetry is 'born of the tension between what [the poet] non-verbally feels and what can be got over in common word-usage to someone who hasn't had his experience or education or travel-grant.'[4] Like most writers in the antimodernist, or realist or readerly tradition, Larkin is, in aesthetic matters, an antiformalist: 'Form holds little interest for me. Content is everything.'[5]

It would be easy enough to demonstrate abstractly that the last-quoted assertion is an impossibly self-contradictory one for a poet to make. A more interesting line of enquiry, however, is to try and define the kind of form Larkin's work actually has, in spite of his somewhat disingenuous denials. (He has claimed, characteristically, that the omission of the main verb in 'MCMXIV',[6] which so powerfully and poignantly creates the sense of an historical moment, poised between peace and war, arrested and held for an inspection that is solemn with afterknowledge, was an 'accident'[7]—as if there could be such a thing in a good poem.) My suggestion is that we can best accomplish this task of defining the formal character of Larkin's verse by regarding him as a 'metonymic' poet.

Poetry, especially lyric poetry, is an inherently metaphoric mode, and to displace it towards the metonymic pole is (whether Larkin likes it or not) an 'experimental' literary gesture. Such poetry makes its impact by appearing daringly, even shockingly unpoetic, particularly when the accepted poetic mode is elaborately metaphoric. This was true of the early Wordsworth, as I argued in Part Two, and it was certainly true of Philip Larkin in his post-*North Ship* verse: nothing could have been more different from the poetry of Dylan Thomas and the other ageing members of the 'New Apocalypse'. Larkin, indeed, has many affinities with Wordsworth (in spite of having had a 'forgotten boredom' of a childhood)[8] and seems to share Wordsworth's 'spontaneous overflow' theory of poetic creation, which T. S. Eliot thought he had disposed of in 'Tradition and the Individual Talent'. 'One should . . . write poetry only when one wants to and has to,' Larkin has remarked; and, 'writing isn't an act of the will.'[9] His poetic style is characterized by colloquialism, 'low' diction and conscious cliché:

Coming up England by a different line
For once, early in the cold new year,
We stopped, and, watching men with number-plates
Sprint down the platform to familiar gates,
'Why, Coventry!' I exclaimed. 'I was born here.'[10]

I lie

Where Mr Bleaney lay, and stub my fags
On the same saucer, and try

Stuffing my ears with cotton-wool, to drown
The jabbering set he egged her on to buy.
I know his habits—what time he came down,
His preference for sauce to gravy, why

He kept on plugging at the four aways—[11]

When I see a couple of kids
And guess he's fucking her and she's
Taking pills or wearing a diaphragm,
I know this is paradise

Everyone old has dreamed of all their lives—[12]

With Wordsworth, Larkin might claim that his 'principal object . . .
was to choose incidents and situations from common life, and to relate
or describe them, throughout, as far as was possible in a selection of
language really used by men, tracing in them truly, though not
ostentatiously, the primary laws of our nature,'[13] though it is from
common urban-industrial life that he usually chooses them—shops,
trains, hospitals, inner-city streets and parks. The gaudy mass-
produced glamour of chain store lingerie—

Lemon, sapphire, moss-green, rose
Bri-Nylon Baby-Dolls and Shorties

provides the occasion for a tentative, uncondescending meditation on
the mystery of sexual allure:

How separate and unearthy love is,
Or women are, or what they do,
Or in our young unreal wishes
Seem to be: synthetic, new,
And natureless in ecstasies. [14]

The topic of death is handled in contexts where modern urban folk face
it, the ambulance and the hospital:

All know they are going to die.
Not yet, perhaps not here, but in the end,
And somewhere like this. That is what it means,
This clean-sliced cliff; a struggle to transcend
The thought of dying, for unless its powers
Outbuild cathedrals nothing contravenes
The coming dark, though crowds each evening try

With wasteful, weak, propitiatory flowers.[15]

Larkin is a declared realist. 'Lines on a Young Lady's Photograph Album', strategically placed at the beginning of his first important collection, *The Less Deceived* (1955), is his 'Musée des Beaux Arts', taking not Flemish painting but snapshots as the examplary art form:

> But o, photography! as no art is,
> Faithful and disappointing! that records
> Dull days as dull, and hold-it smiles as frauds,
> And will not censor blemishes
> Like washing lines and Hall's Distemper boards,
>
> But shows the cat as disinclined, and shades
> A chin as doubled when it is, what grace
> Your candour thus confers upon her face!
> How overwhelmingly persuades
> This is a real girl in a real place,
>
> In every sense empirically true![16]

Like a realistic novelist, Larkin relies heavily on synecdochic detail to evoke scene, character, culture and subculture. In 'At Grass', the past glories of race horses are evoked thus:

> Silks at the start: against the sky
> Numbers and parasols: outside,
> Squadrons of empty cars, and heat,
> And littered grass: then the long cry
> Hanging unhushed till it subside
> To stop-press columns on the street.[17]

In Hull

> domes and statues, spires and cranes cluster
> Beside grain-scattered streets, barge-crowded water,
> And residents from raw estates, brought down
> The dead straight miles by stealing flat-faced trolleys,
> Push through plate-glass swing doors to their desires—
> Cheap suits, red kitchen-ware, sharp shoes, iced lollies,
> Electric mixers, toasters, washers, driers—[18]

After the Agricultural Show

> The carpark has thinned. They're loading jumps on a truck.
> Back now to private addresses, gates and lamps
> In high stone one-street villages, empty at dusk,
> And side-roads of small towns (sports finals stuck
> In front doors, allotments reaching down to the railway);[19]

To call Larkin a metonymic poet does not imply that he uses no metaphors—of course he does. Some of his poems are based on extended analogies—'Next, Please', 'No Road' and 'Toads', for instance. But such poems become more rare in his later collections. All three just mentioned are in *The Less Deceived*, and 'Toads Revisited' in

The Whitsun Weddings (1964) makes a fairly perfunctory use of the original metaphor. Many of his poems have no metaphors at all—for example, 'Myxomatosis', 'Poetry of Departures', 'Days', 'As Bad as a Mile', 'Afternoons'. And in what are perhaps his finest and most characteristic poems, the metaphors are foregrounded against a predominantly metonymic background, which is in turn foregrounded against the background of the (metaphoric) poetic tradition. 'The Whitsun Weddings' is a classic example of this technique.

> That Whitsun, I was late getting away:
>   Not till about
> One-twenty on the sunlit Saturday
> Did my three-quarters-empty train pull out,
> All windows down, all cushions hot, all sense
> Of being in a hurry gone. We ran
> Behind the backs of houses, crossed a street
> Of blinding windscreens, smelt the fish-dock; thence
> The river's level drifting breadth began,
> Where sky and Lincolnshire and water meet.

This opening stanza has a characteristically casual, colloquial tone, and the near-redundant specificity ('One-twenty', 'three-quarters-empty') of a personal anecdote, a 'true story' (compare Wordsworth's 'I've measured it from side to side,/'Tis three feet long, and two feet wide'). The scenery is evoked by metonymic and synecdochic detail ('drifting breadth', 'blinding windscreens' etc.) as are the wedding parties that the poet observes at the stations on the way to London, seeing off bridal couples on their honeymoons:

> The fathers with broad belts under their suits
> And seamy foreheads; mothers loud and fat;
> An uncle shouting smut; and then the perms,
> The nylon gloves and jewellery substitutes,
> The lemons, mauves and olive-ochres that
>
> Marked off the girls unreally from the rest.

Apart from the unobtrusive 'seamy', there are no metaphors here: appearance, clothing, behaviour, are observed with the eye of a novelist or documentary writer and allowed to stand, untransformed by metaphor, as indices of a certain recognizable way of life. There *is* a simile in this stanza, but it is drawn from the context (railway stations) in a way that, we have seen in other chapters, is characteristic of realistic writers using the metonymic mode:

> As if out on the end of an event
>   Waving goodbye
> To something that survived it.

As the poem goes on, Larkin unobtrusively raises the pitch of rhetorical and emotional intensity—and this corresponds to the

approach of the train to its destination: the journey provides the poem
with its basic structure, a sequence of spatio-temporal contiguities (as
in 'Here'). Some bolder figures of speech are introduced—'a happy
funeral', 'a religious wounding'; and in the penultimate stanza a
striking simile which still contrives to be 'unpoetic', by collapsing the
conventional pastoral distinction between nasty town and nice
country:

> I thought of London spread out in the sun,
> Its postal districts packed like squares of wheat.

It is in the last stanza that the poem suddenly, powerfully, 'takes off',*
transcends the merely empirical, almost sociological observation of its
earlier stanzas and affirms the poet's sense of sharing, vicariously, in
the onward surge of life as represented by the newly wedded couples
collected together in the train ('this frail travelling coincidence') and
the unpredictable but fertile possibilities the future holds for them.

> We slowed again,
> And as the tightened brakes took hold, there swelled
> A sense of falling, like an arrow-shower
> Sent out of sight, somewhere becoming rain.[20]

This metaphor, with its mythical, magical and archaic resonances, is
powerful partly because it is so different from anything else in the
poem (except for 'religious wounding', and that has a tone of
humorous overstatement quite absent from the last stanza).

Something similar happens in Larkin's most famous poem, 'Church
Going',[21] where the last stanza has a dignity and grandeur of diction—

> A serious house on serious earth it is,
> In whose blent air all our compulsions meet,
> Are recognized, and robed as destinies

which comes as a thrilling surprise after the downbeat, slightly ironic
tone of the preceding stanzas, a tone established in the first stanza:

> Hatless, I take off
> My cycle-clips in awkward reverence.

That line-and-a-half must be the most often quoted fragment of
Larkin's poetry, and the way in which the homely 'cycle-clips' damps
down the metaphysical overtones of 'reverence' and guarantees the
trustworthy ordinariness of the poetic persona is indeed deeply typical
of Larkin. But if his poetry were limited to merely avoiding the pitfalls
of poetic pretentiousness and insincerity it would not interest us for
very long. Again and again he surprises us, especially in the closing
lines of his poems, by his ability to transcend—or turn ironically

---

*Larkin instructed Anthony Thwaite, then a radio producer, that the poem should be
read holding a carefully sustained note until the very end, when it should 'lift off the
ground', according to David Timms. *Philip Larkin* (1973) p. 120.

upon—the severe restraints he seems to have placed upon authentic expression of feeling in poetry. Sometimes, as in 'The Whitsun Weddings' and 'Church Going', this is accomplished by allowing a current of metaphorical language to flow into the poem, with the effect of a river bursting through a dam. But quite as often it is done by a subtle complication of metre, line-endings and syntax. For example, the amazing conclusion to 'Mr Bleaney':

> But if he stood and watched the frigid wind
> Tousling the clouds, lay on the fusty bed
> Telling himself that this was home, and grinned,
> And shivered, without shaking off the dread
>
> That how we live measures our own nature,
> And at his age having no more to show
> Than one hired box should make him pretty sure
> He warranted no better, I don't know.[22]

Syntactically this long periodic sentence is in marked contrast to the rest of the poem, and marks a reversal in its drift: a shift from satiric spleen vented upon the external world—a Bleaney-world to which the poetic persona feels superior—to a sudden collapse of his own morale, a chilling awareness that this environment may correspond to his own inner 'nature'. This fear is expressed obliquely by a speculative attribution of the speaker's feelings to Mr Bleaney. The diction is plain and simple (if more dignified than in the preceding stanzas) but the syntax, subordinate clauses burgeoning and negatives accumulating bewilderingly, is extremely complex and creates a sense of helplessness and entrapment. The main clause so long delayed—'I don't know'—when it finally comes, seems to spread back dismally through the whole poem, through the whole life of the unhappy man who utters it.

Many of Larkin's most characteristic poems end, like 'Mr Bleaney', with a kind of eclipse of meaning, speculation fading out in the face of the void. At the end of 'Essential Beauty' the girl in the cigarette ad becomes a Belle Dame Sans Merci for the 'dying smokers' who

>   sense
> Walking towards them through some dappled park
> As if on water that unfocussed she
> No match lit up, nor drag ever brought near,
> Who now stands newly clear,
> Smiling and recognizing, and going dark.[23]

We

>   spend all our life on imprecisions
> That when we start to die
> Have no idea why.[24]

Death is, we can all agree, a 'nonverbal' reality, because, as Wittgenstein said, it is not an experience *in* life; and it is in dealing with death, a topic that haunts him, that Larkin achieves the paradoxical feat of expressing in words something that is beyond words:

> Life is slow dying . . .
> And saying so to some
> Means nothing; others it leaves
> Nothing to be said.[25]

The same theme, I take it, forms the conclusion to the title poem of Larkin's most recent collection, *The High Windows*. The poet compares his generation's envy of the sexual freedom of the young in today's Permissive Society to the putative envy of older people of his own apparent freedom, in his youth, from superstitious religious fears.

> And immediately
> Rather than words comes the thought of high windows:
> The sun-comprehending glass,
> And beyond it, the deep blue air, that shows
> Nothing, and is nowhere, and is endless.[26]

8   Postmodernist Fiction

The history of modern English literature, it has been suggested in the foregoing chapters, can be seen as an oscillation in the practice of writing between polarized clusters of attitudes and techniques: modernist, symbolist or mythopoeic, writerly and metaphoric on the one hand; antimodernist, realistic, readerly and metonymic on the other. What looks like innovation—a new mode of writing foregrounding itself against the background of the received mode when the latter becomes stale and exhausted—is therefore also in some sense a reversion to the principles and procedures of an earlier phase. If the critical pronouncements associated with each phase tend to be somewhat predictable, the actual creative work produced is not, such is the infinite variety and fertility of the human imagination working upon the fresh materials thrown up by secular history. But the metaphor/metonymy distinction explains why at the deepest level there is a cyclical rhythm to literary history, for there is nowhere else for discourse to go except between these two poles.

There is, however, a certain kind of contemporary avant-garde art which is said to be neither modernist nor antimodernist, but postmodernist; it continues the modernist critique of traditional mimetic art, and shares the modernist commitment to innovation, but pursues these aims by methods of its own. It tries to go beyond modernism, or around it, or underneath it, and is often as critical of modernism as it is of antimodernism. In the field of writing such a phenomenon obviously offers an interesting challenge to the explanatory power of the literary typology expounded above. The object of this chapter, then, is to attempt a profile of postmodernist fiction and to test the relevance of the metaphor/metonymy distinction to it. Postmodernism has established itself as an *écriture*, in Barthes's sense of the word—a mode of writing shared by a significant number of writers in a given period—most plausibly in the French *nouveau roman* and in American fiction of the last ten or fifteen years, and I shall be concerned here chiefly with the latter. But I shall make reference to texts by British writers where these seem relevant, and I begin with Samuel Beckett, who has a strong claim to be considered the first important postmodernist writer.

Beckett served his literary apprenticeship in the shadow of classical modernism. His earliest publications in prose were a contribution to a symposium on Joyce (1929) and a study of Proust (1930). The opening story, 'Dante and the Lobster', in his first book of fiction, *More Pricks than Kicks* (1934), shows him just beginning to detach himself from the modernist tradition, especially from the technique of Joyce, with whom, of all the modernist writers, Beckett has the closest affinity (and for whom he worked, for a time, as secretary). As it happens, this story deals with the same theme of life/death/time as the texts discussed in Part One. Belacqua, a Dublin student, performs various banal tasks in his day—makes himself a sandwich of burnt toast and gorgonzola cheese for his lunch, attends an Italian lesson, collects a lobster from the fishmonger for his aunt's and his own supper. Among the miscellaneous pieces of information that impinge on his consciousness is the fact that a convicted murderer is to be hanged the next day. Spectacles of pain and misery in the streets on his way home, combined with inner musings on Dante, especially the line from the *Inferno*, '*qui vive la pietà quando è ben morta*',* provoke Belacqua to ask, 'Why not piety and pity both, even down below?', to pray for 'a little mercy in the stress of sacrifice' and to extend his compassion to the convicted murderer:

> Poor McCabe, he would get it in the neck at dawn. What was he doing now, how was he feeling? He would relish one more meal, one more night.[1]

This mood is, however, exposed as a sentimental illusion, for what really shocks Belacqua into a true awareness of pain and death is the discovery that the lobster is still alive and must be boiled in that state so that he may eat it.

> 'Christ!' he said 'it's alive.'
> His aunt looked at the lobster. It moved again. It made a faint nervous act of life on the oilcloth. They stood above it, looking down on it, exposed

---

*'Here pity lives when it is virtually dead.' Belacqua remarks that there is a 'superb pun' on pity/piety.

cruciform on the oilcloth. It shuddered again. Belacqua felt he would be sick.

'My God' he whined 'it's alive, what'll we do?' . . .

'You make a fuss' she said angrily 'and upset me and then lash into it for your dinner.'

She lifted the lobster clear of the table. It had about thirty seconds to live.

Well, thought Belcqua, it's a quick death, God help us all.

It is not.[2]

This conclusion to the story (which I have much abridged) takes place in the aunt's kitchen which, like Dante's Hell, is in 'the bowels of the earth'. The *Divine Comedy* seems to function in Beckett's story much as Homer's *Odyssey* does in *Ulysses*. Belacqua's name (as improbable as Dedalus) derives from *Purgatory*; at the opening of the story he is wrestling with the interpretation of a difficult passage in *Paradise*; and his conversation with his Italian teacher touches on 'Dante's rare movements of compassion in Hell'.[3] The story seems to indicate the ultimate irrelevance of the Christian metaphysic (supremely articulated by Dante) to the problem of suffering and death. It thus reverses the message of Oscar Wilde's 'The Ballad of Reading Gaol'; but Christian symbolism and allusion, especially to the Passion, permeate the climax of the story even if largely disguised under 'low' diction ('Christ!' 'cruciform' 'My God' 'lash into'), evidently to underline the horror of the world when recognized for what it is, a place where one creature lives by the cruel sacrifice of another, right along the chain of being. The identification of the lobster with Christ is clearly signalled earlier in the story when Belacqua, talking to a French teacher, is obliged to use the word *poisson*. 'He did not know the French for lobster. Fish would do very well. Fish had been good enough for Jesus Christ, Son of God, Saviour. It was good enough for Mlle Glain.'[4] Even the hilarious business of Belacqua's lunch fits into the same thematic scheme, inasmuch as Belcaqua's toasting of the bread till it is black, and his handling of the cheese, are portrayed as violent actions perpetrated upon innocent living matter:

> He laid his cheek against the soft of the bread, it was spongy and warm, *alive*. But he would very quickly take that fat white look off its face . . .[5] [my italics]

> He looked sceptically at the cut of cheese. He turned it over on its back to see was the other side any better. The other side was worse. . . . He rubbed it. It was sweating. That was something. He stooped and smelt it. A faint fragrance of corruption. What good was that? He didn't want fragrance, he wasn't a bloody gourmet, he wanted a good stench. What he wanted was a good green stenching rotten lump of Gorgonzola cheese, *alive*, and by God he would have it.[6] [my italics]

The handling of the cheese is proleptic of the aunt's treatment of the lobster at the end of the story: 'She caught up the lobster and laid it on its back. It trembled. "They feel nothing" she said.'[7]

Up to a point, then, 'Dante and the Lobster' responds to the same kind of reading as an episode of *Ulysses*, as a narrative of modern life which alludes to a prior myth that is in some sense a key to its meaning, and in which a superficially gratuitous sequence of banal events is guided towards a final thematic epiphany by discreetly planted *leitmotifs*. But there is a good deal in the text that is not accountable in these terms. The manic, obsessional and eccentric behaviour of the hero, for instance (a long way from the endearing whims and fetishes of Bloom) is in no sense 'explained' by the story. It is funny, but it is also disconcerting. So is, in a different way, the last line of the story: 'It is not.' This is not the first occasion on which the author who 'speaks' the narrative is distinguishable from Belacqua, through whose eyes it is mainly seen, but it is certainly the most emphatically foregrounded— being, in effect, not merely a comment, but a flat contradiction and dismissal of the hero and his hollow epiphany. The author, as it were, scuttles his story in its last line, and this prevents the reader from leaving its uncomfortable implications safely enclosed within the category of 'literature' or 'fiction'. These are features which become progressively more marked in Beckett's fiction (and in postmodernist writing generally), while the 'mythical method' (exemplified by the Dantean parallels) 'of ordering, of giving a shape and significance to the immense panorama of futility and anarchy that is contemporary history' (as T. S. Eliot said of Joyce)[8] disappears, is displaced by a growing insistence that there is no order, no shape or significance to be found anywhere.

Beckett's next work of fiction, *Murphy* (1938) begins:

> The sun shone, having no alternative, on the nothing new. Murphy sat out of it, as though he were free, in a mew in West Brompton . . . He sat naked in his rocking-chair of undressed teak, guaranteed not to crack, warp, corrode or creak at night. It was his own, it never left him. The corner in which he sat was curtained off from the sun, the poor old sun in the Virgin again for the billionth time. Seven scarves held him in position. Two fastened his shins to the rockers, one his thighs to the seat, two his breast and belly to the back, one his wrists to the strut behind. Only the most local movements were possible. Sweat poured off him, tightened the thongs. The breath was not perceptible. The eyes, cold and unwavering as a gull's, stared up at an irridescence splashed over the cornice moulding, shrinking and fading.[9]

This discourse raises a lot of questions in the reader's mind. Some are answered: for instance, Murphy constrains his body in this eccentric manner in order to live more completely in his mind—he is a dedicated solipsist. But how does Murphy manage to tie himself up unassisted? and where is the seventh scarf? More fundamentally, whose voice are we listening to? Who takes pity on 'the poor old sun', and who compares Murphy's eyes to a gull's, and what is the import of these tropes? It is difficult to answer these questions.

If 'Dante and the Lobster' reminds one of Joyce, *Murphy* is Beckett's '1930s' novel. Its drab, historically precise setting (London,

1935), and its subject matter (penniless, alienated young man having difficulties in finding acceptable employment and keeping his girlfriend) have certain affinities with the novels of Isherwood and Orwell (especially *Keep the Aspidistra Flying*) but the experience of reading it is very different. While renouncing the mythic parallelism of Joyce's treatment of Dublin, it also ignores or ridicules the conventions of realism adopted by the representative novelists of the 1930s. There is no local colour in *Murphy*, no evocative synecdochic detail in the descriptions of places and people. The opening of Chapter 2, describing Celia in a list of facts and figures—

Age	Unimportant
Head	Small and round
Eyes	Green
Complexion	White
Hair	Yellow
Features	Mobile
Neck	$13\frac{3}{4}''$

etc.—mocks the conventional novelistic description of physical appearance, as the description of Murphy's grotesque green suit parodies the realistic novelist's reliance on the code of clothing as an index to character.[10] The narrator is for the most part impersonal and aloof, but given to disconcerting interventions, addresses to the reader ('gentle skimmer') and metafictional comments ('Celia, thank God for a Christian name'. . . . 'The above passage is carefully calculated to deprave the cultivated reader'). The predictability of the style and development of the action is extremely low, and although it is a very funny book it is not at all easy to read for this reason. It *resists* reading by refusing to settle into a simply identifiable mode or rhythm, thus imitating, on the level of reading conventions, the resistance of the world to interpretation.

The latter idea becomes explicit in the next novel *Watt* (1953—composed 1942–3), supremely in the episode of the Galls, who appear at the door of the house where Watt is working as a servant to Mr Knott:

> We are the Galls, father and son, and we are come, what is more, all the way from town, to choon the piano.
> They were two, and they stood, arm in arm, in this way, because the father was blind, like so many members of his profession. For if the father had not been blind, then he would not have needed his son to hold his arm, and guide him on his rounds, no, but he would have set his son free, to go about his own business. So Watt supposed, though there was nothing in the father's face to show that he was blind, nor in his attitude, either, except that he leaned on his son in a way expressive of a great need of support. But he might have done this, if he had been halt, or merely tired, on account of his great age. There was no family likeness between the two, as far as Watt could make out, and nevertheless he knew he was in the presence of a father and son, for

had he not just been told so. Or were they not perhaps merely stepfather and stepson. We are the Galls stepfather and stepson—those were perhaps the words that should have been spoken. But it was natural to prefer the others. Not that they could not very well be a true father and son, without resembling each other in the least, for they could.[11]

Uncertainty spreads like the plague through the world of *Watt*. 'The incident of the Galls father and son,' observes the narrator, 'was followed by others of a similar kind, incidents that is to say of great formal brilliance and indeterminable purport. . . . And Watt could not accept them for what they perhaps were, the simple games that time plays with space . . . but was obliged, because of his peculiar character, to enquire into what they meant. . . . But what was this pursuit of meaning, in this indifference to meaning? And to what did it tend? These are delicate questions.'[12] Indeed—but questions absolutely fundamental to Beckett's work. The often-asserted resistance of the world to meaningful interpretation would be a sterile basis for writing if it were not combined with a poignant demonstration of the human obligation to attempt such interpretation, especially by the process of organizing one's memories into narrative form. In the next stage of Beckett's narrative writing, the trilogy of *Molloy* (1951), *Malone Dies* (1951) and the *Unnamable* (1953) (all of which first appeared in French) the impersonal, erratically intrusive and rhetorically unpredictable narrator of the earlier fiction is displaced by a series of first-person narrators, increasingly isolated and deprived of sensory stimuli, desperately trying to make sense of their experience by recalling it. The contradiction between the futility of the effort and the compulsion to make it produces a longing for extinction and silence, which in turn provokes fear and a frantic clinging to the vestiges of consciousness—which is intolerable.

> . . . if only there were a thing, but there it is, there is not, they took away things when they departed, they took away nature, there was never anyone, anyone but me, anything but me, talking to me of me, impossible to stop, impossible to go on, but I must go on, I'll go on, without anyone, without anything, but me, but my voice, that is to say I'll stop, I'll end, it's the end already, shortlived, what is it, a little hole, you go down into it, into the silence, it's worse than the noise, you listen, it's worse than talking, no, not worse, no worse, you wait, in anguish, have they forgotten me, no, yes, no, someone calls me, I crawl out again, what is it, a little hole, in the wilderness. It's the end that is the worst, no, it's the beginning that is the worst, then the middle, then the end, in the end it's the end that is the worst, this voice, that, I don't know, it's every second that is the worst . . .[13]

It would be quite false to suggest that all postmodernist writers share Beckett's particular philosophical preoccupations and obsessions. But the general idea of the world resisting the compulsive attempts of the human consciousness to interpret it, of the human predicament being in some sense 'absurd', does underlie a good deal of postmodernist writing. That is why it seeks to find formal alternatives to modernism as well as to antimodernism. The falsity of the patterns imposed upon experience in the traditional realistic novel is common ground between the modernists and the postmodernists, but to the latter it seems that the modernists, too, for all their experimentation, obliquity and complexity, oversimplified the world and held out a false hope of somehow making it at home in the human mind. *Finnegans Wake* (to take the most extreme product of the modernist literary imagination) certainly 'resists' reading, resists interpretation, by the formidable difficulty of its verbal style and narrative method, and perhaps it has yet to find that 'ideal reader suffering from ideal insomnia' for whom, Joyce said, it was designed. But we persist in trying to read it in the faith that it is ultimately susceptible of being understood—that we shall, eventually, be able to unpack all the meanings that Joyce put into it, and that these meanings will cohere into a unity. Postmodernism subverts that faith. 'Where is the figure in the carpet?' asks a character in Donald Barthelme's *Snow White* (1967), alluding to the title of a story by Henry James that has become proverbial among modern critics as an image of the goal of interpretation; but he adds disconcertingly: 'Or is it just . . . carpet?'[14] A lot of postmodernist writing implies that experience is 'just carpet' and that whatever patterns we discern in it are wholly illusory, comforting fictions.

The difficulty, for the reader, of postmodernist writing, is not so much a matter of obscurity (which might be cleared up) as of uncertainty, which is endemic, and manifests itself on the level of narrative rather than style. No amount of patient study could establish, for instance, whether the man with the heavy coat and hat and stick encountered by Moran in *Molloy* is the man Molloy designated as C, or Molloy himself, or someone else; and Hugh Kenner's description of Beckett 'filling the air with uncertainty, the uncertainty fiction usually dissipates',[15] will apply to a lot of postmodernist writers. We shall never be able to unravel the plots of John Fowles's *The Magus* (1966) or Alain Robbe-Grillet's *Le Voyeur* (1955) or Thomas Pynchon's *The Crying of Lot 49* (1966), for they are labyrinths without exits. Endings, the 'exits' of fictions, are particularly significant in this connection. Instead of the closed ending of the traditional novel, in which mystery is explained and fortunes are settled, and instead of the open ending of the modernist novel, 'satisfying but not final' as Conrad said of Henry James,[16] we get the multiple ending, the false ending, the mock ending or parody ending.

The classic type of the 'closed' ending is that of the crime story in which the detective solves the mystery, reduces to meaningful order the apparently meaningless confusion of clues, and ensures that justice is done. Muriel Spark parodies this convention, and implicitly criticizes the presumption of those (novelists as well as policemen) who play the part of Providence, in novels which disconcertingly readjust the roles of criminal, victim and witnesses. Thus in *The Driver's Seat* (1970) Lyse scatters across Europe in the days before her death a trail of clues which make no sense at all until we grasp that she is in a sense the plotter as well as the victim of the crime. In the same author's *Not to Disturb* (1971) the servants in a luxurious villa on Lake Geneva make their arrangements to profit by a *crime passionelle* which has not yet occurred. Journalists are alerted, statements prepared, contracts negotiated by transatlantic telephone, interviews recorded on tape and film, while the husband, wife and lover are still arguing in the library. The suave butler, Lister, who presides over the whole operation, observes of his employers that 'They have placed themselves, unfortunately, within the realm of predestination.'[17] He excludes two people from the house 'because they don't fit into the story' and the weather (always ready to cooperate with gods and novelists) obligingly eliminates them with a thunderbolt.

In *The French Lieutenant's Woman* (1969) John Fowles presents alternative endings to his story and invites the reader to choose between them. John Barth floats a whole series of possible endings to the title story of his collection *Lost in the Funhouse* (1968), but rejects them all except the most inconclusive and banal. Another story, 'Title', perceptibly influenced by Beckett, contrives not to end at all:

> It's about over. Let the dénouement be soon and unexpected, painless if possible, quick at least, above all soon. Now now! How in the world will it ever[18]

Richard Brautigan adds to the ending of *A Confederate General From Big Sur* (1964) 'A SECOND ENDING', then a third, a fourth and fifth.

> Then there are more and more endings: the sixth, the 53rd, the 131st, the 9,435th ending, endings going faster and faster, more and more endings, faster and faster until this book is having 186,000 endings per second.[19]

The same author concludes the penultimate chapter of *Trout Fishing in America* (1967), entitled 'PRELUDE TO THE "MAYONNAISE" CHAPTER': 'Expressing a human need I always wanted to write a book that ended with the word Mayonnaise.'[20] And accordingly the last chapter consists of the transcript of a letter written in 1952 from 'Mother and Nancy' to 'Florence and Harv' which has the P.S., 'Sorry I forgot to give you the mayonaise [sic].'[21] There is the additional joke that this whimsical human need could have been fulfilled without the last chapter, since the penultimate chapter also ends with the word 'mayonnaise', and the 'MAYONNAISE CHAPTER' is no less arbitrary a way of ensuring that the book ends on that word, since the letter in no way relates to anything that has gone before. Indeed, insofar as the P.S. misspells the word, Brautigan has cheated himself of his intention by transcribing it.

Critical opinion varies about how significantly *new* postmodernism really is. Leslie Fiedler, for instance, thinks it is genuinely revolutionary;[22] Frank Kermode, on the other hand, thinks that it has achieved only 'marginal developments of older modernism'.[23] Both opinions are tenable—both are in a sense 'true'. It depends upon what you are looking for and where you are standing when you are looking. Fiedler is mainly concerned with American literature and culture (in the anthropological sense); Kermode with the international avant-garde in all the arts. Fiedler defines postmodernism primarily as a very recent 'posthumanist' phenomenon, hostile or indifferent to traditional aesthetic categories and values, offering a polymorphous hedonism to its (largely youthful) audience, and unamenable to formalist analysis. Its art is anti-art, and demands 'Death-of-Art criticism'.[24] Kermode, on the other hand, approaches postmodernism as a historian of art and aesthetics and has little difficulty in tracing its theoretical assumptions back to either classical modernism or to the Dadaist schism that developed as long ago as 1916; and he sees the latter tradition as an essentially marginal one, its products more akin to jokes than art, 'piquant allusions to what fundamentally interests us more than they do.'[25] The aim of this chapter is not to try and settle the disagreement, but to try and throw light on the formal principles underlying postmodernist writing.

If Jakobson is right, that all discourse tends towards either the metaphoric or the metonymic pole of language, it should be possible to categorize postmodernist writing under one heading or the other. The theory (crudely summarized) states that all discourse connects one topic with another, either because they are in some sense similar to each other, or because they are in some sense contiguous with each other; and implies that if you attempt to group topics according to some other principle, or absence of principle, the human mind will nevertheless persist in trying to make sense of the text thus produced by looking in it for relationships of similarity and/or contiguity; and insofar as a text succeeds in defeating such interpretation, it defeats itself. It would, I believe, be possible to analyse postmodernist writing in these terms, but perhaps not very profitable. For if we extend the term 'postmodernist' to cover all the writers to whom it seems applicable, we might identify them individually as either metaphoric or metonymic, but it would be difficult to show that their work, considered *collectively*, has any bias towards one pole or the other. Rather it would seem that we can best define the formal character of postmodernist writing by examining its efforts to deploy both metaphoric and metonymic devices in radically new ways, and to defy (even if such defiance is ultimately vain) the obligation to choose between these two principles of connecting one topic with another. What other alternatives might there be? The headings below are intended to indicate some of the possibilities.

Contradiction

> But what is the good of talking about what they will do as soon as Worm sets himself in motion, so as to gather himself without fail into their midst, since he cannot set himself in motion, though he often desires to, if when speaking of him one may speak of desire, and one may not, one should not, but there it is, that is the way to speak of him, as if he were alive, as if he could understand, as if he could desire, even if it serves no purpose, and it serves none.[26]

This passage from *The Unnamable* cancels itself out as it goes along, and is representative of a text in which the narrator is condemned to oscillate between irreconcilable desires and assertions. Famously, it ends, 'you must go on, I can't go on, I'll go on.' If that were rearranged slightly to read, 'I can't go on, you must go on, I'll go on', it would not be at all self-contradictory, but a quite logically motivated and 'uplifting' sequence of despair followed by self-admonishment followed by renewed resolve. As it stands, each clause negates the preceding one. Leonard Michaels approaches this radically contradictory basis for the practice of writing when he says in 'Dostoevsky', 'It is impossible to live with or without fictions.'[27] The religion of Bokonism in Kurt Vonnegut's *Cat's Cradle* (1963) is based on 'the cruel paradox of . . . the heartbreaking necessity of lying about reality and the heartbreaking impossibility of lying about it.'[28]

One of the most emotively powerful emblems of contradiction, one that affronts the most fundamental binary system of all, is the hermaphrodite; and it is not surprising that the characters of postmodernist fiction are often sexually ambivalent: for example, Gore Vidal's sex-changing Myra/Myron Breckinridge,[29] and the central character of Brigid Brophy's *In Transit* (1969), who is suffering from amnesia in an international airport and cannot remember what sex he/she is (the narrator cannot examine his/her private parts in public, but cannot retreat to the privacy of a public convenience without knowing what she/he desires to find out). Henry, the hero of the postmodernist half of Julian Mitchell's duplex novel *The Undiscovered Country* (1968)* is transformed into a woman, and then into a hermaphrodite, and is engaged in the pursuit of a beautiful creature of equally uncertain sex. At the climax of John Barth's allegorical fabulation *Giles Goat-boy* (1966) the caprine hero and his beloved Anastasia survive the dreaded inquisition of the computer WESCAC when, locked together in copulation, they answer the question 'ARE YOU MALE OR FEMALE?' with two simultaneous and contradictory answers, 'YES' and 'NO'.[30]

---

*The other half is realistic or autobiographical in mode. I have written about this work at some length in *The Novelist at the Crossroads* pp. 26–32.

Permutation

Both metaphoric and metonymic modes of writing involve selection, and selection involves leaving something out. Postmodernist writers often try to defy this law by incorporating alternative narrative lines in the same text—for example John Fowles' *The French Lieutenant's Woman* and John Barth's 'Lost in the Funhouse', already cited, Robert Coover's 'The Magic Poker' and 'The Babysitter' in *Pricksongs and Descants* (1969) and Raymond Federman's *Double or Nothing* (1971). This procedure is another kind of 'contradiction', though in practice we are usually able to resolve it by ranking the alternatives in an order of authenticity. A more radical way of denying the obligation to select is to exhaust all the possible combinations in a given field. In the imaginary world of 'Tlön, Uqbar, Orbis Tertius', one of the fables of Jorge Luis Borges that have exercised a potent fascination over many American postmodernist writers, 'Works of fiction contain a single plot, with all its imaginable permutations';[31] and the labyrinthine novel of Ts'ui Pen in Borges' 'The Garden of the Forking Paths' is constructed on similar principles:

> In all fictional works, each time a man is confronted with several alternatives, he chooses one and eliminates the others; in the fiction of Ts'ui Pen, he chooses—simultaneously—all of them. *He creates*, in this way, diverse futures, diverse times which themselves also proliferate and fork. Here, then, is the explanation of the novel's contradictions. Fang, let us say, has a secret; a stranger calls at his door; Fang resolves to kill him. Naturally, there are several possible outcomes: Fang can kill the intruder, the intruder can kill Fang, they both can escape, they both can die, and so forth. In the work of Ts'ui Pen, all possible outcomes occur; each one is the point of departure for other forkings.[32]

By plausibly imagining the impossible, Borges liberates the imagination. Beckett uses permutation in a more limited way and to more depressive effect:

> As for his feet, sometimes he wore on each a sock, or on the one a sock and on the other a stocking, or a boot, or a shoe, or a slipper, or a sock and boot, or a sock and shoe, or a sock and slipper, or a stocking and boot, or a stocking and shoe, or a stocking and slipper, or nothing at all. And sometimes he wore on each a stocking, or on the one a stocking and on the other a boot, or a shoe, or a slipper, or a sock and boot, or a sock and shoe. . . .[33]

and so on, for a page and a half. There are several similar passages in *Watt*, in which every possible combination of a set of variables is exhausted. Probably the most famous example of permutation in Beckett, however, is in *Molloy*, where the eponymous hero wrestles with the problem of distributing and circulating his sixteen sucking stones in his pockets in such a way as to guarantee that he will always suck them in the same order.[34] Beckett's characters seek desperately to impose a purely mathematical order upon experience in the absence of any metaphysical order. In *Murphy* the hero, making his lunch from a packet of mixed biscuits, is torn between his weakness for one particular kind of biscuit and the possibility of total permutability:

> were he to take the final step and overcome his infatuation with the ginger, then the assortment would spring to life before him, dancing the radiant measure of its total permutability, edible in a hundred and twenty ways![35]

When reduced to only two variables, permutation becomes simply alternation and expresses the hopelessness of the human condition. ' "For every symptom that is eased, another is worse," ' opines Wylie in *Murphy*. ' "The horse leech's daughter is a closed system. Her quantum of wantum cannot vary . . . Humanity is a well with two buckets . . . one going down to be filled, the other coming up to be emptied." '[36] In Joseph Heller's *Catch 22* (1961) there is a wounded soldier in the hospital entirely swathed in bandages and connected to a drip-feed bottle and a bottle for waste fluid:

> When the jar on the floor was full, the jar feeding his elbow was empty, and the two were simply switched over quickly so that the stuff could drip back into him.[37]

Discontinuity

One quality we expect of all writing is continuity. Writing is a one-sided conversation. As every student, and every critic, knows, the most difficult aspect of composing an essay or thesis or book is to put one's scattered thoughts into an ideal order which will appear to have a seamless logical inevitability in its progress from one topic to another, without distorting or omitting any important point. This book itself contains innumerable sentences and phrases included not primarily to convey information but to construct smooth links between one topic and another. In fiction, metonymic writing offers a very obvious and readily intelligible kind of continuity based on spatio-temporal contiguities; the continuity of metaphorical writing is more difficult, but not impossible to identify. And as it is by its continuity that a discursive text persuades the reader, implying that no other ordering of its data could be intellectually as satisfying, so it is by its continuity that a work of fiction, if successful, imposes its vision of the world upon the reader, displaces the 'real world' with an imagined world in which the reader (especially in the case of realistic fiction) lives vicariously. Postmodernism is suspicious of continuity. Beckett disrupts the continuity of his discourse by unpredictable swerves of tone, metafictional asides to the reader, blank spaces in the text, contradiction and permutation. Some recent American writers have gone a step further and *based* their discourse upon discontinuity. 'Interruption. Discontinuity. Imperfection. It can't be helped,' insists the authorial voice of Ronald Sukenick's *98.6*[38]

98.6 illustrates the most obvious sign of discontinuity in contemporary fiction—the growing fashion for composing in very short sections, often only a paragraph in length, often quite disparate in content, the breaks between sections being sometimes further emphasized by capitalized headings (as in Richard Brautigan's *In Watermelon Sugar* [1968]), numbers (as in Robert Coover's 'The Gingerbread Man') or typographical devices (like the arrows in Vonnegut's *Breakfast of Champions* [1973]). Vonnegut's later novels and all of Brautigan's are built up in this way, out of sections too short to be recognized as conventional chapters. Donald Barthelme uses bizarre illustrations to break up the text of some of the pieces in *City Life* (1971), and Raymond Federman ingeniöusly varies the typographical layout of *Double or Nothing*, using techniques borrowed from concrete poetry to avoid the odium of

a very direct form of narration without any distractions
without any obstructions just plain
normal
regular
readable
realistic
leftoright
unequivocal
conventional
unimaginative
wellpunctuated
understandable
uninteresting
safetodigest
paragraphed
compulsive
anecdotal
salutory
textual
PROSE   prose   prose   boring
PROSE   PROSE   prose   PROSE plain   PROSE[39]

Leonard Michaels has recently developed what is virtually a new genre: the cluster (it is precisely *not* a sequence) of short passages—stories, anecdotes, reflections, quotations, prose-poems, jokes—each with an individual title in large type. Between these apparently discontinuous passages the bewildered but exhilarated reader bounces and rebounds like a ball in a pinball machine, illuminations flashing on and off, insights accumulating, till the author laconically signals TILT. One such cluster, 'I Would Have Saved Them If I Could', is concerned with the same life/death/time theme in the context of capital punishment—'the condemned prisoner story', Michaels calls it—that we have encountered several times already in this study, but it is quite distinctive in form. It consists of seventeen sections: *Giving Notice*, a brief, bitter comedy of Jewish American life, turning on a son's loss of faith; *A Suspected Jew*, an interpretation of Borges's story 'The Secret Miracle' about a Jewish writer Jaromir Hladik, executed by the Gestapo, who was allowed by God enough time between the firing of the bullets and death to mentally complete his unfinished masterpiece; *The Subject at the Vanishing Point*, a memoir of the narrator's—and author's?—grandfather, a refugee from Polish pogroms; *Material Circumstances*, a hostile vignette of Karl Marx roused to historical wrath by a landlord's insolence; *Business Life*, a wry anecdote of the narrator's uncle who runs successful beauty parlours; *Shrubless Crags*, a quotation from Byron's *The Prisoner of Chillon* about a condemned prisoner; *Song*, a three-line gag about Russian folksongs; *Blossoms*, about the terrifying early experiences of the uncle in Europe; *The Screams of Children*, about Jesus, Hladik, Kafka, the Final Solution; *Heraclitus, Hegel, Giacometti, Nietzsche, Wordsworth, Stevens*, on philosophical systems; *Alienation*, about the relation of Marxism to Christianity; *Lord Byron's Letter*, the transcription of a letter in which the poet gives an eye-witness account of three criminals being guillotined ('the second and third (which shows how dreadfully soon things grow indifferent) I am ashamed to say, had no effect on me as a horror, though I would have saved them if I could'); *Species Being*, a critique of the letter; *Dostoevsky*, a brief account of Dostoevsky's story of being reprieved from sentence of death; *The Night I Became a Marxist*, a mock-Pauline account of conversion; and *Conclusion*, which points out that 'from a certain point of view [that of the dead] none of this shit matters any more'.[40] After several readings a kind of thematic coherence does begin to emerge from this textual collage, epitomized by the sentence quoted earlier from Dostoevsky, 'It is impossible to live with or without fictions.' Fictions, whether literary, theological, philosophical or political, can never make death acceptable, or even comprehensible, yet in a world 'incessantly created of incessant death' (*Conclusion*) we have no other resource. There are degrees of authenticity (Byron's honest exactitude is preferred to Borges's whimsy or Marx's theorizing) but in the end it makes no difference. Such a paraphrase, however, is more than usually misleading, since it is only in the actual reading experience, in the disorientation produced by the abrupt and unpredictable shifts of register from one section to another, that the effects of bafflement, anguish, contradiction are felt. Michaels's exploitation of discontinuity can be more conveniently illustrated by quoting the opening lines of a less complex story, 'In the Fifties':

> In the fifties I learned to drive a car. I was frequently in love. I had more friends than now.
> When Krushchev denounced Stalin my roommate shit blood, turned yellow and lost most of his hair.

I attended the lectures of the excellent E. B. Burgum until Senator McCarthy ended his tenure. I imagined NYU would burn. Miserable students, drifting in the halls, looked at one another.

In less than a month, working day and night, I wrote a bad novel.

I went to school—NYU, Michigan, Berkeley—much of the time. I had witty, giddy conversation, four or five nights a week, in a homosexual bar in Ann Arbor.

I read literary reviews the way people suck candy.

Personal relationships were more important to me than anything else.

I had a fight with a powerful fat man who fell on my face and was immovable.

I had personal relationships with football players, jazz musicians, ass-bandits, nymphomaniacs, non-specialized degenerates, and numerous Jewish premedical students.

I had personal relationships with thirty-five rhesus monkeys in an experiment on monkey addiction to morphine. They knew me as one who shot reeking crap out of cages with a hose.[41]

The 'story' (hardly the right word, but there is no other) continues in the same mode: bald statements of fact which appear to have nothing to connect them except that they belong to the life of the narrator in the 1950s, and seem to have been selected at random from his total experience. There is a kind of recurrent theme—the political impotence of the 1950s—but most of the statements made have nothing to do with it. It's a very risky procedure, but it works because of the casual brilliance of the writing and because the writer persuades us that the discontinuity of his text *is* the truth of his experience. 'I used to think that someday I would write a fictional version of my stupid life in the fifties,' says the narrator at one point, and the implication is that the raw ingredients of that life heaped in front of us constitute a more authentic record than would be any well-made novel.

In the work of Donald Barthelme the principle of *non-sequitur* governs the relationships between sentences as well as between paragraphs. 'Edward looked at his red beard in the tableknife. Then Edward and Pia went to Sweden, to the farm.'[42] The purely temporal continuity of these actions is overwhelmed by the huge difference in scale between them and the absence of any causal connection.

> From his window Charles watched Hilda. She sat playing under the black pear tree. She bit deeply into a black pear. It tasted bad and Hilda looked at the tree inquiringly. Charles started to cry. He had been reading Bergson. He was surprised by his own weeping, and in a state of surprise, decided to get something to eat.[43]

This passage begins with a kind of logical continuity of motivation, but frays out into disparate reactions of Charles—weeping, reading Bergson, feeling hungry—which have nothing to do with Hilda or with each other. One of Barthelme's favourite devices is to take a number of interrelated or contiguous characters, or consciousnesses or conversations, and scramble them together to produce an apparently random montage of bizarrely contrasting verbal fragments ('fragments are the only forms I trust,' a Barthelme character observes).[44] For example, 'The Viennese Opera Ball':

> It is one of McCormack's proudest boasts, Carola heard over her lovely white shoulder, that he never once missed having dinner with his wife in their forty-one years of married life. She remembered Knocko at the Evacuation Day parade, and Baudelaire's famous remark. Mortality is the final evaluator of methods. An important goal is an intact sphincter. The greater the prematurity, the more generous should be the episiotomy. Yes, said Leon Jaroff, Detroit Bureau Chief for *Time*, at the Thomas Elementary School on warm spring afternoons I could look from my classroom into the open doors of the Packard plant. Ideal foster parents are mature people who are not necessarily well off, but who have a good marriage and who love and understand children. The ninth day of the ninth month is the festival of the crysanthemum (Kiku No Sekku) when *sake* made from the crysanthemum is drunk.[45]

Randomness

The discontinuity of the discourse in Brautigan, Michaels, Barthelme, often looks like randomness, but it would be more accurate to say these writers compose according to a logic of the absurd. The human mind being what it is, true randomness can only be introduced into a literary text by mechanical means—for instance the cut-up method of William Burroughs. As he says, 'You cannot will spontaneity. But you can introduce the unpredictable spontaneous factor with a pair of scissors.'[46] The writer cuts up pieces of different texts, including his own, sticks them together in random order and transcribes the result. A similar method of introducing an element of genuine randomness into literature is to issue books in loose-leaf form, the reader being invited to shuffle the sheets to produce his own text (for example B. S. Johnson's *The Unfortunates* [1969]). Such experiments seem to me the least interesting, because most mechanical, way of trying to break out of the metaphor/metonymy system; and I have nothing to add to what I have already said about them elsewhere.[47]

Excess

Some postmodernist writers have deliberately taken metaphoric or metonymic devices to excess, tested them, as it were, to destruction, parodied and burlesqued them in the process of using them, and thus sought to escape from their tyranny. Thomas Pynchon's *Gravity's Rainbow* (1973), for example, takes the commonplace analogy between rocket and phallus and pursues its ramifications relentlessly and grotesquely through the novel's enormous length, while the V motif in the same author's first novel *V* (1963) mocks interpretation by the plurality of its manifestations. Donald Barthelme practices metaphoric overkill more locally, for example in this absurd cadenza of comparisons for the collection of moonrocks in the Smithsonian Institute:

> The moon rocks were as good as a meaningful and emotionally rewarding seduction that you had not expected. The moon rocks were as good as listening to what the members of the Supreme Court say to each other, in the Supreme Court Locker Room. They were as good as a war. The moon rocks were better than a presentation copy of the Random House Dictionary of the English Language signed by Geoffrey Chaucer himself. They were better than a movie in which the President refuses to tell the people what to do to save themselves from the terrible thing that is about to happen, although he knows what ought to be done and has written a secret memorandum about it. The moon rocks were better than a good cup of coffee from an urn decorated with the change of Philomel, by the barbarous king. The moon rocks were better than a ¡huelga! led by Mongo Santamaria, with additional dialogue by St. John of the Cross and special effects by Melmoth the Wanderer.[48]

Richard Brautigan's *Trout Fishing in America* is notable for its bizarre similes, which are based on very idiosyncratic perceptions of resemblance and which frequently threaten to detach themselves from the narrative and develop into little self-contained stories—not quite like a heroic simile, because they are not returned to the original context at their conclusion. For example:

> The sun was like a huge fifty-cent piece that someone had poured kerosene on and then lit with a match and said, 'Here, hold this while I go get a newspaper' and put the coin in my hand, but never came back.[49]

> Eventually the seasons would take care of their wooden names [on grave markers] like a sleepy short-order cook cracking eggs over a grill next to a railroad station.[50]

> my body was like birds sitting on a telephone wire strung out down the world, clouds tossing the wires carefully.[51]

> His eyes were like the shoelaces of a harpsichord.[52]

> The light behind the trees was like going into a gradual and strange department store.[53]

> The creek was like 12,845 telephone booths in a row with high Victorian ceilings and all the doors taken off and all the backs of the booths knocked out.[54]

> The streets were white and dry like a collision at high speed between a cemetery and a truck loaded with sacks of flour.[55]

If these similes strain the principle of similarity to breaking point, the title of the book is used to take the principle of substitution to excess. Trout Fishing in America can be a person:

> And this is a very small cookbook for Trout Fishing in America as if Trout Fishing in America were a rich gourmet and Trout Fishing in America had Maria Callas for a girlfriend and they ate together on a marble table with beautiful candles.[56]

a corpse:

> This is the autopsy of Trout Fishing in America as if Trout Fishing in America had been Lord Byron and had died in Missolonghi, Greece, and afterwards never saw the shores of Idaho again[57]

or the name of a hotel

> Half a block away from Broadway and Columbus is Hotel Trout Fishing in America, a cheap hotel. It is very old and run by some Chinese.[58]

Trout Fishing in America receives letters, and sends replies signed 'Trout Fishing in America'. Trout Fishing in America can be an adjective:

> THE LAST MENTION OF TROUT FISHING IN AMERICA SHORTY[59]
> WITNESS FOR TROUT FISHING IN AMERICA PEACE[60]

Trout Fishing in America can be a pen nib:

> I thought to myself what a lovely nib trout fishing in America would make with a stroke of cool green trees along the river's shore, wild flowers and dark fins pressed against the paper.[61]

Trout Fishing in America, in short, can be anything Brautigan wants it to be.

One equivalent, on the axis of combination, to this excess of substitution, would be the permutation of variables already discussed. But any overloading of the discourse with specificity will have the same effect: by presenting the reader with more details than he can synthesize into a whole, the discourse affirms the resistance of the world to interpretation. The immensely detailed, scientifically exact and metaphor-free description of objects in Robbe-Grillet's writing actually prevents us from visualizing them. That this possibility was inherent in the metonymic method was demonstrated a long time ago by some of the late nineteenth-century realists. Jakobson cites the example of the Russian novelist Gleb Ivanovic Uspenskij, quoting the observation of Kamegulov that in his characterization, 'the reader is crushed by the multiplicity of detail unloaded on him in a limited verbal space, and is physically unable to grasp the whole, so that the portrait is often lost.'[62] The celebrated description of Charles Bovary's school cap in the first chapter of *Madame Bovary* is a more familiar example of what might be called 'metonymic overkill'. Robbe-

Grillet not only overwhelms the reader with more detail than he wants
or can handle, but also (I strongly suspect) ensures that the details will
not cohere. Consider, for example, this description of the harbour
which Mattias is approaching in the first chapter of *Le Voyeur*:

> La jetée, maintenant toute proche, dominait le pont d'une hauteur de
> plusiers mètres; la marée devait être basse. La cale qui allait servir pour
> l'accostage montrait à sa partie inférieure une surface plus lisse, brunie par
> l'eau et couverte a moitié de mousses verdâtres. En regardant avec plus
> d'attention, on voyait le bord de pierre qui se rapproachait insensiblement.
>
> Le bord de pierre—une arrête vive, oblique, à l'intersection de deux plans
> perpendiculaires: la paroi verticale fuyant tout droit vers le quai et la rampe
> qui rejoint le haut de la digue—se prolonge à son extrémité supérieure, en
> haut de la digue, par une ligne horizontale fuyant tout droit vers le quai.
>
> Le quai, rendu plus lointain par l'effet de perspective, émet de part et
> d'autre de cette ligne principale un faisceau de parallèles qui délimitent,
> avec une netteté encore accentuée par l'éclairage du matin, une série de plans
> allongés, alternativement horizontaux et verticaux: le sommet du parapet
> massif protégeant le passage du côté du large, la paroi intérieure du parapet,
> la chaussée sur le haut de la digue, le flanc sans garde-fou qui plonge dans
> l'eau du port. Les deux surfaces verticales sont dans l'ombre, les deux autres
> sont vivement éclairées par le soleil—le haut du parapet dans toute sa
> largeur et la chaussée à l'exception d'une étroite blande obscure: l'ombre
> portée du parapet. Théoretiquement on devrait voir encore dans l'eau du
> port l'image renversée de l'ensemble et, à la surface, toujours dans le même
> jeu de parallèles, l'ombre portée de la haute paroi verticale qui filterait tout
> droit vers le quai.
>
> Vers le bout de la jetée, la construction se complique . . .[63]

But this already sufficiently *compliqué* to make the point. The
published English translation of this passage is as follows:

> The pier, now quite close, towered several yards above the deck. The tide
> must have been out. The landing slip from which the ship would be boarded
> revealed the smoother surface of its lower section, darkened by the water
> and half-covered with greenish moss. On closer inspection, the stone rim
> drew almost imperceptibly closer.
>
> The stone rim—an oblique, sharp edge formed by two intersecting
> perpendicular planes: the vertical embankment perpendicular to the quay
> and the ramp leading to the top of the pier—was continued along its upper
> side at the top of the pier by a horizontal line extending straight toward the
> quay.
>
> The pier, which seemed longer than it actually was as an effect of
> perspective, extended from both sides of this base line in a cluster of
> parallels describing, with a precision accentuated even more sharply by the
> morning light, a series of elongated planes alternately horizontal and
> vertical: the crest of the massive parapet that protected the tidal basin from
> the open sea, the inner wall of the parapet, the jetty along the top of the pier,
> and the vertical embankment that plunged straight into the water of the
> harbor. The two vertical surfaces were in shadow, the other two brilliantly
> lit by the sun—the whole breadth of the parapet and all of the jetty save for one

dark narrow strip: the shadow cast by the parapet. Theoretically, the reversed image of the entire group could be seen reflected in the harbor water, and, on the surface, still within the same play of parallels, the shadow cast by the vertical embankment extending straight toward the quay.[64]

The translator has not made things easier for us by translating *plus lointain* as 'longer', and by using only three English words (*pier, quay* and *jetty*) to translate four French words (*jettée, quai, digue, chausée*)— and not using them consistently, either, translating *jettée* as both 'pier' and 'jetty', and *quai* as both 'pier' and 'quay'. But one can only sympathize with anyone engaged on this task. An obvious procedure for a translator would be to make a sketch or diagram of the harbour, but when I invited students, and subsequently some colleagues in the French Department of my university, to do this, none of them succeeded. The description simply doesn't come together into a visualizable whole.

The last word on metonymic excess may be left to Jorge Luis Borges, who in his story 'Funes, the Memorious', describes a man who, after the shock of an accident, is able to perceive everything that is happening around him and unable to forget anything.

> We, at one glance, can perceive three glasses on a table; Funes, all the leaves and tendrils and fruit that make up a grape vine. He knew by heart the forms of the southern clouds at dawn on 30 April 1882, and could compare them in his memory with the mottled streaks on a book in Spanish binding he had only seen once and with the outlines of the foam raised by an oar in the Rio Negro the night before the Quebracho uprising.[65]

Funes inhabits a world of intolerable specificity and his time and energy are wholly absorbed by the interminable and futile task of classifying all the data of his experience without omission or generalization:

> He was the solitary and lucid spectator of a multiform world which was instantaneously and almost intolerably exact ... I suspect, nevertheless, that he was not very capable of thought. To think is to forget a difference, to generalize, to abstract. In the overly replete world of Funes there were nothing but details, almost contiguous details.[66]

Short Circuit

In Part Two I suggested that at the highest level of generality at which we can apply the metaphor/metonymy distinction, literature itself is metaphoric and nonliterature is metonymic. The literary text is always metaphoric in the sense that when we interpret it we apply it to the world as a total metaphor. This process of interpretation assumes a gap between the text and the world, between art and life, which postmodernist writing characteristically tries to short-circuit in order to administer a shock to the reader and thus resist assimilation into conventional categories of the literary. Ways of doing this include: combining in one work violently contrasting modes—the obviously fictive and the apparently factual; introducing the author and the question of authorship into the text; and exposing conventions in the act of using them. These ploys are not in themselves discoveries of the postmodernist writers—they are to be found in prose fiction as far back as *Don Quixote* and *Tristram Shandy*—but they appear so frequently in postmodernist writing, and are pursued to such lengths as to constitute, in combination with the other devices we have surveyed, a distinctively new development.

Vladimir Nabokov, a transitional figure between modernism and postmodernism, teasingly introduced himself (and his wife) on the perimeter of his fictions as early as his second novel *King, Queen, Knave*, originally published in Russian in 1928. As the coils of the intrigue tighten around the distracted hero, Franz, at a German seaside resort, he notices a vacationing couple talking a language he does not understand and carrying a butterfly net (something of a private joke, this, in 1928, when Nabokov was not yet the world's most famous lepidopterist):

> He thought that they glanced at him and fell silent for an instant. After passing him they began talking again; he had the impression they were discussing him, and even pronouncing his name. It embarrassed, it incensed him, that this damned happy foreigner hastening to the beach with his tanned, pale-haired, lovely companion, knew absolutely everything about his predicament. . . .[67]

In *Pale Fire* (1962) Nabokov plays off the metaphoric and metonymic modes against each other with typical cunning. The novel consists of a poem and a commentary. Normally a poem is fictional and a commentary factual, as verse is a metaphorical and prose a metonymic medium. In *Pale Fire*, however, the prose commentary is more obviously fictive than the poem, in the sense that the commentator Kinbote is a madman suffering from the delusion that he is the exiled monarch of a Ruritanian kingdom called Zembla, while John Shade's poem is a meditation upon entirely credible personal experience. A measure of Kinbote's insanity is the way he perversely and absurdly interprets Shade's poem as a tissue of allusions to his own fantasy; but it would be an oversimplification to say that Nabokov demonstrates the difference between illusion and reality by this opposition between Kinbote and Shade. For one thing, Kinbote's evocation of Zembla has an imaginative power and eloquence which makes us all too eager to suspend our disbelief, and beside it Shade's world seems less interesting. For another, Shade himself is a fiction, an illusion created by a 'real' author, Nabokov, whose well-known personal history corresponds far more closely to Kinbote's than to Shade's. Even the murder of Shade, which, within the limits of the book was 'in fact' committed by an escaped criminal who mistook Shade for the judge who sentenced him, but which Kinbote represents as the error of an assassin sent to kill the exiled king of Zembla, has an origin in Nabokov's own experience, for his father was murdered by political assassins who were attacking someone else.[68] Teasing allusions to the author persist in Nabokov's subsequent novels.

In the last but one of J. D. Salinger's stories about the Glass family, 'Seymour: an Introduction', the narrator, Buddy Glass, mentions that he has written two other stories about his brother Seymour—'Raise High the Roofbeam, Carpenters' (which is no surprise to the reader of the sequence) and 'A Nice Day for Bananafish', which I think *is* a surprise. For 'Bananafish' had no identified narrator, and appeared years before in a collection of *Nine Stories* (1953) by J. D. Salinger, seven of which did not concern the Glass family. Buddy goes on to claim authorship of one of these seven stories, and to refer to a novel of his that sounds very like Salinger's best-seller, *The Catcher in the Rye* (1951). Further on, Buddy refers to criticism of his work and rumours about his private life that are much the same as those provoked by Salinger himself. These revelations have a disorientating effect on the reader. The fiction that Buddy Glass is the author of 'Seymour: an Introduction' is made logically dependent upon the supposition that the J. D. Salinger who we thought wrote 'Bananafish' was the pen name of Buddy Glass, but of course J. D. Salinger's name appears on the title page of both books. Compelled to face the question, who is real, Buddy Glass or J. D. Salinger, common sense tells us the answer, but the rhetoric works in the opposite direction. This deliberate entangling of the myths of the Glass family and the Caulfield family with Salinger's personal history is typical of his later work, where he plays sly games with the reader's assent, stepping up the fictionality of the events as he damps down the literariness of the manner in which he describes them. Purporting to tell us a 'true' family history, and dropping heavy hints that he is the same person as J. D. Salinger, Buddy yet insists again and again on the autonomy of art and the irrelevance of biographical criticism. An extravagantly transcendental philosophy of life involving the endorsement of miracles and extra-sensory perception is put forward in terms of studied homeliness, wrapped around with elaborate qualifications, disclaimers, nods and winks, and mediated in a style that, for all its restless rhetorical mannerism, is strikingly lacking in any kind of 'poetic' resonances. As Ihab Hassan, one of the few critics to have placed Salinger in a postmodernist context, has observed: 'Ungainly, prolix, allusive, convoluted, tolerant of chance, whimsy, and disorder, these narratives define a kind of anti-form. Their impertinent exhortations of reader and writer undercut the authority of the artistic act.'[69]

In their play with the ideas of illusion, authorship and literary convention, however, Nabokov and Salinger maintain a precarious poise. Their narratives wobble on the edge of the aesthetic, but never quite fall off. Modes are mixed, but a certain balance, or symmetry, is preserved. The same is true of Doris Lessing, whose *The Golden Notebook* (1962) and *Briefing For a Descent into Hell* (1971) have certain features in common with their work—the Chinese-box authorship puzzle, for instance, and the reality/fantasy contrast in which the fantasy is more potent than the reality. Present-day American writers are often more slapdash, or less inhibited, in mixing up fact and fiction, life and art. Brautigan's *Trout Fishing in America*, for instance, has many signs of being an unstructured autobiography. The text frequently refers us to the photograph of the author on the front cover, and includes a great many factual documents—letters, recipes, bibliographies, etc. But it also contains extravagantly fictitious episodes such as the one in which the narrator buys a used trout stream from the Cleveland Wrecking Yard:

> It was stacked in piles of various lengths: ten, fifteen, twenty feet, etc. There was one pile of hundred foot lengths. There was also a box of scraps. . . . I went up close and looked at the lengths of stream. I could see some trout in them . . . It looked like a fine stream. I put my hand in the water. It was cold and felt good.[70]

This fantastic event is narrated in a style of sober realism, just as the more banal events in the book are elaborated with fantastic similes. Brautigan leaves to the reader the task of integrating these totally disparate modes of writing. Plainly, he is not bothered.

Kurt Vonnegut uses an apparently artless, improvised mixing of modes to more deliberate thematic effect in *Slaughterhouse 5* (1969). Vonnegut happened to be a prisoner of war in Dresden at the time of the air raid which destroyed it at the end of World War II, and was employed in digging some of the 130,000 incinerated corpses out of the rubble. For years, he confides in his first chapter, he has been trying to make this lump of raw experience into a novel; but such novels have a way of covertly celebrating what they outwardly deplore and being turned into movies with parts for Frank Sinatra and John Wayne. The only way to write an anti-war novel is to write an anti-novel. 'It has to be so short and jumbled and jangled . . . because there is nothing intelligent to say about a massacre.'[71] *Slaughterhouse 5* is a *bricolage* of fragments, short passages that are grim, grotesque and whimsical by turns, which describe the experiences of the very two-dimensional hero, Billy Pilgrim: his war-experiences (which bear a close resemblance to Vonnegut's) his civilian life as a married man and successful optometrist (domestic and social comedy) and his delusions of having been abducted by aliens from the planet Tralfamadore (science-fiction parody). Billy finds the Tralfamadorian concept of time as a field of simultaneous events, from which we are free to select, an answer to the problem of meaningless death which is instanced on almost every page of *Slaughterhouse 5* (invariably accompanied by the laconic comment, 'So it goes') for according to this doctrine (perhaps a parody of Christianity) 'we will all live for ever no matter how dead we may sometimes seem to be.' This concept also provides a justification for the drastic dislocation of chronology in the book, which prevents the reader from locating himself on a narrative line or settling into a single mood, and jumbles together disparate experiences in a way that imitates the incongruities and disjunctions of modern history. Nor are the various planes of the narrative—autobiographical, fictional, fantastic—kept insulated from each other. At his first German prison camp, for instance, Billy Pilgrim and his fellow American POWs are welcomed by a contingent of British veterans who provide a feast that makes the half-starved Americans violently ill. The latrine is crammed with these unfortunates.

> An American near Billy wailed that he had excreted everything but his brains. Moments later he said, 'There they go, there they go.' He meant his brains.
> That was I. That was me. That was the author of this book.[72]

This statement has an interesting double effect. On the one hand it reminds us that the story has an autobiographical, documentary origin, that the author 'was there', and therefore that the narrative is 'true'. On the other hand it simultaneously reminds us that Billy Pilgrim and the author belong to different planes of reality, that we are reading a book, a story, which (whatever its specific proportions of fiction to fact) is necessarily a highly conventionalized, highly artificial construction, and necessarily at a considerable distance from 'the way it was'.

In *Breakfast of Champions*, Vonnegut brings himself as composing author into the 'time present' of the narrative—for example:

> 'Give me a Black and White and water,' [Wayne] heard the waitress say, and Wayne should have pricked up his ears at that. That particular drink wasn't for any ordinary person. That drink was for the person who had created all Wayne's misery to date, who could kill him or make him a millionaire or send him back to prison or do whatever he damn well pleased with Wayne. That drink was for me.[73]

This is what the Russian Formalists called 'baring the device' carried to an extreme, and it is a persistent feature of postmodernist writing.

> The droplets rain from the eaves. The shadow of a cloud dims the snow dazzle. George Washington crosses the Delaware on the walls. I sit at my desk, making this up. . . .

Thus Ronald Sukenick, in 'What's Your Story?'[74] 'I wander the island, inventing it,' begins Robert Coover's story 'The Magic Poker', in which his skill in evoking scenery and generating mystery and suspense is constantly undermined by declarations of his own manipulating presence—the narrator revealed as author:

> Bedded deep in the grass, near the path up to the first guest cabin, lies a wrought-iron poker. It is long and slender with an intricately worked handle, and it is orange with rust. It lies shadowed, not by trees, but by the grass that has grown up wildly around it. I put it there.[75]

'Another story about a writer writing a story! Another regressus ad infinitum! Who doesn't prefer art that at least overtly imitates something other than its own processes? That doesn't continually proclaim, "Don't forget I'm an artifice!" That takes for granted its mimetic nature instead of asserting it in order (not so slyly after all) to deny it, or vice versa?' That is a quite common complaint about the kind of writing I have surveyed in this chapter (especially among British reviewers and critics) but this particular expression of it occurs in a text by one of the most elaborately and ingeniously selfconscious of all postmodernist writers, John Barth;[76] and in context will give little comfort to partisans of traditional realism, one variety of which is amusingly parodied in the following passage:

> C flung away the whining manuscript and pushed impatiently through the french windows leading to the terrace from his oak-wainscotted study. Pausing at the stone balustrade to light his briar he remarked through a lavendar cascade of wisteria that lithe-limbed Gloria, Gloria of timorous eye and militant breast, had once again chosen his boat wharf as her basking place.[77]

The way the narrative tracks its subject through spatial and temporal contiguities with obsessive attention to redundant detail is well-caught, and the characterization of Gloria makes effective fun of the realistic writer's reliance on synecdoche.

The 'manuscript' in this passage is the story itself, entitled 'Life-Story', the trace of a writer's attempts to write a story about a writer who has come to suspect that the world is a fiction in which he is a character—a hypothesis which, if confirmed, would affect both writers, indeed all writers, including Barth. The process of trying to make a story out of this *donnée* provokes various pronouncements about the theory of fiction such as the one quoted above, which seem to be comments upon the fiction but which prove to be part of the fiction. 'Life-Story' is a metafiction cleverly constructed to outmanoeuvre critics of metafiction, since the metafictional frame is continually being absorbed into the picture. This 'regressus in infinitum' is finally arrested by the device of the short-circuit:

> To what conclusion will he come? He'd been about to append to his own tale inasmuch as the old analogy between Author and God, novel and world, can no longer be employed unless deliberately as a false analogy, certain things follow: 1) fiction must acknowledge its fictitiousness and metaphoric invalidity or 2) choose to ignore the question or deny its relevance or 3) establish some other, acceptable relation between itself, its author, its reader. Just as he finished doing so, however, his real life and imaginary

mistresses entered his study; 'It's a little past midnight' she announced with a smile; 'do you know what that means?'[78]

The interruption reveals to him that 'he could not after all be a character in a work of fiction inasmuch as such a fiction would be of an entirely different character from what he thought of as fiction', and the birthday kiss his wife bestows upon him obscures his view of his manuscript and makes him 'end his ending story endless by interruption, cap his pen'.[79] Barth himself has referred to postmodernist writing as 'the literature of exhausted possibility'—or, more chicly, 'the literature of exhaustion',[80] and has praised Borges for demonstrating 'how an artist may paradoxically turn the felt ultimacies of our time into material and means for his work—*paradoxically* because by doing so he transcends what had appeared to be his refutation'.[81] Certainly, in seeking 'some other . . . relation between itself, its author, its reader' than that of previous literary traditions, postmodernist writing takes enormous risks—risks of abolishing itself, if ultimately successful, in silence, incoherence or what Fiedler calls 'the reader's passionate [i.e. non-aesthetic] apprehension and response'.[82] I would certainly not claim that all the texts surveyed in this chapter are equally interesting and rewarding: postmodernist writing tends to be very much a hit-or-miss affair. But many of these books and stories are imaginatively liberating to a high degree, and have done much to keep the possibilities of writing open in the very process of asserting that the most familiar ones are closed. If this assertion were really made good, however—if postmodernism really succeeded in expelling the idea of order (whether expressed in metonymic or metaphoric form) from modern writing, then it would truly abolish itself, by destroying the norms against which we perceive its deviations. A foreground without a background inevitably becomes the background for something else. Postmodernism cannot rely upon the historical memory of modernist and antimodernist writing for its background, because it is essentially a rule-breaking kind of art, and unless people are still trying to keep the rules there is no point in breaking them, and no interest in seeing them broken.

I *

Appendix A

'A Hanging' By George Orwell

[1] It was in Burma, a sodden morning of the rains. A sickly light, like yellow tinfoil, was slanting over the high walls into the jail yard. We were waiting outside the condemned cells, a row of sheds fronted with double bars, like small animal cages. Each cell measured about ten feet by ten and was quite bare within except for a plank bed and a pot of drinking water. In some of them brown silent men were squatting at the inner bars, with their blankets draped round them. These were the condemned men, due to be hanged within the next week or two.

[2] One prisoner had been brought out of his cell. He was a Hindu, a puny wisp of a man, with a shaven head and vague liquid eyes. He had a thick, sprouting moustache, absurdly too big for his body, rather like the moustache of a comic man on the films. Six tall Indian warders were guarding him and getting him ready for the gallows. Two of them stood by with rifles and fixed bayonets, while the others handcuffed him, passed a chain through his handcuffs and fixed it to their belts, and lashed his arms tight to his sides. They crowded very close about him, with their hands always on him in a careful, caressing grip, as though all the while feeling him to make sure he was there. It was like men handling a fish which is still alive and may jump back into the water. But he stood quite unresisting, yielding his arms limply to the ropes, as though he hardly noticed what was happening.

[3] Eight o'clock struck and a bugle call, desolately thin in the wet air, floated from the distant barracks. The superintendent of the jail, who was standing apart from the rest of us, moodily prodding the gravel with his stick, raised his head at the sound. He was an army doctor, with a grey toothbrush moustache and a gruff voice. 'For God's sake hurry up, Francis,' he said irritably. 'The man ought to have been dead by this time. Aren't you ready yet?'

[4] Francis, the head jailer, a fat Dravidian in a white drill suit and gold spectacles, waved his black hand. 'Yes sir, yes sir,' he bubbled. 'All iss satisfactorily prepared. The hangman iss waiting. We shall proceed.'

[5] 'Well, quick march, then. The prisoners can't get their breakfast till this job's over.'

[6] We set out for the gallows. Two warders marched on either side of the prisoner, with their rifles at the slope; two others marched close against him, gripping him by arm and shoulder, as though at once pushing and supporting him. The rest of us, magistrates and the like, followed behind. Suddenly, when we had gone ten yards, the

procession stopped short without any order or warning. A dreadful thing had happened—a dog, come goodness knows whence, had appeared in the yard. It came bounding among us with a loud volley of barks, and leapt round us wagging its whole body, wild with glee at finding so many human beings together. It was a large woolly dog, half Airedale, half pariah. For a moment it pranced round us, and then, before anyone could stop it, it had made a dash for the prisoner, and jumping up tried to lick his face. Everyone stood aghast, too taken aback even to grab at the dog.

[7]   'Who let that bloody brute in here?' said the superintendent angrily. 'Catch it, someone!'

[8]   A warder, detached from the escort, charged clumsily after the dog, but it danced and gambolled just out of his reach, taking everything as part of the game. A young Eurasian jailer picked up a handful of gravel and tried to stone the dog away, but it dodged the stones and came after us again. Its yaps echoed from the jail walls. The prisoner, in the grasp of the two warders, looked on incuriously, as though this was another formality of the hanging. It was several minutes before someone managed to catch the dog. Then we put my handkerchief through its collar and moved off once more, with the dog still straining and whimpering.

[9]   It was about forty yards to the gallows. I watched the bare brown back of the prisoner marching in front of me. He walked clumsily with his bound arms, but quite steadily, with that bobbing gait of the Indian who never straightens his knees. At each step his muscles slid neatly into place, the lock of hair on his scalp danced up and down, his feet printed themselves on the wet gravel. And once, in spite of the men who gripped him by each shoulder, he stepped slightly aside to avoid a puddle on the path.

[10]   It is curious, but till that moment I had never realized what it means to destroy a healthy, conscious man. When I saw the prisoner step aside to avoid the puddle, I saw the mystery, the unspeakable wrongness, of cutting a life short when it is in full tide. This man was not dying, he was alive just as we were alive. All the organs of his body were working— bowels digesting food, skin renewing itself, nails growing, tissues forming—all toiling away in solemn foolery. His nails would still be growing when he stood on the drop, when he was falling through the air with a tenth of a second to live. His eyes saw the yellow gravel and the grey walls, and his brain still remembered, foresaw, reasoned—reasoned even about puddles. He and we were a party of men walking together, seeing, hearing, feeling, understanding the same world; and in two minutes, with a sudden snap, one of us would be gone—one mind less, one world less.

[11]   The gallows stood in a small yard, separate from the main grounds of the prison, and overgrown with tall prickly weeds. It was a brick erection like three sides of a shed, with planking on top, and above that two beams and a crossbar with the rope dangling. The hangman, a grey-haired convict in the white uniform of the prison, was waiting beside his machine. He greeted us with a servile crouch as we entered. At a word from Francis the two warders, gripping the prisoner more closely than ever, half led, half pushed him to the gallows and helped him clumsily up the ladder. Then the hangman climbed up and fixed the rope round the prisoner's neck.

[12]   We stood waiting, five yards away. The warders had formed in a rough circle round the gallows. And then, when the noose was fixed, the prisoner began crying out on his god. It was a high, reiterated cry of 'Ram! Ram! Ram! Ram!', not urgent and fearful like a prayer or a cry for help, but steady, rhythmical, almost like the tolling of a bell. The dog answered the sound with a whine. The hangman, still standing on the gallows, produced a small cotton bag like a flour bag and drew it down over the prisoner's face. But the sound, muffled by the cloth, still persisted, over and over again: 'Ram! Ram! Ram! Ram! Ram!'

[13]   The hangman climbed down and stood ready, holding the lever. Minutes seemed to pass. The steady, muffled crying from the prisoner went on and on, 'Ram! Ram! Ram!' never faltering for an instant. The superintendent, his head on his chest, was slowly poking the ground with his stick; perhaps he was counting the cries, allowing the prisoner a fixed number—fifty, perhaps, or a hundred. Everyone had changed colour. The Indians had gone grey like bad coffee, and one or two of the bayonets were wavering. We looked at the lashed, hooded man on the drop, and listened to his cries—each cry another second of life; the same thought was in all our minds: oh, kill him quickly, get it over, stop that abominable noise!

[14]   Suddenly the superintendent made up his mind. Throwing up his head he made a swift motion with his stick. 'Chalo!' he shouted almost fiercely.

[15]   There was a clanking noise, and then dead silence. The prisoner had vanished, and the rope was twisting on itself. I let go of the dog, and it galloped immediately to the back of the gallows; but when it got there it stopped short, barked, and then retreated into a corner of the yard, where it stood among the weeds, looking timorously out at us. We went round the gallows to inspect the prisoner's body. He was dangling with his toes pointed straight downwards, very slowly revolving, as dead as a stone.

[16]   The superintendent reached out with his stick and poked the bare body; it oscillated, slightly, '*He's* all right,' said the superintendent. He backed out from under the gallows, and blew out a deep breath. The moody look had gone out of his face quite suddenly. He glanced at his wrist-watch. 'Eight minutes past eight. Well, that's all for this morning, thank God.'

[17]   The warders unfixed bayonets and marched away. The dog, sobered and conscious of having misbehaved itself, slipped after them. We walked out of the gallows yard, past the condemned cells with their waiting prisoners, into the big central yard of the prison. The convicts, under the command of warders armed with lathis, were already receiving their breakfast. They squatted in long rows, each man holding a tin pannikin, while two warders with buckets marched round ladling out rice; it seemed quite a homely, jolly scene, after the hanging. An enormous relief had come upon us now that the job was done. One felt an impulse to sing, to break into a run, to snigger. All at once everyone began chattering gaily.

[18]   The Eurasian boy walking beside me nodded towards the way we had come, with a knowing smile: 'Do you know, sir, our friend (he meant the dead man), when he heard his appeal had been dismissed, he pissed on the floor of his cell. From fright.—Kindly take one of my cigarettes, sir. Do you not admire my new silver case, sir? From the boxwallah, two rupees eight annas. Classy European style.'

[19]   Several people laughed—at what, nobody seemed certain.

[20]   Francis was walking by the superintendent, talking garrulously: 'Well, sir, all hass passed off with the utmost satisfactoriness. It wass all finished—flick! like that. It iss not always so—oah, no! I have known cases where the doctor wass obliged to go beneath the gallows and pull the prisoner's legs to ensure decease. Most disagreeable!'

[21]   'Wriggling about, eh? That's bad,' said the superintendent.

[22]   'Ach, sir, it iss worse when they become refractory! One man, I recall, clung to the bars of hiss cage when we went to take him out. You will scarcely credit, sir, that it took six warders to dislodge him, three pulling at each leg. We reasoned with him. "My dear fellow," we said, "think of all the pain and trouble you are causing to us!" But no, he would not listen! Ach, he wass very troublesome!'

[23]   I found that I was laughing quite loudly. Everyone was laughing. Even the superintendent grinned in a tolerant way. 'You'd better all come out and have a drink,' he said quite genially. 'I've got a bottle of whisky in the car. We could do with it.'

[24]   We went through the big double gates of the prison, into the road. 'Pulling at his legs!' exclaimed a Burmese magistrate suddenly, and burst into a loud chuckling. We all began laughing again. At that moment Francis's anecdote seemed extraordinarily funny. We all had a drink together, native and European alike, quite amicably. The dead man was a hundred yards away.

Appendix B

'Michael Lake Describes What the Executioner Actually Faces,'
Guardian 9 April, 1973

[1]   It is doubtful if those who seek the reintroduction of capital punishment have ever seen a hanging. It is a grim business, far removed from the hurly burly of Parliament, from the dusty gloom of the Old Bailey and a million light years away from the murder.

[2]   In New Zealand hangings were always in the evening. There were never any crowds, but three journalists were always summoned to witness the hanging. Their names were published later that night, along with those of the sheriff, the coroner and others, in the Official Gazette. I watched the last hanging in New Zealand.

[3]   Walter James Bolton was a farmer from the west coast of the North Island. He had poisoned his wife. He was 62, and the oldest and heaviest man ever hanged in New Zealand. They had to make sure they got the length of rope right so the drop wouldn't tear off his head.

[4]   I arrived at Mt Eden Gaol, Auckland, at 6 o'clock on a Monday evening. With the other witnesses I was led through the main administrative block, down some steps, and along a wing which it turned out, was a sort of Death Row.

[5]   We were led to the foot of the scaffold in a yard immediately at the end of the wing. The sky was darkening and a canvas canopy over the yard flapped gently in the breeze.

[6]   After a long time, there was a murmuring. Into view came a strange procession; the deputy governor of the prison, leading four warders and among them, walked or rather shambled the hulking figure of Bolton. His arms were pinioned by ropes to his trunk.

[7]   Behind him walked a parson reading aloud. It was with disbelief and shock that I recognised the Burial Service from the Book of Common Prayer.

[8]   High upon the scaffold, 17 steps away, the executioner stood immobile. He wore a black broad-brimmed hat, a black trench coat, and heavy boots, and he was masked. Only the slit for his eyes and his white hands gleamed in the light.

[9]   Bolton was helped up the steps by the warders, who bound his ankles together. The sheriff then asked him if he had anything to say before sentence was carried out.

[10]   Bolton mumbled. After a few seconds mumbling the parson, apparently unaware that the prisoner was talking, interrupted with further readings from the Burial Service.

[11]   I checked my shorthand notes with the other reporters. One, an elderly man who had witnessed 19 hangings, had heard nothing. The other man's shorthand outlines matched my own. He had said: 'The only thing I want to say is . . . .'

[12]   The warders did all the work. They bound him and put a white canvas hood over his head as he stood there, swaying in their grasp. Then they dropped the loop over his head, with the traditional hangman's knot, tidied it up, and stepped back.

[13]   The sheriff lifted his hand and lowered it. The executioner moved for the first and only time. He pulled a lever, and stepped back. Bolton dropped behind a canvas screen. The rope ran fast through the pulley at the top, and then when the Turk's Head knotted in the end jammed in the pulley, the block clanged loudly up against the beam to which it was fixed. The rope quivered, and that was the end of Walter James Bolton.

[14]   A doctor repaired behind the screen which hid the body from us. A hanged man usually ejaculates and evacuates his bowels. In New Zealand, at any rate he also hanged for an hour. Bolton hung while we sat back in the deputy governor's office drinking the whisky traditionally provided by the Government for these occasions—'Who's for a long drop,' asked some macabre wit.

[15]   The city coroner, Mr Alf Addison, an old friend of mine, called us across to his office where we duly swore we had seen the sentence of the court carried out.

[16]   I went back to my newspaper office and wrote three paragraphs. No sensations, I told the night editor, the bloke hadn't made a fuss. Then I went home with a sense of loss and corruption I have never quite shed.

Appendix C

An extract from The Naked Lunch, by William Burroughs

Room like gymnasium. . . . The floor is foam rubber, covered in white silk. . . . One wall is glass. . . . The rising sun fills the room with pink light. Johnny is led in, hands tied, between Mary and Mark. Johnny sees the gallows and sags with a great 'Ohhhhhhhhhhh!' his chin pulling down towards his cock, his legs bending at the knees. Sperm spurts, arching almost vertical in front of his face. Mark and Mary are suddenly impatient and hot. . . . They push Johnny forward onto the gallows platform covered with moldy jockstraps and sweat shirts. Mark is adjusting the noose.

'Well, here you go.' Mark starts to push Johnny off the platform.

Mary: 'No, let me.' She locks her hands behind Johnny's buttocks, puts her forehead against him, smiling into his eyes she moves back, pulling him off the platform into space. . . . His face swells with blood. . . . Mark reaches up with one lithe movement and snaps Johnny's neck . . . sound like a stick broken in wet towels. A shudder runs down Johnny's body . . . one foot flutters like a trapped bird. . . . Mark has draped himself over a swing and mimics Johnny's twitches, closes his eyes and sticks his tongue out. . . . Johnny's cock springs up and Mary guides it up her cunt, writhing against him in a fluid belly dance, groaning and shrieking with delight . . . sweat pours down her body, hair hangs over her face in wet strands. 'Cut him down, Mark,' she screams. Mark reaches over with a snap knife and cuts the rope, catching Johnny as he falls, easing him onto his back with Mary still impaled and writhing. . . . She bites away Johnny's lips and nose and sucks out his eyes with a pop. . . . She tears off great hunks of cheek. . . . Now she lunches on his prick. . . . Mark walks over to her and she looks up from Johnny's half-eaten genitals, her face covered with blood, eyes phosphorescent. . . . Mark puts his foot on her shoulder and kicks her over on her back. . . . He leaps on her, fucking her insanely . . . they roll from one end of the room to the other, pinwheel end-over-end and leap high in the air like great hooked fish.

'Let me hang you, Mark. . . . Let me hang you. . . . Please, Mark, let me hang you!'

'Sure baby.' He pulls her brutally to her feet and pins her hands behind her.

'No, Mark!! No! No! No,' she screams, shitting and pissing in terror as he drags her to the platform. He leaves her tied on the platform in a pile of old used condoms, while he adjusts the rope across the room . . . and comes back carrying the noose on a silver tray. He jerks her to her feet and tightens the noose. He sticks his cock up her and waltzes around the platform and off into space swinging in a great arc. . . . 'Wheeeeee!' he screams, turning into

Johnny. Her neck snaps. A great fluid wave undulates through her body. Johnny drops to the floor and stands poised and alert like a young animal.

‧He leaps about the room. With a scream of longing that shatters the glass wall he leaps out into space. Masturbating end-over-end, three thousand feet down, his sperm floating beside him, he screams all the way against the shattering blue of the sky, the rising sun burning over his body like gasoline, down past great oaks and persimmons, swamp cypress and mahogany, to shatter in liquid relief in a ruined square paved with limestone. Weeds and vines grow between the stones, and rusty iron bolts three feet thick penetrate the white stone, stain it shit-brown of rust.

Notes and References

All page references are to editions actually cited. Where a first edition has not been used, and its date is significant, this is given in square brackets unless already given in the main text. Place of publication is London unless otherwise indicated. 'Harmondsworth' denotes a Penguin edition; other paperback imprints are usually named.

Part One

1   What is Literature?

1. Anthony O'Hear, commenting in *The New Review*, II/13 (1975) p. 66, on an earlier and longer version of this chapter ('A Despatch From The Front', *TNR* I/11 (1975) pp. 54–60). For my reply see *TNR* II/14 (1975) pp. 60–1.
2. For example, John R. Searle, at the beginning of his article 'The Logical Status of Fictional Discourse', *New Literary History* VI (1975) pp. 319–32. See Wittgenstein, *Philosophical Investigations*, I. 66–7.
3. Tzvetan Todorov, 'The Notion of Literature', *New Literary History* V (1973) p. 8.
4. See particularly Richard Ohmann, 'Speech Acts and the Definition of Literature', *Philosophy and Rhetoric* IV (1971) pp. 1–19. Austin discriminates between three kinds of acts that one performs as a speaker: the locutionary (which is simply to say what one says), the illocutionary (which is to use the conventions of a given speech community to perform a specific kind of speech act, e.g. to state, to command, to question etc.) and the perlocutionary (which is to produce a specific effect or consequence by speaking). Ohmann shows that literary texts are abnormal on the illocutionary level, that they appear to work without satisfying Austin's criteria of 'illocutionary felicity'. He therefore proposes that 'A literary work is discourse whose sentences lack the illocutionary forces that would normally attach to them. Its illocutionary force is *mimetic* . . . a literary work *purportedly imitates* (or reports) a series of speech acts, which in fact have no other existence. By doing so, it leads the reader to imagine a speaker, a situation, a set of ancillary events, and so on.' However, Ohmann explicitly limits his definition to 'imaginative' literature, excluding history, science, biography, etc. from his discussion, and is obliged to say that Truman Capote's 'non-fiction novel' *In Cold Blood* is

not a work of literature because it meets all Austin's criteria. John Searle, in the article cited above, uses essentially the same terminology to distinguish between fictional and non-fictional discourse, maintaining that it is impossible to distinguish formally between literary and non-literary discourse.

5. Ruqaiya Hasan, 'Rime and Reason in Literature', *Literary Style*, ed. Seymour Chatman (1971) p. 308.

6. Paul L. Garvin (ed.) *A Prague School Reader on Aesthetics, Literary Structure and Style* (Washington, 1964) pp. vii–viii.

7 Jan Mukařovský, 'Standard Language and Poetic Language' in Garvin, *op. cit.*, pp. 20–3.

8. Hasan *op. cit.* pp. 309–10.

9. Roland Barthes, *Mythologies* trans. Annette Lavers (Paladin edn. St Albans, 1973) p. 36.

10. Ian Watt, *The Rise of the Novel* (1957) pp. 86–96.

11. Garvin, *op. cit.* p. 23.

12. *Ibid.* p. 20.

13. *Ibid.* p. 24.

14. Roman Jakobson, 'Closing Satement: Linguistics and Poetics' in *Style in Language* ed. Thomas E. Sebeok (Cambridge, Mass., 1960) pp. 350–77.

15. For example, of the Russian Futurist poets Jakobson said: 'A number of poetic devices found their application in urbanism.' Quoted by Victor Erlich, *Russian Formalism: History Doctrine* (The Hague, 1965) p. 195.

16. Stanley Fish, 'How Ordinary is Ordinary Language?' *New Literary History*, V (1973) pp. 46ff.

17. Todorov, *op. cit.* pp. 15–16.

18. Fish, *op. cit.* p. 52.

19. *Ibid.* p. 49.

20. Fish's argument begins to falter somewhat as he sees precisely this difficulty looming up:

    'Everything I have said in this paper commits me to saying that literature is language . . . but it is language around which we have drawn a frame, a frame that indicates a decision to regard with a particular self-consciousness the resources that language has always possessed. (I am aware that this may sound very much like Jakobson's definition of the poetic function as *the set towards the message*; but this set is exclusive and aesthetic—towards the message *for its own sake*—while my set is towards the message for the sake of the human and moral content all messages necessarily convey.' (p. 52)

    Literature, here, is identified by a decision to pay particular attention to linguistic form; in order to dissociate this position from Jakobson's (message-minus) position, Fish hastens to say that attention is paid to literary messages for the sake of the kind of content *all* messages necessarily convey. But if all messages are alike in this respect, the only distinguishing characteristic of literary messages must be the attention-worthy form in which the content is expressed: literature as message-plus. Fish cannot in the end find a position outside the message-minus and message-plus definitions he has rejected. It would seem that literature must be *either* one *or* the other.

21. H. G. Widdowson, *Stylistics and the Teaching of Literature* (1975) p. 47.

22. *Ibid.* p. 46.
23. Dell Hymes, 'An Ethnographic Perspective', *New Literary History* V (1973) p. 196.
24. J. M. Cameron, *The Night Battle* (1962) p. 137. I have described Cameron's argument at greater length in *Language of Fiction* (1966) pp. 33–8. Cf. Widdowson, *op. cit.* p. 54: 'Literary discourse is independent of normal interaction, has no links with any preceding discourse and anticipates no subsequent activity either verbal or otherwise. Its interpretation does not depend on its being placed in a context of situation or on our recognition of the role of the sender or of our own role as receiver. It is a self-contained whole, interpretable internally, as it were, as a self-contained unit of communication, and in suspense from the immediate reality of social life.' This incidentally explains why advertisements that use fictional narrative are not axiomatically literary texts—they depend for their interpretation as advertisements on the prior existence of the product and the possibility of purchasing it. There is, however, no reason in principle why advertisements should not acquire the status of literature in the same way as other nonliterary texts, by responding satisfactorily to a literary reading.
25. Northrop Frye, *Anatomy of Criticism* (Princeton, 1957) p. 268.
26. Jonathan Culler, *Structuralist Poetics* (1975) p. 128.
27. Jean-Paul Sartre, *What is Literature?* trans. Bernard Frechtman (New York, 1965) p. 37.

2   George Orwell's 'A Hanging' and 'Michael Lake Describes . . .'

1. Peter Stansky and William Abrahams, *The Unknown Orwell* (1972) p. 224.
2. *Ibid.* pp. 163–4.
3. George Orwell, *The Road To Wigan Pier* (Harmondsworth, 1962) p. 128.
4. Stansky and Abrahams, *op. cit.* p. 205.
5. For a perceptive discussion of this point, see 'The Language Field of Nazism', *Times Literary Supplement*, 5 April 1974, pp. 353–4.
6. Victor Shklovsky, 'Art as Technique', quoted by Robert Scholes, *Structuralism in Literature* (1974) pp. 83–4. Scholes follows the translation of Lee T. Lemon and Marion J. Reis, *Russian Formalist Criticism* (Lincoln, Nebraska, 1965), but emends the final sentences (italicized) for reasons explained in a note.
7. Victor Shklovsky, 'Tristram Shandy: Stylistic Commentary', Lemon and Reis, *op. cit.* p. 57.
8. 'Coming Apart' by James Griffin & Robb Royes of 'Bread'.
9. Ludwig Wittgenstein, *Tractatus Logico-Philosophicus* (1922) 6.4311.

3   Oscar Wilde: 'The Ballad of Reading Gaol'

1. Quotations from 'The Ballad of Reading Gaol' are from Oscar Wilde, *De Profundis and Other Writings* (Harmondsworth, 1973) pp. 231–52.
2. Northrop Frye, *Anatomy of Criticism* p. 195.

3. George Orwell, 'Politics and the English Language' *Collected Essays, Journalism and Letters* (Harmondsworth, 1970) vol. 4, p. 168.

4 What is Realism?

1. See Roman Jakobson, 'On Realism in Art' in *Readings in Russian Poetics* ed. L. Matejka and K. Pormorska (Cambridge, Mass., 1971) pp. 38 ff, for a brilliant demonstration of the relativity of the concept. In his later writings, however, Jakobson's own use of the term implies that it has some kind of stable meaning.
2. *Sunday Times,* 30 June 1974.
3. Quoted in *The Age of Realism,* ed. F. W. Hemmings (Harmondsworth, 1974) p. 166.
4. Hayden White, *Metahistory: the Historical Imagination in Nineteenth Century Europe* (1973) p. 3n.
5. *Ibid.* p. 274.
6. *Ibid.* p. 275.
7. See Tom Wolfe, *The New Journalism; with an anthology edited by Tom Wolfe and E. W. Johnson* (New York, 1973); and my review-article 'The New Journalism?', *The New Review* II/4 (1975) pp. 67–71.

5 Arnold Bennett: 'The Old Wives' Tale'

1. All quotations from *The Old Wives' Tale* [1908] are from the Pan edition (1964).
2. Henry James, 'The New Novel' in *The Future of the Novel* ed. Leon Edel (Vintage edn. New York, 1956) p. 270.
3. Roland Barthes, *Writing Degree Zero,* trans. Annette Lavers and Colin Smith (1967) p. 39.

6 William Burroughs: 'The Naked Lunch'

1. William Burroughs, *The Naked Lunch* (1965) p. 7.
2. David Lodge, 'Objections to William Burroughs', *The Novelist at the Crossroads* (1971) p. 165.

7 The Realistic Tradition

1. Hegel's phrase, applied by Lionel Trilling to Jane Austen's fiction in 'Jane Austen and Mansfield Park', *Pelican Guide to English Literature 5* (Harmondsworth, 1957) p. 128.
2. Gustave Flaubert, *Madame Bovary,* trans. Alan Russell (Harmondsworth, 1950) p. 140.
3. Roland Barthes, 'To Write: an Intransitive Verb?', in *The Structuralist Controversy* ed. R. Macksey and E. Donato (Baltimore, 1972) p. 140.

8 Two Kinds of Modern Fiction

1. Henry James, 'The New Novel' in *The Future of the Novel* p. 271.
2. *Ibid.* p. 273.
3. *Ibid.* pp. 263–4.
4. 'The New Novel' was originally published in two articles entitled 'The Younger Generation' in the *Times Literary Supplement* for 14 March and 2 April 1914.
5. *Ibid.* p. 260.
6. See C. K. Stead, *The New Poetic* (1964) and Cyril Connolly, *Enemies of Promise* (1938).
7. Quoted by Richard Ellmann in *James Joyce* (1959) pp. 360–1.
8. Letter to Hugh Walpole, *The Letters of Henry James*, ed. Percy Lubbock (1922) vol. II p. 246.
9. Virginia Woolf, 'Modern Fiction', *Collected Essays* (1966) vol. II p. 105.
10. Henry James, 'The New Novel' *op. cit.* p. 267.
11. Virginia Woolf, *op. cit* p. 108.
12. See E. M. Forster, *Aspects of the Novel* (1927) Chap. 8; Stuart Gilbert, *James Joyce's 'Ulysses'* (rev. edn., 1957) Part I, chap. 2; and Joseph Frank, 'Spatial Form in Modern Literature', *Sewanee Review*, 1945.
13. Rubin Rabinowitz, *The Reaction Against Experiment in the English Novel, 1950–1960* (1968).
14. Quoted by John Lehmann, *New Writing in Europe* (Harmondsworth, 1940) p. 27.
15. Quoted by George Orwell in 'Inside the Whale', *Collected Essays, Journalism and Letters* (Harmondsworth, 1970) vol. I p. 560.
16. Christopher Isherwood, *Lions and Shadows* (Signet edn., 1968) pp. 159–60.
17. George Orwell, 'Inside the Whale', *op. cit.* I p. 557.
18. John Lehmann, *op. cit.* p. 134.
19. Graham Greene, *Collected Essays* (1969) pp. 115–16.
20. See Greene, *Collected Essays* pp. 23–74.
21. Virginia Woolf, 'Mr Bennett and Mrs Brown' in *Criticism* ed. M. Schorer, J. Miles and G. McKenzie (rev. edn., New York 1958) p. 69.
22. Gordon Haight, *George Eliot* (Oxford, 1968) p. 464
23. See my introduction to George Eliot, *Scenes of Clerical Life* (Harmondsworth, 1973) p. 8.
24. C. P. Snow, *Sunday Times*, 27 December 1953; quoted by Rabinowitz *op. cit.* p. 98.
25. B. S. Johnson, *Aren't You Rather Young To Be Writing Your Memoirs?* (1973) p. 14.
26. Virginia Woolf, 'Mr Bennett and Mrs Brown' *op. cit.* p. 72.
27. Northrop Frye, *Anatomy of Criticism* pp. 26–7.

9 Criticism and Realism

1. Clara Reeve, *The Progress of Romance* (1875) vol. I, Evening vii. Cited in Miriam Allott, *Novelists on the Novel* (1959) p. 47.
2. David Lodge (ed). *Jane Austen's 'Emma': a Casebook* (1968) p. 35.

3. John Bayley, 'Against a New Formalism', *The Word in the Desert (Critical Quarterly* 10th Anniversary No.) ed. C. B. Cox and A. E. Dyson (1968) pp. 66–7.
4. Calvin Bedient, '*Middlemarch*; Touching Down', *Hudson Review* xxii (1969) p. 84.
5. Bedient *op. cit.* p. 71.
6. Mark Schorer, 'Fiction and the Analogical Matrix', *Kenyon Review* 1949. Reprinted in *Critiques and Essays on Modern Fiction 1920–1951* ed. J. W. Aldridge (New York, 1952) p. 91.
7. Malcolm Bradbury, 'Towards a Poetics of Fiction (1) An Approach Through Structure', *Novel* I (1967) p. 50. Mark Schorer's article 'The Humiliation of Emma Woodhouse' is alluded to.
8. Schorer, 'Fiction and the Analogical Matrix' *op. cit.* p. 83.
9. See my 'Crosscurrents in Modern English Criticism' in *The Novelist at the Crossroads* (1971).
10. Schorer, 'Technique as Discovery', *Hudson Review* (1948). Reprinted in David Lodge, ed., *Twentieth Century Literary Criticism* (1972) p. 387.
11. *Ibid.* p. 391.
12. Bayley, *op. cit.* p. 60.
13. *Ibid.*
14. *Ibid.* p. 63.
15. I discuss Kermode's book at greater length in *The Novelist at the Crossroads* pp. 42–5.

10 The Novel and the Nouvelle Critique

1. John Sturrock, 'Roland Barthes—A Profile', *The New Review* I/2 (1974) p. 16.
2. Jean-Paul Sartre, *What is Literature?* Trans. Bernard Frechtman (New York, 1965) pp. 14 and 20.
3. Roland Barthes, *Writing Degree Zero*, trans. Annette Lavers and Colin Smith (1967) p. 66.
4. *Ibid.* p. 69.
5. *Ibid.* p. 72.
6. *Ibid.* p. 84.
7. Roland Barthes, 'To Write: An Intransitive Verb?', *The Structuralist Controversy* ed. R. Macksey and E. Donato (Baltimore, 1972) p. 135.
8. *Ibid.* p. 138.
9. *Ibid.* p. 144.
10. George Orwell, 'Inside the Whale', *op. cit.* p. 557.
11. Barthes, 'To Write: An Intransitive Verb?' p. 141.
12. Eugenio Donato, 'Of Structuralism and Literature', *Modern Language Notes*, LXXXII (1967) p. 571.
13. See G. D. Martin's 'Structures in Space; an account of the *Tel Quel*'s Attitude to Meaning', *New Blackfriars* LII (1971) pp. 541–52 and Chapter 10, ' "Beyond Structuralism": *Tel Quel*', of Jonathan Culler's *Structuralist Poetics* (1974) for an informed discussion of this school.
14. See Ian Watt's *The Rise of the Novel* (1957) for the classic exposition of this view.
15. Peter Caws, 'What is Structuralism?' *Partisan Review* XXXV (1968) p. 82.

16. *Ibid.* p. 85.
17. Roland Barthes, *Critique et Verité* (1966) quoted by Gabriel Josipovici, *The World and the Book* (1971) p. 271.
18. Roland Barthes, 'Criticism as Language', *The Critical Moment* (1964), reprinted in David Lodge. ed. *Twentieth Century Literary Criticism* (1972) pp. 650–1.
19. Eugenio Donato, 'The Two Languages of Criticism', *The Structuralist Controversy* pp. 95–6.
20. Edward W. Said, 'Abcedarium Culturae: Structuralism, Absence, Writing', *Tri-Quarterly* XIX/XXI (1970–71) p. 41.
21. Roland Barthes, 'Style and its Image', *Literary Style* ed. Seymour Chatman (1971) p. 10.
22. *Ibid.* p. 11.
23. Vladimir Propp, *Morphology of the Folktale* (Bloomington, Indiana, 1958). See also his 'Fairy Tale Transformations' in *Readings in Russian Poetics*, ed. L. Matejka and K. Pormorska (Cambridge, Mass., 1971).
24. Tzvetan Todorov, 'The Structural Analysis of Narrative', *Novel*, III (1969) p. 70.
25. Claude Lévi-Strauss, *Structural Anthropology* (New York, 1963) p. 130. Quoted by Neville Dyson-Hudson in *The Structuralist Controversy* p. 232.
26. Claude Lévi-Strauss, *Tristes Tropiques* (New York, 1961) Quoted by Eugenio Donato, *The Structuralist Controversy* p. 90.
27. Philip Young, *Ernest Hemingway: A Reconsideration* (rev. edn., 1966) pp. 1–21.
28. Gabriel Josipovici, *The World and the Book* (1971) p. 309.
29. *Ibid.* p. 133.
30. *Ibid.* p. 139.
31. *Ibid.* p. 307.
32. David Lodge, 'Onions and Apricots; or, Was the Rise of the Novel a Fall From Grace? Serious Reflections on Gabriel Josipovici's *The World and the Book*', *Critical Quarterly* XIV (1972) pp. 171–85.
33. Josipovici, *op. cit.* pp. 260–1.
34. Roland Barthes, *S/Z*, trans. Richard Miller (1975) pp. 5–6.
35. *Ibid.* p. 30.
36. *Ibid.* p. 4.
37. *Ibid.* p. 137.
38. *Ibid.* p. 153.
39. Roland Barthes, 'Style and its Image', *Literary Style* p. 5.
40. Barthes, *S/Z* p. 120.
41. *Ibid.* pp. 54–5.
42. *Ibid.* pp. 80–1.

11   Conclusion to Part One

1. Oscar Wilde, 'The Decay of Lying', *De Profundis and Other Writings* p. 74.
2. *Ibid.* p. 78.

Part Two

1 Jakobson's Theory

1. Victor Erlich, *Russian Formalism* p. 231.
2. Roman Jakobson and Morris Halle, *Fundamentals of Language* (The Hague, 1956) p. 78n.
3. René Wellek and Austin Warren, *Theory of Literature* (Harmondsworth, 1963) p. 195.
4. Roman Jakobson, 'Closing Statement: Linguistics and Poetics', *Style in Language*, ed. Thomas A. Sebeok (Cambridge, Mass., 1960) pp. 350–77.
5. Roman Jakobson, 'Two Aspects of Language and Two Types of Linguistic Disturbances', in Jakobson and Halle, *Fundamentals of Language* p. 58.
6. Roland Barthes, *Elements of Semiology*, trans. Annette Lavers and Colin Smith (1967) p. 63.
7. Stephen Ullmann, *Style in the French Novel* (Cambridge, 1957) p. 214.
8. Richard A. Lanham, *A Handlist of Rhetorical Terms* (Berkeley, 1969) pp. 67 and 97.
9. Jakobson, 'Two Aspects of Language' p. 60.
10. *Ibid.* p. 61.

2 Two Types of Aphasia

1. Jakobson, 'Two Aspects of Language' p. 63.
2. *Ibid.* p. 64.
3. *Ibid.* p. 69.
4. *Ibid.* p. 72.

3 The Metaphoric and Metonymic Poles

1. Jakobson, *op. cit.* p. 76.
2. *Ibid.* p. 78.

4 Drama and Film

1. Stephen Booth, 'On the Value of Hamlet', *Reinterpretations of Elizabethan Drama* (New York, 1969) pp. 137–76.
2. Marshall McLuhan describes some of the relevant research in *The Gutenberg Galaxy* (1962) pp. 36ff.
3. John Harrington, *The Rhetoric of Film* (New York, 1973) p. 138.
4. Sergei Eisenstein, *The Film Sense* (1938); reprinted in *The Modern Tradition: Backgrounds of Modern Literature*, ed. R. Ellmann and C. Feidelson Jnr. (New York, 1965) pp. 163–4.
5. *Ibid.* p. 165.
6. Harrington, *op. cit.* p. 139.
7. Roy Armes, *Film and Reality* (Harmondsworth, 1974) p. 51.

8. George Eliot, *Scenes of Clerical Life*, (Harmondsworth, 1973) p. 53.
9. See chapter 17 of *Adam Bede*.

5　Poetry, Prose and the Poetic

1. Jonathan Culler, *Structuralist Poetics* (1975) p. 161.
2. W. K. Wimsatt, 'One Relation of Rhyme to Reason', *The Verbal Icon* [1954] (1970) pp. 152–66.
3. Roland Barthes, *Elements of Semiology* p. 87.
4. W. B. Yeats, 'Adam's Curse'.
5. Roman Jakobson, 'Closing Statement: Linguistics and Poetics' *op. cit.* p. 358.
6. *Ibid.* pp. 350 and 356.
7. *Ibid.*
8. *Ibid.* p. 358.
9. *Ibid.* pp. 374–5.
10. Jakobson, 'Two Types of Language' pp. 81–2.

6　Types of Description

1. *The Columbia-Viking Desk Encyclopaedia* (New York, 1964).
2. 'The University of Birmingham', *The Guardian* 9 October 1967, p. 4.
3. E. M. Forster, *A Passage to India* [1924] (Harmondsworth, 1959) p. 9.
4. Jakobson, 'Linguistics and Poetics' p. 356.
5. Charles Dickens, *Bleak House* [1852–3] (1892) p. 1.
6. *Ibid.* p. 7.
7. Philip Collins, ed., *Charles Dickens: the Critical Heritage* (1971) p. 273.
8. *Ibid.* p. 272.
9. Charles Dickens, *Oliver Twist* [1837–9] (Harmondsworth, 1966) p. 442.
10. *Ibid.*
11. *Ibid.* p. 443.
12. Quoted by John Carey, *The Violent Effigy: a study of Dickens's Imagination* (1973) p. 130.

8　The Metonymic Text as Metaphor

1. Guy Rosolato, 'The Voice and the Literary Myth', *The Structuralist Controversy* ed. Macksey and Donato p. 202.
2. Ian Gregor, 'Criticism as an Individual Activity: the Approach through Reading', *Contemporary Criticism*, ed. Malcolm Bradbury and David Palmer (1970) p. 195.
3. Arnold Kettle, 'Emma', in *An Introduction to the English Novel* (1951); reprinted in David Lodge, ed. *Jane Austen's 'Emma': a Casebook* (1968) p. 89.

9　Metaphor and Context

1. Richard A. Lanham, *A Handlist of Rhetorical Terms* p. 66.
2. Northrop Frye, *Anatomy of Criticism* p. 136.
3. Aristotle, *Rhetoric* III, 1410b. Quoted by Lanham, *op. cit.* p. 66.
4. Winifred Nowottny, *The Language Poets Use* (1962) p. 68.

5. Graham Greene, *In Search of a Character* [1961] (Harmondsworth, 1968) p. 18.
6. Virginia Woolf, *The Waves* [1931] (Harmondsworth, 1964) p. 94.
7. Gerard Genette, 'Metonymie Chez Proust', *Figures III* (Paris, 1972) p. 53.
8. *Ibid.* pp. 42–3.
9. *Ibid.* p. 45.
10. T. S. Eliot, 'The Love Song of J. Alfred Prufrock'.
11. *Poetry* (Chicago), XXIX (1926). Reprinted in *The Modern Tradition* ed. Ellmann and Feidelson pp. 158–62.
12. Thomas Gray, 'Sonnet on the Death of Mr Richard West', quoted by Wordsworth in Preface to *Lyrical Ballads*.
13. William Wordsworth, Preface to *Lyrical Ballads*. *The Lyrical Ballads 1798–1805*, ed. George Sampson (1959) p. 8.
14. *Ibid.*
15. William Wordsworth, 'Lines written at a small distance from my house, and sent by my little boy to the person to whom they are addressed.' *The Lyrical Ballads* p. 84.
16. Christopher Ricks, 'Wordsworth: "A Pure Organic Pleasure from the Lines" ', *William Wordsworth; a Critical Anthology*, ed. Graham McMaster (Harmondsworth, 1972) p. 513.
17. Samuel Taylor Coleridge, *Biographia Literaria*, chap. 22.
18. Wordsworth, Preface to *Poems* (1815).
19. Lewis Carroll, *Alice Through The Looking-Glass* (1872), Chap. 8.

Part Three

1 James Joyce

1. Barthes, *S/Z* p. 156.
2. *Ibid.* p. 140.
3. *Ibid.* p. 200.
4. James Joyce, *Dubliners* [1914] (Harmondsworth, 1966) p. 7.
5. *Ibid.* p. 9.
6. Richard Ellmann, *James Joyce* (1959) p. 169.
7. Joyce, *Dubliners* pp. 7–9.
8. *Ibid.* p. 13.
9. *Ibid.* p. 10.
10. *Ibid.* p. 11.
11. *Ibid.* p. 15.
12. *Ibid.*
13. *Ibid.*
14. James Joyce, *A Portrait of the Artist as a Young Man* [1916] (Viking Critical edn., New York, 1968) p. 27.
15. *Ibid.* p. 7.
16. *Ibid.* p. 171.
17. *Ibid.* p. 228.
18. Ellmann, *op. cit.* p. 729.
19. Ian Watt, *The Rise of the Novel* (Harmondsworth, 1963) p. 13.
20. Ellmann, *op. cit.* p. 729.

21. Anthony Burgess (ed.) *A Shorter Finnegans Wake* (1966) pp. 7–8.
22. James Joyce, *Finnegans Wake* [1939] (Viking edn., New York, 1962) pp. 213–14.
23. See Edmund Wilson, *Axel's Castle* [1931] (Fontana edn., 1961) p. 188 and A. Walton Litz. *The Art of James Joyce* (1961) p. 113.
24. Hayden White, *Metahistory* p. 372.
25. Joyce, *Finnegans Wake* p. 3. I am heavily indebted to Anthony Burgess's Introduction to *A Shorter Finnegans Wake* pp. 22–3, and vicariously to the several scholars he draws on, for the parenthetical glosses.
26. T. S. Eliot, 'Ulysses, Order and Myth', *The Dial* November 1923, Reprinted in *Criticism*, ed. Schorer, Miles & McKenzie (New York, 1958) p. 270.
27. *Ibid.*
28. Virginia Woolf, 'Modern Fiction', *Collected Essays* II, p. 106.
29. T. S. Eliot, 'The Metaphysical Poets', *Selected Essays* (1961) p. 289.
30. E. H. Gombrich, *The Story of Art* (1952) p. 406.
31. Eliot, 'Ulysses, Order and Myth' pp. 270–1.
32. *Ibid.* p. 270.
33. Walton A. Litz, *The Art of James Joyce* (1961).
34. Stuart Gilbert, *James Joyce's 'Ulysses'* (1930; rev. 1952).
35. Lawrence Sterne, *Tristram Shandy*, Book I, chap. 4.
36. Virginia Woolf, 'Modern Fiction' p. 107.
37. James Joyce, *Ulysses* [1922] (Bodley Head edn., 1954) p. 34.
38. *Ibid.* pp. 34–5.
39. I am indebted to Stuart Gilbert, *op. cit.* (Harmondsworth, 1963) for this gloss.
40. *Ulysses* p. 52.
41. See p. 75 above and note.
42. *Ulysses*, p. 57.
43. *Ibid.* p. 704.
44. *Ibid.* p. 701.
45. Stuart Gilbert, *op. cit.* p. 341.
46. *Ulysses* p. 698.
47. *Ibid.* p. 699.

2 Gertrude Stein

1. Gertrude Stein, *Look at Me Now and Here I am: Writings and Lectures, 1911–45*, ed. Patricia Meyerowitz (Harmondsworth, 1971) p. 21.
2. John Passmore, *A Hundred Years of Philosophy* (Harmondsworth, 1968) p. 105.
3. Gertrude Stein, *Look At Me Now* p. 110.
4. Gertrude Stein, *The Making of Americans* (Harcourt Brace edn. [1934] reprinted 1966) p. 37.
5. *Ibid.* p. 122.
6. *Ibid.* p. 123.
7. *Ibid.* p. 124.
8. *Ibid.* p. 207.
9. *Ibid.* p. 232.
10. *Look At Me Now* p. 102.

11. *Ibid.* p. 25.
12. See Stephen Ullmann, *Style in the French Novel* (Cambridge, 1957) chap. III.
13. See Seymour Chatman, *The Late Style of Henry James* (New York, 1972) and my review in *Novel* VII (1974) pp. 187–9.
14. Roman Jakobson, 'Two Types of Language etc.' pp. 64–5.
15. *Look At Me Now* pp. 124ff.
16. *The Making of Americans* p. 355.
17. *Look At Me Now* p. 109.
18. *Ibid.* pp. 108–9.
19. *Ibid.* p. 105.
20. *The Making of Americans* p. 218.
21. *Look At Me Now* pp. 105–6.
22. *Ibid.* p. 96.
23. *Ibid.* p. 213.
24. *Ibid.* p. 113.
25. *Ibid.*
26. *Ibid.* p. 130.
27. *Ibid.* p. 137.
28. *Ibid.* pp. 161, 163, 170, 171 and 187.
29. *Ibid.* p. 115.
30. *Ibid.* p. 142.
31. *Ibid.* p. 138.
32. Jakobson, *op. cit.* pp. 71–2.
33. Ortega y Gasset, *The Dehumanization of Art and Other Writings on Art and Culture* (New York, 1956) p. 22.
34. Allegra Stewart, *Gertrude Stein and the Present* (Cambridge, Mass., 1967).
35. *The Modern Tradition: backgrounds of modern literature*, ed. R. Ellmann and C. Feidelson Jr. (New York, 1965) pp. 111–12.
36. Ezra Pound, 'A Retrospect', *Twentieth Century Literary Criticism* ed. David Lodge (1972) p. 59.
37. See T. S. Eliot's essays 'Hamlet' and 'Tradition and the Individual Talent' in *Selected Essays*.
38. See Joseph Frank's classic study, 'Spatial Form in Modern Literature' first published in the *Sewannee Review* in 1945.

3 Ernest Hemingway

1. Ernest Hemingway, *A Moveable Feast* (Harmondsworth, 1966) p. 20.
2. Hemingway, *Green Hills of Africa* [1935] (Harmondsworth, 1966) p. 26.
3. Hemingway, *Death in the Afternoon* [1932] (Harmondsworth, 1966) p. 6.
4. Hemingway, *A Farewell to Arms* [1929] (Harmondsworth, 1968) p. 144.
5. Hemingway, *Men Without Women* [1928] (Harmondsworth, 1972) pp. 51–4.
6. *Green Hills of Africa* p. 26.
7. Quoted by Charles A. Fenton, *The Apprenticeship of Ernest Hemingway: the early years* [1954] (New York, 1961) p. 35.
8. *Men Without Women* p. 44.

4 D. H. Lawrence

1. See D. H. Lawrence, *Studies in Classic American Literature* (1924) and Ernest Hemingway, *Green Hills of Africa* pp. 24–5.
2. Lawrence, *Lady Chatterley's Lover*, chap. 9.
3. Lawrence, 'Why the Novel Matters', *Selected Literary Criticism*, ed. Anthony Beal (Mercury edn., 1961) p. 105.
4. Lawrence, *Women in Love* [1921] (Harmondsworth, 1960) p. 126.
5. *Ibid.* p. 123.
6. *Ibid.* p. 209.
7. *Lady Chatterley's Lover* was originally published in Florence in 1928. The first version of the novel was published as *The First Lady Chatterley* in New York in 1944 and the second version, entitled *John Thomas and Lady Jane* was published in London by Heinemann in 1971.
8. Harry T. Moore, *The Intelligent Heart: the Story of D. H. Lawrence* [1955] (rev. edn. Harmondsworth, 1960) pp. 238–9.
9. Barbara Lucas, 'Apropos of *England, My England*', *The Twentieth Century*, March 1961, pp. 288–93.
10. This would correspond to Egbert's weekend leave as described in *England, My England* (Harmondsworth, 1973) p. 35.
11. This passage is deleted (without any indication to that effect) from the relevant letter in D. H. Lawrence, *Collected Letters* ed. Harry T. Moore (1962), vol. 1, pp. 465–9, though Moore quotes part of it in *The Intelligent Heart*, pp. 284–5. It is reproduced here by permission of Yale University, which owns the manuscript. The letter will be printed in full in the complete edition of Lawrence's letters to be published by Cambridge University Press, under the general editorship of James T. Boulton.
12. Emile Delavenay, *D. H. Lawrence: the Man and His Work. The Formative Years: 1885–1919*, trans. Katharine M. Delavenay (1972) pp. 431–4.
13. Letter to Lady Cynthia Asquith, *Collected Letters* ed. Moore, I, p. 364.
14. Lawrence, *England, My England* (Harmondsworth, 1973) p. 7.
15. *Ibid.* pp. 7–8.
16. *The English Review*, October 1915, pp. 238–9.
17. *England, My England* p. 8.
18. *Ibid.* p. 10.
19. *The English Review*, October 1915, p. 239.
20. *England, My England* pp. 10–11.
21. *Ibid.* pp. 12–13.
22. *Ibid.* p. 13.
23. *Ibid.* p. 14.
24. *Ibid.* p. 15.
25. *Ibid.* pp. 15–16.
26. *Ibid.* p. 17.
27. *Ibid.* p. 18.
28. *Ibid.*
29. *Ibid.* pp. 19–20.
30. *Ibid.* p. 19.
31. *Ibid.* p. 20.
32. *Ibid.* pp. 20–1.
33. *Ibid.* p. 31.

34. *Ibid.* pp. 29–30.
35. *Ibid.* p. 7.
36. Graham Hough, *The Dark Sun* [1956] (Harmondsworth, 1961) p. 202.
37. *England, My England* p. 11.
38. *Ibid.* p. 30.
39. Frank Kermode, *Lawrence* (1973) p. 53.
40. Lawrence, *Phoenix II* ed. Warren Roberts and Harry T. Moore (1968) p. 407.
41. *Ibid.* p. 408.
42. *Ibid.*
43. *Ibid.* p. 402.
44. *The English Review*, October 1915, p. 243.
45. *England, My England* p. 32.
46. *Ibid.* p. 33.
47. *Ibid.*
48. W. E. Henley, *For England's Sake* iii, 'Pro Rege Nostro'.
49. Stephen Spender, 'D. H. Lawrence, England and the War' in *D. H. Lawrence, Novelist, Poet, Prophet* ed. Stephen Spender (1973) p. 76.
50. *England, My England* p. 16.
51. *Phoenix II* p. 400.
52. *England, My England* p. 36.
53. *Ibid.* p. 36.
54. *Ibid.* p. 37.
55. *Ibid.*
56. *Ibid.*
57. *Revelation* chap. VI.
58. *England, My England* p. 40.
59. *Ibid.* p. 38.
60. *Ibid.* p. 39.
61. *Phoenix* II p. 383.

5 Virginia Woolf

1. Virginia Woolf, *To The Lighthouse* (1960) p. 225.
2. *Ibid.* pp. 162–3.
3. Richard Ellmann, *James Joyce* p. 87.
4. *To The Lighthouse* p. 249.
5. *Ibid.* pp. 248–9.
6. *The Waves* (Harmondsworth, 1964) p. 248.
7. *The Voyage Out* (Harmondsworth, 1970) p. 123.
8. *Ibid.* p. 301.
9. *Ibid.* p. 215.
10. Quentin Bell, *Virginia Woolf, A Biography; volume II, Mrs Woolf 1912–1941* (1972) p. 72.
11. Virginia Woolf, *A Haunted House and Other Stories* (1943) p. 12.
12. *Jacob's Room* (Harmondsworth, 1965) p. 148.
13. *Ibid.* p. 69.
14. *Ibid.* p. 46.
15. *Ibid.* p. 167.
16. *Ibid.* p. 168.

17. Quentin Bell *op. cit.* p. 106.
18. *Ibid.* p. 107.
19. *Ibid.*
20. Carl Woodring, *Virginia Woolf* (New York, 1966) p. 19.
21. *Mrs Dalloway* (1960) p. 5.
22. *To the Lighthouse* p. 76.
23. *Mrs Dalloway* p. 6.
24. *Ibid.* p. 11.
25. *Ibid.*
26. *Ibid.* p. 33.
27. *Ibid.* p. 35.
28. *Ibid.* p. 36.
29. *Ibid.* pp. 55–6.
30. *Ibid.* pp. 202–3.
31. *Ibid.* p. 201.
32. *Ibid.* p. 203.
33. *Ibid.*
34. *Ibid.* p. 204.
35. Virginia Woolf's Introduction to the Modern Library edn. of *Mrs Dalloway* (New York, 1928), quoted by Jeremy Hawthorn, *Virginia Woolf's Mrs Dalloway* (1975) p. 29.

6   In the Thirties

1. Graham Greene, *The Confidential Agent* (Harmondsworth, 1963) pp. 47–8.
2. *Ibid.* p. 51.
3. George Orwell, *Keep The Aspidistra Flying* (Harmondsworth, 1962).
4. George Orwell, *Coming Up For Air* [1939] (Harmondsworth, 1967) p. 224.
5. Stephen Spender, *The New Realism* (1939) p. 8.
6. Samuel Hynes, *The Auden Generation: Literature and Politics in England in the 1930s* (1976) p. 211.
7. 'Full Moon at Tierz: Before the Storming of Huesca', in *Poetry of the Thirties* ed. Robin Skelton (Harmondsworth, 1964) p. 137.
8. *Coming Up For Air* p. 33.
9. *Ibid.* p. 65.
10. *Ibid.* p. 73.
11. *Ibid.* p. 74.
12. *Ibid.* p. 79.
13. *Ibid.* p. 105.
14. *Ibid.* p. 222.
15. *Ibid.* p. 74.
16. Quoted in Hynes, *op. cit.* p. 271.
17. Christopher Isherwood, *Goodbye to Berlin* [1939] (Harmondsworth, 1965) p. 7.
18. Christopher Isherwood, *Lions and Shadows: An Education In The Twenties* (Signet edn., 1968) pp. 52–3.
19. *Goodbye to Berlin* p. 27.
20. Graham Greene, *The Confidential Agent* p. 111.
21. *Ibid.* p. 142.

22. *Ibid.* pp. 152–3.
23. Richard Hoggart, 'The Force of Caricature' [1953], *Speaking to Each Other* (1970) II p. 49.
24. *Ibid.*
25. *Poetry of the Thirties* pp. 133–6.
26. George Orwell, 'Inside the Whale' [1940], *Collected Essays, Journalism and Letters*, ed. Sonia Orwell and Ian Angus (Harmondsworth, 1970) I, p. 566.
27. Bernard Bergonzi, 'Auden and the Audenesque', *Encounter* XLIV (February 1975) pp. 65–75.
28. *Poetry of the Thirties* pp. 142–3.
29. 'Autumn Journal', *Poetry of the Thirties* pp. 160–1.
30. Rex Warner, 'Hymn', *Poetry of the Thirties* p. 59.
31. 'Musée des Beaux Arts', *W. H. Auden: a selection by the author* (Harmondsworth, 1962) p. 61.
32. *Ibid.*
33. Bergonzi, *op. cit.* p. 70.
34. Hynes, *op. cit.* p. 152.
35. Edward Upward, *The Railway Accident and Other Stories* (Harmondsworth, 1972) p. 83.
36. Graham Greene, *Journey Without Maps* [1936] (Pan edn., 1948) p. 228.
37. Graham Greene, *Brighton Rock* [1938] (Harmondsworth, 1951) p. 128.
38. Graham Greene, *The Power and the Glory* [1940] (Compass Books, New York, 1958) p. 108.
39. Isherwood, *Goodbye to Berlin* p. 7.
40. *Ibid.* p. 8.
41. Graham Greene, *England Made Me* [1935] (Harmondsworth, 1945) p. 9.
42. Graham Greene, *Brighton Rock* (1947) p. 117.
43. Greene, *Brighton Rock* (Harmondsworth, 1951) p. 23.
44. Greene, *The Power and The Glory*. Quoted by Richard Hoggart *op. cit.* p. 48.
45. *Ibid.*
46. *Ibid.*
47. *Ibid.* pp. 47–8.
48. Collected in *The Railway Accident and Other Stories*.
49. See W. H. Sellers' Introduction to *The Railway Accident and Other Stories* pp. 11–12.
50. Isherwood, *Lions and Shadows* p. 12.
51. *Ibid.* p. 43.
52. Isherwood, Foreword to 'The Railway Accident' in *The Railway Accident and Other Stories* pp. 33–4.
53. *Lions and Shadows* p. 43.
54. André Breton, 'What is Surrealism' *The Modern Tradition* ed. R. Ellmann and C. Feidelson Jr. (New York, 1965) p. 606.
55. A. L. Lloyd in *Left Review*. Quoted by Julian Symons, *The Thirties: A Dream Revolved* (1960) p. 94.
56. Breton, *op. cit.* p. 602.
57. I am indebted to William Gaunt for this idea. See his note on 'Time Transfixed' in *Painters of Fantasy* (1974).
58. *The Railway Accident* p. 39.
59. *Ibid.*

60. *Ibid.* p. 40.
61. *Ibid.* p. 61.
62. *Ibid.* p. 13.
63. *Lions and Shadows* pp. 168–9.
64. See Hynes, *op. cit.* pp. 14–15.
65. Quoted in Hynes, *op. cit.* p. 207.
66. 'Journey to the Border' in *The Railway Accident and Other Stories,* p. 125.
67. *Ibid.* p. 151.
68. *Ibid.* pp. 141–2.
69. *Ibid.* p. 171.
70. *Ibid.* p. 138.
71. *Ibid.* p. 193.
72. *Ibid.* p. 195.
73. *Ibid.* p. 197.
74. *Ibid.* p. 204.
75. *Ibid.* p. 200.
76. *Ibid.* p. 220.
77. 'Inside the Whale', *Collected Essays, Journalism and Letters* I, p. 572.
78. Northrop Frye, *T. S. Eliot* (1963); David Lodge, *Evelyn Waugh* (1971).
79. See Evelyn Waugh, 'Ronald Firbank', *Life and Letters* March 1929 (pp. 191–6).
80. Brian Wicker has commented perceptively on this aspect of *A Handful of Dust* in *The Story-Shaped World* (1975) pp. 160–1.
81. Christopher Sykes (*Evelyn Waugh: a biography* (1975) p. 63) records a fascinating passage from Waugh's diaries about the composition of one of his first stories (never reprinted) called 'The Balance': 'I am making the first Chapter a Cinema film and have been working furiously ever since.'

7 Philip Larkin

1. 'The Modern, The Contemporary and The Importance of Being Amis', *Language of Fiction* (1966) pp. 243–67.
2. Quoted in David Timms, *Philip Larkin* (Edinburgh, 1973) p. 60.
3. *Ibid.* p. 109.
4. *Ibid.* p. 21.
5. *Ibid.* p. 62.
6. *The Whitsun Weddings* [1964] (Faber paperback edn., 1971) p. 28.
7. Timms, *op. cit.* p. 112.
8. 'Coming' in *The Less Deceived* [1955] (1973 edn.) p. 17.
9. Quoted in Timms, *op. cit.* p. 61.
10. 'I Remember, I Remember' in *The Less Deceived* p. 38.
11. 'Mr Bleaney' in *The Whitson Weddings* p. 10.
12. 'High Windows' in *High Windows* (1974) p. 17.
13. Wordsworth, Preface to *Lyrical Ballads. The Lyrical Ballads 1798–1805* ed. George Samson (1959) p. 8.
14. 'The Large Cool Store' in *The Whitsun Weddings* p. 30.
15. 'The Building' in *High Windows* pp. 25–6.
16. *The Less Deceived* p. 13.
17. *Ibid.* p. 45.
18. 'Here' in *The Whitsun Weddings* p. 9.

19. 'Show Saturday' in *High Windows* p. 38.
20. *The Whitsun Weddings* pp. 21–3.
21. *The Less Deceived* pp. 28–9.
22. *The Whitsun Weddings* p. 10.
23. *Ibid.* p. 32.
24. 'Ignorance' in *The Whitsun Weddings* p. 39.
25. 'Nothing to be Said' in *The Whitsun Weddings* p. 11.
26. *High Windows* p. 17.

8 Postmodernist Fiction

1. Samuel Beckett, *More Pricks Than Kicks* (Picador edn., 1974) p. 18.
2. *Ibid.* pp. 18–19.
3. *Ibid.* p. 16.
4. *Ibid.* p. 17. The allusion is to the use of the fish as a symbol for Christ by the early Christians.
5. *Ibid.* p. 11.
6. *Ibid.* p. 13.
7. *Ibid.* p. 19.
8. See above p. 138.
9. Beckett, *Murphy* (1963) p. 5.
10. *Ibid.* pp. 52–3.
11. Beckett, *Watt* (1963) p. 67.
12. *Ibid.* pp. 71–2.
13. *The Unnamable* in *Three Novels By Samuel Beckett* (New York, 1965) pp. 394–5.
14. Donald Barthelme, *Snow White* (Bantam edn. New York, 1968) p. 129.
15. Hugh Kenner, *A Reader's Guide to Samuel Beckett* (1973) p. 94.
16. Joseph Conrad, 'Henry James: an appreciation', quoted by Alan Friedman *The Turn of the Novel* (New York, 1966) p. 77.
17. Muriel Spark, *Not To Disturb* (1971) p. 61.
18. John Barth, *Lost in the Funhouse* (Harmondsworth, 1972) p. 117.
19. Richard Brautigan, *A Confederate General from Big Sur* (Picador edn., 1973) p. 116.
20. Richard Brautigan, *Trout Fishing In America* (Picador edn., 1972) p. 150.
21. *Ibid.* p. 151.
22. See Leslie Fiedler. *The New Mutants, Partisan Review* Autumn 1956. Reprinted in Bernard Bergonzi, ed. *Innovations* (1900) pp. 23–45 and the same author's 'Cross The Border—Close That Gap; Postmodernism', *American Literature Since 1900* (1975) ed. Marcus Cunliffe. pp. 344–66.
23. Frank Kermode, 'Objects, Jokes and Art' in *Continuities* (New York, 1968) p. 23.
24. Fiedler, 'Cross the Border etc.' p. 348.
25. Kermode, *op. cit.* p. 20.
26. Samuel Beckett, *The Unnamable, op. cit.* p. 357.
27. Leonard Michaels, *I Would Have Saved Them If I Could* (New York, 1975) p. 137.
28. Quoted by Tony Tanner in *City of Words: American Fiction 1950–1970* (1971) p. 191.
29. Gore Vidal, *Myra Breckinridge* (1968) and *Myron* (1975).

30. John Barth, *Giles Goat-Boy* (1967) p. 672.
31. Jorge Luis Borges, *Labyrinths* (Harmondsworth, 1970) p. 37.
32. *Ibid.* p. 51.
33. Beckett, *Watt* p. 200.
34. Beckett, *Molloy* (1966) pp. 73–9.
35. Beckett, *Murphy* p. 68.
36. *Ibid.* pp. 43–4.
37. Joseph Heller, *Catch 22* (Corgi edn. 1964) p. 16.
38. Ronald Sukenick, *98.6* (New York, 1975) p. 167.
39. Raymond Federman, *Double or Nothing* (Chicago, 1971) p. 85.
40. Leonard Michaels, *I Would Have Saved Them If I Could* pp. 117–48.
41. *Ibid.* pp. 59–60.
42. Donald Barthelme, 'Edward and Pia', *Unspeakable Practices, Unnatural Acts* (Bantam edn. New York, 1969) p. 75.
43. Barthelme, 'Will You Tell Me?', *Come Back, Dr Caligari* (Boston, 1964) p. 47.
44. In 'See The Moon'. Quoted, and amusingly discussed by the author, in *The New Fiction: Interviews with Innovative American Writers* by Joe David Bellamy (1974) pp. 53–5.
45. Barthelme, *Come Back, Dr Caligari* pp. 90–1.
46. Quoted by Tony Tanner, *op. cit.* p. 126.
47. See *The Novelist at the Crossroads* pp. 13–14 and 166–70.
48. Barthelme, 'A Film', *Sadness* (Bantam edn. New York, 1972) p. 78.
49. Brautigan, *Trout Fishing in America* pp. 7–8.
50. *Ibid.* p. 27.
51. *Ibid.* p. 31.
52. *Ibid.* p. 34.
53. *Ibid.* p. 39.
54. *Ibid.* p. 72.
55. *Ibid.* p. 80.
56. *Ibid.* p. 13.
57. *Ibid.* p. 43.
58. *Ibid.* p. 89.
59. *Ibid.* p. 129.
60. *Ibid.* p. 131.
61. *Ibid.* p. 148.
62. Roman Jakobson, 'Two Aspects of Language' p. 80.
63. Alain Robbe-Grillet, *Le Voyeur* (Paris, 1955) pp. 11–12.
64. Alain Robbe-Grillet, *The Voyeur*, translated by Richard Howard (1959) pp. 6–7.
65. Jorge Louis Borges, *Labyrinths* p. 92.
66. Quoted by Tony Tanner in *City of Words* p. 41. The translation differs slightly from that of the Penguin *Labyrinths*, and I have preferred to quote it in this instance because the word 'contiguous' is used.
67. Vladimir Nabokov, *King, Queen, Knave* (1968) p. 259.
68. Nabokov, *Speak, Memory,* (Pyramid edn., New York, 1968) p. 143.
69. Ihab Hassan, *The Dismemberment of Orpheus: Toward a Postmodernist Literature* (New York, 1971) p. 251.
70. Brautigan, *Trout Fishing in America* pp. 142–3.
71. Kurt Vonnegut, *Slaughterhouse 5* (1970) p. 17.
72. *Ibid.* p. 109.

73. Vonnegut, *Breakfast of Champions* (Panther edn., 1975) p. 179.
74. Reprinted in *Superfiction, or the American Story Transformed*, ed. Joe David Bellamy (New York, 1975) p. 254.
75. Robert Coover, *Pricksongs and Descants* (Picador edn., 1973) p. 15.
76. John Barth, *'Life-Story'*, *Lost in the Funhouse* p. 121.
77. *Ibid.* p. 122.
78. *Ibid.* pp. 131–2.
79. *Ibid.* p. 132.
80. John Barth 'The Literature of Exhaustion', *Atlantic* August 1967, p. 29.
81. *Ibid.* p. 32.
82. Leslie Fiedler, 'Cross the Border—Close That Gap' *op. cit.* p. 346.

Index

This index includes the names of all writers, artists, etc. referred to in the text and notes, and explanatory references to certain literary and linguistic terms. These terms are printed in small capitals. **Bold type** page numbers indicate substantial discussion.